W9-CZY-893

Heroes and Legends of Fin-de-Siècle France

In *Heroes and Legends of Fin-de-Siècle France*, Venita Datta examines representations of fictional and real heroes in the boulevard theater and mass press during the fin de siècle (1880–1914), illuminating the role of gender in the construction of national identity during this formative period of French history. The popularity of the heroic cult at this time was in part the result of France's defeat in the Franco-Prussian War in 1870, as well as a reaction to changing gender roles and collective guilt about the egoism and selfishness of modern consumer culture. The author analyzes representations of historical figures in the theater, focusing on Cyrano de Bergerac, Napoleon, and Joan of Arc, and examines the press coverage of heroes and anti-heroes in the Bazar de la Charité fire of 1897 and the Ullmo spy case of 1907.

Venita Datta, professor of French at Wellesley College, where she has taught since 1991, is a specialist of French cultural and intellectual history of the nineteenth and twentieth centuries. She is the author of *Birth of a National Icon* (1999) and has published articles in various journals, including *French Historical Studies*, the *Journal of Contemporary History*, *Historical Reflections/Réflexions historiques*, *French Cultural Studies*, and *CLIO, Histoire, Femmes et Société*. Professor Datta is a recipient of the Chateaubriand Fellowship, awarded by the French government.

More praise for *Heroes and Legends of Fin-de-Siècle France*

"Is there anything new to be learned about the construction of French national identity in the decades before World War I? Datta's thoroughly engaging book shows that there is by exploring the cult of heroes of the day. This strikingly original study finds that the boulevard theater and mass press offered an eager public, anxious about meeting national challenges, a golden age of heroism. A sign of the times was that France's late-nineteenth-century heroes defined themselves more by martyrdom than by conquest. Carefully reading the evidence not only to uncover France's culture wars but also to detect less frequently noted areas of national cohesion, Datta makes many surprising revelations, not the least of which is how many cracks there were in the defense of gender orthodoxies. The success of the Third Republic in overcoming poisonous hatreds and preparing France for its life-and-death struggle comes into focus with this important investigation."
— Lenard R. Berlanstein, University of Virginia

"Through a careful analysis of five *causes célèbres* between the 1890s and the First World War, Venita Datta's new book probes the many levels on which the cult of heroism circulated in the French cultural imagination. By revealing a series of tensions and pretensions surrounding the virility of men, the potential of women, and the meaning of Frenchness, Datta shows how conflicting ideas about the hero divided the very nation they aimed to consolidate. This is a fascinating and indispensable contribution to our understanding of culture and politics at the fin de siècle."
— Christopher E. Forth, author of *The Dreyfus Affair and the Crisis of French Manhood*

"Venita Datta's masterful book gets to the heart of the way heroism and historic symbols of French national unity were dramatized in the press and in theaters at the fin de siècle, mitigating, if not healing, the many political and cultural divisions of the era, while preparing the nation for war."
— Robert Nye, Oregon State University

Heroes and Legends of Fin-de-Siècle France

Gender, Politics, and National Identity

VENITA DATTA

Wellesley College

CAMBRIDGE UNIVERSITY PRESS

CAMBRIDGE UNIVERSITY PRESS
Cambridge, New York, Melbourne, Madrid, Cape Town,
Singapore, São Paulo, Delhi, Tokyo, Mexico City

Cambridge University Press
32 Avenue of the Americas, New York, NY 10013-2473, USA

www.cambridge.org
Information on this title: www.cambridge.org/9780521186520

© Venita Datta 2011

This publication is in copyright. Subject to statutory exception
and to the provisions of relevant collective licensing agreements,
no reproduction of any part may take place without the written
permission of Cambridge University Press.

First published 2011

Printed in the United States of America

A catalog record for this publication is available from the British Library.

Library of Congress Cataloging in Publication data
Datta, Venita, 1961–
Heroes and legends of fin-de-siècle France : gender, politics,
and national identity / Venita Datta.
p. cm.
Includes bibliographical references and index.
ISBN 978-0-521-19595-9 – ISBN 978-0-521-18652-0 (pbk.)
1. Heroes – France – History. 2. Women heroes – France – History.
3. Nationalism – France – History. 4. Sex role – France – History. I. Title.
P96.H462.F84 2011
944.081'2–dc22 2010046889

ISBN 978-0-521-19595-9 Hardback
ISBN 978-0-521-18652-0 Paperback

Cambridge University Press has no responsibility for the persistence or accuracy of URLs
for external or third-party Internet Web sites referred to in this publication and does not
guarantee that any content on such Web sites is, or will remain, accurate or appropriate.

For Sean and Neal

Contents

vii

Acknowledgments

Every book is to some extent a collective endeavor, and this one is no exception. Although the current work begins more or less where the last one ended, it took me some time to figure out where I was going. I am especially grateful to colleagues whom I also count as friends for reading various book abstracts and early drafts: Elinor Accampo, Barbara Day-Hickman, Ruth Harris, William Hitchcock, Raymond Jonas, Dominique Kalifa, Paul Mazgaj, Karen Offen, Jean Pedersen, Mary Pickering, Charles Rearick, Mary-Louise Roberts, Florence Rochefort, Vanessa Schwartz, Gregory Shaya, Willa Silverman, Charles Sowerwine, Mary Lynn Stewart, K. Steven Vincent, and Robin Walz. I am also indebted to a pair of very tough editors, Jo Burr and Ted Margadant, for (repeatedly) obliging me to revise an article that formed the basis of an early chapter.

I offer special thanks to Robert Nye, Christopher Forth, Edward Berenson, Lenard Berlanstein, and Sally Charnow for reading large portions of the manuscript, their lively conversations on fin-de-siècle France, and, above all, for *not* sugar coating their advice. I am grateful for their friendship, and the book is the better for their collegial suggestions.

I express my deep-felt gratitude to my French "family": Doris Khoury-Serres and François and Olivier Serres, for their generosity in hosting me on every single "hit and run" trip to Paris I have taken these past ten years to look at the archives. I also thank Olivier Wieviorka and Vincent Duclert, not only for reading various chapters but also for their hospitality. Our lively dinners were a source of nourishment in all respects.

No words suffice to thank Rachel Fuchs, who has been my friend and mentor ever since we ran away from a rubber chicken banquet nearly seventeen years ago. Rachel is the model of the brilliant scholar, teacher, and colleague. I could not have finished this book without her unstinting advice, support, and affection.

My colleagues in the French Department at Wellesley College graciously agreed to read parts of the manuscript and help me with translations, even during busy semesters. My warm thanks to Catherine Masson and Vicki Mistacco for the former, and to Barry Lydgate, Marie-Paule Tranvouez, Hélène Bilis, Scott Gunther, Andrea Levitt, Michèle Respaut, and the late Nathalie Buchet Ritchey, for the latter.

I also had the good fortune to work with a splendid administrative assistant Sarah Allahverdi and three talented student research assistants: Leslie Viano, Margaret Samu, and Yukti Malhotra. I also thank Bethany Keenan, who helped me secure various documents in France, and Susan Hall, who helped me clean up the manuscript. I could not have completed this project without the support of Wellesley College's liberal leave policy and of the Wellesley College Committee on Faculty Awards. During my last sabbatical, I was lucky to be a scholar in residence at Wellesley's Newhouse Center for the Humanities – my thanks to Tim Peltason and Jane Jackson for making me feel so welcome.

I wouldn't have gotten very far in my research without the help of wonderful librarians and archivists. At Wellesley College, I am grateful for the support of Karen Jensen and Susan Goodman in the Interlibrary Loan Office, as well as of Dale Katzif, Nancy Karis, and Jacqueline Fitzpatrick. In France, I would like to thank Geneviève Morlet and Marie-Odile Gigou at the Bibliothèque Historique de la Ville de Paris; Jean de Preneuf at the Service Historique de la Marine, as well as the librarians at the BNF, Richelieu; the Police Archives of the Préfecture de Paris, and the Bibliothèque Marguerite Durand.

I would also like to acknowledge the debt I owe to a special group of friends: Joanne Berger-Sweeney, Urs Berger, Julie and Hank Donnelly, Margaret Cezair-Thompson, Julie Norem, Jonathan Cheek, Mary Kloppenberg, and Kate Brogan. I thank them for their warmth and affection, especially when I needed them most. I offer thanks as well to Dr. Caroline Block for encouraging me to continue work on my book during difficult circumstances.

Every author needs a sympathetic editor and I am fortunate to have found one in Eric Crahan. I greatly appreciate his enthusiastic (and patient) support of this project. Thanks also to Jason Przybylski for all his advice on how to secure images and permissions.

Last but by no means least, I thank my family, beginning with my husband, Stephen Bold, who has given me much encouragement and listened to my historical ramblings with great patience over the years. His work on the real Cyrano – among the best I have read on the subject (I may be a bit biased) – was a source of inspiration for my own work on Rostand's fictionalized version of the historical figure. Steve also helped with tricky translations and served as my technical advisor. My parents, Y. and Urmil Datta, too have supported all my endeavors, intellectual and otherwise, with enthusiasm and selfless generosity. My brother Sanjay Datta cheered me on as well.

I am also indebted to my sons, Sean and Neal Bold, who seem to have grown up (but not quite, thankfully) during the course of my writing this book. I appreciated their patience when I dragged them to various Parisian haunts, among them, the Père Lachaise Cemetery to see the graves of Sarah Bernhardt and Oscar Wilde and the Sacré-Coeur to look at the Joan of Arc stained-glass windows (it wasn't so bad, was it?). I am also grateful to them for reminding me of what is most important in life – by taking me away from the computer to play – and also for understanding when I needed to get back to my work. This book is dedicated to them.

Introduction

The Fin-de-Siècle Cult of Heroes

The French entered World War I with staunch and grim determination in the summer of 1914. Unlike the often-told story of British soldiers, isolated and alienated from king and country, who continued to fight out of loyalty to their comrades in the trenches rather than a belief in national solidarity, French *poilus* (soldiers), in touch literally and figuratively with the home front, maintained their resolve due to an unshakable faith in the nation.[1] The unity of the French in war, however, belies the fragmented nature of French society during the preceding years, which were marked by political and social conflict. Violent industrial relations, the growth of radical political organizations on both the left and right, along with profound divisions in the body politic born of the Dreyfus Affair – in which a Jewish army officer was falsely accused of treason, culminating in the fiercely divisive separation of church and state in 1905 – all exemplified such disunity. The strong sense of national solidarity among the French during a time of crisis was in large part the result of the fin-de-siècle cult of the hero. Manifesting itself in all areas of national life, especially in the mass press and theater, this heroic cult allowed the French to overcome their differences and rally around the defense of the nation.

[1] Leonard V. Smith, Stéphane Audoin-Rouzeau, and Annette Becker, *France and the Great War, 1914–1918* (New York: Cambridge University Press, 2003; 2008), 11 and 27–30. See a review of the book for *H-France* by Martha Hanna: 3, no. 119 (October 2003), and Jean-Jacques Becker, *1914: Comment les Français sont entrés dans la guerre* (Paris: Presses de la Fondation nationale des sciences politiques, 1977). See also James Joll, who writes about the impact during the years preceding of "the history they [the French] had learnt at school, the stories about the national past which they had been told as children and an instinctive sense of loyalty and solidarity with their neighbors and workmates," *The Origins of the First World War* (New York: Longman, 1984), 189.

Born of defeat and civil war, the Third Republic faced challenges from the left and the right. Those threats coalesced in the Boulanger Affair, which represented an attempt by various political groups to forge unity at the fin de siècle. General Georges Boulanger first came to prominence as war minister in 1886, promoted by Radical politicians as a defender of the common man. Boulanger also appealed to those who desired revenge against Germany. He soon proved to be a huge embarrassment to his left-wing supporters when he nearly involved the country in war with Germany in 1887.[2] They were further chagrined by his negotiations with both monarchists and Bonapartists. When Boulanger won a seat in the Chamber of Deputies as a representative from Paris in January 1889, a coup d'état seemed imminent. At the last moment, however, Boulanger decided not to march on the Elysée palace. Republicans soon took advantage of Boulanger's missed opportunity, issuing a warrant for his arrest in April. The general fled to Brussels before the warrant could be executed and committed suicide on the tomb of his mistress in 1891 – resembling a two-bit player in a melodrama more than a real hero.[3]

The Exposition Universelle of 1889, which took place in the immediate wake of Boulanger's defeat, was another political attempt to forge unity. Marking the centennial of the Revolution, it was the first exhibition to be completely organized under the auspices of the republicans. It offered them an unparalleled opportunity to further links with the revolutionary past and to establish the legitimacy of the new regime. Nevertheless, this enterprise was fraught with difficulties because the moderate republicans and their more left-wing Radical colleagues could not agree on which revolution would be celebrated, that of 1789 or the more controversial Terror of 1793.[4]

---

[2] He was relieved of his duties as minister and posted to the provinces but not before receiving some 100,000 votes in a by election in Paris for which he was not a candidate.

[3] The Boulangist movement, however, played an important role in opposition to the parliamentary republic during the years to come and marked the emergence of a radical revolutionary right as well as the evolution of nationalism from the left to the right. This new nationalism, unlike its left-wing revolutionary counterpart, was exclusive and defensive, as much interested in "internal" enemies as external ones. On Boulangism, see William D. Irvine, *The Boulanger Affair Reconsidered: Royalism, Boulangism and the Origins of the Radical Right in France* (New York: Oxford University Press, 1989); on the revolutionary right, Zeev Sternhell, *La Droite révolutionnaire: Les Origines françaises du fascisme, 1885–1914* (Paris: Seuil, 1978). On nationalism: Raoul Girardet, *Le Nationalisme français, 1871–1914* (Paris: Seuil, 1983).

[4] They concentrated then not on specific events or leaders, many of which and whom were divisive, but on the entire nineteenth century as a product of progress engendered by the Revolution: Pascal Ory, *Une Nation pour mémoire: 1889, 1939, 1989: Trois Jubilés*

The Catholic Church offered its own version of national cohesion when it issued the 1891 encyclical, "Rerum Novarum," in which Pope Leo XIII outlined the need for improving the miserable conditions of the working classes. In yet another encyclical of 1892, "Au Milieu des solicitudes," addressed to the bishops and people of France, he encouraged French Catholics to "rally" to the republican regime by declaring the church neutral with regard to political regimes.[5] The *ralliement* seemed to signal – for a brief time – an end to religious and political strife. The tensions of the Dreyfus Affair, however, would put an end to this alliance and reinstitute the more familiar cry of "no enemies to the left."

For their part, left-wing republicans like Radical-Socialist Léon Bourgeois also attempted to promote national unity – through the doctrine of Solidarism, which they viewed as a bridge between individualism and socialism. By 1900, Solidarism had become the semi-official ideology of the Third Republic, although it had not succeeded in overcoming national conflict.[6] These largely political attempts to find unity were thus not always satisfying. Nor was the recourse to a real-life "hero" like Boulanger, especially when he could not live up to the ideals of heroism. Since such real-life figures did not inspire confidence and ultimately

révolutionnaires (Paris: FNSP, 1992), 159. The 1900 World's Fair in Paris better succeeded in promoting national unity and progress, in large part because the Revolution per se was not the object of focus: see Debora L. Silverman, *Art Nouveau in Fin-de-Siècle France: Politics, Psychology and Style* (Berkeley: University of California Press, 1989), 288–293.

5 The Catholic *ralliés* held between thirty and forty seats in the Chamber of Deputies and were allied with such moderate republicans as Charles Dupuy, Alexandre Ribot, and Jules Méline, all of whom headed governments in the 1890s. Albert de Mun was the most visible of the *ralliés* politicians but more representative were Jacques Piou and Etienne Lamy, both of whom were not members of Parliament during these years: Maurice Larkin, *Religion, Politics and Preferment in France since 1890* (New York: Cambridge University Press, 1995), 7.

6 In common with the Catholics who supported the pope's "new spirit," the Solidarists were inspired by a fear of socialism as well as a recognition that extreme individualism was not sufficient to address the needs of modern industrial society. Léon Bourgeois succeeded Ribot and preceded Méline as prime minister (*président du conseil*), holding the post from 1 November 1895 to 21 April 1896. He won the Nobel Peace Prize in 1920. On Solidarism, see J. E. S. Hayward, "Solidarity: The Social History of an Idea in Nineteenth Century France," *International Review of Social History* 4 (1959): 261–284, and "The Official Social Philosophy of the French Third Republic: Léon Bourgeois and Solidarism," *International Review of Social History* 6 (1961): 19–48. Rosalind H. Williams rightly points out that it would be a mistake to view Solidarism in strictly political terms because it was also seen as a moral concept and applied to consumption as well: *Dream Worlds: Mass Consumption in Late Nineteenth-Century France* (Berkeley: University of California Press, 1982), 270. See also its use to promote French national art: Debora Silverman, 174.

disappointed, French men and women, yearning for cohesion in the face of internecine conflict, turned increasingly to heroes in the fictions of the theater and the press to find a unity "above" politics.

This book examines constructions of heroism during the fin de siècle (1880–1914), the thirty-five-some years preceding the First World War. Exploring the role played by male and female heroes in French society, it links the debates on heroism and gender to the question of national identity. Moreover, it aims to show how and why ordinary French men and women inserted themselves into myths around these national heroes.

Historians disagree about the use of the terms *fin de siècle* and *belle époque* to describe this era, with some preferring the former term for the earlier years, and the latter, to describe those just before the First World War. I myself have referred in this book to the entire period as the fin de siècle, but I do acknowledge that there was a change in atmosphere during the years immediately preceding the war. Not only were the French more united than previously, but they were also more self-confident. They had succeeded in putting an end to their international isolation by forging alliances with the Russians and the British, had successfully amassed a colonial empire, and moreover, had hosted three international world fairs that displayed both their might and innovation. To be sure, the same anxieties that had marked the earlier period – notably a fear of national decline – were still present. Nevertheless, the response to these fears was less morose, more defiant, and diffused with humor more than during the fin-de-siècle period.[7]

Following historians Benedict Anderson and Eric Hobsbawm, who have developed the notion of "imagined" national communities through the "invention of tradition," I argue that the boulevard theater and the mass press were laboratories for the definition of conflicting views of national identity during this time.[8] Both attracted the lower middle-class masses, who constituted the backbone of the Third Republic, as well as elites. Anderson has spoken eloquently of the function of the mass press

---

[7] The term *fin de siècle* was used by contemporaries, whereas *belle époque* is a retrospective term, used in the aftermath of the Great War. Although some historians such as Eugen Weber place emphasis on the fin-de-siècle spirit as distinct from the ten years immediately preceding the war in *France Fin de Siècle* (Cambridge, MA: Belknap Press of Harvard University Press, 1986), 2, others have grouped these years together, among them Roger Shattuck (*The Banquet Years: The Origins of the Avant-Garde in France, 1885 to World War I* [New York: Vintage Books, 1968], 3), calling them the belle époque.

[8] Benedict Anderson, *Imagined Communities: Reflections on the Origin and Spread of Nationalism* (London: Verso, 1991); Eric Hobsbawm and Terence Ranger, eds., *The Invention of Tradition* (Cambridge: Cambridge University Press, 1983; Canto, 1992).

in creating "imagined communities," but the role of the boulevard theater, which had an enormous impact on the social, cultural, and political life of the fin de siècle, should also be illuminated. Recent work by Christophe Charle on the theater in Paris, Berlin, Vienna, and London illustrates the importance of the theater in fin-de-siècle life, especially in France.[9] Premieres of important plays were celebrated in the press as events of national importance, while leading actors and actresses were hailed as celebrities. Indeed, Lenard Berlanstein has argued that some actresses even became symbols of national identity.[10] Questions of national importance were debated in the theater as were issues related to gender. The theater became a forum for discussions about women's roles in French society as well as a place in which new roles could be enacted. The theater thus played an important part in French national life, both as a vehicle for creating national unity and as a motor for revolutionary change.[11]

By examining the tensions among political, commercial, and gender concerns at the time, I argue that both the theater and the press were used by journalists, playwrights, actors, and at times, political leaders to forge national identity around consumption, in the first case, of the news; in the second, of plays. In an attempt to unite a public profoundly divided outside the theater walls, playwrights like Victorien Sardou, Emile Moreau, and Edmond Rostand sought to transform history into a spectacle to be consumed in the boulevard theater and amplified by the mass press. The three most popular heroes of the era – Napoleon, Joan of Arc, and Cyrano de Bergerac, played by the most beloved actors of

[9] Christophe Charle, *Théâtres en capitales: Naissance de la société du spectacle à Paris, Berlin, Londres et Vienne: 1860–1914* (Paris: Albin Michel, 2008). During the late nineteenth century, Paris had more theaters and a greater number of seats available to be sold than the other three cities, 27. See also his "Les Théâtres et leurs publics: Paris, Berlin, Vienne, 1860–1914," in *Capitales culturelles, Capitales symboliques: Paris et les expériences européennes*, ed. Christophe Charle and Daniel Roche (Paris: Publications de la Sorbonne, 2002), 403–420. See also Frederic William John Hemmings, *The Theatre Industry in Nineteenth-Century France* (New York: Cambridge University Press, 1993) and *Theatre and State in France, 1760–1905* (New York: Cambridge University Press, 1994). On the theater of the Ancien Régime, see Jeffrey Ravel: *The Contested Parterre: Public Theater and Political Culture, 1680–1791* (Ithaca, NY: Cornell University Press, 1999).

[10] Lenard Berlanstein, *Daughters of Eve: A Cultural History of French Theater Women from the Old Regime to the Fin de Siècle* (Cambridge, MA: Harvard University Press, 2001), 169–175.

[11] Mary-Louise Roberts, *Disruptive Acts*: The New Woman in Fin-de-Siècle France (Chicago: University of Chicago Press, 2002); Jean Pedersen, *Legislating the Family*: Feminism, Theater, and Republican Politics, 1870–1920 (New Brunswick, NJ: Rutgers University Press, 2003); and Sally Charnow, *Theatre, Politics, and Markets in Fin-de-Siècle Paris: Staging Modernity* (New York: Palgrave Macmillan: 2005).

the day – were heroes for a democratic age. These fictionalized heroes – the subject of three chapters of this book – were all too human and were accessible to fin-de-siècle audiences. In the same manner, incidents like the 1897 Bazar de la Charité fire, in which 125 people, mostly prominent women, were killed, and the 1907–1908 Ullmo treason trial – the focus of two other chapters – were transformed into melodramas by a mass press that often estheticized real-life events. The press turned these events into sensationalized news stories known as *faits divers*, thereby blurring the line between fact and fiction. Ironically, however, the efforts to present unifying figures "above politics" were only partially and temporarily successful, because visions of the hero remained embedded in the politics of the time. Nevertheless, during the years immediately leading up to World War I, public weariness of domestic political quarrels as well as the imminent external threat posed by Germany, which sparked a "nationalist revival," increasingly made such unity independent of political ideologies possible.[12]

The construction of heroes and heroism, essential to an understanding of the emergence of modern French national identity and culture, has been examined by such French historians as Paul Gerbod, Jean-François Chanet, and Christian Amalvi. Their research, however, is largely focused on official celebrations and school manuals, and although they study such female heroes as Joan of Arc, little attention is paid to gender concerns.[13] Similarly, the contributors to Pierre Nora's *Les Lieux de mémoire* (translated into English as *Realms of Memory*), a seven-volume work that examines people, places, and monuments inscribed into France's national memory, do not address the role of gender in the construction of national identity.[14]

My work builds principally on that of such historians as Edward Berenson, Rachel Fuchs, George Mosse, Robert Nye, and Karen Offen, all of whom have made important contributions to the field by developing a conceptual framework for the study of national identity through

---

[12] See Eugen Weber's now classic work, *The Nationalist Revival in France, 1905–1914* (Berkeley: University of California Press, 1968).

[13] Paul Gerbod, "L'Éthique héroïque en France (1870–1914)," *La Revue historique*, no. 268 (1982): 409–429; Christian Amalvi, *Les Héros de l'histoire de France* (Paris: Phot'oeil, 1979), and his *De l'art et la manière d'accommoder les héros de l'histoire de France: Essais de mythologie nationale* (Paris: Albin Michel, 1988); Jean-François Chanet, "La Fabrique des héros: Pédagogie républicaine et culte des grands hommes de Sedan à Vichy," *Vingtième Siècle*, no. 65 (January–March 2000): 13–34.

[14] Pierre Nora, ed., *Les Lieux de mémoire*, 3 vols. (Paris: Gallimard, Quarto, 1997; the volumes were originally published from 1984 to 1992).

the lens of gender.[15] Recent publications dealing with masculinity, my own earlier work and that of Christopher E. Forth among them, have concentrated on images of male heroes rather than female ones and have focused in particular on the Dreyfus Affair.[16] While giving the Affair its due, I expand the debate about heroes beyond the Affair to other causes célèbres of the period. Although the Affair led to the articulation of two opposing visions of the hero, it does not encompass all aspects of the debate on heroism at this time, in particular, discussions about female heroism.

Historians of France have generally viewed this period as male dominated, despite the "crisis of masculinity" that many middle-class males of the time experienced. Yet as scholars of feminism have illustrated, the same years were instrumental for the feminist movement in France. These two discursive strands of French historiography need to be woven together for a more complete view of the period, as do the threads of political, cultural, and gender history. Some men expressed their fear of female domination in the public sphere in the form of a vociferous anti-feminist, and, at times, misogynist backlash, while others sought to democratize formerly aristocratic notions of honor and manhood. Nevertheless, there is ample evidence of new roles for women in French society and a tacit acceptance of the "female" heroic traits of self-sacrifice and devotion beyond their traditional associations with motherhood. Despite rhetoric to the contrary, women were increasingly rehabilitated and incorporated into a vision of the nation, both as symbols of national

[15] Edward Berenson, *The Trial of Madame Caillaux* (Berkeley: University of California Press, 1992); among her numerous works, see Rachel G. Fuchs, *Contested Paternity: Constructing Families in Modern France* (Baltimore: Johns Hopkins University Press, 2008), and with Elinor Accampo and Mary Lynn Stewart, eds., *Gender and the Politics of Social Reform in France, 1871–1914* (Baltimore: Johns Hopkins University Press, 1995); George L. Mosse, *Nationalism and Sexuality: Middle-Class Morality and Sexual Norms in Modern Europe* (Madison: University of Wisconsin Press, 1985); Karen Offen, "Depopulation, Nationalism, and Feminism in Fin-de-Siècle France," *American Historical Review* 89, no. 3 (June 1984): 648–676. With the exception of Edward Berenson, who has recently completed *Heroes of Empire: Five Charismatic Men and the Conquest of Africa* (Berkeley: University of California Press, 2010), none of these scholars concentrate specifically on heroes, although Robert A. Nye, whose research represents an important underpinning for my work, defines traditional notions of heroism at this time. See his pathbreaking *Masculinity and Male Codes of Honor in Modern France* (Berkeley: University of California Press, 1998).

[16] See my *Birth of a National Icon: The Literary Avant-Garde and the Origins of the Intellectual in France* (Albany: SUNY Press, 1999); and Christopher E. Forth, *The Dreyfus Affair and the Crisis of Manhood* (Baltimore: Johns Hopkins University Press, 2004).

identity and as spectators of plays in the boulevard theater and readers of the mass press.

I begin my study of heroes by examining the historical context of the fin de siècle in which the cult of the hero emerged. Next, I proceed to explore fin-de-siècle notions of heroism in the theater and the press, focusing on the role of mass culture in forging national identity as well as that the culture of melodrama in shaping contemporary understandings of heroism.

I. The Nation and the Cult of Heroes

The nation is a soul, a spiritual principle. Two things, which, truth be told, are but one, constitute this soul, this spiritual principle. One is in the past, the other in the present. One is the possession in common of a rich heritage of memories; the other is active consent, the desire to live together, the will to continue to value the undivided heritage passed down. ... The nation, like the individual, is the result of a long past of efforts, of sacrifices, and of devotion. The cult of ancestors is the most legitimate of cults; ancestors have made us what we are. A heroic past, great men, glory. ... This is the social capital upon which the idea of the nation is founded. To share past glories, a common will in the present; to have done great things together, to desire to do so again, here are the essential conditions for the making of a people. We love in proportion to the sacrifices we have taken on, the ills we have suffered. ... A nation is thus a great solidarity, constituted by the feeling of sacrifices made and those that lie ahead.[17]

Ernest Renan, "Qu'est-ce qu'une nation?" Lecture delivered
at the Sorbonne, 11 March, 1882.

When the well-known philosopher Ernest Renan spoke these words, in the wake of the defeat in the Franco-Prussian War and the annexation of the two provinces of Alsace and Lorraine, he was addressing not only his audience at the Sorbonne but also his German audience across the Rhine. In opposition to such German thinkers as Johann Gottlieb Fichte, he was arguing for a nation defined not by race, religion, language, or economic considerations, but rather by a democratically constructed union created from common experiences and a sense of solidarity. In the atmosphere of what one historian has described as "the culture of defeat," Renan was essentially turning defeat on its head, arguing in favor of France's moral superiority over its German victor.[18] In addressing his countrymen

---

[17] An excerpt of this text is reproduced in Raoul Girardet, *Nationalismes et Nation* (Brussels: Editions Complexe, 1996), 137–139.

[18] Wolfgang Schivelbusch, *The Culture of Defeat: On National Trauma, Mourning, and Recovery*, trans. Jefferson Chase (New York: Picador, 2004), 125.

and women, Renan exhorted them to unite around the newly established Third Republic, a regime born of defeat and the civil war of the Commune. For Renan, as well as his contemporaries, heroism in the past, present, and future played a key role in forging national identity. Great men (and some women) sacrificed themselves for the glory and survival of the nation, and, moreover, served as examples for the ordinary French men and women who shared in these sacrifices.[19]

The fin de siècle then was a formative period for the forging of French national identity. Modern French national identity, as we understand it today is a relatively recent phenomenon, a product of both the Revolution and especially the Third Republic, whose leaders sought to establish the new regime's legitimacy by forging links with the past, first and foremost with the French Revolution.[20] Accordingly, during the Third Republic's early years, its leaders instituted republican symbols – adopting the "Marseillaise" as the national anthem and establishing July 14 as a national holiday. They also sought to replace the influence of the Catholic Church, passing legislation on civil marriage; relegalizing divorce; and establishing secular, compulsory, and free primary schools. The schools, along with a massive (the Freycinet Plan) program of railroad and road building, as well as universal military service, and the concomitant emergence of mass culture, thereby transformed a nation of "peasants into Frenchmen," a process brilliantly described by historian Eugen Weber.[21]

Another means by which the regime sought to establish its legitimacy was through the cult of heroes. In the years following defeat in the Franco-Prussian War, the cult of the hero gained great popularity in France. The contemporary exaltation of the army and the intense interest in both dueling and sports served to promote the heroic ideal. The cult of the hero manifested itself in the curriculum of the primary schools as well

[19] As historian David Bell notes, there is no female equivalent for the term *grand homme* because "grande femme" means a big woman rather than a great one! David A. Bell, *The Cult of the Nation in France: Inventing Nationalism, 1680–1800* (Cambridge, MA: Harvard University Press, 2001), 127. On the cult of *grands hommes*, see Jean-Claude Bonnet, *Naissance du Panthéon: Essai sur le culte des grands hommes* (Paris: Fayard, 1998).

[20] David Bell places the origins of the nation in the eighteenth century. National identity is, of course, always in flux. Nevertheless, the idea of an abstract identity, which means that one is French first and foremost, with personal affiliations of gender, religion, and ethnicity relegated to the private realm, is a legacy of the French Revolution.

[21] Eugen Weber, *Peasants into Frenchmen: The Modernization of Rural France, 1870–1914* (Stanford, CA: Stanford University Press, 1976). See also a critique of Weber's work in James Lehning, *Peasant and French: Cultural Contact in Rural France during the Nineteenth Century* (New York: Cambridge University Press, 1995).

as in literature and the arts. The search for heroes was the consequence of a widespread sense of national inferiority vis-à-vis Germany and a desire to promote heroes for the expansion of the empire, as well as the product of collective guilt with regard to the egoism and selfishness of modern consumer culture. Both these fears fueled the contemporary crisis of masculinity in France, which was further exacerbated by the decline in the national birthrate and the emergence of the New Woman, who challenged traditional gender roles.[22] The close associations of the notion of honor and the culture of the sword also help to explain the particular resonance of military heroes. Certainly, civilian heroes were also celebrated, but it was the cult of the military hero that held sway.

In his study, *The Culture of Defeat*, Wolfgang Schivelbusch has described what he calls a "gender reversal" between France and Germany in the wake of the Franco-Prussian war, arguing that the loss in the war transformed France into a maiden in distress, while a united Germany thereafter assumed the male role.[23] Schivelbusch is undoubtedly right that France was henceforth seen as a maiden in distress, even by some of her own countrymen and women, but it is worth noting that France was associated with the so-called "feminine" influences of civilization long before the loss in the war. Nevertheless, it is true that the cult of the hero was deemed all the more necessary after France's stunning defeat to the Germans. The hero provided a means by which to avenge France's humiliation in the war. For her countrymen and women, France may have lost on the field of battle, but she still possessed a proud tradition of honor and glory.

The republican state as well as the Catholic Church, which were often at loggerheads, both promoted various figures, each establishing its own "Pantheon" of heroes.[24] The republican pantheon undoubtedly contained more men of letters like Victor Hugo, "pantheonized" in 1885,

---

[22] See Nye, *Masculinity and Male Codes of Honor*, 225; and Berenson, *The Trial of Madame Caillaux*, 186–198. See also the important study by Annelise Maugue, *L'Identité masculine en crise au tournant du siècle, 1871–1914* (Paris: Rivages, 1987; Payot, 2001).

[23] According to Schivelbusch, before the Franco-Prussian war, Germany – in particular, Prussia – was celebrated by such nineteenth-century thinkers as Germaine de Staël as the representative of a literary and "feminine" culture, while France led by the Napoleonic armies was seen as a conquering male hero: Schivelbusch, *The Culture of Defeat*, 120. It is true that the two countries are seen today, at least by Americans, as respectively male and female. A recent *New York Times* article discussed this gendering: Nina Bernstein, "For Americans, It's French Sissies vs. German He-Men," *New York Times*, 28 September 2003.

[24] Indeed, the Pantheon itself was the object of struggle between the republicans who claimed it for the republic, and Catholics, who viewed this appropriation as a desecration of the former Church of Sainte-Geneviève. The Pantheon reverted to the republicans

and scientist Louis Pasteur, along with generals of the revolutionary and Napoleonic eras.[25] Its Catholic counterpart, on the other hand, exalted saints (Joan of Arc and Sainte-Geneviève), aristocratic military heroes of the Ancien Régime (who were associated with the Catholic Church), and kings. Both groups, however, admired military heroes, who had special resonance in an age of defeat.

For the newly established, hotly contested Third Republic, the cult of heroes was a way to cement national solidarity as well as to establish its legitimacy and roots in the past, even the more distant past of the Ancien Régime. In many ways, the search for heroes was ecumenical, because republican leaders wished to present the Third Republic in the context of continuity, not rupture with the past. Witness the favorable treatment of kings and other figures of the Ancien Régime in Ernest Lavisse's monumental history of France, which was read by countless generations of schoolchildren at the primary and secondary levels, earning Lavisse the title of *instituteur national* (national schoolteacher).[26] More than republican heroes, the Third Republic needed national heroes who could unify in their persons both the idea of an eternal nation and that of the modern republic.[27]

Writers played a key role in promoting the cult of heroes, not least among them, the most popular novelists and playwrights of the day, Maurice Barrès, Edmond Rostand, Victorien Sardou, and his collaborator Emile Moreau. Barrès, known as the "Prince of Youth" before he became a deputy from the city of Nancy and a bulwark for the nationalist right, celebrated "professors of energy" who exemplified French grandeur, singling out Napoleon Bonaparte and poet-statesman Victor Hugo. Barrès called Napoleon an "exciter of the soul," whose "contact had the

in 1881 and was reinaugurated with the death of Victor Hugo in 1885. See Mona Ozouf's essay: "Le Panthéon," in Pierre Nora, ed., *Les Lieux de mémoire*, vol. 1 (Paris: Gallimard, Quarto: 1997), 155–178.

[25] Even the Socialists established their own "pantheon," Gerbod, 417.

[26] Jean-François Chanet, "La Fabrique des héros," 14. In the surveys launched by the *Almanach du drapeau*, the most popular heroes cited were Joan of Arc and Napoleon, with the generals of the Revolution (Marceau, Hoche, etc.) coming in third: Gerbod, 419. On Lavisse, see Pierre Nora's, "Lavisse, instituteur national," in *Les Lieux de mémoire*, vol. 1, 239–276.

[27] As Edward Berenson observes, "individuals who unified in themselves the nation and the Republic like the king's two bodies under the *Ancien Régime*, one to represent an eternal stable France, and the other, to represent the modern changing Republic." "Unifying the French Nation: Savornan de Brazza and the Third Republic," in *Music, Culture and National Identity in France 1870–1939*, ed. Barbara Kelly (Rochester, NY: University of Rochester Press, 2008), 20.

power to make souls great."[28] As for Hugo, he represented the "mystical leader," "the modern soothsayer," who had become a "sacred" "god."[29] Barrès also sought contemporary role models and thought he had found a savior in General Boulanger but was sorely disappointed.

Members of the avant-garde, many of whom were disciples of Barrès – at least before the Dreyfus Affair led to a parting of ways – also promoted the cult of heroes, especially intellectual ones. They praised such foreign writers as Thomas Carlyle, whose work *On Heroes, Hero-Worship, and the Heroic in History* was translated into French in 1887, and Friedrich Nietzsche, whom they viewed as the source of "energy" in a decadent, corrupt society. Nietzsche, in particular, was the object of a cult in France during the fin de siècle. Young writers were fascinated by Nietzsche's writings on the "superman" or "overman," especially the idea of the superiority of the artist, which allowed them to feel like Nietzschean "masters" in a world in which they were actually quite insignificant. Role models Nietzsche and Carlyle resonated with these writers because both men spoke of the special role in society of men of thought.[30]

The fascination with heroes was not limited to male authors, although it is the former who have been studied more in this regard than their female counterparts. It seems only logical that women writers too were affected by the widespread discourse on degeneration and that they, in common with their male counterparts, sought their own models of energy. Poet and novelist Anna de Noailles, who was fascinated by the figure of Napoleon – himself a role model for Nietzsche – wrote of the great hero in her poetry. Poet Gérard d'Houville, the daughter of Parnassian poet José-Maria de Heredia, was influenced by her father's famous collection of poems *Les Trophées*, which celebrated male classical heroes, and translated this need for heroes into a quest for feminine role models, in particular, her own female ancestors, in her poetry. Playwright Marie Lenéru was also interested in heroes, devoting an entire study to the revolutionary Saint-Just. As for Daniel Lesueur, one of the most popular novelists and journalists of the era, she celebrated female heroism both in her articles for the feminist newspaper *La Fronde* and in her best-selling novels.[31]

[28] Barrès, *Les Déracinés* (Paris: Ed. 10/18 Union générale d'éditions, 1986), 168–169.
[29] *Les Déracinés*, 332–333.
[30] See *Birth of a National Icon*, 17–38 and 39–64, and Christopher E. Forth, *Zarathustra in Paris: The Nietzsche Vogue in France, 1891–1918* (De Kalb: Northern Illinois University Press, 2001), 15–44.
[31] I have written about women writers and their interest in Napoleon in "Superwomen or Slaves? Women Writers, Male Critics, and the Reception of Nietzsche in Belle-Epoque

Although heroes of the age were increasingly secular, they did not simply replace older saintly figures, at least not for Catholics, but coexisted alongside them.[32] The fin de siècle also witnessed a mystical Catholic revival, as evidenced by the sacred heart cult and the vogue of pilgrimages to Lourdes.[33] The republicans themselves were not free from a certain religious fervor – viewing themselves as the apostles of a new state religion, and in some respects, mirroring their opponents.[34]

Moreover, in the atmosphere of defeat that followed the French loss in the war, the idea of turning a loss in battle into a moral victory involved a form of martyrdom. It is for this reason that the heroes who resonated at the time with the French public were not necessarily victorious military figures but rather martyred ones, thus not the conquering general Napoleon but rather the post-Waterloo figure, described by his biographer Emmanuel de Las Cases as Prometheus chained to his rock on Saint-Helena; not the triumphal maid who led the French to victory against the English in the Hundred Years War but rather the imprisoned girl, burned at the stake for heresy; not the brilliant swordsman Cyrano de Bergerac, who fought off one hundred men in battle and similarly cut down his opponents with his razor-sharp wit, but rather the world-weary man who won neither fame nor the woman he loved. Added to this triumvirate of the most beloved heroes of the age, all of whom who bridged the gap between left and right to some extent, were the chevalier Roland, who sacrificed his own life to save Charlemagne's forces, and Vercingétorix, the Gaulish chieftain who bore defeat to the Romans with grace and courage. The former was the hero of the epic tale *La Chanson de Roland* – which became a part of the republican school curriculum in the 1880s – and the latter was immortalized in Ernest Lavisse's primary school textbooks.[35] Indeed, such notions

France," *Historical Reflections/Réflexions historiques* 33, no. 3 (Fall 2007): 421–447. See especially 425–426.

[32] Moreover, the republicans created their own heroic cult, creating new lay saints for a democratic age. See Berenson, "Unifying the Nation," 19–20.

[33] David Bell makes a similar point about the rise of nationalism not being opposed to a decline in religion: 7–9; 23. On the sacred heart cult, see Raymond Jonas, *France and the Cult of the Sacred Heart: An Epic Tale for Modern Times* (Berkeley: University of California Press, 2001). On Lourdes, see Ruth Harris, *Lourdes: Body and Spirit in the Secular Age* (New York: Viking, 1999), and Suzanne K. Kaufman, *Consuming Visions: Mass Culture and the Lourdes Shrine* (Ithaca, NY: Cornell University Press, 2005).

[34] See Avner Ben-Amos, *Funerals, Politics and Memory in Modern France, 1789–1996* (New York: Oxford University Press, 2000).

[35] Vercingétroix, the Gaulish chieftain who undertakes the unsuccessful resistance to Roman conquest, poses, in the words of Schivelbusch, "the question of defeat as historical necessity," whereas Roland and Joan are "martyr-heroes of an ultimately successful cause,"

of heroism as self-abnegation and sacrifice for the greater good were themselves akin to religious martyrdom. Thus, there was ample room for common ground on heroes who could unite the nation and contribute to national regeneration.

Although contemporary playwrights might depict these heroes as legendary and heroic, they also depicted them as all too human, a quality that brought these transcendent figures down to earth for the fin-de-siècle's increasingly democratic audiences. When Félix Duquesne portrayed Napoleon in Sardou's 1893 production of *Mme Sans-Gêne*, he was dressed (or rather – undressed) in his dressing gown during much of the play. He was depicted not as the conquering military hero but as a loving husband afraid he might be cuckolded. Similarly, Sarah Bernhardt represented Joan of Arc as a vulnerable young girl whose all too human frailties made her destiny that much more remarkable. Likewise, the great poet and warrior Cyrano, completely in command in front of an audience, was tongue-tied and undone when he encountered the woman he loved, Roxane. Even as playwrights showed their characters' human side, they took pains to idealize, even sanitize, their lives. As Bernhardt herself noted, audiences did not want to see the sordid reality of historical figures but rather better versions of themselves, played by the most celebrated and charismatic actors of the age.[36]

In addition to heroes of the past, the French in a democratic age also looked to heroes in everyday life, whose actions were amplified not only in books and magazines but also and especially by the mass press.[37] Whereas heroes of the Ancien Régime, with the notable exception of Joan of Arc, had been aristocratic, the heroes of the Revolution were of modest origin, just like the *nouvelles couches* or lower middle classes promoted by the Third Republic. The Académie française even distributed annual prizes (*prix de vertu*) for "daily acts of courage," thereby encouraging the idea that the ordinary man, woman, and even child (like

---

166. On Roland, see Schivelbusch, 142–147. A colonial hero who could turn defeat into victory was Jean-Baptiste Marchand. See Edward Berenson, "Fashoda, Dreyfus and the Myth of Jean-Baptiste Marchand," *Yale French Studies* (special issue, ed. Dan Edelstein and Bettina R. Lerner) 111 (2007): 129–142.

[36] Sarah Bernhardt, *Ma double vie* (Paris: Phébus, 2000), 99–100.

[37] Gerbod, 424. The eighteenth-century cult of great men already held a measure of democratization because the philosophes distinguished between military heroes (illustrious men) who were so exceptional that their deeds could not be duplicated by the ordinary man or woman, and the "great man" whose everyday acts could serve as an example, model, and guide for others: Bell, 116–117.

the revolutionary hero Joseph Bara, who died fighting the royalists) could become a hero.[38] The Third Republic, wishing to be inclusive, promoted heroes from all social classes – from the peasant girl Joan of Arc and the working-class heroes of the Bazar de la Charité fire, to the parvenu Napoleon, and finally, to the elite women in the Bazar de la Charité fire and the aristocrat Cyrano. Although aristocratic males might make some republicans uncomfortable, aristocratic heroes like Cyrano de Bergerac could be adopted, as long as they were identified either with the greater good of the French nation or with the democratic ideals of the period.

Jews too were incorporated to some extent in the national consensus, in particular, actress Sarah Bernhardt, who played Joan of Arc twice in important national productions, as well as Napoleon's doomed son, who died of tuberculosis at the age of twenty-one, in Edmond Rostand's 1900 play *L'Aiglon*. There was also unity around the anti-hero Charles-Benjamin Ullmo, the naval ensign convicted of treason in 1908, whose Jewish identity was downplayed in favor of a view that depicted him as a fallen French hero and as a symbol of the dangers to the national body of drugs and loose women.

Finally, women too were celebrated as heroes, although the best-known heroes of the age – with the notable exception of Joan of Arc – were male. Women were repeatedly mentioned in compendia of heroes of the time, not only saintly women in the past (by Catholics) but also by republicans, who praised the women who had played supporting roles in both the Revolution and the Franco-Prussian War.[39] Thus, there clearly was an effort by contemporaries, on both the left and right, to include women as heroes who would form part of a national consensus, especially if these female heroes could be subordinated to their male counterparts.[40] Furthermore, certain heroic traits, for example, those of self-sacrifice and abnegation, were coded as feminine, a view reinforced by associations with Christianity. Yet such "female" heroic traits, whether possessed by a man or woman, were acceptable as long as they could be harnessed to the male notion of honor. The nation was the product of the sacrifice of

[38] Gerbod, 419.

[39] Gerbod, 421–422.

[40] Denis Provencher and Luke Eilderts illustrate in their study of gender in the Lavisse manuals how representations of women heroes, especially Joan, were ambivalent because Joan needed to be represented both as a hero and as a young girl. This tension often led to a contradiction between text and image, which was certainly the case of Bernhardt's Joan: "The Nation According to Lavisse: Teaching Masculinity and Male Citizenship in Third-Republic France," *French Cultural Studies* 18, no. 1 (2007): 46–49.

every citizen and the cult of heroes all-encompassing, incorporating both genders and a variety of classes.

Competing Notions of the Hero: The Dreyfus Affair and Beyond

Rationality, long considered a bourgeois male trait – as opposed to the sentimentality and irrationality of women – was used to assert male superiority over women and colonized men, especially in the educational system. There emerged during the late nineteenth century, however, a competing discourse about manhood, promulgated in part by medicine and the sciences, which celebrated strong male bodies. Indeed, those who promoted such materialist discourses often blamed the soft "civilizing" aspects of modern society for diminishing the manhood of the very same "superior" men.[41] Tensions also existed within biomedical discourse. While the medical community destabilized traditional notions of gender – especially with research on male hysteria – the same practitioners also buttressed the traditional order by minimizing the incidence of male hysteria and projecting it on working-class and or foreign male bodies.[42] Thus, although the notion of honor was harnessed to manhood, the definitions of manhood were not always the same.

Not only were bourgeois notions of manhood contested from within, they were also contested from without, first and foremost by women, who challenged male superiority and difference by entering traditionally male-dominated spheres. The Camille Sée school law of 1880 led to a fourfold increase in the number of lycée degrees held by women. These years also saw the first women doctors and lawyers, although their actual presence in the field was quite modest compared to the contemporary fascination for such figures.[43] Finally, although there is a long tradition of women writers in France, this period witnessed a real upsurge in the numbers of

---

[41] Christopher E. Forth, "*La Civilisation* and Its Discontents," in *French Masculinities: History, Culture and Politics*, ed. Christopher Forth and Bertrand Taithe (New York: Palgrave Macmillan, 2007), 86–87.

[42] Mark Micale, *Hysterical Men: The Hidden History of Male Nervous Illness* (Cambridge, MA: Harvard University Press, 2008), 206–208.

[43] Anne Sauvy, "La Littérature et les femmes," in *Histoire de l'édition française. Vol. 4: Le Livre concurrencé: 1900–1950*, ed. H-J. Martin and R. Chartier (Paris: Fayard, 1991), 269–270. See also Juliette M. Rogers, "Feminist Discourse in Women's Novels of Professional Development," in *A "Belle Epoque"? Women in French Society and Culture, 1890–1914*, ed. Diana Holmes and Carrie Tarr (New York: Berghahn Books, 2006), 184–186. On women's writing, see the anthology by Vicki Mistacco, *Les Femmes et la tradition littéraire: Anthologie du Moyen Age à nos jours*, 2 vols. (New Haven, CT: Yale University Press, 2006).

women writers, in part, due to the new school law.[44] Women also increasingly appropriated male discourses of honor as well as role models for their own ends. Feminist Arria Ly, for example, used the notion of honor to argue in favor of women fighting duels, as did women seeking restitution from men who had impregnated them.[45] Women writers like Anna de Noailles, Gérard d'Houville, Marie Lenéru, and Daniel Lesueur turned Nietzschean misogynist discourse on its head in a variety of ways and argued in favor of women's freedoms, constructing an image of the New Woman whose actions challenged the conventional bourgeois order of the day. Although they might not explicitly use the term, their heroines were *superwomen*, who dominated in some way the men with whom they were involved.[46]

Bourgeois notions of masculinity were also challenged by other outsiders – male bohemians and members of the avant-garde. Bohemians (not all bohemians were members of the avant-garde and not all members of the avant-garde were bohemians) contested the ideal of work that defined the bourgeois male and instead celebrated art and freedom from conventions. Similarly, some writers and artists of the avant-garde celebrated emotion and feeling, although they were careful to distinguish themselves from the irrationality of women. Indeed, some even argued that an excess of intellect led to moral and physical decline.[47] Some decadent writers

---

[44] Octave Uzanne noted in 1894 that there were 1,219 women members of the Société des gens de lettres and 32 members of the Société des auteurs dramatiques: Uzanne, quoted by Béatrice Slama, "Femmes écrivains," in *Misérable et glorieuse: La Femme du XIXème siècle*, ed. Jean-Paul Aron (Brussels: Editions Complexe, 1984), 214. Contemporary press reports at the time of Daniel Lesueur's candidacy to the Société des gens de lettres board (Lesueur was the first woman elected to the executive board of the society and later served as its vice-president) indicated that for 800 members of the association, 80 were women: "Les Candidatures féminines," *Le Figaro*, 25 March 1900 (Dossier Lesueur, Bibliothèque Marguerite Durand). Anne-Marie Thiesse notes that although 2–3 percent of writers overall were women, 17 percent were authors of "popular novels": *Le Roman du quotidien: Lecteurs et lectures populaires à la Belle Epoque* (Paris: Le Chemin Vert, 1984), 183–184. Although it is difficult to establish exact figures of women writers during this period, it is clear that men of the time noticed the phenomenon; witness the veritable flood of studies on women writers, among them, works by Charles Maurras, Jean de Gourmont, Paul Flat, and Jules Bertaut.

[45] Andrea Mansker, "Shaming Men: Feminist Honor and the Sexual Double Standard in Belle Époque France," and Rachel G. Fuchs, "Paternity, Progeny, and Property: Family Honor in the Late Nineteenth Century," both in *Confronting Modernity in Fin-de-Siècle France: Bodies, Minds and Gender*, ed. Christopher Forth and Elinor Accampo (New York: Palgrave Macmillan, 2010), 169–191 and 150–168, respectively.

[46] Datta, "Superwomen or Slaves?" 424.

[47] On Bohemians and manhood, see Michael L. Wilson, "'Capped with Hope, Clad in Youth, Shod in Courage': Masculinity and Marginality in Fin-de-Siècle Paris," in *Confronting*

like Anatole Baju, the editor of a journal called *Le Décadent*, praised the increasing refinement and feminization of men, which they associated with the divine.[48]

Competing notions of manhood came to the fore during the Dreyfus Affair. In 1894, the Jewish army captain Alfred Dreyfus was accused of selling documents to the Germans. Despite his protestations of innocence, he was tried in a secret court-martial trial, convicted (based on documents neither he nor his lawyer had viewed), and subsequently sentenced to life imprisonment on Devil's Island in French Guyana. Two years later, Lieutenant Colonel Georges Picquart, who had been named chief of the intelligence services, learned that the real culprit was another officer, Major Walsin Esterhazy, and, furthermore, that the documents incriminating Dreyfus had been fabricated. Picquart was viewed with disdain by his superiors and transferred to Tunisia, while the real traitor was protected by army leaders, who engaged in a cover-up. The government and the army refused to reopen Dreyfus's case, although Esterhazy was tried and acquitted. Only in the wake of the acquittal, when prominent novelist Emile Zola published an open letter, "J'Accuse," to the French president in the newspaper *L'Aurore*, on January 13, 1898, did the Dreyfus case became a full-scale national affair. Due to the efforts of Dreyfusards like Zola, another trial for Dreyfus was ordered, although the military court once again found the army captain guilty – this time with the unlikely explanation of "extenuating circumstances." The affair culminated with the French president pardoning Dreyfus. In 1906, France's supreme court, the Cour de Cassation, overturned the guilty verdict and Dreyfus was reintegrated into the French army.

The Dreyfus Affair still resonates in France today. Not only did it mark the entry of intellectuals as a group into public life, but it also signaled the crystallization of a modern anti-Semitic movement and, with it, the birth of the Zionist movement. Furthermore, it illustrated the power of the press and, moreover, led to a new configuration of political forces, which eventually led to the separation of church and state in 1905. Not least of all, it left its imprint on national memory and was incorporated into a mythology for the left and the right, both

Modernity in Fin-de-Siècle France: Bodies, Minds and Gender, ed. Christopher Forth and Elinor Accampo (New York: Palgrave Macmillan, 2010), 192–212. On the avant-garde and manhood, see Datta, *Birth of a National Icon*, 118–126.
[48] Baju, quoted in Micale, 210.

of which viewed it as a key defining moment and a model for future confrontations.[49]

While the Affair was debate about ideas, specifically about competing notions of national identity, those notions were embedded in opposing views of heroism and manhood. Dreyfusards, that is, partisans of Dreyfus, extolled reason, moral courage, and intellectual qualities, praising such heroes as Emile Zola, who risked his career and reputation, and Colonel Picquart, who defied his superiors to state the truth. Although Picquart was a military man, it was his intellectual qualities as well as his willingness to forsake hierarchy in order to obey his conscience that Dreyfusards praised. For Dreyfusards, heroism and manhood was thus defined by independence of thought, whereas for anti-Dreyfusards, a real hero was often a military man who respected discipline and established institutions like the army and church. He also displayed physical courage, engaging in daring exploits.[50] Anti-Dreyfusard heroes included such men as Colonel Hubert Henry. The plebian officer, promoted for his courage rather than his intellect, forged documents to convict Dreyfus and later committed suicide, thus becoming a martyr for the anti-Dreyfusard cause. Each group, moreover, asserted that its opponents were less than real men and attempted to depict them as effeminate and homosexuals. Dreyfusards perhaps were more defensive about their manhood than their opponents, given contemporary discourses on male bodies and the detrimental effects of a "soft" intellectual life.[51]

Despite these very real differences, there was a great deal of common ground in the construction of heroes. Both sides concurred about the role of heroes in the quest for national revival. Indeed, the two groups agreed on certain heroic traits: courage, whether moral or physical, and

[49] I have written at length in my earlier work that the Dreyfus Affair marked the culmination of a process begun in the avant-garde during the years preceding the Affair. Moreover, the mythology of the Affair has obscured the fact that despite very real differences between the values expressed by the opposing groups, they shared similar ideas – not only a belief in the role of intellectuals in public life but also shared views about honor and manhood. On the universal importance of the Affair, see Louis Begley, *Why the Dreyfus Affair Matters* (New Haven, CT: Yale University Press, 2009). See also Ruth Harris, *Dreyfus: Politics, Emotion and the Scandal of the Century* (New York: Metropolitan Books, 2010) for another important new treatment of the Affair.

[50] The philosophes in the eighteenth century had already distinguished between merely eminent men, including military heroes, who had accomplished brave acts, and great men, whose entire lives were to serve as an example for their fellow men. This definition was not always maintained and the two categories were often nearly collapsed: Bell, 117.

[51] Datta, *Birth of a National Icon*, 149–159; Forth, *The Dreyfus Affair*, 67–102.

disinterestedness – the idea of self-sacrifice and abnegation for the greater good. Furthermore, there was some overlap in the heroes extolled by the two groups. Dreyfusards *did* admire some military heroes, not only Colonel Picquart but also colonial leaders Savornan de Brazza and Jean-Baptiste Marchand – the latter two of whom were equally celebrated by anti-Dreyfusards.[52] Moreover, such anti-Dreyfusards as Maurice Barrès praised both Napoleon, the man on horseback, and poet Victor Hugo, dubbing them "professors of energy." Both sides also asserted male superiority over women, although they allowed for the possibility of female heroism.

Although the Dreyfus Affair witnessed an apotheosis of the *male* hero in French society, it was part of a longer and broader process of nation building and of the construction of heroes. An examination of the larger context of the fin de siècle also allows us to view the process by which the conflicts about heroes during the years before and during the Dreyfus Affair increasingly gave way to a national consensus – which also included women – in the years immediately preceding the First World War. Moreover, the tensions between competing notions of heroes as well as the common ground around them, which played out in larger national discussions of heroes in the mass press and the theater at the fin de siècle, illustrate not only how complex those notions were but also how often they were destabilized.

II. Heroes, Mass Culture, the Theater, and the Press

"The theater is a great mystery ... it is not our fault if people have sometimes turned it into a charade; if they have denigrated this festival of the crowd, transforming it into a society game. ... It is not our fault if people have forgotten what is sacred in the theater." These words lamenting the commercialization of the theater at the fin de siècle are those of Edmond Rostand, in his reception speech to the Académie française on June 4, 1903.[53] There is a certain irony to these remarks, because since Rostand himself benefited from the same commercialization that he criticized here. In a similar vein, Maurice Talmeyr, writing for the conservative *La Revue des deux mondes* in September of the same year, noted

---

[52] On Brazza, see Berenson, "Unifying the French Nation," and on Marchand, "Fashoda, Dreyfus and the Myth of Jean-Baptiste Marchand."

[53] *Discours de Réception à l'Académie française, le 4 juin 1903* (Paris: Charpentier et Fasquelle, 1904), 29.

the ubiquity of the penny press: "Let us imagine that we are returning from a ball. It is between six and seven o'clock in the morning, and we glimpse from the back of our carriage the spectacle of a Parisian street. Workers are heading off to work; delivery men go by on their carts, concierges open their doors. We meet milkmen and women carrying bread. And what do we observe? All of these people, or nearly all, are reading the newspaper."[54] Here, Talmeyr lamented the popularity of the *roman-feuilleton* or serialized story among the new readers of newspapers.[55] Just four years later, this view was echoed by a reporter for the Socialist newspaper *L'Humanité*. In an article entitled, "Comment on lance un feuilleton," journalist André Morizet not only decried the importance of the *feuilleton* in the paper, but he also held women responsible for this development: "The *feuilleton* in the newspaper is the domain of the woman.... Woe to those newspapers whose *feuilletons* do not have the approval of the housewife! ... The husband in order to obtain some peace will abandon his preferred paper, and we will know, by the decline in circulation, the importance of the homemaker."[56] If Talmeyr denigrated the influence of the popular classes in defining tastes, Morizet focused his ire on women, held responsible for the decline of standards. He also expressed the fear that henceforth women would control both purchasing power and public discourse. These writers, from three different points on the political spectrum, shared a common distrust of the urban mass culture exemplified by the penny press and the boulevard theater. Although these two venues, whose reach was far and wide, were ideal places to construct heroes, both were also symbols of the perceived dislocations of modernity, of which mass consumption was a notable example.

Rostand, Talmeyr, and Morizet were not alone. Both members of the avant-garde like Nietzsche and cultural conservatives, among them, anti-Semite Edouard Drumont, railed against the commercial theater and the press, which they represented as inauthentic, overrun by the masses, overly "feminine," and unheroic.[57] The department store, in particular,

---

[54] Maurice Talmeyr, "Le Roman-Feuilleton et l'esprit populaire," *La Revue des deux mondes* 17 (September 1903): 203.

[55] The *roman-feuilleton* had, of course, been around for much longer, dating from the earlier part of the nineteenth century.

[56] Morizet, "Comment on lance un feuilleton," *L'Humanité*, 28 October 1907.

[57] On Nietzsche and his criticisms of the commercial theater and of the masses, see Andreas Huyssen, *After the Great Divide: Modernism, Mass Culture, Postmodernism* (Bloomington: Indiana University Press, 1986), 50–51. On women as symbols of modernity, specifically consumerism, see Rita Felski, *The Gender of Modernity* (Cambridge, MA: Harvard University Press, 1995), 61–90.

fueled male fears of the voracious woman consumer, whose "lust" for objects "depleted" the resources – both financial and sexual – of her husband, thereby disrupting the economic and sexual hierarchy between the sexes.[58] Nowhere is this more evident than in Zola's 1883 novel *Au Bonheur des dames*, in which the writer celebrated the department store, describing its activity as the "poetry of modern life," but in which he also depicted women consumers as out of control and sexually crazed. Even republicans like Zola viewed with ambivalence the consumer culture that accompanied the rise to power of the bourgeois Third Republic. Although they admired certain aspects of industrialization and production, they tended to see consumption as a threat to "disinterestedness" (both a republican and a heroic trait) and the civic ideal of the republic.[59]

Consumption, linked to female desire, was juxtaposed to male self-control. It threatened to feminize males who could be both swept up in a desire to consume and rendered helpless by the consuming women around them.[60] Consumption not only threatened to bring women into the public sphere, but it also had the potential to invade the interior of the home, seen as the last bastion against the corrupting influences of brute individualism. Thus, the private interests of the marketplace individual were seen as antithetical to the social duties of the republican citizen, although these tensions were reconciled by the moral and aesthetic management of the woman consumer through the civilizing influence of taste. The female consumer was thus tamed, presented as an artist of the interior and the commodity as an art object. The marketplace itself became an artistic arena. Such a view also gave women a public role in the new consumer society and incorporated them into the national consensus.[61]

Similarly, for elite males, consumption was coded as art, if it could be channeled into the category of collecting. Represented as creative, collecting

[58] Felski, 74.

[59] Williams, 315–316.

[60] See David Kuchta on "the great masculine renunciation," that is, the adoption by aristocratic males of a frugal and sober ideal both in dress and consumption. Kuchta writes: "The masculine language of industry and frugality emerged as part of eighteenth-century aristocratic men's claims to a political and cultural hegemony which had the intent and effect of excluding lower and middle-class men, and all women, from the formal institutions of power." "The Making of the Self-Made Man: Class, Clothing, and English Masculinity, 1688–1832," in *The Sex of Things: Gender and Consumption in Historical Perspective*, ed. Victoria de Grazia and Ellen Furlough (Berkeley: University of California Press, 1996), 56. See also Felski, 73–74, on the all-"consuming" female.

[61] Lisa Tiersten, *Marianne in the Market: Envisioning Consumer Society in Fin-de-Siècle France* (Berkeley: University of California Press, 2001), 2–7, and Debora Silverman, 186–189.

was also rational and therefore manly, because it implied both an investment and a "hunt" for objects and a calculation as to how they might be obtained. Such an enterprise even pitted males in "duels" with one another for the acquisition of these objects.[62] In these ways, the dangers of consumption for men but especially for women were minimized and associated with a higher ideal, that of the construction of family and nation.

As for the middle classes and lower middle classes, both male and female, their consumption in the department store could also be linked to a higher purpose. Like the republican school, the department store was responsible for homogenizing French society and forging national identity around certain kinds of consumption. The department store was a "cultural primer" that laid down for the rising middle classes the models and codes of behavior of the Parisian upper middle classes. Through their consumption, these classes could themselves "become" bourgeois.[63]

Despite such rhetoric, however, consumption clearly threatened masculinity at this time, implying as it did the increasing importance of women in society. Moreover, this consumption did not entirely mitigate the image of the feminizing influences of consumerism on middle-class and lower middle-class men who no longer had ties to the land or to manual work, especially the bureaucrats and clerks belonging to the *nouvelles couches* promoted by the Third Republic. These men were derided for their lack of manhood by Maurice Barrès in his best-selling 1897 novel *Les Déracinés*. Intellectuals too were singled out for their effeminacy at this time; hence their fascination for heroes and their importance in promoting heroes during this period. For men of the *nouvelles couches*, as for those of other classes who frequented the theater and read the mass press, heroes were a way of offsetting the "feminizing" influences of consumption.[64] These

---

[62] Consumption, as Leora Auslander writes, "while necessary [for both sexes] to the economic health of the country, was understood as potentially profoundly disruptive of the libidinal economy, capable of deregulating and destabilizing the family and the society." "The Gendering of Consumer Practices in Nineteenth-Century France," in *The Sex of Things: Gender and Consumption in Historical Perspective*, ed. Victoria de Grazia and Ellen Furlough (Berkeley: University of California Press, 1996), 103. Women were thus both consumers and a commodity, linking in the minds of many men of the time the kleptomaniac and the prostitute: Felski, 64. See also the excellent review essay by Mary-Louise Roberts, "Gender, Consumption and Commodity Culture," *American Historical Review* 103, no. 3 (June 1998): 817–844.

[63] Michael Miller, *The Bon Marché: Bourgeois Culture and the Department Store* (Princeton, NJ: Princeton University Press, 1981), 183.

[64] Men from the lower classes apparently rejected the notion that their consumption was feminizing: Christopher E. Forth, *Masculinity in the Modern West: Gender, Civilization and the Body* (New York: Palgrave Macmillan, 2008), 156.

heroes gave them license to consume the fruits of mass culture and at the same time claim to associate themselves with higher ideals. For women, the cult of heroes offered new possibilities for female heroism and also allowed them to participate in the construction of national identity.[65] By identifying themselves with heroes in the theater and the press, men as well as women could pretend to possess such traits, especially because the heroes promoted in the theater and the press were better versions of the ordinary man or woman. Moreover, the use of heroic figures to market such commodities as soap, liqueurs, and candy, although ironic, is not unsurprising; it served both to offset consumerism's apparently feminizing capacity and as a way of harnessing consumerism to the "selfless" ideals of heroism.

Although Rostand may have decried the state of the theater at the fin de siècle, he also celebrated its importance in French culture and society.[66] For Rostand, the theater had a sacred quality. The mystery to which he referred was undoubtedly the medieval mystery play depicting biblical stories, which originated with performances by clergy members but eventually involved the entire community.[67] The medieval mystery play then was a communal affair, in some ways a replica of the sacred communion shared by all within the church walls. For Rostand, the theater in his own time was also a sacred trust, a communal activity, but it no longer revolved around the Catholic Church. Rather, it was a celebration of the cult of the nation. Although he might not explicitly say so, Rostand, in all of his major plays, from *Cyrano* (1897), to *L'Aiglon* (1900) and to *Chantecler* (1909), attempted to unite his compatriots around the nation and its heroes.

Rostand was right about the power of the theater at the fin de siècle. The shared experience of the theater was immediate and communal in a way that no newspaper could ever be, even if the solitary readers were reading in a public space.[68] The theater in Paris during this time could

---

[65] Auslander distinguishes between males who participate in political identity and women, excluded from the political arena, who contribute to national identity (102–103). Although such a distinction is useful, I would observe that there was considerable overlap between "political" and "national" identity.

[66] I examine Rostand as a celebrity author in an essay, "Heroes, Celebrity and the Theater in Fin-de-Siècle France: *Cyrano de Bergerac*" in *Constructing Charisma: Celebrity, Fame and Power in Nineteenth-Century Europe*. ed. Edward Berenson and Eva Giloi (New York: Berghahn Books, 2010), 155–164. On the commercialization of the theater at the fin de siècle, see Charle, *Théâtres*, 13, 37.

[67] Not incidentally, it included members of various guilds who could "advertise" their wares by the props and costumes used.

[68] Charle, *Théâtres*, 11.

reach a public wider than that of readers of best-sellers, who numbered 100,000, whereas hit productions, which had 300 performances or more, could easily reach up to five times as many people.[69] Indeed, Rostand's *Cyrano de Bergerac*, which beat all records of the day, celebrating its 1,000th performance in 1913, attracted millions of spectators.[70]

The boulevard culture of Paris offered more possibilities to women than ever before, not only the glittering shop windows of the department stores, which provided their own spectacle, but also the theater.[71] There is clear evidence that women and girls frequented the theater in greater numbers, especially in the late nineteenth century. As acting became a more respectable profession, theatergoing became a more feminized cultural event.[72] Women's magazines of the time, obviously destined for female fans, began celebrating actresses as role models for ordinary "respectable" women. Actresses as upright *bourgeoises* became a marketable commodity, to be consumed in the same way as their plays.[73] Moreover, as the celebrity interviews with these actresses illustrate, they were increasingly playing roles that would be more palatable to family audiences.

The 1864 decree, which lifted government control over the numbers of theaters during the waning years of the Second Empire, led to a commercialization of the theater. Not only did it contribute to an increase in the numbers of theaters, but it also was responsible for the creation of a market that privileged the tastes of the masses, culminating in a decline of literary, classical genres. While the newly emergent middle and lower middle classes increasingly frequented the theater, more popular audiences abandoned it in favor of cheaper entertainments like the café-concert, the circus, and sporting events. The "haussmannisation" of the theater resulted in the removal of theaters from the more populist eastern areas of Paris – the Boulevard du Temple, which housed many of these theatres, was known as the Boulevard du crime – toward the newly transformed western sections of the city. This move led to a sharp increase in the prices of tickets.[74] At the same time, improvements in urban transportation within Paris as well as the construction of railroads and roads

---

[69] Charle, *Théâtres*, 404.

[70] Hemmings, *The Theatre Industry in Nineteenth-Century France*, 3.

[71] See Vanessa Schwartz's *Spectacular Realities: Early Mass Culture in Fin-de-Siècle Paris* (Berkeley: University of California Press, 1998).

[72] Berlanstein, 168.

[73] Berlanstein, 209–236.

[74] Charle, *Théâtres*, 36–37, 45.

facilitated access to Paris from other parts of the country, allowing individuals from the provinces and outlying areas to frequent the theater. The ease of access, coupled with the centralization of French culture, meant that the provincial theater, in comparison with Paris, had little to offer.[75] Thus, a visit to Paris to see the latest theater success was obligatory, as was a visit to the department store.[76] Foreigners also frequented the theater, especially during the world fairs of 1889 and 1900, although less often than earlier, given the presence of other entertainments where knowledge of French was not required. At any rate, these entertainments all earned Paris the reputation of the capital of spectacle, and, indeed, the "capital of the nineteenth century."[77]

The press amplified the successes of the theater, not only reporting on the hits of the day but also reproducing parts of plays, and sometimes the plays in their entirety. It also reported on the private lives of the actors and actresses who incarnated the most popular roles, bringing the world of the theater into the lives of even those who could not afford to go to the theater regularly.

In the age before the advent of the cinema and radio, the influence and power not only of the theater but also of the print press was unprecedented. The 1881 press law, which established freedom of the press, as well as innovations in printing and production techniques that significantly reduced costs and made the reproduction of images easier, led to the spectacular rise of the press at the fin de siècle. The increasing literacy of the French public, a result of the Ferry school laws of the 1880s, and improvements in transports further contributed to the emergence of the press, the penny press, in particular. The four major newspapers of the time, *Le Petit Parisien* (known as the paper with the largest circulation worldwide), *Le Petit Journal*, *Le Journal*, and *Le Matin* together sold roughly four million copies in 1912.[78] Moreover, these papers, although produced in Paris, were widely disseminated in the provinces, with a significant portion of their sales taking place there, making them truly national in scope. At the same time, there emerged a vibrant regional press, which did not compete with the national press but coexisted

---

[75] First runs of national plays often began in the provinces in other countries: Charle, *Théâtres*, 15, 45.

[76] Miller, 169.

[77] Charle, *Théâtres*, 27, 38. In the words of Walter Benjamin, "Paris was capital of the nineteenth century."

[78] Christophe Charle quotes these figures from Bellanger in *Le Siècle de la presse (1830–1939)* (Paris: Seuil, 2004), 160.

alongside it. Not only did the local papers report on national events, linking the local to the national, but they also reproduced articles of note in the national papers.[79] Given the country's population of thirty-nine million people on the eve of World War I, the newspaper's reach was truly phenomenal, with the four leading papers reaching one out of two adults in France.[80] No less an observer than sociologist Gabriel Tarde noted that the press had the power to create a public out of disparate individuals who shared a common sense of belonging through the newspaper, even as they maintained their individual, including political, differences.[81] Tarde thus anticipated Benedict Anderson's "imagined communities" by nearly a century.[82]

Together, the national and local press contributed to a homogenization of the French public and the forging of a common sense of national identity.[83] The major papers sought to attract the greatest number of readers; this did not necessarily make them apolitical, as they did not hesitate to engage in national debates of interest to their readers. The four major papers did, however, seek to unite the public around a national consensus, one that celebrated French grandeur.[84]

The newspapers also attracted a wide public by publishing sensationalized stories, both in the form of the *roman-feuilleton* and the *fait divers*. As Morizet further lamented in his diatribe against the *feuilleton*, it interrupted the monotony of everyday existence by celebrating the melodramatic: "It is the melodrama that breaks up the monotony of working-class lives."[85] Melodrama, a more populist genre, declined in the theater (as the theater became more exclusive) at the fin de siècle, its hegemony challenged by other genres – among them, the bourgeois drama (*drame bourgeois*), one-act vaudeville plays (*vaudevilles*), historical plays, and comedies – and its aesthetics, by the avant-garde theater. Nevertheless, the melodramatic mode continued to inform plays of the time, even when

---

[79] Marianne M'sili, *Le Faits divers en république: Histoire sociale de 1870 à nos jours* (Paris: CNRS Editions, 2000), 143; Charle, *Le Siècle de la presse*, 156–157. On the *fait divers*, see also David H. Walker, *Outrage and Insight: Modern French Writers and the "Fait Divers"* (Oxford: Berg, 1995).

[80] Berenson, *Madame Caillaux*, 209.

[81] See Tarde's essay "Le Public et la foule," in *L'Opinion et la foule* (Paris: PUF, 1989), 42–43.

[82] See Berenson's excellent analysis of the press and its role in forging national community, including heroes, in "Unifying the French Nation," 20–23.

[83] Msili, 146.

[84] Charle, *Le Siècle de la presse*, 157; Berenson, "Unifying the French Nation," 20–21.

[85] Morizet.

they explicitly rejected melodrama as a genre. Moreover, melodrama was increasingly taken up by the new penny press that published the serialized *feuilletons*, read by women and the more popular classes, as the diatribes of Morizet and Talmeyr against the genre illustrate.[86]

The newspaper was a sexually divided space such that *faits divers*, trials, and dramatic public representations of private events occupied the intermediate zone separating the masculine space of politics from the feminine space of the serialized novels, which was located below the fold of the newspaper.[87] On the one hand, fictional accounts in the *feuilleton* were often portrayed in a realistic fashion, and on the other, *faits divers* were increasingly presented as fiction, thus leading to a blurring between fact and fiction.[88] Contemporaries were primed to view certain events as they would fictional accounts, complete with the heroes and villains of melodrama.

To understand how and why contemporaries of the fin de siècle were so ready to view contemporary events as melodramas, it is helpful to examine briefly the history of melodrama in France. In his seminal work on the melodramatic imagination, literary scholar Peter Brooks shows that the melodramatic mode was born in France in the aftermath of the Revolution, at the moment that marked the final dissolution of the sacred as defined by the church and the monarchy.[89] In the wake of this

[86] This avant-garde theater, both Naturalist and Symbolist, however, was generally intended for a small circle of initiates rather than for mass audiences: Charnow, *Theatre, Politics, and Markets in Fin-de-Siècle Paris*. On the various popular genres in the theater during the nineteenth and early twentieth centuries, Charle, *Théâtres*, 73. See pp. 224–226 for the decline of the melodrama at the fin de siècle. See Charle, *Théâtres*, 289, and *Le Siècle de la presse*, 143–166, for melodrama in the press.

[87] Thiesse, *Le Roman du Quotidien*, 183–184. This link between fiction and reality is an important one. In "Presse et culture de masse en France (1880–1914)," *Revue historique*, 605 (January–February 1998), Christian Delporte argues that the *fait divers* represented a middle ground between pure fiction and reality, favoring the identification of the reader with the individuals in the story. Slowly, it took the place of the popularity of *roman-feuilleton* as an argument for increasing sales, 104. He also notes that the daily paper was destined for all members of the family, including women who had heretofore been excluded from reading the papers, 110.

[88] Schwartz, 32–33. See also Marie-Ève Thérenty, who argues that a circular relationship existed between literature and journalism as the same individuals moved freely between the two genres. She notes, moreover, that this movement contributed both to making the newspaper more literary at this time (*littérarisation*), and to the fictionalization of daily life, which she describes as the "poetics of the quotidian," *La Littérature au quotidien: Poétiques journalistiques au XIXème Siècle* (Paris: Seuil, 2007), 18–25.

[89] One should note that Brooks characterizes melodrama as a mode rather than as a genre: Peter Brooks, *The Melodramatic Imagination: Balzac, Henry James, Melodrama,*

upheaval, the melodramatic mode emerged, representing, in part, the urge for moral certainties but grounding them in personal and individual terms.[90]

The modern world of the late nineteenth century was marked by the decline of religion and traditional interests and the concomitant rise of new elites, along with increased industrialization, the rapid growth of cities, and the advent of technology. In such a society, the power of melodrama to describe real-life events was comforting and seems understandable, just as it was in the aftermath of the Revolution. The increasingly "spectacular" aspect of modernity only heightened the predilection for the melodramatic mode, which was grounded in the visual. Thus, melodrama, in particular, but all exaggerated fictional modes, informed the public's view of real-life events and promoted a desire for larger-than-life heroes. [91]

Fin-de-siècle images of heroism (and its opposite) were shaped by the press and the theater, both of which disseminated theatrical notions of heroes. French men and women of the time sought heroes in the serialized *feuilletons* of the mass press and in the plays of the boulevard theater and even modeled their own behavior and that of their contemporaries on what they read and saw onstage. The journalist from *L'Humanité*, writing in 1908, observed: "How true it is … [that] the book and the theater act on modern manners! … There are people who only dress, speak, laugh, live, and die as one does in novels. Others, even more numerous, model their gestures on what they have seen in the theater … with postures and vocal inflections borrowed from the Comédie française or the Ambigu [a theater that specialized in melodramas]."[92] No wonder then

and the Mode of Excess (New Haven, CT: Yale University Press, 1976; 1995), vii, 45. See also James R. Lehning, *The Melodramatic Thread: Spectacle and Political Culture in Modern France* (Bloomington: Indiana University Press, 2007).

90 Melodrama, which depicts the world in Manichean terms, pits the pure individual against the evil villain. The most famous practitioner of melodrama was Pixérécourt, known, not incidentally, as the "Corneille of the boulevards." Pixérécourt's heroics were more exteriorized, simplified, and hyperbolic than those of Corneille and were represented onstage in a more "spectacular" and visual way than in Corneille's classical theater: Brooks, 24–27.

91 This is also the view of Thérenty, who notes that all types of literature from the theater to the novel to the literary journal rivaled the newspaper to represent the "poetics of the quotidian," 26.

92 V. "Le Triomphe de Sherlock Holmes," *L'Humanité*, 8 June 1908, p. 2. The same writer lamented the pernicious role of the press and the theater, calling them, "La Mauvaise Ecole," *L'Humanité*, 17 November 1907 (front page, above the fold). This piece was signed V. Snell.

that French men and women, whose worldview was shaped in no small measure by the fictions of the theater and the press, looked to these venues both for a celebration of the glories of the past and as a national unity "beyond" politics.

In this book, I explore constructions of heroism through the course of five chapters. The first and last, which examine real-life heroes and anti-heroes in the mass press, serve as bookends for the three middle chapters on heroes in the theater. Given that the focus of this book is thematic, I do not always proceed chronologically. The overall narrative, however, represents a chronological process, by which heroes and anti-heroes increasingly became objects of a national consensus, especially during the years immediately preceding the First World War.

I begin Chapter 1 with an analysis of the Bazar de la Charité fire in May 1897. A real-life incident, it was covered obsessively by the mass press, which represented the major players as characters in a melodrama, and inspired a national debate about decadence, regeneration, and heroism. Class warfare and religious differences, expressed in the differing images of the aristocratic female victims, their male working-class rescuers, and the male aristocratic villains, the *gardénias*, who allegedly deserted the women, reflect the extent of the divisions in French society on the eve of the Dreyfus Affair.

In the next three chapters, I study heroes in the theater to illustrate how historical figures were fictionalized in the theater by authors and publicists who sought to transform history into a spectacle to be consumed in the boulevard theater and amplified by the mass press. In Chapter 2, which examines the reception of Edmond Rostand's *Cyrano de Bergerac*, I once again explore the role of aristocratic men in French society, this time through the lens of a fictionalized aristocratic hero. An immediate critical and popular success, *Cyrano* played to full houses during the height of the Dreyfus Affair, uniting within the theater walls a public profoundly divided outside them. Even though Rostand himself was a Dreyfusard, Cyrano had admirers on both sides of the Affair. Both Dreyfusards and anti-Dreyfusards could celebrate Cyrano and claim him as one of their own, the first group because he illustrated that the pen was mightier than the sword, and the second, because he was a military hero. A closer examination of the play, however, reveals a more equivocal portrait of Cyrano. Cyrano's physical deformity, along with his inability to declare his love for Roxane, undercut his "heroism." As he would in his 1900 play *L'Aiglon*, Rostand thus destabilized contemporary ideals of heroism and manhood as much as he celebrated them.

In the following two chapters, I continue my study of heroes in the theater by focusing on Napoleon and Joan of Arc. Like Cyrano, both were military heroes, and, moreover, figures of defeat whose losses transformed them into martyrs and symbols of national resistance against such traditional enemies as England, as well as the new, ever-increasing threat posed by Germany. Despite such similarities, however, many differences separate the two most popular heroes of the time. Napoleon ultimately symbolized the tradition of French national grandeur, while Joan, abandoned by king and country, represented a more problematic legacy of female virtue and goodness in a corrupt male world.

In Chapter 3, I examine the way in which writers and critics of the fin de siècle exploited the Napoleonic legend for different political and cultural ends. Concentrating on Victorien Sardou's (with Emile Moreau) *Madame Sans-Gêne* (1893), Maurice Barrès's *Les Déracinés* (1897), Edmond Rostand's *L'Aiglon* (1900), and Gyp's novel *Napoléonette* (1913), I argue that following the defeat of Boulangism, the Napoleonic legend was divorced from party politics and experienced a revival in popular culture. Proponents and detractors of the Third Republic, who represented Napoleon as a figure of national unity, used the legend both to criticize their enemies and as a vehicle for exploring anxieties about gender and fears about the processes of democratization.

I proceed in Chapter 4 to a discussion of a female military hero, Joan of Arc, in part, to juxtapose the major female hero of the period to the most important male one. This chapter discusses the way in which Joan of Arc, the subject of both military and religious legend, was transformed into an object of popular consumption, focusing on two of the best-known productions of the fin de siècle: Jules Barbier's *Jeanne d'Arc*, with music by Gounod, performed in 1890, with Sarah Bernhardt in the title role, and *Le Procès de Jeanne d'Arc*, by Emile Moreau, staged at the Théâtre Sarah-Bernhardt in 1909, with Bernhardt again playing the lead. As in the case of Napoleon, the commodification of Joan occurred against the backdrop of a struggle to appropriate her by the left and right. The figure of Joan also revealed fears about changing gender roles. The deliberate choice of Bernhardt to portray Joan of Arc, not once but twice, demonstrates that the search for heroes was not uniquely a male enterprise. This chapter, along with the previous ones, complicates our notions of heroism, particularly female heroism. Furthermore, Joan, in common with Cyrano, but unlike Napoleon (although Rostand's *L'Aiglon* came close), managed to unite fin-de-siècle audiences "above politics," and thus marks a step forward in forging a unified national consensus on the eve of World War I.

In Chapter 5, devoted to the 1907–1908 espionage case of naval ensign Charles-Benjamin Ullmo, I return once again to a real-life event covered in detail in the mass press. Anti-Semites, who did not fail to note Ullmo's Jewish origins, drew strong parallels between the Dreyfus and Ullmo cases, but Ullmo and Dreyfus could not have been more different. Unlike Alfred Dreyfus, the innocent, discreet family man, Ullmo, by his own admission, was a flamboyant bachelor with drug and gambling problems as well as an expensive mistress. The Ullmo trial was a failed replay of the Dreyfus Affair, because contemporaries rejected the divisions of the Dreyfus era. Captivated by the press's account of Ullmo's betrayal of honor and country for love, they depicted the naval officer as a tragic anti-hero and as a symbol of the dangers of national decline. Although the events of the Ullmo case took place slightly before the staging of the second Joan of Arc play in 1909, I end with an actual historical event to illustrate the extent to which fact and fiction had become blurred and, indeed, collapsed such that the French public could consume the Ullmo affair both as a *fait divers* and as an incident in a national melodrama. Like the second Joan of Arc play, the Ullmo case marks an important step in healing the wounds – if only temporarily – of the Dreyfus Affair, allowing the French to forge national unity on the eve of the First World War.

Gender, Class, and Heroism in the Bazar de la Charité Fire of 1897

At number 23, rue Jean-Goujon, just off the bustle of the Champs-Elysées, stands Notre-Dame de la Consolation, an imposing church built in the Louis XVI style. Even Parisians, if they were to find themselves on this quiet street around the corner from the métro stop Alma-Marceau, would be hard-pressed to know that the church was built on the site of what contemporaries of the fin de siècle viewed as one of the greatest disasters of the time. Reading the plaque at the entrance of the church, they would learn that Notre-Dame de la Consolation represents an ex-voto offering to the 125 victims, nearly all of them prominent women, who perished in the Bazar de la Charité fire on May 4, 1897.[1]

Billed as the society event of the season, the Bazar de la Charité was a yearly charity bazaar patronized by wealthy aristocratic and bourgeois Catholic women. Founded in 1885 to raise money for Catholic organizations by entrepreneur Henry Blount and presided over by the Baron de Mackau, a leading Catholic politician who had rallied to the republic, the Bazar de la Charité was held in a common venue for an entire month. Its organizers and attendees, who were there by invitation only, represented,

---

[1] The figure of 125 – not 126 as most contemporary reports indicated – is confirmed by Pierre Nicolas, who has compiled a *Martyrologe du Bazar de la Charité*, a prosopographic dictionary of the victims of the fire (Paris: Ed. Pierre Nicolas, 2000). Only five of the victims were grown men. This low figure was the cause of considerable controversy. Calls to build Notre-Dame de la Consolation coincided with the inauguration of the Sacré-Coeur. See Raymond Jonas, *France and the Cult of the Sacred Heart: An Epic Tale for Modern Times* (Berkeley: University of California Press, 2001). It is perhaps no accident that Notre-Dame de la Consolation was built in the Louis XVI style since the king was seen by Catholics as a martyr par excellence. A large sum to build the church was donated by the American-born wife of Boni de Castellane.

in the words of *Le Matin*, "the phone directory of the nobility and of 'le Tout-Paris.'"[2]

The bazaar had previously occupied different venues, most recently on the rue de la Boétie in the eighth arrondissement. In 1897, the organizers decided to move the bazar to the rue Jean-Goujon (between nos. 13 and 15), near what is now the avenue Franklin Roosevelt on the site of large, empty lot lent to them. The lot was located next to the stables of the Baron Rothschild and looked out in the back over a hotel, L'Hôtel du Palais.[3] With a view to cutting costs, the bazaar organizers had constructed a large temporary wooden structure that occupied the length of the lot. The structure, built quickly, with little regard for safety, was made of pine. Inside the structure was a diorama of an old-fashioned Parisian street, which was to house the twenty-two booths in the charity bazaar.[4] On the second day of the bazaar, the organizers decided to install a projector, which caught fire shortly after 4:15 PM.[5] Although there were a number of exits, two in the front as well as three in the back, the rapid spread of the fire would make it difficult for the 1,200 people trapped inside to get out.[6] Within a matter of minutes, the entire structure had burned to the ground.

According to eyewitness reports, people were pushing and shoving each other to get out, in the process knocking down others, who then created a barrier for those seeking to exit the building. Many of the individuals who escaped the fire emerged from the building with their clothes on fire; a number of them did not survive their injuries. Local residents came to the rescue of the victims, including the employees of the Rothschild stables, who doused the victims with water; workers passing by the scene,

---

[2] Unsigned article from *Le Matin* from 5 May 1897 called "Ce qu'était le Bazar de la Charité." Unless otherwise noted, all newspaper articles cited without authors are unsigned.

[3] The site was viewed as ideal; not only was it located in a fashionable part of town but the venue had been loaned free of charge by Michel Heine. The organizers felt they could raise more money by cutting down on overhead expenses.

[4] There was a certain irony in having a replica of a medieval street housed in a structure in the heart of the recently Haussmannized Paris.

[5] The exact time was disputed, but most contemporaries agreed that the fire occurred after 4 and before 4:30 PM. This was one of the first *faits divers* that involved a new technology – the cinema. My thanks to Professor Vanessa Schwartz for reminding me of this fact.

[6] The exact number of attendees at the time of the fire was contested, with the organizers indicating that there were more than 1,600 people. They would, naturally, be interested in inflating the number to minimize the number of deaths. Most accounts in the press, however, cite the lower figure of 1,200.

who ran into the burning building; and the staff of the Hôtel du Palais, two of whom rescued more than one hundred people through a barred window overlooking the back end of the Bazar de la Charité lot.

The tragedy of the Bazar de la Charité captured the public imagination, in large part because of the status of the victims, one of whom was the Duchesse d'Alençon, the sister of the Austrian empress as well as the wife of a member of the Orléans family. Indeed, the press covered the event extensively, even obsessively. Despite initial calls for solidarity, discussions about the fire quickly disintegrated into a political struggle pitting partisans of the secular republic against those who supported the Catholic Church. The conflicts of the Bazar de la Charité fire sounded the death knell of the *ralliement*, the fragile coalition that allied moderate republicans to moderate Catholics and former monarchists who had "rallied" to the regime, although the fire did not itself lead to the collapse of this alliance. One of the most important *faits divers* of the fin de siècle, the Bazar de la Charité fire illuminates the importance of the mass press in the creation of national identity at this key moment in French history; yet it was not Benedict Anderson's unified "imagined community" but rather a profoundly divided nation that was exposed by the fire, despite concerted efforts toward unity around the idea of a community in mourning.[7]

The political conflicts articulated during the Bazar de la Charité fire, overlaid by class tensions, were also embedded in the most important debate of this cause célèbre, which centered on the heroism of the victims and their rescuers. While Catholics exalted the female victims as heroes who had sacrificed their lives in aid of Catholic charities, populists simultaneously extolled the virtues of their working-class rescuers and cast

---

[7] In his now classic work, *Imagined Communities: Reflections on the Origin and Spread of Nationalism* (London: Verso, 1983; 1986), Benedict Anderson speaks of the "mass ceremony" of reading performed daily by an individual who knows that others "of whose existence he is confident, yet of whose identity he has not the slightest notion" are doing the same, 38. In his article titled "News, Public, Nation," *American Historical Review* 107, no. 2 (April 2002), Michael Schudson offers an important corrective to Anderson's remarks by noting that although newspapers can create a sense of national community, different newspapers present different readings of the same events or even cover different events. Thus, a national community can be created by such a dialogue. Schudson further observes that news is "not only the raw material for rational public discourse [à la Habermas] but also the public construction of particular images of self, community, and nation," 484. The importance of studying the press not only for content but also for form is also at the heart of the enterprise undertaken by editors Dean de la Motte and Jeannene M. Przyblyski in their volume of essays *Modernity and the Mass Press in Nineteenth-Century France* (Amherst: University of Massachusetts Press, 1999), 4.

aspersions against the male aristocrats who had survived the fire. In fact, the press coverage of the fire is not only revelatory of the class warfare and religious differences that contributed to the divisions in French society on the eve of the Dreyfus Affair but it also sheds light on the construction of images of male and female heroism, shaped by the gender anxieties of the period.[8]

Finally, the events of the Bazar de la Charité fire highlight the increased blurring of fact and fiction as well as the importance of theatrical conventions in the culture of the time. Not only did the tragedy elicit an outpouring of printed materials – newspaper articles as well as street literature composed of songs, caricatures, and broadsides – it also inspired fictional accounts, among them, a "mystery play," written by a Catholic priest in 1899.[9] The best known of the fictional accounts, however, is a short story

[8] Michel Winock, "Un Avant-goût d'apocalypse: L'Incendie du Bazar de la Charité," in *Nationalisme, antisémitisme et fascisme en France* (Paris: Seuil, 1990), 83–102, is especially interested in the link between the fascination of the public for this horrifying yet titillating spectacle and the theme of decadence in literature and art of the period, although he also treats the theme of class warfare and representations of female and male heroism. I myself concentrate on the representations of male and female heroism as well as the construction of national identity in the press. In this chapter, I am working from the press coverage of the fire, much of it culled from the files in the Paris Police Archives (BA1313–1314), supplemented by my own systematic reading of such newspapers as *La Libre Parole, Le Figaro, La Croix, Le Matin, Le Temps, L'Illustration*, and *Le Petit Parisien*, along with reports from the Police Archives, and documents from the Bibliothèque Historique de la Ville de Paris (BHVP) Actualités and print collections. The contents of the BA1313–1314 boxes have been switched around, as I observed on two separate visits in 2004 and 2005 to the archives. I will therefore refer to all materials from these files by both numbers. Another recent treatment of the fire is Geoffrey Cubitt, "Martyrs of Charity, Heroes of Solidarity: Catholic and Republican Responses to the Fire at the Bazar de la Charité, Paris, 1897," *French History* 21 (2007): 331–352. See also Frederick Brown, *For the Soul of France: Culture Wars in the Age of Dreyfus* (New York: Knopf, 2010), 231–250. For other accounts on the fire, see an essay by Louis Sapin, "L'Incendie du Bazar de la Charité," pp. 271–332 in *Prélude à la Belle Epoque*, ed. Gilbert Guilleminault (Paris: Denoël, 1956) and Dominique Paoli, *Il y a cent ans: L'Incendie du Bazar de la Charité* (Paris: Mémorial du Bazar de la Charité, 1997).

[9] See Jean-Paul Clébert's *L'Incendie du Bazar de la Charité: Roman vrai* (Paris: Denoël, 1978). Clébert, using eyewitness testimony in the press, has fictionalized the story by presenting the "thoughts" of the various actors involved. See also Louis-Marie Dubois, *L'Incendie du Bazar de la Charité: Mystère en deux tableaux* (Paris: Librairie salésienne, 1899). The Actualités collection at the BHVP on the fire contains a wealth of such images. I offer my deep-felt thanks to Mme Geneviève Morlet, who facilitated my access to these documents. Particularly striking is the wealth of visual imagery both in the regular press and especially in the illustrated press, among them, representations of the Bazar de la Charité before and after the fire and commemorative ceremonies, as well as images of the rescuers and victims. At least three issues of the illustrated supplement to *Le Petit Journal* depict the victims and rescuers. See the numbers from 16 and 23 May as well as 6 June 1897: Figures 1.1–1.4).

by Paul Morand from 1946, which tells the tale of an adulteress, thought to have perished in the fire, identified by the pearl necklace she has given her wastrel lover Clovis, who dies in the fire while trying to pawn it to an attendee of the Bazar. During the fire, Clovis attempts to make his way out, pushing and hitting the women there, thereby giving lie to his "heroic" name. Thus, the melodramatic representations in the press of the "heroic" aristocratic women, the "simple" working-class heroes, and the supposedly "cowardly" male aristocrats marked contemporaries long after, among them Morand, who as a child remembered witnessing some of the events.[10]

A Press and Public of Voyeurs?

Members of the press were almost instantly on the scene; the organizers had telephoned the authorities soon after the fire began and someone alerted the newspapers, who sent their best reporters to cover the incident. One of *Le Figaro*'s most experienced journalists stated that he had never witnessed anything as horrible, even during the Franco-Prussian War.[11] Newspapers were filled with firsthand accounts of the women emerging from the fire, half-naked, writhing in pain.[12] These reporters also wrote harrowing descriptions bordering on voyeurism when they recounted scenes of families attempting to identify the charred remains of their loved ones at the Palais de l'Industrie, which had been set up as a makeshift morgue.

   Some of the writers seemed to take perverse pleasure in describing these grim scenes, which the public appeared to find thrilling. Newspapers reported of individuals claiming to be the servants or relatives of the dead women to gain access to the Palais de l'Industrie.[13] Thus, national mourning was also accompanied by titillation with regard to the dead women's bodies. These upper-class private women's bodies, literally and figuratively undressed, were a site for public

[10] Morand's story ends abruptly with the wife returning home, having no way of explaining to her husband where she was [waiting in her lover's apartment for his return] nor how her necklace came to be found in the ruins of the fire: Paul Morand, "Le Bazar de la Charité," in *A la fleur d'oranger* (Vevey: Les Clés d'or, 1946).

[11] "La Catastrophe d'hier," *Le Figaro*, 5 May 1897.

[12] Such Dantesque descriptions haunted the Romantic imagination, as Winock has noted, 86–87. I would add that they were akin to the "ecstasy of suffering" associated especially with female Catholic saints.

[13] See, for example, "Odieux commerce," *La Libre Parole*, 7 May, and "Odieux," *L'Autorité*, 8 May.

fantasy, their undergarments depicted in minute detail. Female servants played a key role in identifying their mistresses' bodies by their clothing or jewelry, offering a tantalizing glimpse into the private world of the upper classes.[14] The women's clothing was described as were their physical traits. One unidentified woman's body was depicted as having hairy legs and an abdomen marked by the signs of childbearing. Another was described as having a voluminous belly.[15] Such descriptions bordered on the obscene, and Michel Winock has aptly described these accounts as fetishistic necrophilia.[16] It might seem strange at first glance to compare the French public's morbid fascination with these upper-class women's bodies to that of the British public for the eviscerated bodies of Jack the Ripper's victims nearly ten years earlier – the women in the Ripper case were prostitutes, unlike the virtuous Catholic women victimized by the fire. Nevertheless, both sets of women had become objects of public consumption (Figures 1.1, 1.2).[17]

The sites of the disaster became objects of curiosity, attracting large crowds every day. *Le Gaulois* of May 9 mentioned in particular the American and English tourists who flocked to the scenes, and *L'Echo de Paris* of May 10 spoke of these tourists – easily recognized by their ubiquitous Baedeker guides – who went to great lengths to attempt to view the dead bodies.[18] According to *Le Jour*, near the site of the tragedy, *camelots* were hawking and singing newly composed songs about the incident, and *La Libre Parole* of May 7 added that these street peddlers were also selling tops, combs, and other wares.[19] Thus, the rue Jean-Goujon and the Palais de l'Industrie, where the dead bodies were housed, had become both objects and sites of consumption. Crowds also gathered around Notre-Dame on the day of the official ceremony to commemorate

[14] Thus revealing "les dessus" and "les dessous de la bourgeoisie." See Philippe Perrot's book of this title, translated into English as *Fashioning the Bourgeoisie: A History of Clothing in the Nineteenth Century*, trans. Richard Bienvenu (Princeton, NJ: Princeton University Press, 1994).

[15] See, for example, *Le Figaro* of 7 May, which described in this manner the remaining unidentified women's bodies. The more sober *Le Temps* also engaged in such reporting.

[16] Winock, 88.

[17] See Judith Walkowitz, *City of Dreadful Delight: Narratives of Sexual Danger in Late-Victorian London* (Chicago: University of Chicago Press, 1992), in particular, the chapter on "Jack the Ripper," 191–228.

[18] "Rue Jean-Goujon," *Le Gaulois*, 9 May and "Pages d'agenda," *L'Echo de Paris*, 10 May, respectively. Still other papers spoke of vendors who fabricated objects retrieved from the fire to sell them to gullible tourists.

[19] "La Catastrophe de la Rue Jean-Goujon," *Le Jour*, 6 May 1897 and "La Foule," *La Libre Parole*, 7 May.

FIGURE 1.1. "The Site of the Bazar de la Charité Fire," front cover of *Le Petit Journal*, supplément illustré, May 16, 1897. Author's collection.

FIGURE 1.2. "The Corpses Pulled out of the Ruins," back cover of *Le Petit Journal*, supplément illustré, May 16, 1897. Author's collection.

the dead and the reports in the Police Archives indicate that many unau-thorized individuals managed to get in with forged tickets.[20]

In his work on *badauds* (gawkers) and the making of a mass public, Gregory Shaya has argued that such crowds, represented in the press, con-stituted a national community of mourning and empathy independent of politics and class.[21] Although it is true that there was a national commu-nity of mourning and sorrow depicted in the press during the Bazar de la Charité fire, such calls for solidarity and mourning were, in part, rhetoric that belied the reality of deep-rooted political and social divisions of French society at the time. Instead, it was an attempt to forge such unity especially because it was lacking.[22] A crowd linked by a shared interest in a *fait divers*

[20] See BA 1313–1314: Report signed André from 12 May entitled "Au sujet du service religieux célébré à Notre-Dame pour les victimes du Bazar de la Charité." The agent reported that President Faure and Minister Barthou had trouble getting in because of the crowds.

[21] "The *Flâneur*, the *Badaud*, and the Making of a Mass Public in France, circa 1860–1910," *American Historical Review* 109, no. 1 (February 2004): 62. Indeed, an unsigned article in *Le Figaro* of 9 May, written no doubt by Jules Huret, who reproduced it in his book on the fire, was entitled "Paris en deuil."

[22] That is not to say that this sense of community outside of class and politics might not emerge, as was the case during the Ullmo spy case of 1907–1908. Dominique Kalifa

could splinter into different political factions. The sympathetic crowds of *badauds* who visited the site of the tragedy at the rue Jean-Goujon, as well as the sensation-seeking onlookers who tried to argue their way into the Palais de l'Industrie, where the dead bodies were housed, were also readers of particular newspapers with their own political philosophies.[23]

The Press, Partisan Politics, and the Nation

The first reactions were ones of horror, and all the newspapers began with the idea of pity for the victims and calls for national unity. The anonymous author of an article in *Le Soir* expressed this sentiment, noting too that all were equal in the face of death.[24] Yet many of these statements in favor of national solidarity were fraught with partisan overtones. Lucien Millevoye, who wrote for *La Patrie*, which billed itself as "the organ of national defense," couldn't prevent himself from disparaging republican politicians. Deploring the divisions of the last twenty-five years, he called for unity.[25] Given his repeated criticism of the parliamentary republic, however, Millevoye's call for an end to social divisions seems a bit disingenuous. In an earlier article, he had spoken in the same breath of miners lost in accidents and the cream of Parisian society lost in the Bazar de la Charité fire.[26] André Vervoort, writing on May 6 in *Le Jour*, a moderate republican newspaper, concurred. In such circumstances, there were no distinctions between the rich and the poor.[27] But in another article in *Le Jour* of May 10, the anonymous author, who complained that the rich were talking of solidarity in suffering but were too egotistical to think about miners and workers, exhorted these privileged individuals to read

notes that such *faits divers* served to create a sense of community during an era of great social and political division. See *L'Encre et le sang: Récits de crimes et société à la Belle Epoque* (Paris: Fayard, 1995), 283–284.

[23] Edward Berenson notes that political crowds corresponding to the readership of different newspapers also existed at this time. See "Fashoda, Dreyfus and the Myth of Jean-Baptiste Marchand," *Yale French Studies* (special issue, eds. Dan Edelstein and Bettina R. Lerner) 111 (2007): 129–142. Similarly, in her work on female criminals, Ann-Louise Shapiro questions the idea of a so-called neutral context of *fait divers* and the *roman feuilleton*, arguing that the readers of the stories still inhabited an imaginary universe informed by politics and culture: *Breaking the Codes: Female Criminality in Fin-de-Siècle Paris* (Stanford, CA: Stanford University Press, 1996), 46.

[24] "La Politique," *Le Soir*, 11 May.

[25] Lucien Millevoye, "Le Respect de la mort," *La Patrie*, 9 May 1897.

[26] Millevoye, "Deuil public," *La Patrie*, 6 May 1897: "public mourning makes no difference."

[27] André Vervoort, "L'Hectacombe," *Le Jour*, 6 May 1897.

León Bourgeois's work on Solidarism.[28] As for the "right thinking press," *Le Figaro* noted that the women who had perished in the fire had died while trying to raise money to help the poor.[29]

Most of the populist newspapers, however, were a little more skeptical about the idea of national solidarity, no matter the social status of the victims.[30] A. Bouceret, writing in the anti-clerical *La Lanterne* of May 6, defended the poor, saying that they would never reproach their fellow citizens for thinking that the nation was lamenting the death of rich women while the poor died in mining and other work-related accidents. Bouceret himself noted that there was no danger inherent in the jobs of these women, whereas the miners and other workers faced peril on a daily basis. He also took a potshot at the conservative press, calling on Catholics to show sympathy if a fire were ever to take place at the Grand-Orient, killing scores of freemasons.[31] One left-wing paper went even further. Louis Dubreuilh of *La Petite République* dismissed the victims of the fire: "The thing is, you see, that it is no longer about workers' lives snuffed out by a firedamp explosion [in a mine]; it's about the existence of leaders, plutocrats and sensualists who have been touched by egalitarian death."[32] Dubreuil's colleague from *La Petite République* observed that the Bazar de la Charité had been a "monarchical demonstration" and that one would do well to think of the sufferings of the poor, because the date of the fire, May 4, coincided with the anniversary of the 1891 Fourmies massacre, in which workers celebrating May Day (as well as women and children) were killed by government troops.[33]

---

[28] "Le Sacrilège du Père Ollivier," *Le Jour*, 10 May. Léon Bourgeois's work on Solidarism was first published in *La Nouvelle Revue* in 1895 and in volume form under the title *Solidarité* a year later.

[29] "La Presse révolutionnaire," *Le Figaro*, 6 May 1897. The author of this unsigned article wrote: "The admirable creatures [who] died holding out their hands to the lost children of Belleville or of la Villette [poor areas of Paris] ... They went to a great deal of trouble for the offspring of those who vote for the likes of M. Faberot and M. Jaurès [left-wing, Socialist leaders]." He thus reproached the left-wing press for not banding together around national mourning.

[30] The anonymous journalist for *Le Jour* wrote that based on his observations of the crowds at the site of the tragedy, the disaster was too "exclusively worldly and aristocratic" to stir the sympathy of the working classes: "Autour du sinistre," 9 May 1897. I would like to thank Professor Gregory Shaya for pointing this reference out to me.

[31] A. Bouceret, "Tribune libre," *La Lanterne*, 6 May 1897.

[32] Dubreuilh, quoted by Lucien Victor-Meunier in "Le Respect de la douleur," *Le Rappel*, 6 May 1897. This journalist lambasted the *Petite République* reporter.

[33] Albert Gouillé, "Prenez garde!" *La Petite République*, 6 May 1897. Maurice Allard, writing in *La Lanterne* of 8 May ("L'Idée du *Gaulois*") expressed similar sentiments. In the wake of the appeal launched by *Le Gaulois* and *Le Figaro* (subsequently only

Even the ceremony to commemorate the dead was fraught with such political tensions. On May 9, an official ceremony was held at Notre-Dame, attended by republican officials, including President Félix Faure and Minister of the Interior Louis Barthou. Presiding over the ceremony was the Dominican (one of the congregations disbanded by the republicans) Père Ollivier, not known for his republican sympathies. As the republican papers reported, Père Ollivier had several years earlier compared republicans to cheese: "the more there are, the more it stinks." The priest used the occasion, which was ostensibly a manifestation of national unity – the presence of republican leaders at a public and official religious ceremony was unprecedented – to chastise the current regime. The tragedy of the Bazar de la Charité, he claimed, was a lesson from God, indeed, a chastisement of the French people, who had forsaken Christian traditions in favor of the false promise of progress and technology:

You [God] wanted to teach a tremendous lesson to the pride of this century, in the course of which man speaks endlessly of his triumph over you. You have turned against him [man] the conquests of his science, so vain, when it is not associated with yours; as well as the flame that he claims to have snatched out of your hands like the Prometheus of antiquity.

The punishment, according to Père Ollivier, although merited – France had forsaken her Christian traditions – was not in vain, if she could find her way back to the Catholic Church.[34] The sacrifice of the women's bodies then was a way to redeem the body of the nation.

The republican papers were scandalized by Père Ollivier's speech. Most of these papers wondered, as did the journalist for *La Paix*, why republican leaders had agreed to co-organize the service at Notre-Dame with the Catholic Church, because this act violated the neutrality of the state in religious matters.[35] In another editorial, the same journalist, G. Barbézieux, castigated the Dominican priest, representing him as a relic of the past. Barbézieux concluded his article by warning against such dangerous manifestations by the church at a time when reactionary forces planning

Le Figaro would organize the list of donors) to raise the money that was lost due to the fire, Allard noted that all the charities were Catholic ones, including aid to Catholic schools. Republican papers, he felt, would be hard-pressed to contribute to such a fund-raising enterprise.

[34] He went on to talk about God's vengeance during the Commune. I have quoted Père Ollivier's speech from Jules Huret's book *La Catastrophe du Bazar de la Charité (4 mai 1897)* (Paris: Juven, 1897), 148–150, but the speech was reproduced in all the major newspapers the following day.

[35] Editorial "Un Jeu dangéreux," signed G. Barbézieux, from 6 May 1897.

the imminent fall of the republic were reorganizing.[36] In his opinion, the republican leaders had been ambushed by the church.[37]

Nor could the various political factions agree on the meaning of the fire itself. While some on the right, like François Coppée, recently converted to Catholicism and soon to be a leader of the Ligue de la Patrie Française, viewed it as a failure of science, others, especially those in the left-wing press, contested this view of the futility and failure of science and progress, as did Jean Mérac, writing for the moderately republican *La Paix*.[38] Thus, the fire exposed a variety of conflicts in French society; it revealed tensions between the bourgeois republic and the working classes, for whom the regime had done little, by illustrating that the latter, who suffered deaths on a regular basis in work-related disasters, could not command the same national attention and respect as the prominent victims of a charity bazaar. It also made secular republicans uneasy about the seemingly cozy relationship between the moderately republican Méline regime and Catholics. Not only had the Méline cabinet violated the religious neutrality of the state in organizing a national funeral for the victims at Notre-Dame but the Catholics involved had also behaved badly, using the occasion of the fire to claim that it was divine retribution against the republican regime.

Working-Class Heroes

One of the most obvious signs of social conflict that marked this period was the representation in the different papers of the victims of the fire and their rescuers, mostly illustrative of the national debate about heroism as

---

[36] Barbézieux, "Le Sermon du Père Ollivier, " *La Paix*, 10 May 1897: "The Notre-Dame speech was to be expected, issuing from the head and heart of this Dominican from the Middle Ages, lost soul in our century of elevated philosophical reasoning. Father Ollivier is the dying past which rises up, in a supreme effort against contemporary society; it is the last combat of the Church, which, no longer able to change minds, finding itself up against the indifference of the public and invincible Science, tries using terrorism and scare tactics."

[37] See "Le Guet-apens" in the 11 May 1897 issue of *La Paix*, signed by Z.

[38] "We have stolen fire from the heavens; we are the masters of electricity which we have made into a fairy-like and charming plaything for our amusement. And voilà! We had no idea that we were merely children playing with matches," declared François Coppée in "L'Incendie du Bazar de la Charité," *Le Journal*, 5 May. For his part, Jean Mérac, in "L'Homme et le malheur" in *La Paix* of 6 May, wrote: "Man, even though he is a dwarf, will emerge a titan from this long battle. ... But, let us not be discouraged. The ambition of Prometheus is beautiful enough to be kept alive, from one age to the next, in spite of the chains which bind our hero to his rock of punishment."

well as evolving gender roles. The populist papers all called for special honors and decorations for the modest working-class heroes – plumbers, coachmen, and cooks – who had come to the aid of the aristocratic women. For the left, the working men represented the redemption of the body politic.[39] A number of these papers used the heroism of the working-class men to criticize republican politicians. Henri Rochefort, writing in *L'Intransigeant*, called for a Legion of Honor for "the intruder [gêneur] Gaumery," the cook who had saved dozens of women by pulling them through the window of the hotel that overlooked the Bazar de la Charité lot, contrasting his heroism to the parading by republican leaders of their decorations.[40] Gaumery was celebrated in the press for his modesty. When he was congratulated by the editor of *Le Figaro* for his bravery, he replied: "We only did our duty. Anyone would have done the same in our place. But, that's quite enough. It is time to return to our pots and pans. It is not every day that dinner gets made by itself."[41] The naiveté and simplicity of this working-class hero thrilled the press. Not only did the papers quote this statement, so too did they publish photos and other images of Gaumery dressed in his chef uniform (Figure 1.3).

In an article from May 6, the author praised the courage of two guards, whose names were not mentioned in the article, who died saving others: "The two guards knew their Duty. They had the heroism to go forth into the fire, although with two steps back, they could have saved their lives. ... Now their plebeian remains are indistinguishable from those of the patricians. ... Let us celebrate them, these two obscure heroes, companions in death of the grandest ladies of France, [these men] who must also have had blue blood in their veins, (and) the blood of a proud race, for having gone forth so proudly to battle the flames!"[42] Some conservatives

---

[39] In his essay "A Muse for the Masses: Gender, Age, and Nation in France, Fin de Siècle," *American Historical Review* 109, no. 5 (December 2004): 1456, David Pomfret notes the power of working-class women to redeem the nation. A similar argument could be made for the redemptive power of their male counterparts. See Edward Berenson: *The Trial of Madame Caillaux* (Berkeley: University of California Press, 1992), 194. In both cases, members of the working class represented the "true" uncorrupt France, which had been tainted by the bourgeoisie and upper classes. In the aristocratic imagination, however, the worker could be seen as a symbol of irrational violence.

[40] "Le Gêneur Gaumery," *L'Intransigeant*, 8 May 1897.

[41] Quoted by Jules Huret, 19. Many of the papers also praised the heroism of the hotel's owner, Mme Roche-Sautier, whose coolheaded thinking had led to the escape plan. This image of a vigorous "in-charge" female was perhaps more acceptable in a woman who worked for a living than it was in a bourgeois or aristocratic woman.

[42] "Notes parisiennes," *La Paix*, 6 May.

LA CATASTROPHE DE LA RUE JEAN-GOUJON (Les sauveteurs)

FIGURE 1.3. "The Catastrophe of the Rue Jean-Goujon (The Saviors)," front cover of *Le Petit Journal*, supplément illustré, May 23, 1897. Author's collection.

praised the working-class heroes, commenting on the devotion of servants to their masters, as did Joseph Cornély in *Le Gaulois* of May 6: "Such episodes honor the masters as much as the servants, because it is the goodness of the former which gives rise to the devotion of the latter. They prove that the precursors of the shock troops of barbarism, the uhlans [German soldiers] of future savagery, have not yet succeeded in damaging the cement that binds – no matter what is said – French society."[43]

Later in the month, various ceremonies celebrating the heroes took place; one such celebration was a banquet organized by André Vervoort, editor of the populist newspaper *Le Jour* on May 20.[44] Another was the official ceremony held by Interior Minister Louis Barthou on May 21 to distribute medals and other decorations to the rescuers. Finally, another banquet and ceremony was held at the Hotel de Ville on June 6. Songs were written in honor of the heroes, and their names were published in the newspapers.[45] In some of the articles of this time, journalists sniped that there were too many rescuers and that some of them had invented their exploits.[46] Although papers of various political leanings used the heroism of the rescuers to make different statements about the nation, they were unanimous in the way they described the heroism of these working-class men. During the mid-nineteenth century, French masculinities were fractured, embedded both in class differences and geography. At the time of the Third Republic, while such differences remained, official rhetoric increasingly sought to diminish them, instead attempting to incorporate all classes and regions to create a national masculine ideal.[47] Several themes were repeated in the course of reporting on these ceremonies.

---

[43] J. Cornély, "Les Domestiques," *Le Gaulois*, 6 May.

[44] *La Croix* noted acidly in an article of 22 May that banquets were inappropriate and that the organizers of *Le Jour* would have done better to convoke the heroes to a mass.

[45] "La Croix d'Honneur de l'ouvrier" celebrated the Legion of Honor received by the coachman Georges. One of the stanzas read: "We must help each other while on earth / regardless of fortune or stature / We are equal and are brothers / Similar is our blood / For the suffering class / That toils in the workshop / Let us lighten the Cross of the worker." The last stanza of the song exhorted French women to make more French heroes: Paris Police Archives, BA1313–1314.

[46] *La Libre Parole*, "La Question des sauveteurs" of 3 June mocked the "false rescuers" who had received decorations and monetary rewards but did not deserve them. Only ten people really merited the term *rescuers*, wrote the journalist who signed E.C. See also Alfred Capus, "Les Sauveteurs du lendemain," *Le Figaro*, 6 June.

[47] Bertrand Taithe, "Neighborhood Boys and Men: Changing Spaces of Masculine Identity in France, 1848–1871," in *French Masculinities: History, Culture and Politics*, ed. Christopher E. Forth and Bertrand Taithe (New York: Palgrave Macmillan, 2007), 67–83.

The rescuers were described as "disinterested." They had saved lives at great peril to their own and for no monetary recompense. Moreover, they were not publicity seekers.[48] It is for this very reason that many of the papers, citing the authority of public opinion, demanded that these heroes be rewarded both materially and symbolically.

Whereas the earlier articles concentrated on the men who had helped women escape through the window of the Hôtel du Palais – Gaumery, the *chef de cuisine*, along with his assistant Vauthier, as well as the plumber Piquet, and the roofer's apprentice Desjardins – the later articles focused almost exclusively on the unemployed coachman Georges, who had displayed visceral courage by running into the burning building eleven times to rescue victims of the fire. The various newspapers' depictions of Georges were nearly identical. As in the case of Gaumery, the words "good boy" and "modest" were repeated in all of them. The press widely reported Georges's surprise at receiving the Legion of Honor. They also noted approvingly that the newly decorated Georges had received a comfortable government job and pension, because no bourgeois could accept getting into a coach driven by a recipient of the Legion of Honor.

A number of reporters paid Georges a visit at his humble rooms in a building located in the seventh arrondissement, speaking with his landlady and colleagues. Describing him as a devoted family man, they reported with sentimentality that Georges, a single parent, took good care of his three-year-old son. One such article by Eugène Tardieu in *L'Echo de Paris* described the open, frank physiognomy of this "simple child of Paris": "Georges has a clean-shaven face, with a soft and energetic expression, grey eyes with a malicious gleam." Indeed, pictures and drawings of him show a youthful and clean-shaven thirty-seven-year-old man, looking slightly uncomfortable in an ill-fitting suit. Such a portrait, both the description and the image, fit the press's idea of a humble working-class hero (Figure 1.4). Tardieu also noted that Georges was more proud of his profession than of his decoration. Moreover, when praised for his courage, he responded modestly, "Bah! We did what we could."[49] The working-class accents of his speech were widely reported in the papers, as were those of Gaumery.

---

[48] The word *réclame* is repeated in a number of the articles by journalists who wrote that in an age of materialism, such devotion was exemplary. Indeed, in a letter to the newspaper, Mme Roche-Sautier felt the need to defend her honor after one newspaper claimed that she was selling to tourists the bars of the window leading to her hotel.

[49] Eugène Tardieu, "Actualités," *L'Echo de Paris*, 23 May. See also articles from *Le Matin* of 22 May and those of *Le Jour*, *Le Journal*, and *L'Intransigeant* from 23 May.

FIGURE 1.4. "The Saviors of the Bazar de la Charité: The Coachman Georges Being Decorated by the Minister of the Interior," front cover of *Le Petit Journal*, supplément illustré, June 6, 1897. Author's collection.

Fact or Fiction? Melodrama and the Bazar de la Charité

Tardieu also remarked on Georges's resemblance to the playwright Victorien Sardou, known for his melodramas. Such a comparison is interesting, especially in light of the melodramatic aspects of the whole affair. Another commentator in the press had noted that decorating a coachman seemed to be a scene right out of a boulevard melodrama.[50] This theme of melodrama is a recurring one in the Bazar de la Charité fire and was an important frame of reference for contemporaries of the period. Real events were turned into spectacle, akin to a play attended at the boulevard theaters, which attracted mass audiences.[51] As in the theater, the public was riveted by these real-life incidents, with the *fait divers* serving as a middle ground between pure fiction and reality. At any rate, the nature of both the *fait divers* and the theater encouraged the identification by readers and playgoers with the "characters" in the story. The populist press, given the radical origins of the melodrama, was perhaps more likely to see things in this way – from the doomed aristocratic heroines and the valiant working-class heroes, to the mustache-twirling villains of the piece, the aristocratic *gardénias*, who supposedly caned their way out of the fire, at the expense of their female companions. (The term *gardénias* referred to the elegance of idle society men whose sole purpose in life was to attend balls and parties, ride in the Bois du Boulogne, and search for eligible rich women to marry.) The ironies of such heroism as well as the lack thereof appealed to the popular imagination, just as it must have appalled elites of the time. Catholics attached to Christian traditions might well have seen the events as a passion play, which substituted the suffering of the women for that of Christ.[52] In both cases, however, the theatricalization and estheticization of political events was evident.[53]

---

[50] Victor de Cottens, "En passant," *Soir*, 22 May. In his book on the Bazar de la Charité fire, based on press coverage of the affair, Jules Huret described the bazaar as the "théâtre de la catastrophe," 14.

[51] Vanessa Schwartz, *Spectacular Realities: Early Mass Culture in Fin-de-Siècle Paris* (Berkeley: University of California Press, 1998), 12.

[52] See Judith Walkowitz's tour de force analysis of the press in *City of Dreadful Delight*. Based on her reading of the work of Peter Brooks (*The Melodramatic Imagination* [New Haven, CT: Yale University Press, 1976]), she notes that during the nineteenth century, "melodrama came to serve as a primary imaginative structure for a wide array of social constituencies," 86.

[53] Jean-Yves Mollier in an essay, "La Littérature et presse du trottoir à la Belle Epoque" in *La Lecture et ses publics à l'époque contemporaine: Essais d'histoire culturelle* (Paris: PUF, 2001), speaks of the estheticization of politics at this time and observes that the right

Yet for the national melodrama that the events of the Bazar de la Charité represented, the supposedly cowardly behavior of the aristocratic males was problematic. How could it be that the sons of the noble chevaliers of France had deserted their posts, leaving the heroics to working-class males? Even more important, it was not the fair maidens of melodrama who needed saving; rather, the women themselves had performed valiant acts, coming to France's rescue, thereby preserving her honor.

The *Gardénias* or the Crisis of Masculinity?

After the initial reports about the victims and their working-class rescuers, the newspapers turned their attention to the small number of male victims in the fire, only 5 out of 125, mostly elderly.[54] Although these men had died saving the lives of their female companions (for example, Dr. Feulard, who went in to save his wife and back again, unsuccessfully this time, to save his daughter, and old war hero General Munier, who died of his injuries shortly after making his way out of the burning edifice), many in the press wondered about the role of their compatriots. Stories about the young, elegant aristocratic *gardénias*, who had supposedly made their way out of the fire by using their canes to knock women down, began circulating in the press, reaching a fever pitch on May 16 and 17. Even well-respected newspapers like *Le Temps* repeated such stories, as did publications whose clientele included the so-called *gardénias*, among them *Le Gaulois*, *Le Figaro*, and *L'Echo de Paris*. The fear of aristocratic male cowardice touched a nerve as this theme was widely invoked in fin-de-siècle decadent literature – witness the notoriety of Joris-Karl Huysmans's *Des Esseintes* after the publication of *A Rebours* in 1884.[55] One of the first of these articles was a mordant piece by Gyp, published in *La Libre Parole* of May 9. Gyp's fictional marquise, responding to the young aristocrat who tells her that 200 men were in attendance at the Bazar de la Charité, is relieved that more men were not there: "Thank goodness there weren't more of them since if there had been, all of the women would have been burned."[56]

during the Dreyfus Affair (I would add the left too) was obliged to treat current events as a melodrama, representing traitors as villains in boulevard plays, 153.

[54] Doctors Feulard and Rochet, two elderly merchants, and General Munier. Two young boys, ages four and eleven, were also victims.

[55] I owe this observation to Professor Ruth Harris.

[56] Gyp, "A Bâtons rompus," *La Libre Parole*, 9 May. This was the first of three such articles, in which Gyp expressed her thoughts via her fictional aristocratic characters. See also "Nouveau Jeu" from 16 May, in which two little girls "play" at being the woman who perishes in the fire and her male companion who flees in a cowardly fashion.

Naturally, the numbers of those attending the Bazar de la Charité were contested. Initial newspaper reports put these numbers at 1,200 with 200 of them men. Subsequently, however, these numbers were challenged, especially by the organizers of the bazaar, who had a vested interest in minimizing the proportion of deaths and in reducing the number of men among the attendees. A man identified only as "an intimate friend" of one of the committee members furnished the reporter for *Le Temps* with a written document stating that the committee members estimated the presence of 1,600–1,700 people at the Bazar de la Charité before the fire broke out,[57] although other witnesses cited different figures, with the painter Jean-François Raffaëilli claiming that some 1,200–1,300 people were present and the Abbé Gaultier Delaubry putting the figure at 700.[58] The number of men there, given the rumors, was especially delicate. Here again, Mackau and other organizers and participants of the bazaar estimated the numbers at forty or so, with only a small proportion of these being society men. The actual figure for those in attendance, including the numbers of men, is impossible to establish, now as it was then. Séverine, writing for *L'Echo de Paris* on May 13, opted for 100 men, the average between the high and low, an estimate that seems reasonable in the absence of definitive proof.[59]

Some of the initial accounts of the surviving victims seemed to confirm speculation about the unchivalrous behavior of the men at the Bazar de la Charité. A number of newspapers quoted testimony of those present, including that of Raffaëilli, who told the press about the injury his daughter had suffered, as well as that of mother and daughter Mme and Mlle Von den Henvel, who told the reporter for *L'Echo de Paris* about the bad behavior of some of the men present.[60]

Even the judge in charge of the investigation into the fire, Bertulus, unintentionally confirmed such rumors by making a statement that earned him the ire of many in the press. When asked by the journalist for *L'Eclair* about the progress of the inquiry, the hapless magistrate complained that when

---

[57] "Une Enquête sur l'incendie du Bazar de la Charité," *Le Temps*, 11 May.

[58] Raffaëilli told *Le Temps* ("L'Incendie du Bazar de la Charité," 15 May) that there were 1,200–1,300, of whom 100–120 were men. In the same article, Germain Lecour, the Baron de Mackau's secretary, claimed that there were twenty-five to thirty men, maximum, there. The Abbé Gaultier Delaubry spoke with *La Croix* of 19 May: "La Catastrophe: Et les hommes?"

[59] Séverine, "Qu'ont fait les hommes?" *L'Echo de Paris*, 13 May.

[60] Mme von den Henvel and her daughter survived the fire and told the reporter for *L'Echo de Paris* what they had seen: "I saw men who seemed stark raving mad who struck out with their canes in order to make their way forward," quoted by Huret, 27.

he asked the women to tell him how the fire started, he had to stop them because all they could talk about were the brutal acts of the men present![61] Other stories seemed to belong to the realm of the apocryphal, especially those that told of broken engagements between couples because the fiancé had supposedly left his beloved behind in order to save himself.[62] Given the number of eyewitnesses who testified to improper male behavior, it is very likely that such incidents, although limited, took place, although it is impossible to know for sure at a distance of more than a century. Even the police reports of the time contain the echo of such accusations although, as their authors stated, there was no proof, with rumors circulating about the supposed cowardly conduct of the Baron de Mackau and the Duc d'Alençon, among others.[63] What is perhaps more important for the historian of *mentalités* (mentalities), however, is the impact that these stories had on the public imagination, because it offers a unique perspective on the gender anxieties of the period and their impact on national identity.

The fact that aristocratic men had supposedly been wanting in courage sounded the major theme of the articles published, a failing that was juxtaposed to the heroism of their female companions as well as to that of the women's working-class rescuers. Such accusations of cowardice were not to be taken lightly at a time when honor was of great importance, especially in the wake of the French defeat in the Franco-Prussian War. Bourgeois and upper-class males, increasingly disconnected both from physical activity

---

[61] The quote given by Bertulus to *L'Eclair* was repeated widely in the press. See, for example, the quote and indignant reactions from the following papers: "Ce n'est pas possible," *Le Voltaire*, 16 May and "Poursuites nécessaires," by Maurice Allard, *La Lanterne*, 16 May.

[62] See "Reconnaissance," signed G. in *Le Jour*, 15 May and "Preuve d'amour," by Alfred Capus in *Le Figaro*, 17 May.

[63] A report from 13 May (signed Aspic) read: "Several victims who are still being treated, are determined, once they have recovered, to protest against the way in which the gentlemen present conducted themselves, at the time of the disaster. It appears that M. de Mackau acted in a particularly cowardly manner, and only saved himself by pushing all of those around him. Other gentlemen cleared the way by distributing blows left and right." The agent concluded that a scandal would ensue: "All of these details will become known, since at this moment, now that tempers are calm, the unfortunate behavior of many of those [males] present is becoming clear, and this will very soon prove to be a rather spicy scandal for members of the aristocracy." In another report from Aspic from the next day, 14 May, the agent repeated the rumor that Père Delabarre, one of the editors for *La Croix* (whose offices were in back of the site of the fire and whose staff helped save numerous individuals), could testify to the bad conduct of many men who had used their canes to hit women and young girls in order to escape. Another agent, Mortaiss, in a report from 15 May recounted the following story: "Henceforth, the word on the street is: 'Only the servants displayed courage.'" Paris Police Archives, BA1313–1314.

and ties to the land, were already on the defensive with regard to their masculinity, particularly vis-à-vis working-class males who engaged in manual labor. Hence the call for real men of action in the novels of writers as different as Emile Zola and Maurice Barrès. Although these tensions did not fully emerge until the Dreyfus Affair, all the elements were already present in the national discussions of the Bazar de la Charité fire.[64]

Many in the press, and not only in the populist press, mocked the aristocrats, dubbing them the "chevaliers of fear" or "the royal runaways" or even "the false fleers of the *grand monde*."[65] So delectable was this idea of the *gardénias* that popular songs of the period played upon this theme. One such song, "La Grande Complainte sur l'incendie de la rue Jean-Goujon" ("The Great Lament of the Fire on the Rue Jean-Goujon"), commented: "The old French gallantry / made light of it [the disaster of the fire]." Another entitled "Le Sauvetage du Baron d'Escampette: Chevalier et Baron de la Trouille" by Marius Réty mocked the aristocratic Gontran who fled from the scene of the fire: "In order not to be grilled / The proud marquis of panic ... / In a noble gesture / Transforming his cane into a club / Lost no time // Courageously leaving the scene!" The moral of the story – to be safe, a woman had to enter a bazaar with a worker on her arm – was recounted in the last stanza of the song: "As one would have it / When venturing forth / To a bazaar, without risk of danger / A valiant knight is of no use / To any woman / Not accompanied by a roofer / Or even a brave plumber!" The refrain, to be repeated in a spoken voice, was, "Hot! Hot! B ... arrons!" (the implication being that the word expected would be "bastard").Yet another song, "Les Chevaliers de la Frousse" similarly denigrated the manhood of the elegant "chevaliers" who did nothing to save their women: "It is not the salons / That will give us men / It is not the salons / That show us what we are worth / Go to the [working-class] suburbs / To see what we are worth / Go to the [working-class] suburbs / That's where you will get help." To find real men, one had to go to the working-class quarters of Paris.[66]

Caricaturists for the satirical press also had a field day. One such image from *La Silhouette*, "The Gardenias of the Rue Jean-Goujon" represents men with canes and top hats – symbols of their class – trampling over women and young girls in order to escape the fire. The caption reads

---

[64] On images of the intellectual hero and the military hero, see my *Birth of a National Icon: The Literary Avant-Garde and the Origins of the Intellectual in France* (Albany: SUNY Press, 1999), 135–182.

[65] Albert Cellarius, "Le Royal-Fuyard: sauve qui peut," *Le Jour*, 16 May and "Les Faux fileurs du grand monde" in *L'Intransigeant*, 18 May.

[66] All three songs are located in the Paris Police Archives, BA 1313–1314.

"Gentlemen of the 'Fin-de-Siècle'" (Figure 1.5). The term *fin de siècle* was used by contemporaries, most notably Max Nordau, to deplore the degradation of contemporary manners.[67] Another image from *Le Journal comique* of June 6 entitled "O Tender Gardenias!" depicts an elegant monocled man and a young woman with the tip of a cane sticking out from her head being tended by a nurse. The caption, a conversation between the young woman and the man reads: *Woman*: "I didn't see you, the day of the disaster of the Bazaar ..." *Man*: "Pardon me, I was near the door with several members of my circle" (Figure 1.6).

Despite such mockery, however, the theme of upper-class cowardice was no laughing matter. Many in the press lamented the fact that the exploits of these "descendants of the Crusades" contrasted so poorly with those of their noble ancestors, noting that the aristocracy had historically been closely associated with the army.[68] How could members of a class "whose muscular strength had been legendary in the past" have used their physical force to injure women, asked the anonymous journalist for *L'Eclair* in his column of May 14. Like many who compared the site of the tragedy to a field of battle, this reporter likened the losses at the fire to those at Agincourt, with one important difference – it was men who had died at Agincourt.[69]

Many deplored such contemporary manners, comparing the events of the fire to the recent incidents at the Ecole des Beaux-Arts in which male students, protesting the entry of women, had organized a noisy protest (charivari) and yelled "Shout down the women!" Such behavior at this sensitive moment was doubly embarrassing. Whereas most in the press decried such manners and hoped to offer new lessons in proper male comportment to the young generation,[70] the journalist for the monarchist *Le Soleil* blamed women for their plight. Although he admitted that self-preservation did not justify such behavior, he felt it important to note that this shameful attitude was symptomatic of new behavior in a France

[67] There is no date on the image. These gentlemen are beating a hasty retreat and the word *croisées* (meaning crossroads) in the title could be a play on the word *croisade*, meaning crusade – in which their ancestors had acquitted themselves honorably. Because the word is italicized here, it could also refer to a proper name or a publication. On the meaning of *fin de siècle*, see Eugen Weber, *France Fin de Siècle* (Cambridge, MA: Belknap Press of Harvard University Press, 1986), 9–15.

[68] Aristocratic men were seen as literally having war in their blood. See Robert A. Nye, *Masculinities and Male Codes of Honor in Modern France* (Berkeley: University of California Press, 1998), 15–30.

[69] "Et les hommes?" *L'Eclair*, 14 May.

[70] See "Egoïsme masculin," *Le Temps*, 15 May.

FIGURE 1.5. Bobb, "The Gardenias of the Rue Jean-Goujon," *La Silhouette* (no date).

Caption: "Gentlemen of the 'Fin-de-Siècle.'" Courtesy of the Bibliothèque Historique de la Ville de Paris, Actualités collection.

FIGURE 1.6. "O Tender Gardenias!" *Le Journal comique*, June 6, 1897.

Caption: Woman: "I didn't see you, the day of the disaster of the Bazaar."
Man: "Pardon me, I was near the door with several members of my circle ..."
Courtesy of the Bibliothèque Historique de la Ville de Paris, Actualités collection.

that had always been generous and respectful to women. Indeed, men had a "divine mission" to protect women whose physical frailty had made men their protectors. Nevertheless, he felt that the contemporary decline of the cult of the woman, which he viewed as a sign of national decadence and weakness, was the fault of feminists, who insisted on being treated as equals:

Speaking frankly, women are partly responsible for this evolution. Scorning, all of sudden, the men that surrounded them, no longer wishing to be the object of a cult which had become annoying and insipid, they have become determined to make themselves more masculine. They have adapted boyish manners which contrast singularly with their [female] countenance. ... Then came the excursions [with men], on horseback, on bicycles, the promiscuity of a friendship that does not even end at the door of the cabarets of Montmartre.

He continued: "Woman in abandoning this role of sovereign, of mystery, of muse, has diminished herself considerably, to the detriment of man himself." Moreover, men of the time had become too feminized, too cosseted and protected and condemned to idleness. He praised the army as an institution that made men. In the end, he noted, women's mission was maternity, and it was the gender confusion of the time that had led to the current situation.[71] Although others undoubtedly shared this retrograde view, not many in the press dared to hold women responsible for the plight of those who died in the fire. More progressive commentators like H. Hostein, writing in *France* of May 16 about the incidents, observed that men did not know what to make of women's changing roles in society: "We either place her too high, through a servile adoration or we reduce her to the condition of a mere slave." He exhorted his male colleagues to treat women better: "Come on, men; let us be better and, above all, more just toward women!"[72]

Female Heroes

Hostein's comment was perceptive. Moreover, it had implications that he perhaps did not fully realize or articulate. What touched a nerve in the Bazar de la Charité fire was the fact that in the popular imagination, if not necessarily in actuality, gender roles had been reversed in a sort of grotesque carnival. In this world turned upside down, it was the women

---

[71] "Quelle est la cause?" by Furetières in *Le Soleil*, 16 May.
[72] H. Hostein, "La Politique," *France*, 15 May.

who had displayed courage and the men who had behaved like stereotypical women. Making up a balance sheet in her piece for *L'Echo de Paris* on May 13, Séverine concluded that it was women and young girls who kept their cool, citing the bravery of the young girl Mlle de Froissard, who saved an elderly relative and a young cousin. In contrast with the abundance of female heroic acts, the balance sheet for men was rather meager.[73] The press was filled with accounts of the heroism of the women present. Many newspapers cited the devotion of daughters, among them Mlles de Heredia (the daughter of the poet) and Morado, both of whom refused to leave until they were able to extricate their mothers. So too were there numerous mothers who ran back in to save their children, in the process losing their lives. Many of the conservative papers also cited the courage of the nuns who organized the rescue of women over the wall leading to the offices of *La Croix*, waiting until last to save themselves. Nearly all the commentators praised female chivalry and gallantry. In contrast, the men had done little or nothing, concluded the anonymous writer for *L'Eclair* on May 14, observing that these men had lost their honor.[74]

The reporter for *Le Temps* in an article entitled "Egoïsme masculin" from May 15 lamented that "the majority of men, in contrast with women, supposedly had only enough virility necessary for overturning obstacles." They had used their superior physical force in a cowardly way. Furthermore, they had only displayed their self-interest in this case and in the Beaux-Arts incident. If things had really happened this way, "there is nothing more humiliating for the male self-image and one hardly knows how to characterize such a dereliction of duty and of the chivalrous traditions of our race," the reporter concluded. In a similar fashion, Albert Rogat, writing in *France* of May 15, opposed moral courage to physical force, decrying that the men had not displayed the former and, moreover, had used their superior force to save themselves: "One is ashamed to admit it, that given their physical force, their moral energy, one had the right to expect better of them." According to Rogat, these men no longer knew anything "but the animal instinct of [self-]preservation."[75]

Real courage for many of these male commentators was defined as keeping one's presence of mind, no matter the circumstances, and was contrasted to brute force. Gender norms of the period generally defined males by their rationality and ability to keep their wits about them,

[73] Séverine, "Qu'ont fait les hommes?" *L'Echo de Paris*, 13 May.
[74] "Et les hommes?" *L'Eclair*, 14 May.
[75] Rogat, "Et les hommes?" *France*, 15 May.

although a number of writers, Maurice Barrès, Henry Bérenger, and Friedrich Nietzsche, along with philosopher Henri Bergson, praised feeling and emotion. Some even defined these traits as heroic, using them to attack "dried up" rationalists who thought and therefore could not act.[76] Whereas some males might have valorized emotion in men, comparing it to *cran* or guts, descriptions of women by males of various political classes and persuasions did not always give women the same benefit of the doubt. When women were defined as emotional, their emotionalism was depicted as irrational and animalistic – witness the contemporary descriptions of crowds as "feminine." It is for this reason that a commentator like Rogat was especially pained that it had been the women who had maintained their sangfroid, in contrast to the men, who had acted like unthinking beasts. Many articles in the press referred to the fleeing men as "wild animals."[77] Comparing the events of the fire to the incidents at the Ecole des Beaux-Arts, the author of "Egoïsme masculin" found that it was "a very painful and disconcerting symptom" of the degradation of contemporary manners, and he exhorted his compatriots to double their energies to combat such aberrations for the honor of the nation.[78]

In "Leur héroïsme," published in *La Libre Parole* on May 13, Jules Delahaye spoke of "the most beautiful page in the history of women! So beautiful that one would like to have found more men [up to this standard of heroism] for the honor of men!" His confrere from *La Libre Parole*, Gaston Méry, in an article entitled "Et les hommes?" of May 12, too had contrasted the behavior of elite males to the heroism and nobility of the women who had died saving loved ones.[79] The aristocratic men, acting like "bêtes humaines" – note the reference to Zola's famous work – had abandoned their womenfolk to save themselves. Like captains of a ship, they should have been the last to leave and should have

---

[76] Barrès and Bérenger, who expressed such fears of an excess of intellect, went on to take opposite sides in the Dreyfus Affair. Similarly, future anti-Dreyfusard Charles Maurras shared with future Zionist Max Nordau a fear of extreme emotionalism, which both associated with degenerate art. Thus, these differing views of manhood and honor cut across religious, social, and political lines: *Birth of a National Icon*, 122–125.

[77] See "Poursuites nécessaires" by Maurice Allard, *La Lanterne*, 16 May.

[78] "Egoïsme masculin," *Le Temps*, 15 May. See also Rogat, who spoke of "the honor of our sex and our race."

[79] Gaston "Et les hommes?" *La Libre Parole*, 12 May: "Yet they were there, only five minutes earlier! They posed simpering, monocles in place, around these women, who exquisitely, asked them for charity. Ah yes, one must have the courage to say it, these gentlemen abandoned these ladies to save their own skin!"

gone down with the ship, if necessary. Thus, their mere survival was a sign of their dereliction of duty. Indeed, he and others praised the Duchesse d'Alençon for her devotion to duty. She could easily have fled but had been heard telling her companions to escape while she stayed to help others.

Méry praised the "simple women" who had no responsibilities but who had exhibited "an admirable courage and selflessness."[80] Méry implicitly insulted women in the same breath as he praised them by describing them as "simple." H. de Kerohant, the journalist for the royalist *Le Soleil*, was even more explicitly derogatory. Although he celebrated the women for their "energy" and "sangfroid," he concluded, perhaps not realizing that he was contradicting himself, in the following fashion: "Yes, in all classes of society, women know how to be heroic because they have heart. The head is often light – a birdbrain – but the heart is good."[81] Here he was undercutting the heroism of the women by defining it as a visceral reaction of the heart, of emotion, and even self-interest, implying that the women had simply gone in to save loved ones. Moreover, he implied that the qualities of the "head" were male, suggesting that male heroism was "rational."[82] Kerohant's uneasiness with gender blurring is evident. How could the women display energy and presence of mind and still be, as he dubbed them, "birdbrains" (*tête de linotte*)? He also noted – somewhat defensively – that one needn't exaggerate the qualities of the heroic women. Men, after all, were capable of courage too.[83] The journalist for *L'Echo de Paris* of May 15 expressed similar sentiments, albeit from a different perspective. Acknowledging that women too could be brave, he lamented sorrowfully, "Courage and abnegation are not the exclusive prerogative of our sex, as recent events have all too sadly illustrated."[84]

Catholic Martyrs

Whereas the secular newspapers concentrated on the heroism of the women who had died or survived saving loved ones, emphasizing filial or motherly duty, they also commented on the intrinsic heroic qualities of the women involved. Catholics, however, tended to emphasize the

---

[80] Méry.
[81] H. de Kerohant "Ce n'est pas possible," *Le Soleil*, 18 May.
[82] As we have seen, not all men shared this view of male heroism.
[83] Kerohant.
[84] "Encore les hommes?" *L'Echo de Paris*, 15 May.

martyrdom of the women who had perished in the fire.[85] Père Olliver had scandalized republicans by declaring that the fire was retribution for a France that had lost its way. Comparing the women's sacrifice to that of Christ, who had died for other men's sins, these Catholics called upon a long tradition associating women with Christ's suffering.[86] According to Père Paul Fesch, the author of an homage to the victims entitled *Mortes au champ d'honneur: Bazar de la Charité*, women's role was to suffer: "'Women have a celestial instinct for adversity,' said Chateaubriand. It is true; it seems that God created them, saying: 'You will live on earth in order to suffer and to console.'"[87] Such sentiments were to be found in all the Catholic commentary of the fire. Edouard Drumont in *La Libre Parole* asked why the mainstream republican press was so surprised and shocked by these sentiments, which were part of Catholic doctrine.[88] The association of suffering with women, however, was not unique to Catholics. Even the reporter for *Le Figaro* commented, "The hearts of women, steeped in goodness, charity, and an aptitude for sublime sacrifices, are generally worth more than those of men, [who are] always troubled by aggressive thoughts, bitterness, excessive severity or ambition."[89]

Because the date of the fire was close to the May commemorations of Joan of Arc and, moreover, the month of May corresponded to celebrations of the Virgin Mary, it is not surprising that many observers, especially Catholics, compared the sacrifice of the women victims to that of Joan herself, among them Père Ollivier in his sermon at Notre-Dame: "Oh dear and noble victims! ... you appear to us like Joan of Arc on the red [smoke] clouds of the stake, surrounded by light and rising

---

[85] I am thinking of the coverage in *La Croix* and in the various commemorative books in honor of the victims, written by Catholic laypeople or clergy. For a complete list of these works, see the catalog of the BHVP.

[86] See Richard D. Burton's study *Holy Tears, Holy Blood: Women, Catholicism, and the Culture of Suffering in France, 1840–1970* (Ithaca, NY: Cornell University Press, 2004); and Ruth Harris, *Lourdes: Body and Spirit in the Secular Age* (New York: Viking, 1999), 306–307. See also Suzanne K. Kaufman, *Consuming Visions: Mass Culture and the Lourdes Shrine* (Ithaca, NY: Cornell University Press, 2005), 140–144. Elinor Accampo, writing about Nelly Roussel, notes that the feminist also used this theme to liberate women from the burden of childbearing. See Accampo's essay "Private Life, Public Image: Motherhood and Militancy in the Self-Construction of Nelly Roussel, 1900–1922," in *The New Biography: Performing Femininity in Nineteenth-Century France*, ed. Jo Burr Margadant (Berkeley: University of California Press, 2000), 223.

[87] Père Paul Fesch, *Mortes au champ d'honneur: Bazar de la Charité* (Paris: Flammarion, 1897), 14.

[88] Drumont, "L'Expiation," *La Libre Parole*, 11 May.

[89] "A Propos des sauveteurs," *Le Figaro*, 22 May.

toward a glory where the Inspirer of your charity and the Remunerator of your sacrifice awaits you."[90] Père Paul Fesch observed that, like Joan, the women had fallen on the field of battle: "They too have fallen, these noble women on the field of battle; their souls have soared, not by driving back a bloodthirsty enemy, but by attempting to save, through their charity, the life of the unhappy sons of France – which is also a [way of] defending the nation."[91] In an age when heroes were often absent, the women had shown the world that France still was capable of producing them: "You have shown the entire universe that our native soil is not sterile because it always produces heroes who shed their blood valiantly on the field of battle."[92]

But this comparison might actually have had a subversive value, not recognized by the reverend fathers, since Joan was not only the young Catholic maiden who saved both king and country but also a cross-dressing woman who defied the gender roles of her time. Surely, this view of Joan of Arc was not lost on feminists of the time.[93] Sarah Bernhardt, who depicted Joan on the stage twice, was well aware of the double nature of the heroine she sought to represent.[94] Thus, despite the attempts by many conservative papers to depict the women as martyrs and victims, the comparison with Joan of Arc only reinforced the idea that women could be heroes too and, moreover, in a way that did not necessarily correspond to strictly delineated gender categories.

[90] Quoted in Huret, 150.

[91] Fesch, 324.

[92] Fesch, 5. The use of the word *sterile*, given the fear of depopulation and interest in women bearing children, is no accident.

[93] Ruth Harris has persuasively argued against a monolithic vision of Catholicism marked by "paternalist repression." Although the Church did put women in subordinate positions, it also "offered them a world of opportunity and found a means of cultivating their loyalty and energies": *Lourdes*, 361. Indeed, as she observes (in a conversation with the author), the descriptions of the women who perished in the fire were similar to those of Catholic women who endured physical and emotional hardships to travel to Lourdes to help the poor and ill. Thus, there is a long tradition in the Catholic Church of strong women. In speaking of the female *miraculées* who went to Lourdes, Suzanne Kaufman likens them to New Women, stating that they transgressed traditional female models of the time based on modesty and self-abnegation, "embracing instead an assertive feminine subject." This double nature made the *miraculée* appealing to many devout Catholic women of the time: *Consuming Visions*, 161. Following this logic, one could argue that the double appeal made Joan attractive not only to Catholics but also to some feminists.

[94] See Mary Louise Roberts, *Disruptive Acts: The New Woman in Fin-de-Siècle France* (Chicago: University of Chicago Press, 2002), 210–212.

Whitewash or National Solidarity?

If there was uneasiness about the role of the women in the fire, the discomfort with that of men was even greater, leading to the eventual waning of the stories about the *gardénias*. Some of the women survivors who had initially spoken of being hit or shoved by men seeking to get out either recanted or denied ever having implied that their men had acted other than honorably. Indeed, the whole *gardénia* affair ended in a whitewash in the wake of an inquiry conducted by the society paper *Le Gaulois*. Lest contemporaries charge that the paper was simply doing the bidding of its aristocratic clientele, the editors announced that truth was their objective and that *Le Gaulois* sought to be the paper of all the French people ("de tous les braves gens").[95]

Le Gaulois interviewed the organizers of the bazar, including the Baron de Mackau and Henry Blount, as well as three *commissaires*, the men who were supposed to oversee the counters, and finally, a number of women and two priests who were in attendance. According to the testimony of eyewitnesses, many of the men there, including Blount and Mackau, about whom rumors had circulated in the press, had displayed great courage in working to save lives. Perhaps less convincing are the declarations of the women interviewed who claimed they saw no acts of male brutality and – those of men and women alike – who claimed that only half a dozen men were present at the time of the fire. Finally, the two priests interviewed noted that there were only 600–700 people in attendance, thereby contradicting the estimates of 1,600–1,700 given by Mackau and other members of the committee, a discrepancy that was fully exposed by the populist press.[96]

Class tensions certainly framed the comments in the populist press about the unexpected denouement of the gardenia affair. The anticlerical *Le Jour* published a piece on May 28 called "On serre des coudes" in which the reporter deplored "the reawakening of the esprit de corps of the royalist-Catholic salons" that had led to the present conclusion of events. The anonymous author jeered at the account published in *Le Figaro* of an eyewitness who claimed that the young men present might have "pushed a little" with their canes, as one did at the theater. In an earlier article of May 20, *Le Jour* had accused the society papers of

---

[95] "Le Rôle des hommes au Bazar de la Charité," *Le Gaulois*, 19 May. This *enquête* was conducted by Georges Foucher. The disclaimer about speaking for the entire nation, not just the well-heeled clientele of the *Le Gaulois*, did not sway critics of the newspaper.

[96] "Le Rôle des hommes au Bazar de la Charité."

both having begun the rumors about the *gardénias* and of then hushing them up. This reporter for *Le Jour* wondered how republican journalists could hear the rumors of society folk, if not from society papers. He went on to point out the contradictions in *Le Gaulois*'s coverage and the questions its inquiry left unanswered. The fact that the *Gaulois* reporter Georges Foucher, interviewing Jean-François Raffaëilli, who refused to back down about his story of impropriety on the part of some men, had added an editorial comment questioning the accuracy of the painter's statements especially earned the ire of the journalist from *Le Jour*: "It turns out that you can't be a real man of the world, except by failing to reveal – or ignoring – the violence of the little gardenias."[97]

Henri de Rochefort commented in *L'Intransigeant* that the society women insisted on believing in the heroism of men of their class because they had no other alternative but to do so. How else could they justify marrying their daughters off to such men?[98] Like Rochefort, the iconoclast aristocrat Gyp, who felt more at home with the "populo" than those of her own class, wrote in "Revirement," the third of her vignettes about the events, that accusing the men meant creating a disruption of society life. At the end of her story, the men are "graciously" pardoning the dead women for putting men in the position of behaving badly.[99] Later that year, when the Baron de Mackau, along with the two workers from the cinema firm that had provided the projector, was tried for responsibility in the fire, the left-wing press had a field day. Mackau, whom they felt was responsible for running the Bazar de la Charité, had been placed on the same footing as the two lowly employees: Bellac the projectionist and his assistant Bagrachow. Mackau was fined a mere 500 francs, whereas the two others were given suspended sentences, respectively, of one year in prison with a fine of 300 francs, and eight months in prison with a fine of 200 francs.[100] André Vervoort had earlier predicted such an occurrence, noting that Mackau occupied a strategic position in the Chamber of Deputies, serving as liaison between the Catholic right and the republican cabinet. He thus benefited from "certain favors of the State."[101]

---

[97] "Les Gardénias: Le Rôle des hommes au Bazar," *Le Jour*, 20 May.

[98] Henri Rochefort, "Les Animaux malades de la peste," *L'Intransigeant*, 16 May.

[99] Gyp, *La Libre Parole*, 3 June.

[100] The reports in the police files document the sentencing, which was, of course, also covered by the press.

[101] André Vervoort, "Les Coupables," *Le Jour*, 8 May 1897. Such sentiments were also shared by Georges Clemenceau, who railed against *les grosses légumes* (big cheeses) in his piece "Après le sinistre," *La Justice*, 13 May.

In his essay on the Bazar de la Charité, Michel Winock argues that the theme of gender warfare was replaced by class warfare in the wake of the recanting of the society women.[102] I would argue, however, that the two are inextricably linked, with the theme of gender lying at the heart of the class warfare conducted in the press. As much at stake as class solidarity was gender solidarity. The fact that women displayed bravery and men cowardice contradicted the gender norms of the period. It is in part for this reason that mainstream papers accepted the minimizing of the actions of the elite men and sought instead to point to the heroism of the men there, that of elite and working-class males alike.

For their part, the two prominent female journalists, Gyp and Séverine, who went on to take opposing positions during the Dreyfus Affair, upheld the honor of the women in the fire by maintaining their critical views of the male *gardénias*. One wonders how this played to the female readers of the press at this time, whose numbers had increased during these years, especially in the case of the Bazar de la Charité fire, in which many of the principals were women.[103]

In contrast, the middle-class males who wrote for the major newspapers as well as middle-class republican politicians, while in agreement about male working-class heroism and that of the women, soon became uneasy with this image of cowardly aristocratic males. Although aristocrats themselves played an increasingly smaller role in French society and politics under the republican regime, aristocratic notions of male honor still held sway and were firmly ingrained in the Third Republic's notion of national honor. Most bourgeois men thus aspired to aristocratic ideals, and if male members of the aristocracy were found wanting, their behavior would reflect badly on middle-class men as well.[104] Thus, men in key positions of power in the Third Republic, in the press as well as in the political sphere, had a vested interest in protecting male aristocrats because in doing so they were protecting themselves as well as the nation. In light of the loss of honor in the Franco-Prussian War, the French felt

---

[102] Winock, 92.

[103] Christian Delporte notes that the daily paper was destined for all members of the family, including women who had heretofore been excluded from reading the papers. He affirms (p. 110), as does Anne-Marie Thiesse, that women tended to read the *roman-feuilleton*, whereas men concentrated on politics and the *fait divers*. See Thiesse's *Le Roman du quotidien: Lecteurs et lectures populaires à la Belle Epoque* (Paris: Le Chemin Vert, 1984), 20. I would argue that women did read the coverage of the Bazar de la Charité fire (judging by the letters received by editors of various papers), not only because women were the principals in the tragedy but also because this real-life event had become fictionalized.

[104] See Nye, 150–151, and Berenson, *Madame Caillaux*, 182–187.

self-conscious vis-à-vis Germany. Indeed, many of the commentaries noted that the loss of elite male honor would humiliate the French even further in German eyes.[105]

In the end, national solidarity won out, because the valor of elite males also reflected on that of the French nation itself.[106] Not unsurprisingly, papers like *Le Gaulois* led the charge, cleverly eliding the honor of the aristocratic men with that of the nation. Thus, Georges Foucher, commenting on the necessity of an inquiry, observed: "To diminish in any way the country's reputation for chivalry and courage is to threaten its very nature."[107] Similarly, Colomba, writing for *L'Echo de Paris* of May 18, although denouncing the behavior of some men present, cautioned against judging an entire class by the conduct of a few individuals, especially a class that had always given France valiant soldiers. The article ended with a plea for a calming of social tensions.[108] These calls for national solidarity, along with pressure on the aristocratic women not to break ranks, were responsible for the gradual waning of the *gardénia* story, although populist papers could be forgiven for claiming that class unity alone had been responsible for ending the whole affair, especially given the self-congratulatory tone of the society papers.[109]

Georges Foucher in *Le Gaulois* of May 20 noted smugly, "So ends our inquiry, undertaken in order to respond, less in France than abroad, to a campaign that by appearing to dishonor some individuals, could end up casting suspicion on the courage of all French men."[110] A few days later, on May 28, members of *Le Gaulois*'s editorial staff pronounced

---

[105] See, for example, Foucher's concluding comments in "La Fin de notre enquête," *Le Gaulois*, 20 May: "Thus concludes our inquiry, undertaken to respond – less in France than abroad – to a campaign, which under the guise of dishonoring certain persons, could throw suspicion on the courage of all French men." Such sentiments support Richard Thomson's claim that *revanche* was more important than has been depicted by historians: *The Troubled Republic: Visual Culture and Social Debate in France, 1889–1900* (New Haven, CT: Yale University Press, 2004), 170–171.

[106] As Edward Berenson notes, gender loyalty could take precedence over religious and therefore political loyalty: *Madame Caillaux*, 192.

[107] "Une Enquête nécessaire, by G.F. (Georges Foucher) in *Le Gaulois* of 18 May. He also noted that *Le Gaulois*, which had been "faithful to its tradition of profound respect for women, had fulfilled, as best it could, the sweetest of duties in paying homage to the noble women."

[108] Colomba, "Chronique," *L'Echo de Paris*, 18 May.

[109] The waning of the story was also due to fatigue; by the end of the month, the Bazar de la Charité fire was no longer front-page news. Earlier, the death of the Duc d'Aumale (on 7 May) had temporarily knocked the Bazar de la Charité story off the front pages of some of the more sober newspapers, *Le Temps* among them.

[110] Georges Foucher, "La Fin de notre enquête," *Le Gaulois*, 20 May.

themselves happy first as French men and then as journalists that the presiding judge Bertulus had also cleared the men present at the bazaar of all
charges.[111] Conservative Catholic Joseph Cornély, writing for *L'Echo de
Paris* of May 22, was also relieved, striking a sycophantic note in thank-
ing *Le Gaulois* for proving that upper-class men were valiant. Cornély
went on to note that there was only one man present for twenty women,
which explained why only five men died. He also further minimized male
injuries by pointing to the fact that women's clothing easily caught fire.
The final assault to female bravery in the fire, however, was the brazen
comment that women were subject to emotion that paralyzed them, but
men, with their military training, had the requisite sangfroid to escape.
Having gone on the offensive against women, the reporter went on to
criticize those (referring to the left-wing republicans) who sought to keep
the upper bourgeoisie and aristocracy out of public life. They had already
been eliminated from political life and now were being deprived of their
hereditary reputation for bravery by those who would incite fratricidal
hatreds.[112]

Such journalists were no doubt the targets of Gyp's article "Revirement,"
but most in the press, like Lucien Millevoye in *La Patrie* of May 23,
sounded a more conciliatory note, urging his compatriots to forget for
a moment those who did not do their duty and concentrate instead on
those sons of the people who upheld the reputation of the country. These
men were the future soldiers of France. Despite the threats that came
from across the Rhine, the French were still a noble and valiant race.[113]
Le Matin, known for its measured reporting of the case, noted in an article of May 21 titled "Les Nerfs de Paris" that public opinion evolved too
quickly. Moreover, the French loved stark oppositions. First, there were
calls to accord accolades to the heroes such that too many decorations
and recompenses were distributed. Then, there was a current of opinion
hostile to society men, and finally, when the actions of the working men
were called into question, those of their aristocratic compatriots were

[111] "La Légende des gardénias," *Le Gaulois*, 28 May.
[112] J. Cornély, "Enquête," *L'Echo de Paris*, 22 May. Not all journalists for *L'Echo de Paris*
felt that way. On 22 May, Simone, in her "Pages d'agenda," wrote a fictional letter to
one of the working-class heroes, Dhuy, explaining the absence of aristocratic women at
a banquet for the working-class heroes, by saying that it was harder for these women to
recognize that they owed their lives to a "cesspool cleaner" than to admit that they had
received "blows from a cane" from a gentleman.
[113] Lucien Millevoye, "Le Courage civique," *La Patrie*, 23 May: "A race which steadfastly
cherishes the cult of valor, who loves and honors it for this virile sentiment, will [know
how to] fight, will [know how to] die."

rehabilitated. This article raised an interesting point. Although the working-class heroes did not have to be discredited for aristocratic males to be rehabilitated, clearly, for the "good" of the nation, all classes of French males had to be represented as heroic.

The Power of the Press

The coverage of the gardenia incident in the press also reveals the power that contemporaries gave to the newspaper and its primary importance henceforth in national life. As the gardenia story unfolded, many in the press, including *Le Radical*, *Le National*, *L'Intransigeant*, *France*, and *La Libre Parole*, were calling for the names of the men who had conducted themselves dishonorably. The reporter for *La Libre Parole*, Gaston Méry, was especially aggressive in pursuing this story. Not only did he demand names but he also claimed that they were well known in society circles and threatened to publish them.[114] Similarly, H. Hostein writing for *France* of May 16 joked about publishing the names so as to give these gentlemen "good press" (*bonne presse*).[115] Some like Henri Rochefort in *L'Intransigeant* doubted the good faith of the system,[116] and the anonymous journalist for *Le National* of May 17 even went so far as to declare that if Parisians had these men in their hands, they would have lynched them.[117]

All these articles calling for names declared that public opinion demanded it. Méry, like others in the press, reacted with indignation to Bertulus's suggestion that the men could not be pursued by law. Alexandre Hepp even declared that in the absence of justice through the courts, publishing the names would have to suffice: "public opinion will compensate for the weakness of the system, and we will settle, however reluctantly, for the stocks."[118] These journalists, taking the role of the Fourth estate very seriously, thus threatened to mete out punishment in the court of public opinion if such justice could not be served in the court of law.[119]

---

[114] Méry mentioned publishing the names in nearly all of his articles. See especially "Et les hommes," *La Libre Parole*, 12 May.

[115] H. Hostein, "La Politique," *France*, 16 May.

[116] Henri Rochefort, "On demande les noms," *L'Intransigeant*, 8 May.

[117] "Les Muscadins impunis," *Le National*, 17 May.

[118] Alexandre Hepp, "Homicide par prudence," *Le Journal*, 14 May.

[119] This development provides an interesting comment on Sarah Maza's thesis that earlier in the eighteenth century, the way that such justice was carried out was in the female-dominated world of court society, that is, public opinion of those who mattered. Later,

Although journalists never went as far as accusing individual men, they did mention the names of the men believed to be in attendance during the fire, thereby obliging those named to recount their actions that day or deny having been there. Here again, the reactions of the men whose names were published in the newspapers illustrate the power of the press at the time. Many wrote letters to the editors of the papers to clear their names, asking that they be published. And, of course, *Le Gaulois*, claiming to speak for the entire nation, undertook an inquiry to clear the names of the men suspected. Finally, the newspapers used their power to consult the people directly to raise money for the charities affected by the fire. *Le Figaro* undertook this task, publishing daily lists of the contributors and the sums donated, in the end raising a great deal of money. Commenting on the 589,000 francs they had raised for charities, the editors of *Le Figaro* noted in a self-congratulatory fashion, "Yes, the press is a great and noble thing, greater and even more noble on those days when its strength is applied on behalf of all that need it ... it is able to find its way into other hearts, giving to so many who are unaware of each other's existence, to so many people of good will who are seeking each other out, the chance to meet, to work toward a common goal."[120] This description of the press is remarkably similar to that of Benedict Anderson's "imagined community" of newspaper readers.

The Bazar de la Charité and the *Ralliement*

The events of the Bazar de la Charité represent an important affair of public opinion, one that foreshadows the battle waged in the press during the Dreyfus Affair a few months later. Historians have long spoken of the Dreyfus Affair as the first affair of national opinion formed by a powerful press. The events of the Bazar de la Charité illustrate that such habits and mechanisms by which individuals resorted to the press to dispense justice or to right the wrongs of the judicial system were already in place.

as the century came to a close, such justice would move to the male-dominated public assemblies and courts of law: *Private Lives and Public Affairs: The Causes Célèbres of Prerevolutionary France* (Berkeley: University of California Press, 1993), 314. In the case of the Bazar de la Charité fire, justice, which could not be dispensed in a court of law, was to be carried out in the court of public opinion, this time extending to the masses, by a press powerfully poised to play the role of national arbiter.

[120] "580,000 francs!" *Le Figaro*, 10 May. The eventual sum would be more than a million francs. See *Le Figaro* of 29 May. In addition, nearly one million francs were donated anonymously to the Comité du Bazar de la Charité. Eventually, the press learned that the donor had been Mme Lebaudy, the sugar heiress.

The events of the Bazar de la Charité fire also mark one of the last times that the coalition of the *ralliement* would hold together. On May 29, an interpellation of the Méline cabinet took place in the Chamber of Deputies, ending in a vote of confidence of 296 votes to 231. Although the Cabinet survived, the polemics during this debate were heated, with deputy Georges Berry asking why the police hadn't intervened to stop the bazar, given the presence of a fire hazard. Barthou, the minister of the interior, replied as he had done on previous occasions, that the event was private and therefore the government had no jurisdiction there. Next, deputy Vallé asked why a republican government had participated in a religious ceremony and how Père Olliver, a member of a disbanded congregation with a reputation for polemics, had been allowed to give an unvetted speech. The anti-clerical paper *La Petite République* mocked Méline's answers to these questions and commented bitterly that it was now clear that Méline had chosen "monarchists disguised as those who have rallied to the republic" over other republicans to his left. The Catholic deputy Denys Cochin's defense of the Méline cabinet seemed to confirm suspicions on the left that the Méline cabinet was working hand in hand with the "clericals." One of the more dramatic moments occurred when Albert de Mun, calling for social peace in wake of the tragedy, was shouted down by the left as the *fusilleur* (responsible for the repression of Communards) of the Commune.[121]

A few short months later, in the wake of the Dreyfus Affair, the *ralliement* would be a memory of the past, as the theme of republican defense once again asserted itself. Faure would be dead (February 1899), replaced by the more left-wing Emile Loubet. Similarly, the moderate republican Jules Méline, who had done much on the government end to encourage the support of Catholics, lost his post as prime minister to the Radical Henri Brisson, who as president of the Chamber of Deputies had incurred the wrath of Catholics by denouncing Père Ollivier's sermon in a session of May 18, and by having his speech distributed and posted throughout the country.[122] Despite pressure from groups left of the Méline cabinet and those to the right of the *ralliés* (those who had rallied to the republic), this fragile coalition did not fall apart over the

---

[121] "La Chambre," by Civis, *La Petite Republique*, 30 May. *Le Figaro* and *Le Temps* were, of course, much more sympathetic to the Cabinet and critical of Berry and the other deputies who had initiated the interpellation. See *Le Figaro* and *Le Temps* of 30 May.

[122] See *La Croix*'s concerted campaign against Brisson. One article compared him to the bomb-thrower Vaillant. Not to be outdone, *La Croix* and other Catholic groups printed Ollivier's sermon and distributed it as well.

Bazar de la Charité fire. As some noted in the left-wing press, the Baron de Mackau, himself a deputy (from the Orne region), occupied a strategic position as mediator between the moderates in power and the *ralliés*.[123]

On June 25, the question of the bazaar came up again in the Chamber, this time, with regard to voting additional funds for the medals distributed and for the ceremonies at Notre-Dame. Once again, deputies on the extreme left used the occasion to rail against the violation of government neutrality in religious matters. In the end, the credits were voted 375 to 80.[124]

Conclusion

The tragedy of the Bazar de la Charité fire should have been an occasion for national unity. It was among the first important *faits divers* covered by a mass press that had become a major force in French society. Although the press contributed to creating a sense of national community in terms of the "consumption" of the titillating and horrifying aspects of the events, its coverage also revealed and, at times, exacerbated deep-rooted political, social, and cultural tensions in French society – indeed, conflicting visions of the nation. The representations of the victims and the rescuers were colored by these divisions. For the populist press – those who would go on to become both Dreyfusards and anti-Dreyfusards – the working-class heroes were the "real" men of France. Unlike the corrupt republican politicians and the cowardly society men who survived the fire, they knew their duty. Through their selflessness and devotion, they contributed to a renewal of a France suffering from decadence and decline, which they associated with both republican elites and the upper classes. For Catholics and moderate republicans, however, these working-class heroes were more a sign of national unity, and some conservative commentators even went as far as expressing their belief that the devotion in the fire of servants to masters amply illustrated the goodness of the latter.

Whereas the left celebrated the redemptive and heroic qualities of working-class men, Catholics viewed the sacrifice of the aristocratic

---

[123] See the recent biography of Mackau by Eric Phélippeau, *L'Invention de l'homme politique moderne: Mackau, l'Orne et la République* (Paris: Belin, 2002).

[124] One deputy, Trouillot, proposed that the sum be reduced by 100 francs in order to censure the government for having participated in a religious ceremony, while another, Hubbard, supported a motion to reject the credits. Once again, Denys Cochin intervened in the defense of the Cabinet, asking for a truce in the wake of such national tragedy. See the article by Pas-Perdus in *Le Figaro* of 26 June: "La Chambre: Encore le Bazar de la Charité."

women victims' bodies as a means to redeem the body politic. In the eyes of Catholics, the sacrifice of the aristocratic women who perished in the fire was akin to the sacrifice of Joan of Arc, who died to save king and country. These women expiated the sins of a France that had abandoned its Catholic traditions. Secular newspapers, especially anti-clerical ones, while exalting the victims as exemplars of French womanhood, contested this idea of expiation, even as they shared a fascination with their Catholic counterparts for the victimhood of the women. Indeed, this image of the women as passive victims dominates discussions of their actively heroic acts.

If the depiction of male heroism was subject to class warfare, the representation of female heroism seemed to be the object of some consensus, because the ideal of the selfless mother and daughter corresponded to both Catholic and republican views of women. Thus, despite differing views of the nation, a common set of expectations about male heroism as superior to female heroism united both sides. These assumptions had been so shaken by the gender confusion of the time that the behavior of Catholic women in the traditional feminine milieu of charity was conflated in the popular imagination with that of their New Women sisters, who transgressed gender norms by expressly rejecting the traditional roles of wives and mothers.[125] As the press depicted it, the events of the Bazar de la Charité fire revealed glimpses of a world turned upside down in which women showed more courage than men. Nothing less than the honor of France demanded the righting of this situation. It is for this reason that those in the mainstream, Catholics and non-Catholics alike, sought the rehabilitation of the *gardénias*, which was thus the result of gender solidarity as much as the product of class solidarity. After all, the men who wrote for the mainstream press, along with most republican politicians, were middle-class males, who in aspiring to aristocratic codes of male honor, had as much at stake as the maligned *gardénias*. Even those writing for the populist newspapers, scoffing at this whitewash, as they dubbed it, would probably have asserted the superiority of male heroism, as represented by working-class men, to female heroism, as it was incarnated by the aristocratic women.

[125] See Roberts, p. 8, on the distinction between a New Woman and a feminist. The latter chose to emphasize the roles of women as wives and mothers. Diana Holmes and Carrie Tarr tend to see more overlap between feminists and New Women than Roberts: "New Republic, New Women? Feminism and Modernity at the Belle Epoque," in *A 'Belle Epoque'? Women in French Society and Culture, 1890–1914*, ed. Holmes and Tarr (New York: Berghahn Books, 2007), 20.

The events of the Bazar de la Charité fire, however, illustrated the cracks in strictly delineated gender ideals, challenging contemporary gender stereotypes, not only of the weak female victim and the strong male hero but also of the very nature of heroism. In the end, it was the women who had displayed actual heroism unlike many of the men. Not only could women be heroes, but certain "female traits" – among them, self-sacrifice and abnegation – were heroic. These ideals may have fit the image of the ideal woman of the time, but they also corresponded to the characteristics of heroism. In an increasingly selfish and consumer-oriented society, heroes sacrificed themselves for the greater good. As numerous articles indicated, the women in the fire had fallen on the "battlefield" of charity, in the process of helping others. Despite rhetoric to the contrary, national discussions of heroism in the Bazar de la Charité fire announced the increasing acceptance in the years to come of the traditional female traits of self-effacement and sacrifice, as long as they were linked to the notion of honor, the quintessential male trait.

Furthermore, the paradigm that pitted weak, emotional females against strong, rational males was called into question. Not only were the women in the fire coolheaded, but it was the males who had "lost their heads." Many in the press repeatedly mentioned the "sangfroid" of the male rescuers, contrasting their cool with the "panic" of the female victims, even as they cited examples to the contrary. Those who attempted to minimize or deny female heroism, depicting it as a passive act, the product of the heart, or self-interest – the women had gone in to save loved ones – rather than a conscious choice, were faced with the fact that the emotion of the women in the fire had been transformed into *cran* or guts, a quality associated with courage and heroism. Although male heroes were traditionally exalted for their mental faculties, especially for keeping their heads in a dangerous situation, physical courage could be seen as guts, a heroic male virtue, as it was in the descriptions of the male working-class heroes. Thus, despite efforts by some observers and participants in the Bazar de la Charité fire to draw clearly delineated gender lines, the actual events illustrated the destabilization of those boundaries, a process further examined in the following three chapters on Cyrano de Bergerac, Napoleon, and Joan of Arc.

One could argue that the tensions present during the Bazar de la Charité fire fueled subsequent attempts to find heroes in French society. Indeed, the impassioned debates during the Dreyfus Affair brought the question of heroes even more dramatically onto the national stage. Although Alfred Dreyfus himself fit the Dreyfusard view of the hero, he did not comport himself as a theatrical hero, thereby disappointing his supporters and the public. Such disappointments in real life led, in part, to the search for heroes in the boulevard theater of the time, as illustrated by the popularity of the fictionalized Napoleon and Joan of Arc, portrayed by the greatest stars of the era. Witness too the phenomenal success of Edmond Rostand's *Cyrano de Bergerac*, which played to sellout audiences, just a few months after the fire – at the height of the Dreyfus Affair. *Cyrano de Bergerac* would, in some measure, rehabilitate the aristocratic male, who had lost much ground in the real-life incident of the Bazar de la Charité fire, albeit through the auspices of a fictionalized aristocratic hero whose opposition both to absolutist power and foppish aristocrats endeared him to democratic audiences of the time.

2

Cyrano: A Hero for the Fin de Siècle?

Just a few short months after the incidents of the Bazar de la Charité fire, a male aristocrat was once again on center stage, this time, in the theater itself. Yet Cyrano de Bergerac, the eponymous hero of Edmond Rostand's play, redeemed – by timing if not necessarily through the intention of the author – the gardenias whose honor had suffered greatly.[1] First presented on the Parisian stage on December 27, 1897, just two weeks prior to the publication of Zola's "J'Accuse," on January 13, 1898, *Cyrano de Bergerac* became an immediate critical and popular success and played to full houses during the height of the Dreyfus Affair, uniting within the theater walls a public profoundly divided outside them.

Since the fin de siècle, *Cyrano* has become one of the most beloved and most often staged plays in the history of the French theater.[2] Translated

---

A small portion of this chapter has appeared in my article "Heroes, Celebrity and the Theater in Fin-de-Siècle France: *Cyrano de Bergerac,*" in *Constructing Charisma: Celebrity, Fame and Power in Nineteenth-Century Europe*, ed. Edward Berenson and Eva Giloi (New York: Berghahn Books, 2010), 155–164, and is reproduced with permission from Berghahn Books.

[1] Rostand had begun writing before the fire, but as a keen observer of the national scene, he had to have been influenced by the national debates about manhood and honor at the time.

[2] Much has been written about Rostand, especially since the centenary of *Cyrano*. Among the numerous books, see Sue Lloyd, *The Man Who Was Cyrano* (Bloomington, IN: Unlimited Publishing, 2002); Jacques Lorcey, *Edmond Rostand*, 3 vols. (Paris: Atlantica, 2004); Jean-Baptiste Manuel, *Edmond Rostand, écrivain imaginaire* (Paris: Atlantica, 2003); Marc Landry, *Edmond Rostand: Le Panache et la gloire* (Paris: Plon, 1986); Caroline de Margerie, *Edmond Rostand ou le baiser de la gloire* (Paris: Grasset, 1997). The work closest resembling my own is that of Jean-Marie Apostolidès, *Cyrano: Qui fut tout et qui ne fut rien* (Paris: Les Impressions nouvelles, 2006). I have consulted the Rostand, Coquelin,

into countless foreign languages, it has been adapted for the cinema, most recently, in the 1990 Rappeneau film, in which Cyrano was portrayed by the ubiquitous Gérard Depardieu. The centennial of *Cyrano de Bergerac* in 1997 inspired numerous festivities, among them two different revivals of the play, an exhibition organized in conjunction with the Bibliothèque Historique de la Ville de Paris and a great number of articles in the leading newspapers and weekly magazines. In 2006, Cyrano was revived at the Comédie française and, a year later, played to sellout audiences on Broadway, with Kevin Kline in the lead role. American audiences perhaps know the Cyrano story best through its retelling by Steve Martin in the 1987 film entitled not Cyrano but *Roxanne*. In the original story, Cyrano, a poet-soldier, is in love with his cousin, the *précieuse* Roxane. Unable to declare his love for her, he ends up wooing her for a handsome but inarticulate young nobleman named Christian, writing love letters to her in Christian's stead. When Christian dies in battle, Cyrano vows to keep his secret; only when Cyrano himself is dying does Roxane finally learn the true identity of the man she has loved all these years.

It is no exaggeration to state that *Cyrano de Bergerac* has become a *lieu de mémoire*, because both the play and its eponymous hero have been absorbed into the French national consciousness.[3] Although a flawed hero, Cyrano corresponds to the image the French have, or, more accurately, would like to have, of themselves. In fact, French commentators have compared Cyrano to historical figures from Vercingétorix to De Gaulle, all of whom have borne defeat with grace.[4] Without denying the universal appeal and timelessness of *Cyrano de Bergerac*, it is clear that the play was very much a product of its time and Cyrano a hero for the fin de siècle, symbolic of a France wounded by the Franco-Prussian War and already preparing for the next battle. More than any other of the time, this play exemplifies the prevailing zeitgeist and offers us a valuable tool for exploring notions of heroism during the years that preceded the First World War.

This chapter examines the reception of Edmond Rostand's *Cyrano de Bergerac*, focusing on the political, social, and cultural context in which the play was presented and received. Despite the fact that Rostand himself

---

and Cyrano dossiers at the BNF Richelieu, and ART and Actualités collections at the Bibliothèque Historique de la Ville de Paris and have also conducted a systematic review of the major newspapers of the period.

[3] Pierre Nora, ed., *Les Lieux de mémoire*, 3 vols. (Paris: Gallimard, 1984–1992; Quarto, 1997).

[4] See Marc Lambron, "Le Mythe Cyrano," *Le Point*, no. 916 (9 April 1990): 8–12.

was a Dreyfusard, Cyrano had admirers on both sides of the Affair. Both Dreyfusards and anti-Dreyfusards could celebrate Cyrano and claim him as one of their own, the first group because he illustrated that the pen was mightier than the sword, the second, because he was a military hero.

A closer examination of the play, however, reveals a more equivocal portrait of Cyrano. Cyrano's physical deformity, his enormous nose, along with his inability to declare his love for Roxane, undercut his "heroism." A man who would never consummate his love could not correspond to the ideal fin-de-siècle male, who was supposed to regenerate the nation by siring as many male children as possible. In fact, the relationship between Cyrano and Christian conjures up the specter of homoeroticism, or at the least, of a type of male bonding that was suspect in the masculine culture of the time. Both are incomplete halves who make a whole as a couple; only together can they secure Roxane's affections. As he would two years later with *L'Aiglon*, Rostand destabilized contemporary ideals of heroism and manhood as much as he celebrated them. A secondary theme of the play, celebrity and success, also preoccupied contemporaries of the fin de siècle, in particular, Rostand himself, who decried both, instead exalting pure artistic values as incarnated by his hero. Yet the phenomenal success of the play – many critics called it an apotheosis – garnered the playwright the very fame he denounced and earned him the status of a national icon.[5] The first part of this chapter examines the role of gender in shaping notions of the hero in *Cyrano de Bergerac*, whereas while the second part analyzes the impact of fame and success on contemporary constructions of heroism.

Heroes, Honor, and the Culture of the Sword

An exploration of the culture of the sword, which gave rise to Cyrano's resounding success, should precede an examination of the play as well as the specific circumstances in which it was represented and received. In light of the military defeat in the Franco-Prussian War, contemporary

[5] Emile Faguet, writing about Rostand's induction to the French Academy ("L'Académicien d'aujourd'hui") in *Le Gaulois* of 4 June 1903, referred to Rostand as a "young Athenian god." He continued: "Heroism is also – sometimes – a form of youth." Although I am using fame and celebrity interchangeably here, in the case of Rostand, I am aware that the first rests on the accomplishments of the person considered, whereas the second refers to "a person whose name, once made by the news, now makes the news." Irving Rein, Philip Kottler, and Martin Stoller, *High Visibility* (New York: Dodd Mead, 1987), 15. See *Constructing Charisma: Celebrity, Fame and Power in Nineteenth-Century Europe*, ed. Edward Berenson and Eva Giloi (New York: Berghahn Books, 2010).

Frenchmen, fearing a loss of manhood, looked to France's aristocratic past, in particular, to the chivalric ideal, which they associated with honor and manhood. Furthermore, they linked these notions to the revival of the nation. Middle-class men of the time – Rostand among them – emulated certain aristocratic ideals, especially the notion of honor, which they opposed to the values of the marketplace, even when, they, like Rostand himself, succeeded and benefited from them. Robert Nye observes that the celebration of the chivalric ideal in France during the nineteenth century was largely the work of liberal and progressive thinkers, who associated themselves with a "richer and deeper moral heritage than could be derived from the egotistic doctrines of liberal economics and legal individualism."[6] Moreover, they could also claim for themselves the quality of courage that underlined the chivalric ideal and was the basis of the French patriotic tradition. This chivalric ideal was not inconsistent with the middle-class values of work and egalitarianism. Contemporaries felt that the culture of the sword should hold sway in a democracy, and some even asserted that fencing had done as much to advance equality as the "Declaration of the Rights of Man."[7] Indeed, the late nineteenth century witnessed more duels than any other time in French history, with the exception of the seventeenth century, the setting for Rostand's play.[8]

The close associations of the notion of honor and the culture of the sword also help to explain the particular resonance of military heroes. Certainly, civilian heroes were also celebrated, but it was the cult of the military hero that held sway – the three most important heroes of the time being Joan of Arc, Napoleon, and Cyrano. Yet these three military heroes were not always seen as larger than life but flawed and human. Cyrano's grandeur lies not in his conventionally "heroic" qualities but rather in his panache, that is, his dignity and verve in face of adversity, as Rostand himself explained in his speech to the Académie française: "What is panache? It does not suffice to be a hero to possess it. Panache is not grandeur but

[6] Robert A. Nye, *Masculinity and Male Codes of Honor in Modern France* (Berkeley: University of California Press, 1998), 150; see also Edward Berenson, *The Trial of Madame Caillaux* (Berkeley: University of California Press, 1992), 182–187, who argues that French politicians may have adopted "aristocratic" mores of dueling in order to acquire legitimacy in the eyes of those not used to being governed by members of the middle and lower middle classes, 184.

[7] Nye, 155 and 167.

[8] On duels, see Nye, especially chapters 8 and 9, and Berenson, *Madame Caillaux*, 167–198, and 200–207. See also Jean-Noël Jeanneney, *Le Duel: Une Passion française, 1789–1914* (Paris: Seuil, 2004).

something more that moves beyond it. It is something that flutters, [it is] excessive, a bit rebellious ... panache is the spirit of bravura."[9]

Cyrano was a hero who appealed to wounded French pride in the wake of the loss of the Franco-Prussian War, as were Joan of Arc, and even the conquering hero Napoleon, who was also ultimately defeated. Even if representations of these heroes contained a more defiant tone in the years immediately preceding the First World War, they were, in the end, all vanquished heroes.[10]

Setting the Stage: The Real Cyrano and the Seventeenth Century

In creating his hero, Rostand generally followed the outlines of the real Cyrano's (Hercule-Savinien Cyrano de Bergerac, 1619–1655) life. He was present at the siege of Arras and was known for his bravery; he even appears to have fought off numerous attackers at the Porte de Nesle, as Rostand depicts in Act 2. Moreover, the soliloquy to the moon in Act 3 was no doubt inspired by one of Cyrano's best-known writings, *Voyage dans la lune*, a work seen by many contemporaries of Rostand as a precursor of Jules Verne's stories. But Rostand also glossed over some real-life details, including Cyrano's freethinking tendencies – he was a disciple of materialist philosopher Pierre Gassendi – as well as his most probable homosexuality and syphilis in order to create the fictional hero in love with Roxane.[11]

Rostand set his play during the seventeenth century, an age in which France dominated the European continent, and, moreover, a period distant enough in time for most of his compatriots to have accepted it as part of

---

[9] Edmond Rostand, *Discours de Réception à l'Académie française, le 4 juin 1903* (Paris: Charpentier et Fasquelle, 1904), 22–23.

[10] The noted critic and professor at the Ecole Normale Supérieure, Ferdinand Brunetière, wrote the following about France in 1640 (albeit a few years after the height of *Cyrano's* popularity): "Having recovered from the civil war, victorious in Spain, France witnessed at this time, around 1640, a new awareness, more profound and clear, of the solidarity of all of its parts, of a sense of unity." Quoted by Ralph Albanese, *Corneille à l'école républicaine: Du Mythe héroïque à l'imaginaire politique en France: 1800–1950* (Paris: L'Harmattan, 2008), 154.

[11] A young critic, Emile Magne, taxed Rostand with historical inaccuracies, to which Rostand wittily replied that there were no anachronisms that were unintended and that he could certainly point out one or two more that Magne had missed in his diatribe against the play. See Stephen C. Bold, "Rostand's *Cyrano de Bergerac* and Seventeenth-Century France," paper presented at the WSFH, Boston, November 1998, 3. Bold states that Rostand was creating parallels between his own fin de siècle and the baroque period of the seventeenth century, suggesting that Cyrano was in many ways similar to Barrès's "professeur d'énergie," that is, a leader with panache, 10.

the national heritage. For the French of the fin de siècle, still smarting from the loss of the Franco-Prussian War and diminished international status, the swashbuckling age of Louis XIII represented French grandeur. The war with Spain depicted in the play nearly ended in defeat in the same way that the Franco-Prussian War did. The action described in the fourth act of the play – the siege of Arras (1640) – however, represented an important turning point in hostilities: the French averted near defeat and then proceeded to victory. Rostand's contemporaries of the turn of the century must have looked upon these events with a certain amount of nostalgia and envy.

It is not the "classical age" of Louis XIV's personal reign (1660–1680) that Rostand celebrated in the play but rather the France of Louis XIII, also exalted in such earlier works as Alexandre Dumas père's *Les Trois Mousquétaires* and Théophile Gautier's *Le Capitaine Fracasse* and *Les Grotesques*, all of which served as models for Rostand. Opportunities for heroism were abundant in the earlier part of the era; once Louis XIV came to power and consolidated the centralizing policies of Cardinal Richelieu, his father's chief minister, there was little room for personal initiative or heroism.[12]

During the fin de siècle, especially in the years leading up to the First World War, the works of Corneille as well as the playwright himself were enshrined in the school programs and manuals of the Third Republic. This celebration was in part an attempt to link the Third Republic to the legacy of the Ancien Régime, particularly that of the seventeenth century, viewed as a great age in French history, and neatly dovetailed with the efforts of such republican historians as Ernest Lavisse. The popularity of Corneille, however, transcended left/right political differences. Although monarchists might emphasize Corneille's Christian qualities and republicans his progressive ones, both sides could agree that Corneille's work served as a heroic example for schoolchildren. Not only did he represent the incarnation of national grandeur, but his work was also part of the national patrimony.[13] Corneille then was a symbol of national honor,

---

[12] Paul Bénichou, *Morales du grand siècle* (Paris: Gallimard, 1948), 17. For Cyrano and the baroque tradition, see Bold, 6. Cyrano in some respects resembles Rodrigue, the larger-than-life hero of *Le Cid*. I am indebted to Professor Bold for his insights into seventeenth-century culture.

[13] Some, like Catholic Victor Laprade, even saw Corneille as an antidote to modern commercial literature as well as against the pernicious influences of foreign literatures, not only of the past, like Shakespeare and the German Romantics, but also current influences as promoted by the avant-garde: Albanese, 142.

and his heroes, who exemplified disinterestedness, honor, and sacrifice, were held up as examples to French schoolchildren of the time. Yet these heroes, as other contemporaries observed, were abstract and in some ways unattainable. Indeed, some contemporaries like Jules Lemaître called Corneille "our great professor of energy" and fellow critic Emile Faguet compared Corneille's heroes to Nietzschean supermen, while still others, like Catholic critic Victor Laprade, saw France itself as a Cornelian hero, condemned to a stark choice between heroism and oblivion.[14] This tension between abstraction and unattainability on one hand and the need to emulate them on the other perhaps influenced theatergoers, raised on these values in their schoolbooks, to seek human, flawed heroes in the theater. Rostand, ever attuned to his time, was undoubtedly well aware of the various contemporary writings on Corneille; he attempted to reconcile in *Cyrano de Bergerac* not only the Ancien Régime and the Third Republic but also the values of disinterestedness, honor, and sacrifice as represented by Corneille with the audience's desire to see humanized heroes. Thus, Cyrano, from a literary point of view, was more like the baroque hero of the preclassical period, given his celebration of excess, wit, and panache, although he shared some qualities of the classical hero, because he displayed great honor and courage, and, moreover, bore his unrequited love for Roxane stoically.[15]

A republican writer, but one who was enamored of French history, Rostand sought to link the Third Republic to the legacy of the Ancien Régime, a delicate balancing act also undertaken by leading republican historian Ernest Lavisse.[16] Rostand's Cyrano was an aristocrat but one whose disdain of the absolutist monarchy and foppish aristocrats allied him with the democratic ideals of the Third Republic. In this way, Rostand sought to reconcile France's present with its past, doing so much more successfully in this play than two years later when he undertook a similar feat with the Napoleonic legacy in *L'Aiglon*. A critical and popular success, *Cyrano de Bergerac* appealed both to critics who could approve of the aristocratic values (as opposed to those of the marketplace) that he represented and to popular audiences who

[14] Cited in Albanese: Victor Laprade, 142; Faguet, 158; Lemaître, 148.
[15] Even Rostand's use of the *alexandrin*, typically associated with the classical tradition, was not a servile pastiche but in essence a tweaking of this tradition: Bold, 7. One should note too that the play was seen as a success, not because of its use of prose, rare for the theater at this time, but rather in spite of it: see Gaston Jollivet, "La Poésie au théâtre," *Le Gaulois*, 4 January 1898.
[16] Nye, 150–151, and Berenson, *Madame Caillaux*, 187–189.

sympathized with his rejection of the centralizing monarchy and of powerful patrons.

Not only were the play's values of honor and manhood associated with the aristocratic culture of the Ancien Régime, but the play was also linked culturally to the past in the eyes of such critics as Jules Lemaître, who saw *Cyrano de Bergerac* as the culmination of three centuries of French art, comparing Rostand to Corneille and Hugo.[17] Others, like noted critic Emile Faguet, who saw the play as the harbinger of a new era in which France would reign supreme, declared in *Le Journal des débats* that *Cyrano de Bergerac* and its author announced the opening of the twentieth century in "a brilliant and triumphant manner" and that Europe would finally look upon France with envy.[18] The ultrapatriotic critic of *Le Journal* went even farther, proclaiming that Cyrano announced the reawakening of nationalism in France.[19] Whether viewed as part of a long French tradition or as the sign of a new French literature, the play was acclaimed as a source of French pride. The word "pride" is repeated so often in reviews that it is clear that critics were fulfilling a need to reclaim France's lost honor.[20] One such commentator, the journalist Silvio, writing for the conservative newspaper *Le Gaulois*, noted that Rostand himself was the source of such pride, calling him a Bonaparte of the theater, who won all his battles.[21]

Heroes, National Identity, and the Theater

The celebration of national honor in the theater illustrates the important role the theater played in the cultural, social, and political life of fin-de-siècle France and suggests that we look beyond official celebrations, parliamentary debates, and school manuals for a complete understanding

---

[17] Jules Lemaître, "Revue dramatique," originally published in *La Revue des deux mondes*, (1 February 1898), reproduced in *Impressions de théâtre*, 10ème série (Paris: Société française d'imprimerie et de librairie, 1898), 336.

[18] Emile Faguet, *Le Journal des débats*, 3 January 1898.

[19] Georges Thiébaud, *Le Journal*, 10 January 1898. According to this critic, *Cyrano* "trumpeted forth like a brass band in red pants."

[20] Critics' reviews of the play were hyperbolic. One such example was Léon Kerst, a journalist for *Le Petit Journal* from 29 December 1897 ("Premières Représentations"), who called the play a "restorative bath." Yet another, Dom Blasius, writing for *L'Intransigeant* ("Premières Représentations") of 30 December 1897, observed: "Only a poet, a real and great poet, a man of taste and wit, like M. Rostand was capable of bringing about in this year of our Lord 1897, such a revolution."

[21] Silvio, "Silhouette parisienne," *Le Gaulois*, 28 December 1898.

of discussions about national identity at this time. Two of the most popular heroes of the era, Napoleon and Joan of Arc, along with Cyrano,
the obscure seventeenth-century poet-soldier, were fictionalized by playwrights and played by the most popular actors of the day. Whereas the
former were well-known historical figures, it was Rostand who made the
real-life Cyrano a household name. Given Rostand's view of the theater
as a "sacred" space, it is surely no accident that he opened his own play
with a "play within a play," set in the theater of the seventeenth century.[22] Rostand was tipping his hat not only to the theater of the past
but also to the importance of the theater and its audiences in his own
time. Additionally, the theme of acting and performing are pivotal for the
play. Thus, when Cyrano forbids the actor Montfleury from appearing on
stage in Act 1, it is because the latter is a bad actor; moreover, Cyrano's
"performance" in front of the audience (in the same act) is seen as more
authentic than the one represented onstage.

Images of heroes at this time were shaped in large part by a literary
culture in which theatrical conventions flourished.[23] Nevertheless, the
three most important heroes of the day, rather than being represented
as legendary figures, were made all too human. At the same time, these
heroes were idealized and played by the most charismatic actors of the
age. In part, the legendary panache of Cyrano was the panache of the
actor Constant Coquelin (1841–1909), for whom Rostand had specifically written the part (Figure 2.1).

Born in Boulogne, Coquelin was of humble origins, the son of a baker
and pastry maker. Having little interest in baking, he left home for Paris,
where he entered the Conservatoire and made his first appearance on
stage at the Comédie française. He was known for his resemblance
to playwright Molière and also for his strength and physical prowess,
along with his prodigious memory. As in the case of Sarah Bernhardt,
countless photographs and caricatures were published of him so that he
was recognizable to the average French man or woman. Journalists who
wrote about him referred to the heroism of the actor learning his lines, as
well as his "cerebral labor" and "mission to incarnate" his role.[24] When
Coquelin died in 1909, most of the articles devoted to him described

---

[22] Rostand, *Discours de Réception à l'Académie française*, 29.

[23] See Emile Faguet's review of the revival of Cyrano in 1900, in which he comments that
the French have a habit of looking for "men of salvation" in the theater as well as elsewhere: "La Semaine dramatique," *Le Journal des débats*, 21 May 1900 (BHVP, ART
collection).

[24] Henri de Weindel, *Le Gaulois* of 29 March 1898.

M. COQUELIN

Rôle de *Cyrano de Bergerac*

CYRANO DE BERGERAC

FIGURE 2.1. Constant Coquelin as Cyrano, courtesy of Bibliothèque Nationale de France, Paris (BNF).

FIGURE 2.2. The poet and the actor: Rostand's funeral oration at the Coquelin funeral, January 1909, courtesy of the BNF.

the actor as a quintessential French hero, who died as he had lived, "in action." Although Coquelin's funeral in 1909 was not a state event, many political personalities were in attendance, as were colleagues from the world of the theater. Foremost among them were his friends Sarah Bernhardt, with whom he toured the United States in a production of *Cyrano* (she played Roxane), and Rostand, who delivered a eulogy celebrating the actor (Figures 2.2 and 2.3).[25]

Heroes were perceived to be antidotes to rampant consumerism, even when they themselves – Joan and Napoleon, as well as Cyrano – became objects of commodification. These then were democratic heroes for the age of mass culture. Real-life heroes were transformed into objects of popular consumption, consumed on stage every night. In the case of the one-hundredth performance of *Cyrano*, Raguneau pastries, named for Cyrano's *patissier* friend in the play, were passed out to audience members so that they could literally consume the play.[26] On the one hand, heroes were

---

[25] There is a dossier on Coquelin at the BNF Richelieu: Rt6620, as well as articles published at the time of his death. See *Le Monde illustré* from 6 February 1909: "Constant Coquelin." *Comédia*, the paper devoted to the theater, reproduced all the eulogies in its 30 January 1909 issue. See also "Grand Comédien, grand philanthrope," in *Théâtre* (15 January–15 February 1909) in BHVP, *Dossier d'actualités*. The reporter from the *New York Times* mentioned that the president of France had sent his personal secretary to Coquelin's deathbed to pay respects to the great author: "Elder Coquelin Dies of Acute Embolism," *New York Times*, 28 January 1909.

[26] Aiglon candies and writing paper were popular at this time, as were Joan of Arc products.

FIGURE 2.3. Constant Coquelin and Sarah Bernhardt, courtesy of the BNF.

made appealing and charismatic by celebrated actors, and on the other, reduced to their human qualities and rendered more accessible. A symbiotic relationship thus operated between actor and the hero portrayed. The actor imbued the character played with celebrity; in turn, the heroic qualities of the character were transferred to the actor in the role.[27]

[27] See Henri de Weindel in *Le Gaulois* of 29 March 1898 (BNF Richelieu SR: 951530, 1898 Dossier). Such a transferral was also in evidence when Bernhardt played Joan and l'Aiglon. This powerful act of "creation" for both Bernhardt and Coquelin was coded as masculine. See Mary-Louise Roberts, *Disruptive Acts: The New Woman in Fin-de-Siècle France* (Chicago: University of Chicago Press, 2002), 174–176.

These heroes, like the actors who portrayed them, became, with the help of the press, mass marketing and publicity techniques, "intimate strangers" to an entire nation.[28] Furthermore, in a time of national division, heroes as played by celebrated actors represented a national unity "above politics." This was certainly the case of Cyrano and Coquelin.[29] Similarly, Sarah Bernhardt's Joan succeeded in uniting audiences during a time when the left and right were grappling for control of Joan's destiny. To some extent, the recourse to heroes in the theater was a result of this political polarization, as critics, actors, and playwrights acknowledged. In great measure, the ability to unite was based on the talents of actors Coquelin and Bernhardt, both of whom were considered national icons. Unity within the theater worked better in some cases than others. Despite calls for heroes "above politics," many of them – in particular, Napoleon – remained embedded in the politics of the time. In the end, Napoleon, if not Cyrano and Joan, was more successfully co-opted by the nationalist right.

Rostand and the Dreyfus Affair

Although it was written before the height of the Dreyfus Affair, *Cyrano de Bergerac*'s success must be set against the backdrop of the Affair. While the play appealed to partisans on both sides, Rostand himself was a Dreyfusard. Rostand's son Maurice writes of his father's ardent Dreyfusard beliefs: "My father was a Dreyfusard of the first hour, he was a Dreyfusard with passion, courage, and an energy that illustrates that if he had wanted to go into politics, he would have done so with aplomb."[30] He also describes his father's patriotism and dedication to the army as well as stating that the women in the house, Mme Rostand and

---

[28] See Richard Schickel, *Intimate Strangers: The Culture of Celebrity* (New York: Doubleday, 1985). See also Lenard Berlanstein, *Daughters of Eve: A Cultural History of French Theater Women from the Old Regime to the Fin de Siècle* (Cambridge, MA: Harvard University Press, 2001), 209–236, and Roberts, especially, 169–174, both of whom explore this theme. See also Lawrence M. Friedman, *The Horizontal Society* (New Haven, CT: Yale University Press, 1999). On women celebrities, see Lenard Berlanstein, "Historicizing and Gendering Celebrity Culture: Famous Women in Nineteenth-Century France," *Journal of Women's Studies* 16, no. 4 (2004): 65–91.

[29] In a survey published in *Le Journal* shortly before the outbreak of hostilities, readers, asked to name their favorite hero, overwhelmingly cited Cyrano, ahead of Jean Valjean and D'Artagnan: cited by Rosemond Gérard (Rostand), *Edmond Rostand* (Paris: Charpentier, 1935), 18–19.

[30] Maurice Rostand, *Confession d'un demi-siècle* (Paris: La Jeune Parque, 1948), 48.

her mother, were anti-Dreyfusards. This family tension, no doubt, also contributed to Rostand's modest stance, for which he was reproached by friends and acquaintances like Jules Renard and Léon Blum.[31]

The author of an article in *L'Aurore* on March 7, 1898, noted Rostand's standoffish attitude (*un peu dédaigneuse*) vis-à-vis involvement in the Affair.[32] Rostand had at first refused Georges Clemenceau's request to sign the petition in favor of Zola, claiming that a poet better served his art by signing poems than manifestoes.[33] *L'Aurore* quoted him as telling an acquaintance (not identified but undoubtedly Jules Renard, who subsequently wrote to Rostand to apologize for leaking this information to the press): "I would not have written *Cyrano*, if I had to subsequently disavow my work, by not approving a man who is the *lone voice against the crowd*. If I have not signed the list presented to me, it is because I did not approve of the form in which it was conceived. … And in any case, I have the habit of only signing what I myself have written."[34] Rostand was probably worried about the impact of signing a public petition on the popularity of his play. Theater authors were at the mercy of the public for their success. Aside from avant-garde playwrights, who were almost all Dreyfusards, most theater authors were indifferent to the Affair and were on the whole apolitical, more concerned with their personal material success than with an ideological debate.[35] Finally, whatever his own personal preferences, Rostand, who respected the army, was undoubtedly pleased that partisans on both sides could find something to admire in Cyrano, because he would attempt a similar tightrope act two years later with *L'Aiglon*.

Rostand especially admired Lieutenant-Colonel Picquart, the officer who uncovered the falsified documents implicating Dreyfus, as the article

---

[31] Jules Renard, *Journal*, vol. 2 (Paris: Union générale d'éditions, 1984), 518.

[32] Léon Parsons, "L'Opinion d'un poète," *L'Aurore*, 7 March 1898.

[33] Margerie, 128.

[34] Parsons, *L'Aurore*, 7 March 1898. These quotes were leaked to Parsons by Rostand's friend Jules Renard, an ardent Dreyfusard frustrated by his friend's public reticence. Margerie cites an apologetic letter from Renard to Rostand on his revealing the playwright's Dreyfusard beliefs to the press, 128.

[35] Christophe Charle, *La Crise littéraire à l'époque du naturalisme: Roman, théâtre, politique* (Paris: PENS, 1979), 169–171. Most avant-garde authors appealed to small coteries rather than a wider public and thus were not subject to the same pressures as authors who depended on mass audiences. See my *Birth of a National Icon: The Literary Avant-Garde and the Origins of the Intellectual in France* (Albany: SUNY Press, 1999), 17–38, and Sally Charnow, *Theatre, Politics, and Markets in Fin-de-Siècle Paris: Staging Modernity* (New York: Palgrave Macmillan, 2005), 115–150.

from *L'Aurore* quoting Rostand indicated: "Apart from Emile Zola, there is a man whom I admire greatly. It is Colonel Picquart. He has been braver than a general on the battlefield."[36] Picquart shared some of Cyrano's qualities; like Cyrano, he disdained authority by risking his career and the disapproval of his military superiors for a "disinterested" truth. For Joseph Reinach, the great historian of the Affair, Picquart had "refused to prostitute his conscience," while fellow Dreyfusard Francis de Pressensé found him to be a martyr in his sacrifice for his principles.[37] Such descriptions could easily fit Cyrano himself; no wonder then that Rostand found Picquart a fascinating and sympathetic figure.

Ironically, *Cyrano de Bergerac*'s success may have worked against the modest Alfred Dreyfus, who could not compete with theatrical heroes. Unlike Picquart, Dreyfus was never able to exhibit Cyrano's panache, one reason that contributed to contemporaries' viewing Picquart as a hero and Dreyfus as a victim, despite the great courage the latter also displayed.[38] Conventions of the theater prevented them from valuing the lack of Dreyfus's "performance" and for confusing content with style.[39] As Joseph Reinach observed, they wanted a performance "to give them goose bumps or the delight of a melodramatic show," concluding that "an actor was needed and he [Dreyfus] was a soldier."[40] Dreyfus played by an actor like Coquelin then might have elicited more sympathy – indeed actor and theater director André Antoine, in attendance at the Rennes trial, claimed he could have done a better job than Dreyfus in moving his audience![41] Unlike heroes of melodrama, Dreyfus exhibited a stoic calm

---

[36] Parsons.

[37] Datta, *Birth of a National Icon*, 154.

[38] One of the first works Dreyfus read after his pardon and release was *Cyrano*, which he enjoyed immensely, as he indicated to Jules Huret in an interview for *Le Figaro*, republished in Jules Huret, "Le Voyage d'Alfred Dreyfus," *Tout yeux, tout oreilles* (Paris: Charpentier, 1901), 358.

[39] "It was ... inevitable that in a country where the esthetics of the theater dominates, that in this affair, where everything, for the last two years, had the appearance of drama, the inability of Dreyfus to express his emotions and his lack of charisma worked to his detriment once again" (Joseph Reinach, *Histoire de l'Affaire Dreyfus*, vol. 2 [Paris: Editions Robert Laffont, 2006], 508–509).

[40] Reinach, 508–509.

[41] Victor Basch quoting Antoine in "Alfred Dreyfus et l'Affaire," *Cahiers des Droits de l'Homme* (31 July 1935), 503, cited by Françoise Basch, *Victor Basch: De l'affaire Dreyfus au crime de la Milice* (Paris: Plon, 1994), 68–69. Dreyfus himself recognized the public's need for theatricality on his part in his memoirs: Alfred Dreyfus, *Carnets (1899–1907)* (Paris: Calmann-Lévy, 1998), 182–183. See also Vincent Duclert's discussion of this point: *Alfred Dreyfus: L'Honneur d'un patriote* (Paris: Fayard, 2006), 741–742.

not appreciated by contemporaries who wanted their heroes to display both emotion and verve, like Cyrano himself.[42]

The same journalist from *L'Aurore*, who had begun his article chiding Rostand for his refusal to publicly engage in the Affair, noted approvingly that the playwright had finally spoken and, moreover, had done it in a poetic manner. During a gala performance of *Cyrano* at the Théâtre de la Porte Saint-Martin for the students of the Collège Stanislas (Rostand's high school) and their families, Rostand addressed the young men with the following verses: "Be little Cyranos / If darkness falls, fight your way out against the shadows / Shout frantically when things go badly: It is evil / Be in favor of beauty, BE AGAINST THE MULTITUDES!" [in capital letters in the original][43] This exhortation was seen by contemporaries as a Dreyfusard statement, and true to Rostand's fashion, it was expressed in the most apolitical terms possible and in verse.

Although Rostand waited until November 1898 to sign a public Dreyfusard manifesto – a petition in favor of Picquart – he did attend the premiere of Romain Rolland's *Les Loups* in the company of Picquart on May 18, 1898, at Lugné-Poe's Théâtre de l'Oeuvre.[44] Not only was attending the play with a noted Dreyfusard figure a public and courageous act, but the play itself was controversial. Rolland, seeking to unite audiences – perhaps in the same way as *Cyrano* – had transposed the action of the Dreyfus Affair to the equally controversial period of the French Revolution. Despite Rolland's intentions to present a play "above politics," it was hailed as a Dreyfusard manifesto and roundly condemned

---

[42] Other fin-de-siècle conventions of heroism also worked against Dreyfus. Male heroes, unlike female ones, were perceived as active agents. They could be victims but they had to have chosen their sacrifice. Georges Clemenceau, the editor of *L'Aurore*, noted that the real hero of the Affair was Picquart because he had chosen to tell the truth about the military cover-up, knowing full well the consequences of his actions. The undated quote from Clemenceau states: "Dreyfus was the victim, Picquart the hero," quoted in Vincent Duclert, *L'Honneur d'un patriote*, 27. See also Clemenceau's article on Dreyfus, in which he emphatically represents him as a victim who needs saving by Dreyfusards: "L'Interrogatoire," *L'Aurore*, 8 August 1899.

[43] Parsons. The original line in French reads: "Criez épurduement lorsque c'est mal: C'est mal!" Could this have been a play on words since the word "mal" (evil) and "mâle" (male) are homonyms? In other words, it was an act of manhood to denounce evil. Rostand ended this discourse by exhorting these young men not to be afraid to appear ridiculous, yet ironically, Cyrano is afraid to appear ridiculous and so does not declare his love for Roxane.

[44] He also signed a petition protesting Zola's suspension from the Legion of Honor: Lloyd, 155. On Rostand signing Picquart's petition, see Joseph Reinach, *Histoire de l'Affaire Dreyfus*, vol. 2, 221.

by the anti-Dreyfusards in the audience, who also jeered at Rostand and Picquart.[45] As for Dreyfusards, they acclaimed Picquart, who was the real hero of the day, as an embittered Rolland observed, writing that the "real spectacle" took place offstage.[46]

In the wake of this joint public appearance, such conservative newspapers as *Le Jour* and *La Patrie* attempted to launch a campaign against Rostand – with little success, although they did succeed in securing the cancellation of a reception for the Rostands at the Collège Stanislas.[47] The fact that these anti-Dreyfusard partisans were unable to affect the popularity of the play is telling, because it illustrates the public's desire to reject partisan politics in favor of unity in the theater. Nevertheless, only a handful of people were allowed to be "above the fray," as Rolland learned to his chagrin. It seems that Rostand's politics were overlooked or pardoned by anti-Dreyfusards because they admired his work and believed it to be patriotic.[48] Anti-Dreyfusards would also praise *L'Aiglon* two years later, and if Rostand received criticism, it came, as had criticism for *Cyrano*, from the avant-garde, the majority of whose members were Dreyfusards.

Heroism and Manhood at the Fin de Siècle

As *Cyrano*'s popularity during the Dreyfus Affair illustrates, the play's preoccupations – in particular, its articulation of the notions of heroism and manhood – were very much those of the fin de siècle, despite the fact that *Cyrano de Bergerac* is set in the seventeenth century. Indeed, the entire play can be seen as a meditation on heroism, with Rostand

---

[45] The performance resulted in altercations between the Dreyfusards and anti-Dreyfusards present. See Antoinette Blum, "*Les Loups* au Théâtre de l'Oeuvre: le 18 mai 1898," *Revue d'histoire littéraire de la France* 6 (November–December 1976): 883–895, and "*Les Loups* de Romain Rolland: Un Jeu théâtral sur l'histoire," *French Review* 66, no. 1 (October 1992): 59–68, and my "Romain Rolland and the Theater of the Revolution: A Historical Perspective," *CLIO* 20, no. 23 (Spring 1991): 213–222.

[46] See Romain Rolland's account in his *Mémoires* (Paris: Albin Michel, 1956): "The real performance is not on stage but in the theater itself," 294.

[47] Rolland, 295.

[48] "Les Dreyfusards à 'l'Oeuvre,'" *La Libre Parole* of 19 May 1898 (unsigned), noted that Picquart was in attendance at the Oeuvre performance without comment and without mentioning that he was accompanied by Rostand. Others were not so lucky. Henry Bauër, who hosted both Rostand and Picquart in his box, ultimately lost his post as drama critic for *L'Echo de Paris* when he published a review of the play in the avant-garde journal *La Revue blanche*, after *L'Echo de Paris* had refused the article.

simultaneously celebrating and undermining heroic qualities.[49] The first part of this section examines Cyrano as a hero who combines the traits of a military hero with those of an intellectual hero, thereby appealing both to anti-Dreyfusards and Dreyfusards, whereas the second explores the ways in which Cyrano represents the gender ambiguity of the period, along with Rostand's own reservations about honor and manhood.

Despite the different types of heroes exalted during the fin de siècle, heroism was founded, above all, on physical and moral courage. Moreover, heroism implied self-control and scorn of danger, both male qualities (this despite the popularity of Joan of Arc).[50] Heroes, who believed in honor and duty, exhibited an exceptional strength of will and practiced discipline and sacrifice made not for selfish reasons but for the greater good of the collectivity – most often, the nation. Cyrano's disdain of aristocratic privilege and patronage, his independence of thought, his wit, and his mastery of oratory made him a quintessential French hero. Contemporary accounts all emphasize his *French* qualities; furthermore, his bravery, both physical and moral, satisfied both anti-Dreyfusards and Dreyfusards. Cyrano incarnated the culture of honor, which transcended religious and political differences.[51] Moreover, he was a great orator and thus a master of words, qualities greatly admired in a culture that values literature and writers.

As a means of national reconciliation, Cyrano was much more successful than had been the "national mourning" around the Bazar de la Charité fire. Unlike the aristocratic gardenias, whose honor could not easily be rehabilitated, Cyrano could redeem the honor of the aristocratic males. Furthermore, Cyrano united in his person the heroic exploits of the working-class men of the Bazar de la Charité fire with the heroic ideals of the male aristocrats. Cyrano's noble origins and his identification with the downtrodden allowed for a national reconciliation in a way that the events of the Bazar de la Charité fire, which exposed social, political, and religious tensions, never could.

An immediate reason for Cyrano's popularity during the Affair then was that he combined the traits of a military hero, in particular, loyalty and bravery in combat, celebrated by anti-Dreyfusards, with an independence of spirit and a refusal to follow the crowd, moral qualities

---

[49] The word *hero* is used three times in the first act alone.

[50] Paul Gerbod, "L'Éthique héroïque en France (1870–1914)," *La Revue historique*, no. 268 (1982): 424–425. Ironically, heroes who were supposed to shore up gender differences only succeeded in pointing to the blurring of such distinctions.

[51] Berenson, *Madame Caillaux*, 192.

celebrated by Dreyfusards. Although anti-Dreyfusards admired military heroes and Dreyfusards, civilian heroes, these categories were not mutually exclusive. Anti-Dreyfusard writer Maurice Barrès, for example, yearned for an "intellectual Bonaparte" who could combine the qualities of the great general with those of the great writer Victor Hugo. Whereas the real-life General Boulanger did not fulfill this promise – indeed, his suicide on the grave of his mistress was melodramatic and perhaps even "womanly" – the fictional Cyrano certainly did.[52] Dreyfusards, on the other hand, held up military man Colonel Picquart as a hero; although they emphasized his moral courage and his intellectual qualities rather than his physical and military prowess, they too held up patriotic, republican military heroes.

The fact that Rostand himself, acutely attuned to the temper of the age, sought to unite these qualities is nowhere more in evidence than in the first act of the play: the Vicomte de Valvert (the man to whom Richelieu's nephew the Duc de Guiche wishes to marry off Roxane so that he may make her his mistress) taunts Cyrano about his big nose, and Cyrano, responding, accompanies each thrust and parry of his sword with a cut of his wit, simultaneously carrying on a verbal and a physical duel. In comparison with Cyrano, Valvert, despite his outward elegant appearance, cuts a poor figure, lacking any wit himself, and Cyrano reproaches him for this lacuna, telling him, "Vous auriez bien dû rester neutre."[53] This sentence is ambiguous; Cyrano could either be telling Valvert that he should have remained neutral or that he should have been born neutered, because the word in French has double meaning. Thus, Valvert's manhood is challenged by Cyrano, who believes that wit and mastery of words are male qualities. So too is independence of thought. Cyrano, refusing aristocratic and royal patronage, claims that it is unmanly.[54]

Writers of the age, Rostand among them, were on the defensive with regard to their masculinity in light of contemporary fears of an overly intellectualized France, Rostand perhaps especially so, given his own

---

[52] See Barrès's *Les Déracinés*, originally published in 1897 (Paris: Union générale d'éditions, 1986), 165–167. Despite his political differences with Rostand, Barrès admired him immensely, as his *Cahiers* illustrate: *Mes Cahiers: 1896–1923* (Paris: Plon, 1994), 402.

[53] Act 1, Scene 4, *Cyrano de Bergerac*, preface by Patrick Besnier (Paris: Gallimard, 1983; 1999), 105. The word *neutre* is also a grammatical term, meaning neither male nor female. Generally, when the French talk about being neutered, they use the word *sterilization*, but given Rostand's use of word play, the implication that Valvert is not sufficiently manly is most definitely present.

[54] Cyrano observes: "le cou s'effemine" (the neck becomes effeminate), 192.

frailty. In fact, he had a physical and nervous breakdown in the wake of *Cyrano*'s resounding success.[55] He would again explore the topic of masculinity two years later in *L'Aiglon*. Rostand destabilized the Napoleonic legacy by representing the doomed son as a neurasthenic – played, moreover, by a female actor, the legendary Sarah Bernhardt. In Cyrano, however, Rostand sought an ideal who combined his own talents as a writer with the strong physical traits he himself lacked. Dreyfusard intellectuals were at a disadvantage compared to anti-Dreyfusards when it came to laying claim to masculinity, losing the battle of rhetoric in this area to their opponents.[56] Given such a situation, Cyrano's simultaneous literary talents and his physical strength must have resonated in particular with them. Anti-Dreyfusard intellectuals, for their part, could also revel in this combination, because, like their Dreyfusard counterparts, they too shared concerns about the unmanly intellectual.

Cyrano: The Anti-Hero?

Yet Rostand simultaneously celebrated and destabilized contemporary norms of honor and manhood, perhaps in a way that his audiences did not fully recognize, as both *Cyrano* and *L'Aiglon* were exalted as symbols of French nationalism, often by individuals whose politics were at odds with his own. In some ways, Cyrano resembles the typical manly hero. He wields his sword, a symbol of male potency, with great prowess. He exhibits his valor when he fights off one hundred men in an ambush at the Porte de Nesle offstage in the second act. One must also address the question of his large nose, typically associated with the size of a man's penis. Patrick Besnier, writing in the introduction to his annotated edition of *Cyrano de Bergerac*, notes that Cyrano mocks his nose for all sorts of reasons, but not "that one ... [because] it is the only one that counts."[57] Finally, like other celebrated heroes of the time, Cyrano also possesses great moral courage. When Roxane praises him for his exploits at the

---

[55] Rostand himself was subject to neurasthenia. When he fell ill in 1900, he was advised by his doctor to move away from Paris. It is partly for this reason that he eventually moved to the Basque country and had his villa built there. There is an entire file on the Cambo house in the Rostand dossier at the BNF Richelieu: Rf 71.534. On intellectuals and their defensiveness about manhood, see Datta, *Birth of a National Icon*, especially 117–182, and Christopher E. Forth, *The Dreyfus Affair and the Crisis of French Manhood* (Baltimore: Johns Hopkins University Press, 2004), especially 21–102.

[56] Forth, 11.

[57] Patrick Besnier, "Préface," to the folio edition of *Cyrano de Bergerac*, 25.

Porte de Nesle, he tells her he has done better since that event, referring to his agreeing to protect his erstwhile rival, Christian.[58]

In many ways, Cyrano is not a typical manly hero.[59] Indeed, the aristocratic passion for dueling, for some observers of the era, might even be seen as effeminate, because it implied that a man was emotional, fragile, and prone to slights and thus felt compelled to enter into a duel.[60] Such gender instability was already in evidence during national discussions of the previous year around the events of the Bazar de la Charité fire, when aristocratic men had shown the "womanly" qualities of fear and panic, while women had displayed both "sangfroid" and "cran," two traits generally associated with male heroism. By the time of the Ullmo trial in 1908, views of manhood were destabilized to the point that contemporaries could accept both typically "male" and "female" traits in a military man. As for Cyrano, he incarnates the notion of sacrifice and self-abnegation, two typically female traits; furthermore, his martyrdom to assure Roxane's happiness could even be seen as priest-like, even Christ-like.[61] Social commentators of the period, particularly republican ones, regularly associated Christianity with female (and "Oriental") traits, which they opposed to the male Western ideals of chivalry.[62] One such commentator, L. Jeudon, also used Darwinian theories to root honor in manhood, which he defined as the desire of males to win females through sexual prowess and valor in combat. Female animals watched such "spectacles" and "applauded" them.[63] Although Cyrano is successful in combat, he is, of course, a failure in love, and by such standards, not sufficiently manly, as critic Jules

[58] Act 2, Scene 6, p. 171.

[59] When Cyrano throws his purse at the audience in Act 1, thereby depriving himself of a month's pension, he claims to do so for the sake of the beauty of the gesture, thus recalling the bravura of certain anarchist bomb throwers whose actions had captivated the public's imagination a few years earlier. While their acts, admired for the "beauty of the gesture," appealed to some writers of the age, most members of the French public, including serious anarchist thinkers, found their deeds decidedly unheroic. See my "Passing Fancy? The Generation of 1890 and Anarchism," *Modern and Contemporary France*, no. 44 (January 1991): 3–11.

[60] Berenson, *Madame Caillaux*, 184–185. See also Robert Nye's review essay "Western Masculinities in War and Peace," *AHR* (April 2007): 430, in which he examines the ways that military men in war expressed their "feminine" qualities in their nurturing and protection of fellow soldiers.

[61] My thanks to Professor Lenard Berlanstein, to whom I owe this latter observation.

[62] See L. Jeudon, *La Morale de l'honneur* (Paris: Félix Alcan, 1911), 95 and 117. Although this text postdates the publication of *Cyrano*, it accurately reflects ideas common to the fin de siècle.

[63] Jeudon, 79. See Edward Berenson's interesting discussion of this point, *Madame Caillaux*, 88.

Lemaître recognized when he called him a "would-be lover who was only able to love by proxy, and who was not loved."[64] Lemaître also noted Cyrano's "sublime abnegation," a quality also underlined by reviewer Alfred Athys of *La Revue blanche*, who too was aware of Cyrano's unheroic qualities: "Cyrano is one of these minor heroes, all the more moving because they are not essentially heroic, whose suffering is to lack in grace and genius, who are sublime mediocrities."[65]

Unable to consummate his relationship with Roxane, Cyrano could actually be seen as half of a couple with Christian. Nowhere is this "coupling" more evident than in the scene in Act 2 (Scene 10) that seals their pact. Christian sighs that he would like to better express himself, while Cyrano responds that he would like to be good looking: "Let us [together] become a hero out of a novel," proposes Cyrano to Christian. Furthermore, when Cyrano offers the hapless cadet his services, he even uses the word "compléter" [to complete], telling him: "Will you complete me as I complete you/ ... I will be your wit, you will be my beauty."[66] Nevertheless, in common with each other, these two men, brave in battle, claim that they "tremble" before the woman they love, and neither can "perform" (the word can be used both ways) properly before her. Christian needs Cyrano to "act" in his stead, and Cyrano can only "perform" the role of the hero in front of an audience, indeed, literally on stage in the theater, when he takes the place of actor Montfleury in Acts 1 and 2, and especially, in the pivotal balcony scene where he woos Roxane – ostensibly for Christian. In the end, neither Christian nor Cyrano consummates his love with Roxane – Christian because he is sent off to battle, where he dies, and Cyrano because he is unable – and later, unwilling – to declare his love for Roxane.

Cyrano is thus not a typical hero: he is not a successful lover; his sacrifice is more "female" than "male"; and finally, he forms a couple with Christian as much as with Roxane. In the end, he does not die a hero's death on the field of battle but instead laments while he is dying that he was struck from behind by a lackey. Furthermore, his nose, a metonym for his manhood, gets in the way of his being successful in love, because it renders him ridiculous. Cyrano expresses his fear of appearing ridiculous a number of times in the play and uses his wit and his sword to silence those who would mock him for his appearance. He prefers to make fun

---

[64] Jules Lemaître, 341–342.
[65] Alfred Athys, *La Revue blanche* 15 (15 January 1898): 153.
[66] Act 2, Scene 10, p. 209.

of his own nose rather than permitting others to do so. This preoccupation, linked to a loss of honor and manhood, was common among males of the fin de siècle, who often fought duels to avoid being derided. In light of such concerns, critic Henry Bauër's observation that Cyrano's "excess of candor and male virtue" rendered him ridiculous has special resonance.[67] Despite his efforts, Cyrano *is*, in the end, ridiculous. Finally, Cyrano is all talk and no action; his epitaph is, after all, as he himself states, "He who was everything and nothing."[68] Action as opposed to thought was seen by most contemporaries – although perhaps not by a writer like Rostand – as a male quality par excellence.

Nor is Christian himself a typical hero, although he looks like one from the novels of seventeenth-century author Honoré d'Urfé, in the words of Roxane.[69] He thus fits the conventional literary mode of heroism, but appearances, as Cyrano explains to the Vicomte de Valvert in the first act, are deceiving. Christian, a military man, lacks wit and cannot speak for himself, needing another man to stand in his stead. As one reviewer observed, Christian is but a puppet controlled by another man.[70] Such an image at the time was a code word for unmanliness. A few years earlier, Oscar Wilde had been dismissed as a puppet by those who feared his homosexuality, and Alfred Dreyfus himself was sometimes represented as a puppet by anti-Dreyfusards, trying to dismiss his credibility by calling into question his honor and manhood.[71] Yet Christian is not unintelligent nor is he lacking in noble qualities. In fact, he dies a hero's death at Arras. Realizing it is Cyrano whom Roxane prefers, he enters into battle, looking for death, thus sacrificing himself both for his country and for the woman he loves. Here again, this selfless act (Christian's name is significant) could be seen as more "female" than male, because since a real "man" might well have chosen to fight Cyrano for Roxane.[72]

If Cyrano and Christian form a couple, so too, of course, do Cyrano and Roxane. Like Cyrano, she loves wit and words – indeed, their

---

[67] Henry Bauër, "Premières Représentations," *L'Echo de Paris*, 30 December 1897 (BNF Richelieu SR: 951530,1897 Dossier).

[68] Act 5, Scene 6, p. 415.

[69] Act 2, Scene 5, p. 167.

[70] In "Les Premières: *Cyrano de Bergerac*," published in *La Fronde* of 29 December 1897, Jeanne Marnière calls Christian a "pantin" and a "mannequin," two different words for puppet.

[71] See Datta, *Birth of a National Icon*, 117–134.

[72] It seems that the French preferred selfless heroes to strictly "macho" ones at this time, perhaps in part because such "sacrifice" was seen as redemptive.

excess – and shares Cyrano's ideas about love.[73] Nevertheless, she marries Christian, who leaves for war without consummating their marriage. Although she cannot at first see beyond appearances, Roxane does in the end redeem herself, telling Christian that she loves his wit more than his looks, a declaration that sends him off to die a hero's death. Moreover, she shows great courage by making her way past enemy Spanish soldiers in order to deliver food to the cadets and to see her husband again, thereby recalling the figure of Sardou's Mme Sans-Gêne, who served as *vivandière* in the Napoleonic army. Nevertheless, even though she ventures onto the field of battle, she does not challenge traditional notions of masculinity and femininity, because since her bravery and sacrifice are made not in the name of honor or the nation (although her actions could be seen as patriotic) but rather for love.[74] Like Cyrano, she too is steadfast in her affections, retreating to a convent after the death of her husband. These qualities of sacrifice and courage redeem Roxane, making her more appealing to fin-de-siècle audiences – to men, who, as critic René Doumic noted, putting themselves in the place of Cyrano, could easily imagine feeling anger for her because she preferred another man to them – and women, who might otherwise have been jealous of her beauty.[75]

By all accounts, the play's popularity cut across gender lines. Although he does not get the girl, Cyrano sacrifices all in the name of love, which is undoubtedly what made him appealing to women in the audiences. Jeanne Marnière, reviewing the play for the feminist newspaper *La Fronde*, viewed Cyrano as a symbol of "courage, valor, moral beauty [and] noble energy."[76] Her fellow reporter at *La Fronde*, Marie-Anne de Bovet, in an article entitled, "Les Cadets de Gascogne," of January 5, 1898, praised the heroic sacrifice of the men in battle, thus highlighting the popularity of military heroes at the fin de siècle. She even declared that the battle scenes at Arras would appeal most to the crowds who might otherwise be indifferent to the beauties of the love story, stating, "the beauty of carnage is that which speaks to the soul of the crowd." Although she claimed she was not glorifying war or military heroes, she did hold them up for special admiration, declaring

---

[73] I owe this observation to Professor Stephen Bold.

[74] I wonder, however, how Bernhardt playing the role of Roxane to Coquelin's Cyrano on tour in the United States might have affected the image of the character.

[75] Doumic, "Cyrano de Bergerac," *Le Théâtre nouveau* (Paris: Perrin, 1908), 329.

[76] Jeanne Marnière, "Les Premières: *Cyrano de Bergerac*," *La Fronde*, 29 December 1897.

that their sacrifice, although not more noble, was more beautiful than
that of the doctor or engineer who saved lives, because it was a sacrifice with "panache."[77]

In an article entitled "Les Femmes et la paix," also of January 5, another
reporter for *La Fronde*, Maria Pognon, vehemently opposed the appeal of
heroism in battle and instead praised heroes of both sexes who performed
useful services to humankind, citing the work of doctors and nurses. The
army appealed to male vanity, she claimed, whereas the heroism of civilian heroes was disinterested. For Pognon, moral courage was more admirable than physical courage, which she defined as an animal courage of
a "beast in delirium." In common with the reactions of Dreyfusard and
anti-Dreyfusard men, these three women had different reactions to the
"heroic sacrifice" of Cyrano and other soldiers in battle, yet all seemed to
admire Cyrano's supreme sacrifice for love. Furthermore, despite Bovet's
declaration about the inability of crowds to appreciate the finer points
of the play, it appears from other reviewers' responses and descriptions
of audience reactions (both men and women) that the balcony scene and
the last scene of revelation are those that moved contemporary audiences
the most.

Men, for their part, could especially admire Cyrano's physical bravery and even his "disinterestedness," a heroic quality par excellence at
this time, yet they could also feel superior to him. René Doumic noted
that Cyrano was a mediocre figure but that the public liked underdogs
and felt indulgent toward them. Cyrano's excess of panache, according
to Doumic, made them smile and want to protect him.[78] Because Cyrano
was flawed, they could in some sense feel superior to him. At the same
time, men in the audience could admire Cyrano, knowing that even if
they could never match his sacrifice, such a French hero existed.

Not only was Cyrano a hero with whom audiences could identify, so
too was the play itself accessible to fin-de-siècle audiences, who could
share in the author's glory. In his review of the play, Jules Lemaître
noted: "Are we not the equals of the poet himself – except for one thing,
of quite little importance: the faculty for artistic creation, which is only a
happy accident and which does not necessarily imply superiority of intelligence? The beauty of a work of art is nothing if it is not recognized and

---

[77] Bovet, who was the daughter of military man, became an anti-Dreyfusard and resigned
from the staff of the Dreyfusard *La Fronde* in September 1898. My thanks to Elizabeth
Everton for sharing this information with me.
[78] Doumic, "Cyrano de Bergerac," 330–331.

felt, and is, in a sense, the work of all."[79] Thus, the success of the play was due in no small measure to the simultaneous accessibility of the play's hero and its author.

Fame and Success at the Fin de Siècle

Although the major theme of *Cyrano de Bergerac* is heroism, it is also a commentary on celebrity and consumer culture, with Cyrano seen as an antidote to the burgeoning consumer culture of the age. Critic Charles Donos, writing in *Les Hommes d'aujourd'hui*, exalted Rostand as a heroic example, calling him "a conqueror of popularity, who has understood during our contemporary period of money-worship, how to explain to the multitude sentiments of admiration and enthusiasm for a hero ... ch only in bravura, wit, love and abnegation."[80] Similarly, Emile Faguet wrote that this play was destined to "console us for all the industrial literature in which we are mired."[81]

The contemporary fear of modern consumer society manifested itself not only in the debate concerning heroes, masculinity, and national identity, but also in discussions about the role of the writer in French society. Thus, another reason for *Cyrano*'s success was that its exaltation of independence of thought and freedom of action and rejection of facile fame struck an important chord among many writers of the fin de siècle.

During the late nineteenth century, writers from all ends of the political spectrum, from monarchist Charles Maurras and anti-Semite Edouard Drumont, on the one hand, to anarchists Paul Adam and Octave Mirbeau, on the other, feared for their status in a democratic society. They blamed the "industrialization" of literature, that is, the overproduction of materials for an insatiable but mediocre public lacking in taste, and the concomitant dominance of money in the new society, for the decline in the status of the writer. Deploring a society that valued industrialists and politicians over men of thought, avant-garde writers banded together in the 1880s and 1890s. Defining themselves as an "intellectual aristocracy," they proposed to restore the grandeur and dignity of the writer in France, lost with the rise of the marketplace.[82]

---

[79] Lemaître, 345–346.
[80] Charles Donos, *Les Hommes d'aujourd'hui*, 9, no 465, no. date, BHVP, ART collection.
[81] Emile Faguet, *Le Journal des débats*, 3 January 1898.
[82] Datta, *Birth of a National Icon*, 65–84.

As we have seen, both Dreyfusards and anti-Dreyfusards valued independence of thought and freedom of action, which is precisely what Cyrano celebrates in his famous "non merci" (no thank you) speech, in which he outlines his philosophy.[83] The Duc de Guiche, offering Cyrano his patronage, declares that a poet is a luxury (Act 2, scene 7). Cyrano counters by declining such patronage, instead declaring that a true poet and hero had to maintain his independence. Here, Rostand was expressing his unease over a newly democratic society in which fame and celebrity often took precedence over real art. Rostand, like other writers of his day, especially those of the avant-garde, feared that those who were celebrated were not necessarily the best. In Cyrano's time, writers would have had to flatter a wealthy protector. During the fin de siècle, the protector's role would have been taken over by that of the mass public, to whom writers, especially those in the theater, would have to appeal to succeed. Rostand feared then the pedestrian tastes of the multitudes.

At the same time, however, Rostand rejected the isolation of avant-garde writers, with whom he shared this unease about popular success. Although Cyrano rejected money, patronage, and protection in favor of destitution, danger, and independence, in his non merci speech, Rostand through Cyrano also rejected retreat into the small coteries of the avant-garde and even referred in the original French text to the illustrious predecessor of the contemporary avant-garde journal *Le Mercure de France*.[84] Small wonder then that most reservations with regard to the play came from the avant-garde. A number of avant-garde critics were rather cautious in their reviews; not surprisingly, the critic from *Le Mercure de France* was downright insulting, claiming that Rostand had perfected the art of bad writing.[85] In part, the cool reception had to do with Rostand's jibe, but it also was linked to the success of *Cyrano* among the established critics as well as with the public.[86] As Jules Lemaître

[83] Commenting on this scene, the poet Catulle Mendès wrote: "The hour, triumphant and admirable, has come ... when poets are indeed the masters of Paris," *Le Journal*, 29 December 1897.

[84] Act 2, Scene 8.

[85] A. F. Herold, "Les Théâtres," *Le Mercure de France* 25 (February 1898): 594. See also the reviews published in other avant-garde journals: Jacques des Gachons in *L'Ermitage* 26 (January–June 1898): 236–237, who described "the good bourgeois folk [who] since fill the theater with their lyrical bravos," and Alfred Athys, "La Quinzaine dramatique," *La Revue blanche* 15 (15 January 1898): 150–154.

[86] These critics claimed that Cyrano represented the revival of French youth and a welcome antidote to the vogue of foreign literatures, and Symbolist and Naturalist theater promoted by the avant-garde. See especially Francisque Sarcey's review in *Le Temps* of 3 January 1898.

noted in his review, *Cyrano*, unlike Hugo's *Hernani* and Corneille's *Le Cid* to which it was compared, did not face the challenge of not being understood, and it is this reproach that underlies avant-garde criticism of the play.[87]

Ironically, of course, although the play decried material success and fame, it earned its author those very same things. Avant-garde writers undoubtedly found this tension somewhat unsettling; their reviews include a certain amount of sniping against the *commerçants* (tradesmen) who made the play a huge success and against the self-congratulatory reactions of the established, bourgeois critics. But it should be said that members of the avant-garde often sought the very fame they denounced and thus some of their reactions may be attributed to professional jealousy. In many ways, Rostand was like his hero (Figure 2.4). Although both Cyrano and his author Rostand denounced fame, they both needed a public to survive. Rostand was obviously fascinated with failure, because all his heroes, Cyrano included, were *ratés* (failures) to some extent.[88] Despite his bravery and heroism, Cyrano loses his love Roxane and despite his great talent, gains no literary fame, being surpassed by writers of lesser talent. This situation is exacerbated by his tragic flaw, his nose. Thus, his wit and bravery must compensate for his physical deformity. Yet Cyrano's wit and mastery of words were a means of extracting revenge, as Marc Lambron, writing in *Le Point* a few years back, noted, commenting that Cyrano represented "this national propensity to see a speech as an emblem of resistance."[89] Rostand himself saw Cyrano as an ideal, a symbol of purity, who battled the crass values of the marketplace represented by those who succeed in his place.

Rostand's ambivalent attitude toward his success is, of course, revelatory of the ambivalence many celebrities of all eras have felt toward fame. They simultaneously feed on it for their egos and creativity and deplore its invasive aspects. But the case of Rostand and *Cyrano de Bergerac* also tells us something about the way celebrity was experienced and viewed in fin-de-siècle France, as well as its role in creating national heroes at this time. Members of the literary elite, to which Rostand belonged, were wary of fame and quick success, traits they associated with material and modern culture, and designated as simultaneously "vulgar" and "American."

---

[87] Lemaître, 344.
[88] This is the theme of his *Les Musardises*.
[89] Lambron compared Cyrano's act of resistance to De Gaulle's speech of 18 June 1940 (p. 8), but he also could have compared Cyrano's eloquence to Zola's revolutionary act in publishing "J'Accuse."

FIGURE 2.4. Edmond Rostand, ca. 1900; Adoc-photos/Art Resource, New York.

They clearly feared being overrun by the "questionable" tastes of the masses. Rostand's supporters worked in vain to convince other literati that mass appeal and early success did not go hand in hand with superficiality and lack of artistic merit.

Popular audiences of the time, who flocked to such plays as *Cyrano de Bergerac*, however, did not share these views about democracy and celebrity, holding up famous actors like Coquelin or Bernhardt as role models. Theatergoers of the fin de siècle reveled in the culture of celebrity and felt great sympathy for the new heroes of the democratic age, ones with whom they could identify. Not only were the heroes these actors represented viewed as accessible – better versions of the ordinary man or woman – but the success of the actors who portrayed the heroes also illustrates the possibilities of social promotion as promulgated by the meritocratic republic.[90] Although Rostand himself belonged to an elite, his actors, Coquelin and Bernhardt, came from the popular classes. In the case of Rostand himself, these theatergoers and readers of the mass press, imbued with a national tradition that venerates writers, were fascinated by the creator of their beloved Cyrano and viewed him as a national hero. Although they might not all aspire to his fame and fortune, they could vicariously share in it. The success of Rostand was due, in part, to the complicity his audience felt with the great writer because his work was accessible to them. Like his creator, Cyrano was an aristocratic hero with populist tendencies who appealed to the democratic masses of the fin de siècle.

Conclusion

Cyrano de Bergerac, unlike the Bazar de la Charité fire just seven months earlier, became the means of national reconciliation at a time of great political conflict, uniting in the theater audiences who were weary of political infighting during the height of the Dreyfus Affair. The epony-mous Cyrano's appeal lay in his incarnation of national glory. Yet Cyrano, like other popular heroes of the time – the real-life female heroes of the Bazar de la Charité fire – as well as Joan of Arc and even Napoleon as he was depicted in the fin-de-siècle theater, also transgressed gender norms of the period. Certain heroic traits, notably self-control and scorn of danger, were viewed as male qualities, whereas others – self-sacrifice and abnegation – were seen as typically "female" characteristics. How then do we reconcile the popularity of sensitive, democratic heroes who blurred gender lines with the "crisis of masculinity" during the fin de siècle? The concerns about honor and manhood *were* acute; witness the battle that pitted Dreyfusards and anti-Dreyfusards, both of whom laid claim to real honor and manhood. Furthermore, some male anxieties did indeed manifest themselves in a misogynist and anti-feminist backlash on the part of certain writers. Social commentator L. Jeudon had described women as the spectators of the duels among men, and sociologist Gabriel Tarde even blamed women, along with the mass press, for the rise in duels, thereby expressing a fear of the increased influence of women in French society.[91]

---

[90] Berlanstein, *Daughters of Eve*, 219.
[91] For a discussion of this point, see Berenson, *Madame Caillaux*, 188–189. Women also increasingly read the mass press, especially the *feuilletons*: see Anne-Marie Thiesse, *Le*

Despite such manifestations of misogyny, the pervasive popularity of heroes who blurred gender categories complicates our understanding of the crisis of masculinity, suggesting, as Lenard Berlanstein has observed, that a real "breakthrough in understandings of gender" was made at this time.[92] The popularity of such sensitive heroes also signals profound changes in the way that women and traditional "female" traits were viewed in French society; already in the Bazar de la Charité fire, female heroism had been acknowledged, however grudgingly.[93] Although most males did not advocate abandoning the traditional role of women as wives and mothers – Roxane, after all, was no New Woman – women at the fin de siècle were increasingly incorporated into an understanding of the nation both as theatergoers and as role models and symbols of national identity. Roxane serves as an "ear" for Cyrano and Christian and therefore is a symbol of the increasingly female audiences of the time.[94] Furthermore, in an era in which French honor was sorely tested, any figure, male or female, who brought glory to the nation, was celebrated.[95] Perhaps the crisis of masculinity was due less to the rise of women in the public sphere than to the loss of the war.[96] Such an explanation would account for the simultaneous appeal of sensitive and military heroes, and moreover, of heroes who faced their destiny with dignity. The fates of Napoleon, Joan, and Cyrano all mirrored France's situation at the fin de siècle – hence, in part, their success with contemporary audiences.

By literally and figuratively thumbing his nose at the rest of Europe, Cyrano foreshadowed the nationalist revival that preceded the Great

---

Roman du quotidien: Lecteurs et lectures populaires à la Belle Epoque (Paris: Le Chemin Vert, 1984), 20.

[92] Berlanstein, 239. See also Ann-Louise Shapiro, who argues that although women's rights certainly were not complete by the fin de siècle, the republic had begun to redefine the meanings of citizenship, in particular, female citizenship: *Breaking the Codes: Female Criminality in Fin-de-Siècle Paris* (Stanford, CA: Stanford University Press, 1996), 215. This is also the view of such historians of gender and feminism as Rachel Fuchs, Karen Offen, Mary Lynn Stewart, and Elinor Accampo.

[93] Although the 1889 World's Fair celebrated the cult of the republican man and science in the very masculine symbol of the Eiffel Tower, just eleven years later, during the 1900 World's Fair, the values being celebrated were feminine and aristocratic: Debora Silverman, *Art Nouveau in Fin-de-Siècle France: Politics, Psychology and Style* (Berkeley: University of California Press, 1989), 285–314.

[94] There is sufficient qualitative evidence to suggest that women attended the theater in greater numbers at this time than earlier in the century.

[95] Berlanstein, 204.

[96] Berlanstein, 239.

War.[97] This revival, along with a desire to find unifying heroes in the theater and fiction, also manifested itself in a renewal of the Napoleonic legend. Appropriately enough, the legend witnessed its apogee with Rostand's 1900 play *L'Aiglon*. Once again, Rostand's creation – brought to life this time by Sarah Bernhardt – reflected the temper of the age.

[97] Eugen Weber, *The Nationalist Revival in France, 1905–1914* (Berkeley: University of California Press, 1968).

3

"L'Appel au Soldat": Visions of the Napoleonic Legend in Popular Culture

Although the real Cyrano was an obscure historical personage transformed into one of France's leading heroes at the fin de siècle, the figure of Napoleon, like Joan of Arc, already occupied a large place in the French collective national consciousness as a *lieu de mémoire*.[1] Nevertheless, as

L'Appel au soldat is the title of Maurice Barrès's 1900 novel. An examination of the Boulangist episode, it comprises the second volume of Barrès's trilogy of *romans de l'énergie nationale*. The title, which evokes the perceived need for a military hero, can easily refer to the other works on the Napoleonic legend examined here. An earlier version of this chapter, "'L'Appel au soldat': Visions of the Napoleonic Legend in Popular Culture of the Belle Epoque," was published in *French Historical Studies*, 28: 1–30. Copyright 2005, Society for French Historical Studies. Reprinted by permission of the publisher, Duke University Press.

[1] No less than three articles are devoted to different aspects of the Napoleonic legend, one on the soldier Chauvin, a second on the Napoleonic Code, and a third on the *retour des cendres*, that is, the return of Napoleon's remains to France under the July Monarchy: Pierre Nora, ed., *Les Lieux de mémoire* (Paris: Quarto, 1997); "Le Code Civil" by Jean Charbonnier is published in Volume 1 of the Gallimard Quarto edition, pp. 1331–1352; "Le Soldat Chauvin," written by Gérard de Puymège, and "Le Retour des cendres" by Jean Tulard are published in Volume 2 of the Quarto edition, pp. 1699–1728 and 1729–1754, respectively. Missing, however, is an article on the Napoleonic legend in literature. Perhaps this omission occurs because so much has been published elsewhere on the impact of the Napoleonic legend on writers of the early nineteenth century, particularly those dating from the Restoration and July Monarchy. Among the many works published, see especially J. Lucas-Dubreton, *Le Culte de Napoléon, 1815–1848* (Paris: Albin Michel 1960), as well as the many works of the doyen of Napoleonic scholars, Jean Tulard, in particular, *L'Anti-Napoléon: La Légende noire de l'Empereur* (Paris: Julliard, 1965) and *Le Mythe de Napoléon* (Paris: Armand Colin, 1971). The last few years have witnessed a revival of studies on Napoleon and the Napoleonic legend. See the biography by Steven Englund, *Napoleon: A Political Life* (Cambridge, MA: Harvard University Press, 2004). On the legend and Napoleonic cults, Natalie Petiteau, *Napoléon, de la*

in the case of Joan, the Napoleonic legend witnessed a revival during the late nineteenth and early twentieth centuries. Military heroes, as the popularity of Cyrano, Napoleon, and Joan illustrate, had special resonance at this time and were, moreover, a part of a republican effort to recuperate the past.[2] In this chapter, the theme of the military hero is explored once again, through an examination of the way in which writers and critics exploited the Napoleonic legend for different political and cultural ends. Whereas numerous works on the military aspects of the Napoleonic legacy exist, representations of the Napoleonic legend in the popular culture of the fin de siècle constitute a relatively little-studied phenomenon.[3]

Although it focuses mainly on the theater, this chapter also includes a discussion of two key novels on the Napoleonic legend, without which an understanding of the Napoleonic legacy at this time would not be complete. Concentrating on Victorien Sardou's (with Emile Moreau) *Madame Sans-Gêne* (1893), Maurice Barrès's *Les Déracinés* (1897), Edmond Rostand's *L'Aiglon* (1900), and Gyp's *Napoléonette* (1913), it argues that following the defeat of Boulangism, the Napoleonic legend was divorced from party politics and experienced a revival in popular culture. Proponents and detractors of the Third Republic, who represented Napoleon as a figure of national unity, used the legend both to criticize their enemies and as a vehicle for exploring anxieties about gender and fears about the processes of democratization. Reduced to a minor

mythologie à l'histoire (Paris: Seuil, 1999); Sudhir Hazareesingh, *The Legend of Napoleon* (London: Granta Books, 2004) and *The Saint-Napoleon: Celebrations of Sovereignty in Nineteenth-Century France* (Cambridge, MA: Harvard University Press, 2004); and Philip Dwyer, *Napoleon: The Path to Power* (New Haven, CT: Yale University Press, 2008), who not only studies how Napoleon himself constructed his own legend but also presents a psychobiography of Napoleon as a young man.

[2] Jean-François Chanet, "La Fabrique des héros: Pédagogie républicaine et culte des grands hommes de Sedan à Vichy," *Vingtième Siècle* 65 (January–March 2000): 14.

[3] On the importance of the cultural legacy of the Napoleonic phenomenon, see Malcom Crook and John Dunne, "Napoleon's France: History and Heritage," *Modern and Contemporary France* 8, no. 4 (November 2000): 429, and Annie Jourdan's *Napoléon: Héros, imperator et mécène* (Paris: Aubier, 1998), which examines the images of Napoleon in the painting, sculpture, and historiography of the earlier part of the nineteenth century. Fewer works exist on the gender implications of the Napoleonic legacy. A notable exception is Michael J. Hughes's essay, "Making Frenchmen into Warriors: Martial Masculinity in Napoleonic France," in *French Masculinities: History, Culture and Politics*, ed. Christopher E. Forth and Bertrand Taithe (New York: Palgrave Macmillan, 2007), 51–66. Hughes argues that when Napoleon became ruler of France, he restored the warrior virtues of aristocracy to the army, thereby extending these virtues to all French men and thus to the French nation. The ideal man at this time was a soldier who was, moreover, aggressively heterosexual, 55–61.

character, the new fictional Napoleon was not a world-historical figure but rather an intimate one fashioned by each individual's needs and consumed as popular entertainment. The chapter begins with an examination of the evolution of the Napoleonic legend over the course of the nineteenth century before proceeding to an analysis of the four works themselves.

The Napoleonic Legend

The period from 1890 until the First World War witnessed a flowering of the Napoleonic cult in France.[4] For the first time, the Napoleonic period became the subject of serious academic history, as the writings of Albert Vandal, Frédéric Masson, Henry Houssaye, and Hippolyte Taine illustrate.[5] With the notable exception of Taine, these historians were admirers of Napoleon. Nevertheless, the most significant arena for the revival of the Napoleonic cult was in literature, in particular, the theater, and in the fine arts.[6] Artists like Edouard Detaille (1848–1912) celebrated Napoleonic victories in their paintings, while writers as diverse as Victorien Sardou, Maurice Barrès, Gyp, Paul Déroulède, and Edmond Rostand were all seduced by the Napoleonic legend. Sardou's *Madame Sans-Gêne* (1893), the story of a washerwoman who becomes a duchess and wife of a Napoleonic marshal, and Rostand's *L'Aiglon* (1900), with Sarah Bernhardt in the title role, played to full houses, while memoirs about the Napoleonic period sold briskly.[7] In the year 1893 alone, several plays with a Napoleonic theme were presented on the Parisian stage, among them Sardou's *Madame Sans-Gêne* at the Vaudeville, along

---

[4] Robert Gildea, *The Past in French History* (New Haven, CT: Yale University Press, 1994), 102. The destruction of the Great War changed the minds of most French men and women about the glories of war. By 1921, in a survey conducted by *Le Petit Parisien*, Napoleon had fallen to fourth place as a great nineteenth-century French figure. See R. S. Alexander, "The Hero as Houdini: Napoleon and Nineteenth-Century Bonapartism," *Modern and Contemporary France* 8, no. 4 (November 2000): 466. Nevertheless, the centenary of Napoleon's death in 1921 was an opportunity to celebrate the French victory in the First World War: Hazareesingh, *The Legend of Napoleon*, 263.

[5] Taine's *Origines de la France contemporaine*, published in 1890, contained a detailed portrait of Napoleon. See Pieter Geyl, *Napoleon: For or Against*, trans. Olive Renier (New Haven, CT: Yale University Press, 1967).

[6] Gildea, 103.

[7] See Philip Dwyer, "Public Remembering, Private Reminiscing: French Military Memoirs and the Revolutionary and Napoleonic Wars," *French Historical Studies* 33, no. 2 (Spring 2010): 231–258.

with Alphonse Lemonnier's *Madame la Maréchale* at the Théâtre de l'Ambigu (and then at Château-d'Eau), Léopold Martin-Laya's *Napoléon* at the Théâtre de la Porte-Saint-Martin, and Charles Grandmougin's *L'Empereur* at the Théâtre des Poètes. "Always him! He is everywhere!" exclaimed Ernest de la Vogüé, who noted that the "avalanche" of publications on the First Empire was both the cause and effect of the heightened interest in the period.[8]

During the fin de siècle, the figure of Napoleon became a multifaceted cultural icon for writers across the political spectrum, from the republican left to the nascent nationalist right. It can easily be demonstrated that the Napoleonic legend was already in place during the emperor's own lifetime; it was certainly cemented shortly after his death, following the publication of *Le Mémorial de Sainte-Hélène* in 1823.[9] Moreover, the legend was never singular but rather plural; indeed, the power of the Napoleonic legend was its very elasticity. The figure of Napoleon, although related to Bonapartism, has to a great extent escaped party politics, thus allowing divergent groups to see in Napoleon what they desired and to lay claim to his historical legacy.[10] During the July Monarchy, different visions of Napoleon were used by opponents and partisans of the regime, with the former emphasizing the revolutionary heritage of the "little corporal" and the latter highlighting Napoleon's imperial legacy in order to associate the lackluster regime with Napoleonic military grandeur.[11] The July Monarchy thus divorced the Napoleonic legend from Bonapartist politics; such so-called depoliticization made possible the return of Napoleon's remains

---

[8] Ernest de la Vogüé, "Un Portrait de Napoléon," *La Revue des deux mondes* 117 (15 May 1893): 443.

[9] Some historians distinguish between a Napoleonic "myth," which he created himself, including in *Le Mémorial de Sainte-Hélène*, and a legend, which sprang up after 1815: Hazareesingh, *The Legend of Napoleon*, 4. For an overview of the history of the Napoleonic legend, see Jean-Pierre Rioux, "L'Aigle de légende," *L'Histoire*, no. 124 (July–August 1989): 94–100 and Gildea, 89–111.

[10] Alexander, "The Hero as Houdini," 457.

[11] See Barbara Ann Day-Hickman, *Napoleonic Art: Nationalism and the Spirit of Rebellion in France (1815–1848)* (Newark: University of Delaware Press, 1999). In *The Spectacular Past: Popular History and the Novel in Nineteenth-Century France* (Ithaca, NY: Cornell University Press, 2004), Maurice Samuels argues that the years from 1815 to 1848 saw the greatest concentration of plays about Napoleon, with the period from August 1830 to August 1831 constituting an apogee, 119–120. He also notes that although plays produced during the fall of 1830 had associated Napoleon with the revolutionary tradition, those from the winter presented Napoleon as a unifying figure, at the same time that Bonapartists became dissatisfied with the July Monarchy, 128.

to the Invalides by a regime that feared the revolutionary legacy of Napoleon and was determined to exclude the masses from politics.[12]

The fin de siècle witnessed a similar phenomenon. The Napoleonic legend was used by writers who were proponents as well as detractors of the Third Republic, but whereas in the earlier period Napoleon had been represented as either a revolutionary or a champion of authority and order, during the turn of the century, both sides attempted to represent him as a figure of national unity. Although they succeeded in separating Napoleon from Bonapartism as a political movement, they most definitely put the legend to work for their own political ends.[13]

The fin-de-siècle cult of heroes explains, in part, the tremendous popularity of the Napoleonic legend, whether the representation was literary or otherwise. Critic Téodor de Wyzewa noted the need for secular heroes in an age of de-Christianization. Moreover, the republican search for heroes among the men of the Revolution was fruitless because these figures proved controversial on closer examination. Napoleon, however, stirred up fewer controversies. In other words, the Napoleonic legacy was sufficiently ambiguous to reunite different factions. As Wyzewa shrewdly observed, "We do not love him for himself, but through him, we fulfill our need to love."[14] And Napoleon himself had claimed in *Le Mémorial de Sainte-Hélène* that he was the national unifier.

Moreover, as Francis Magnard, writing in 1894, observed, the First Empire evoked images of a heroic time, long past, of "the old-fashioned art of war, heroic and personal." Such personalized warfare, which promoted individual heroism, had been replaced by impersonal warfare based on geometry and mathematical precision.[15] At the time that Magnard wrote his article, the French army was undergoing profound changes that would eventually lead to the events of the Dreyfus Affair. Traditionalists in the army feared not only the increasingly democratic, republican, money-oriented society the army was supposed to protect, but also the rise of the technocratic officer, often found in the artillery,

---

[12] Gildea, 95–96.

[13] Hazareesingh, *The Legend of Napoleon*, also argues that by the fin de siècle, the Napoleonic legend was no longer part of an "overarching political project" but rather a way of cementing national unity, with the republicans firmly involved in such efforts, 261.

[14] Wyzewa, "Trois Historiens de Napoléon Ier," *La Revue bleue* 41, no. 23 (2 December 1893): 728–729. See also an article published in *Le Gaulois* by former Boulangist deputy Jules Delafosse, "Le Culte des héros," *Le Gaulois*, 28 March 1900.

[15] Francis Magnard, "La Résurrection d'une légende," *La Revue de Paris* (1 February 1894): 107.

who had been promoted for his intellectual attributes rather than for his raw courage. Alfred Dreyfus, it should be remembered, was an artillery officer.[16]

The rise of General Boulanger may also be explained by the contemporary desire for heroes. As Magnard noted perceptively, the popularity of the Boulangist movement represented a contemporary quest for a "professor of energy," albeit an aborted one. The poor general, in Magnard's words, had been but a "musketeer" at a time when France needed a true hero.[17]

The view of Napoleon as a figure "above politics" was only possible in the wake of the defeat of Boulangism and the decline of Bonapartism as a viable political movement.[18] Once the real would-be Napoleon was safely offstage, republican politicians, who feared the man on horseback, could enjoy representations of him in the theater. The premiere of *L'Aiglon* was attended by members of the imperial family as well as by such republican leaders as René Waldeck-Rousseau, Léon Bourgeois, and Louis Barthou.[19] Similarly, for opponents of the Third Republic, the defeat of Boulanger increased their desire for a national savior; because they could not find one in the present and in real life, they looked to their imaginations and to the past.

Given the controversial nature of the French Revolution, it was difficult to turn it into a subject for popular entertainment; witness the uproar over Sardou's 1891 *Thermidor*, which ended in a parliamentary debate, after Sardou, a moderate republican, repeatedly praised the early achievements of the Revolution but roundly condemned the excesses of the Terror.[20] After the defeat of Boulanger and the decline of the Bonapartist

---

[16] On the army, see William Serman, *Les Officiers français dans la nation (1848–1914)* (Paris: Aubier Montaigne, 1982).

[17] Magnard, 110.

[18] Magnard, 102. On Bonapartism, see John Rothney, *Bonapartism after Sedan* (Ithaca, NY: Cornell University Press, 1969), and Karen Offen, *Paul de Cassagnac and the Authoritarian Tradition in Nineteenth-Century France* (New York: Garland, 1991). On Boulangism, see Philippe Levillain, *Boulanger, fossoyeur de la monarchie* (Paris: Flammarion, 1982) as well as an excellent review essay by Paul Mazgaj, "The Origins of the French Radical Right," *French Historical Studies* 15, no. 2 (Fall 1987): 287–315.

[19] Magnard, 104.

[20] Sardou's exaltation of Danton and concomitant condemnation of Robespierre and his followers were greeted by disturbances during the play's second performance at the Comédie Française and then subsequently banned by the government, which claimed to maintain public order. This move led to a parliamentary debate in which Radicals, led by Georges Clemenceau, used the play as an excuse to rupture the budding alliance between

party, however, Napoleon could serve both as a rallying point for writers across the political spectrum and a profitable topic for popular consumption. Indeed, Sardou next turned his attentions to the Napoleonic legend, staging *Madame Sans-Gêne* in 1893.

Such "depoliticization" of the Napoleonic legend was announced by significant developments in historiography, notably the 1887 publication in *La Revue des deux mondes* of Hippolyte Taine's essay on Napoleon, which sparked the Napoleonic revival.[21] The article, which ultimately formed the basis for the second volume of Taine's *Origines de la France contemporaine*, caused an uproar to the surprise of its author and his contemporaries because it portrayed the emperor as an ogre. Despite the decline of the Napoleonic legend following France's defeat in the Franco-Prussian War, Taine's savage depiction touched a national nerve. Contemporaries realized that whatever their political opinion of Napoleon, he represented "an essential element of our national heritage."[22] No longer the subject of polemics, Napoleon was henceforth the purview of professional historians rather than contemporaries of the Empire, whether these contemporaries were for or against the Empire.[23]

The study of Napoleon as an object of historical study led in some ways to the distancing of the historical Napoleon, yet this distancing was accompanied by a heightened interest among historians in the emperor's personal life. Frédéric Masson's *Napoléon et les femmes* and Arthur Lévy's *Napoléon intime* were highly successful, as were the various memoirs of the period. The study of Napoleon's private life brought him closer to the public, and he therefore became fair game for appropriation by littérateurs. If a cause and effect between historical trends and literary developments is impossible to ascertain, one can speak of a convergence

the Opportunist republicans and monarchists who had rallied to the republic. Claiming that the Revolution was a "bloc," Clemenceau appealed to republican solidarity, forcing more moderate republicans, who had favored overturning the ban, into voting to uphold it to preserve the republican alliance between Opportunists and Radicals. On this event, see Eugen Weber, "About *Thermidor*: The Oblique Uses of Scandal," *French Historical Studies* 17, no. 2 (Fall 1991): 330–342, and Steven M. Beaudoin, "'Et les beaux rêves d'avenir?' Victorien Sardou and Fin de Siècle Attitudes on the French Revolution" (M.A. thesis, University of Maine, 1990).

21 Hippolyte Taine, "Napoléon Bonaparte," *La Revue des deux mondes* 79 (15 February 1887): 721–752. The second part of the article was published on 1 March 1887 in Vol. 80.

22 Magnard, 102.

23 Gustave Larroumet, "Un Nouveau 'Retour des cendres,'" originally published on 15 October 1893, was subsequently reproduced in *Nouvelles Études de la littérature et d'art* (Paris: Hachette, 1894), 188–189. See also de Vogüé, 444.

of the literary and historical representations of Napoleon that announced a supposedly depoliticized and more intimate Napoleon.

In both the theater and the museum of the fin de siècle, the personal emotions of the country's leaders were more important to the public than a dry depiction of historical and political events.[24] Indeed, the period saw a rise in the popular interest in visual representations of historical scenes; witness the "o-rama" craze (for panoramas and dioramas) and the popularity of the wax museum. Similarly, in the boulevard theater, history was made into a spectacle that could be consumed by socially diverse audiences. This was certainly the case of the Bernhardt productions of Joan of Arc; similarly, the spectacular nature of *Cyrano de Bergerac* contributed to its success among audiences who reveled in the glories of the past. Like the panoramas of the Musée Grévin, the historical scenes represented in the theater constituted popular, democratic history that bridged the distance between the past and the present by accentuating the personal attributes of public figures.

Interestingly enough, the Napoleon of many of the fictional works of the fin de siècle did not occupy center stage but was reduced to a minor, indeed, a supporting character. In *Headless History*, Linda Orr argues that the French Revolution constitutes a "black hole" in French literature. Although French works of fiction in the nineteenth century could not directly take on the French Revolution, they did indirectly approach "the traumatic space of the Revolution."[25] The same could easily be argued of Napoleon. Earlier in the century, such novels as Balzac's *Le Colonel Chabert* and Stendhal's monumental *Le Rouge et le noir* only treated him indirectly.

For writers of the fin de siècle seeking to use Napoleon as a symbol of reconciliation, especially those with liberal republican leanings, it was nearly impossible to represent the emperor in his full glory. To incorporate Napoleon into the national memory, they had to reduce him to a shadow of himself – it was perhaps no accident that one of the most popular representations of Napoleon during this time took place at the puppet theater run by the denizens of Le Chat Noir (could the use of

---

[24] Vanessa R. Schwartz's work on the historical tableaux of the Musée Grévin has informed my thoughts about the representation of history in the theater of the time. On the Musée Grévin, see *Spectacular Realities: Early Mass Culture in Fin-de-Siècle Paris* (Berkeley: University of California Press, 1998), 142–144. On the o-rama craze, see especially 157–162.

[25] Linda Orr, *Headless History: Nineteenth-Century French Historiography of the Revolution* (Ithaca, NY: Cornell University Press 1990), 17.

a puppet to depict Napoleon be a way of undermining both his manhood and authority?).[26] In Sardou's *Madame Sans-Gêne*, Napoleon is unclothed during most of the play, that is, clothed only in his dressing gown, divested thus of his power, both political and military. The real "hero" of the piece is the former-washerwoman-turned-duchess, symbol of the meritocratic Third Republic. Similarly, in Rostand's *L'Aiglon*, the major character is Napoleon's son, who is but a pale imitation of his father. Napoleon himself is represented by the ghosts of his soldiers on the battlefield of Wagram and also by the metonym of his famous bicorne hat, which Metternich addresses in a delirious daydream, thinking that the emperor has returned to life. Here again, the real hero of the play is an everyman, the *grognard* (Napoleonic soldier), Flambeau, who represents the ideals of the Revolution. In these two plays, liberal republican authors appropriated the Napoleonic legend, by "undressing" Napoleon, both literally and figuratively. The only way for these republicans to reconcile the figure of Napoleon with the republic was to reduce him to human size and to emphasize his legacy of meritocracy and revolutionary messianism.

Even in works authored by integral nationalists, Napoleon is addressed only via his so-called descendants. The seven young protagonists in *Les Déracinés* are represented as potential heirs of Napoleon who must take from him the lessons offered by this "professor of energy." In fact, the entire passage of the novel takes place around the Emperor's *tomb*. Similarly, in Gyp's *Napoléonette*, Napoleon is represented through the fictionalized legacy of his goddaughter. Such a shift in the focus of the legend to heretofore minor players not only allowed writers of varying political persuasions to present Napoleon more easily as a figure of national unity, but it also allowed them to use the legend as a vehicle for exploring the various cultural forces at play during the period, especially concerns about gender and fears about the processes of democratization amid emerging mass politics and culture.

It is no coincidence, then, that the fin de siècle also marked Napoleon's transformation from a world-historical figure to a more intimate one

---

[26] Jonas Barish notes that the vogue for marionettes at the time was a response to a need to detheatricalize the theater from the posturing of actors but was also a way to retheatricalize it from the paralyzing effects of realism: *The Antitheatrical Prejudice* (Berkeley: University of California Press, 1981), 344. The Chat Noir also represented Joan of Arc in the shadow puppet theater in 1900: Jann Pasler, *Composing the Citizen: Music as Public Utility in Third Republic France* (Berkeley: University of California Press, 2009), 663.

to be fashioned to each individual's needs and consumed as popular entertainments by a public that craved images of a heroic past.[27] Indeed, the premieres of Sardou's *Madame Sans-Gêne* and Rostand's *L'Aiglon* were considered events of national importance and covered extensively by the national press.[28] Like earlier Romantic authors, the writers of the fin de siècle emphasized their individual visions of Napoleon, but instead of concentrating exclusively on the conquering hero, they presented an intimate portrait that detailed his personal life. Such a presentation of Napoleon was naturally fraught with contradictions. In an age that decried the "crisis of masculinity," Napoleon incarnated a manly image from a bygone, glorious era, yet at the same time, this person was reduced to his human foibles. Finally, although Napoleon was exalted as a hero for a time sorely in need of heroes, he was simultaneously reduced to a supporting player and, moreover, to an ordinary man, confronted with his own personal problems. As such, he was a true hero for the democratic age.

In examining the different political and cultural uses made of the Napoleonic legend by writers and critics of the fin de siècle as well as the reception of these works by the general public, I begin with the popular Sardou play *Madame Sans-Gêne* (1893), which signaled the arrival of a more intimate Napoleon, presented as a figure on the boulevard stage, and then proceed to study Barrès's highly influential *Les Déracinés* (1897). In this first novel of the trilogy of *romans de l'énergie nationale* (novels of national energy), published shortly before the height of the Dreyfus Affair, Barrès presented Napoleon as a "professor of energy," an exemplar for his countrymen, but also as a mythical and personal figure, a Napoleon of the soul. Barrès's *Les Déracinés* not only confirmed the trend toward a more personalized figure, to be shaped by each individual, but also marked the arrival of an integral nationalist Napoleon. Supposedly a figure of national reconciliation, this Napoleon was nevertheless contrasted with the corrupt opportunist republic abhorred by Barrès. Next, I examine the best-known and most popular of the works on the Napoleonic legend, *L'Aiglon* (1900), which represents the apotheosis of the Napoleonic legend during the fin de siècle. This work, like Rostand's

[27] On the commodification of history during an earlier period, see Samuels, especially 63–106.
[28] Jean Pedersen has highlighted the important role of the theater in national discussions about social and political issues, indeed, about national identity, in her book *Legislating the Family: Feminism, Theater, and Republican Politics* (New Brunswick, NJ: Rutgers University Press, 2003).

earlier play *Cyrano de Bergerac* (1897), became synonymous for most contemporaries with France itself. Nevertheless, despite the author's intentions, the play was more successfully co-opted by the right than the left in the wake of the Dreyfus Affair. *L'Aiglon* also highlights tensions in the Napoleonic legend, for although it was heralded by many on the right as an example of the glory and power of Napoleon, its hero was a weak young man, hardly the virile figure of Barrès's dreams. Finally, I examine Gyp's *Napoléonette* (1913), which also reflects the development of a more intimate Napoleon, depicted in the novel as the heroine's godfather, as well as of an integral nationalist hero, a process begun by *Les Déracinés* and further strengthened in the wake of *L'Aiglon*. Like *Madame Sans-Gêne*, *Les Déracinés*, and *L'Aiglon*, *Napoléonette* sheds light on the gender anxieties of the time and the public hunger for heroes up until the eve of the First World War.

These four works trace the process by which Napoleon was divorced from Bonapartism and incorporated into the national patrimony. In addition, they illustrate the Napoleonic legend's ambiguity, which undoubtedly constitutes its power to capture the hearts and minds of writers and the public of the fin de siècle, regardless of their political affiliation. In this sense then, the legend did succeed in being "above politics."

Madame Sans-Gêne

Madame Sans-Gêne tells the story of Catherine (née Hubscher) Lefebvre, a washerwoman who had once known the young General Bonaparte. She later serves as *vivandière* in the Napoleonic army and many years after becomes a duchess, when her husband becomes a marshal of France. The first act of the play is set on August 10, 1792, the date of the forced abdication of Louis XVI, with the rest of the action of the play taking place nearly twenty years later, at Napoleon's Imperial Court. The washerwoman-*vivandière*, now a duchess, is as frank as ever.[29] Her time at the

---

[29] There was a real Catherine Lefebvre (née Hubscher) [her tomb is located at the Père-Lachaise Cemetery], a regimental laundress whose husband, François Joseph Lefebvre, became a marshal of France. She was a frank speaker just as Sardou depicted her in his play. But it is Sardou who dubbed her "Madame Sans-Gêne." The real "Madame Sans-Gêne," who received her sobriquet from Napoleon himself, was Marie-Thérèse Figueur, who donned male clothing to follow Napoleon into battle. Given the gender ambiguities of the fin de siècle, it is interesting that Sardou chose to combine the biographies of these two historical figures to create his own theatrical character. On Figueur, see Robert Ouvrard, ed., *Histoire de la Dragonne* (Paris: Cosmopole Editions, 2005), 177 (footnote 6). My thanks to Professor Barbara Day-Hickman for pointing this source out to me.

court has not succeeded in refining her, to the point that an embarrassed Napoleon asks her husband to divorce her. The husband refuses, and Catherine, through her resourcefulness, candor, and charm, succeeds in convincing the emperor of her true worth. In a somewhat convoluted subplot, she even saves the emperor from executing a man he believes has cuckolded him.

Although most critics considered *Madame Sans-Gêne* a slight play, they acknowledged its ability to captivate and amuse audiences as well as the historical accuracy of the décor and costumes, for which Sardou was well known[30] (Figures 3.1 and 3.2). A number of critics noted that the play missed opportunities to analyze social and political issues seriously. Instead, the characters of Catherine and Napoleon are at times caricatural, their lines played for laughs – although the fact that Catherine (played by actress Gabrielle Réjane), a woman, stands up to Napoleon is not without political implications for the modern reader.[31] But as Jules Lemaître observed, despite taking Sardou to task for his lack of seriousness, such a presentation was exactly what one expected of a play at the Vaudeville; audiences of the boulevard theater would have had trouble with a more serious play.[32]

Some critics reproached Sardou for depicting too coarse a parvenu, not to mention too humble a Napoleon, while others defended the historical accuracy of this characterization. A reviewer of *Madame Sans-Gêne* praised Sardou's representation of the emperor as more "real" and "human" than legend would have it, thus explaining the appeal of numerous recent works on Napoleon, both historical and fictional.[33]

---

[30] See, for example, reviews by Camille Bellaigue in *La Revue des deux mondes* 120 (15 November 1893): 459–461, and Francisque Sarcey, *Quarante Ans de théâtre* (Paris: Bibliothèque des annales politiques et littéraires, 1901), 154–161, originally published on 30 October 1893. For more on *Madame Sans-Gêne*, see James Lehning, *The Melodramatic Thread: Spectacle and Political Culture in Modern France* (Bloomington: Indiana University Press, 2007), 55–59.

[31] Lehning observes that Catherine combines the private virtue of a woman with the public virtue of a (male) citizen, but that Napoleon's approval of her stems not from these qualities but from her ability to play a man's game of court intrigue, 55–56. I would add that the game of intrigue was seen by revolutionary leaders as a female game, associated especially with aristocrats and the monarchy, a fact that leads me to a more ambiguous gender reading of the play and its characters.

[32] See Jules Lemaître's review, originally published on 5 November 1893 and republished in *Impressions de théâtre*, 8ème série (Paris: Société française d'imprimerie et de librairie, 1897), 187–198.

[33] Ange Galdemar, "Madame Sans-Gêne avant le rideau," *Le Gaulois*, 27 October 1893.

FIGURE 3.1. Félix Duquesne as Napoleon in Victorien Sardou's *Madame Sans-Gêne*, courtesy of the BNF.

A more intimate, less grandiose emperor was thus a hero for a democratic age; he was, in many ways, like everyone else.[34] Not all critics, however, subscribed to this point of view. In his review of *Madame Sans-Gêne* published in *La Revue bleue*, Jacques du Tillet claimed that Sardou's

[34] Wyzewa, 730.

FIGURE 3.2. The cast of Sardou's *Madame Sans-Gêne*, courtesy of the BNF.

Napoleon was both crass and ridiculous. Tillet was embarrassed by so intimate a portrait; how could such a man, little more than Sardou's puppet, have been the hero of Austerlitz?[35]

Tillet, however, was in the minority. Most observers, like Henry Fouquier, who himself had written a play about Napoleon, clearly understood that the popularity of the Napoleonic legend was primarily a literary phenomenon. The character of Napoleon, he claimed, was perfect for either tragedy or comedy. Even a depiction of his faults was not inconsistent with legend.[36] Weighing in on the quarrel between Masson and Sardou on the historical accuracy of *Madame Sans-Gêne*, Fouquier explained that it did not really matter.[37] Instead of the tragic reality of history, the theater represented a comforting legend. The role of literature was to stick to the essentials of history, not to lose itself in

---

[35] Tillet, *La Revue bleue* 52, no. 19 (4 November 1893): 605. During the Oscar Wilde trial, one French critic described the Irish poet as a "puppet," thereby impugning his honor and manhood. See my *Birth of a National Icon: The Literary Avant-Garde and the Origins of the Intellectual in France* (Albany, NY: SUNY Press, 1999), 128.

[36] Henry Fouquier, "Le Retour de Sainte-Hélène," *Le Figaro*, 30 November 1893.

[37] Masson and Sardou had each accused the other in the popular press of historical inaccuracies in their respective works.

details.[38] Thus, in the court of public opinion, the litterateur had clearly triumphed over the historian. A more literary, humanized Napoleon had been firmly implanted in the cultural landscape of the period.

But Sardou's depiction of Napoleon as an ordinary man (he believes that his wife is cheating on him but learns that she is faithful) had potential to diminish his image. The conquering hero of Austerlitz was reduced to a jealous husband clothed in his dressing gown for much of the play. Sardou's Napoleon was perhaps more human and intimate, but he had also been robbed of his grandeur and virility. Sardou had accused Masson of creating a Napoleon for "those with delicate sensibilities," but his own Napoleon seemed even less manly. In the highly charged atmosphere of the fin de siècle, a man who even feared being cuckolded could be said to have lost his honor and manhood.[39]

Despite his republican leanings, Sardou, unlike Barrès and Gyp, and perhaps more like his fellow playwright Rostand, was less interested in offering a certain political view of Napoleon than in presenting a Napoleon for popular entertainment and profit.[40] His "take" implicitly celebrated the democratic qualities Napoleon represented, as Catherine and her husband were symbols of the social mobility promulgated by the Revolution and Napoleon himself, as well as by the leaders of the Third Republic. Such mobility would also be seen favorably by the newly democratized audiences who attended the boulevard theater in large numbers. As commentators of the time noted, Sardou had a gift for determining what was popular and capitalizing on it – indeed, the play was revived in 1900 during the Universal Exhibition and was performed more than two hundred times during this period.[41]

Like *Thermidor, Madame Sans-Gêne* had a life independent of its author. Despite Sardou's intentions to present an "apolitical" and intimate Napoleon, the play nevertheless elicited a great deal of attention from those who used it to criticize the current regime. The critic writing in Edouard Drumont's populist, militarist, and anti-Semitic *La Libre Parole* believed that the entire worth of Sardou's play rested in

[38] Fouquier. On the same theme, see Paul Costard, "La Légende au théâtre," *Le Gaulois*, 6 March 1900, and "La Vérité au théâtre," signed by Le Passant, in *Le Figaro* of 20 March 1900.

[39] See Robert A. Nye, *Masculinity and Male Codes of Honor in Modern France* (Berkeley: University of California Press, 1998).

[40] On the use of the Napoleonic legend for profit during an earlier period, see Samuels, 143–145.

[41] Lehning, 55.

its evocation of the grandeur of the imperial period.[42] Explicit in this statement was a disdain of the mediocrity of contemporary political leaders. Writing in the monarchist *Le Gaulois* of November 21, 1893, Gaston Jollivet observed that at no other time in French history had the public been more disposed to interest in seeing "men and events of the monarchy," particularly in light of such recent scandals as the Panama Affair. It is interesting to note that a royalist was here laying claim to the Napoleonic legacy, but this development reflected, in part, the Bonapartist alliance with royalists. For Jollivet, the last twenty years of the republican regime, which he defined as "prosaic," were incompatible with "our national genius" and thus contributed to the people's desire for refuge in the fictions of the theater.[43]

This reference to fiction and, moreover, to the theater is telling. Not only was a more literary Napoleon emerging at this time, but the theater, in particular, seemed to be a special vehicle for the popularity of the Napoleonic legend, a view echoed by John Grand-Carteret, the author of *L'Aiglon en images dans la fiction poétique et dramatique*.[44] Like other observers of the time, Grand-Carteret explained the popularity of the legend in the theater as essentially a product of democracy, denigrating the general public as the "eternal mob" and condemning its desire to consume historical images without having to think seriously about the consequences of historical events. Sounding like certain commentators of our own day who deplore the popularity of television and the internet to the detriment of reading, Grand-Carteret claimed that the "crowd" expected to be entertained without being challenged.[45]

Grand-Carteret's elitist comments are revelatory of the ambivalence felt by many contemporaries, both conservative and progressive, about democratization and the arrival of mass consumer society. Despite their different perspectives on bourgeois modernity, republicans and antirepublicans often agreed about the dangers of consumer culture, although the latter associated their attacks on consumerism with the corruption of the republic.[46]

---

[42] Félicien Pascal, *La Libre Parole*, 28 October 1893.

[43] Gaston Jollivet, "La Monarchie au théâtre," *Le Gaulois*, 21 November 1893.

[44] John Grand-Carteret, *L'Aiglon en images dans la fiction poétique et dramatique* (Paris: Charpentier et Fasquelle, 1901), 8.

[45] Grand-Carteret, 11.

[46] On the female consumer as a potential social danger, see Lisa Tiersten, *Marianne in the Market: Envisioning Consumer Society in Fin-de-siècle France* (Berkeley: University of California Press, 1998), 16.

L'Aiglon (Acte II) *Leçon de tactique*
Le Duc de Reichstadt (Mᵐᵉ Sarah-Bernhardt) et les petits soldats de bois

FIGURE 3.3. Sarah Bernhardt with Napoleonic artifacts on the set of *L'Aiglon*, courtesy of the BNF.

Other commentators also noted the commercialism that accompanied the Napoleonic cult, including Magnard, who referred to the popularity of not only First Empire furniture but also Napoleonic relics: "Today, the Napoleonic cult is widespread, simultaneously illustrated and reinforced by the commercial spirit of well-informed merchants."[47] Sarah Bernhardt bought Napoleonic artifacts at considerable expense to make the sets of *L'Aiglon* more authentic (See Figure 3.3.).[48] Grand-Carteret himself added that in the wake of Rostand's play, merchants wishing to capitalize on the craze were hawking "Aiglon writing paper" and "Aiglon candies," just as they had capitalized on the popularity of *Cyrano* two years earlier.[49] Ironically, the commercialism that was in part responsible for the revival of the Napoleonic cult was also cited

[47] Magnard, 106. Wyzewa too noted the commercial nature of the cult, citing the popularity of the Empire style, 728.
[48] Marc Andry, *Edmond Rostand: Le Panache et la gloire* (Paris: Plon, 1986), 101.
[49] Grand-Carteret, 2.

by many writers as the reason that France needed heroes. In a materialist age, the hero represented "disinterestedness" and public good. For these individuals, the Napoleonic legend, a symbol from their past, alleviated their anxieties even as purveyors of the legend like Sardou and Rostand capitalized on the development of mass consumption to sell their works.

Les Déracinés

Maurice Barrès initially saw in Boulanger a national unifier, a man above political factions, and, moreover, a bulwark against parliamentary machinations, a view he expressed in an 1888 article entitled "M. le Général Boulanger et la nouvelle génération."[50] He wrote of his disappointment in *L'Appel au soldat*, which chronicles the Boulangist saga.[51] Disillusionment about Boulanger, the would-be Napoleon, led Barrès, like Gyp, back to the original. In *Les Déracinés* (1897), Barrès devoted a chapter to Napoleon that is one of the most powerful encomiums ever written to the late emperor. In it he sends his young Lorrainers, recently arrived in Paris, on a pilgrimage to Napoleon's tomb, underlining the emperor's particular appeal to youth: "Napoleon's tomb, for twenty-year old French men, is not a place of peace … it is the crossroads of all energies, which we call audacity, will, and appetite."[52] To these "grandsons of the soldiers of the *Grande Armée*," seeking to reconcile their thoughts with meaningful action, Napoleon represents a worthy example.[53]

Barrès spoke in *Les Déracinés* not of the Napoleon of history, described by artists, historians, and writers, but rather of myth, *le Napoléon de l'âme* (the Napoleon of the soul), who has the power to "electrify souls" throughout the ages. He is, in Barrès's words, "an exciter of spirits" who inspires others to action.[54]

Barrès also claimed that Napoleon, unlike the protagonists of the novel, remained true to his origins and ideas, even when it meant forsaking his teachers. Barrès was referring here not only to his young *déracinés*, who must rid themselves of the uprooting influence of their neo-Kantian teacher Bouteiller, but also to himself and his increasing distance from his own *maîtres* Hippolyte Taine and Ernest Renan. For

---

[50] Barrès, *La Revue indépendante* (April 1888), 59–60.
[51] Barrès, *L'Appel au soldat* (Paris: Plon, 1926), 226.
[52] Maurice Barrès, *Les Déracinés* (Paris: Union Générale d'éditions, 10/18, 1986), 165.
[53] Barrès, *Les Déracinés*, 174.
[54] Barrès, *Les Déracinés*, 167–168.

Barrès, Napoleon, who married his ideas to action, represented the ideal hero, as did the poet-statesman Victor Hugo. In contrast with the young men, who are lost in a "disassociated," "decerebrated," and "feminized" France, Napoleon, the virile hero, established order in a country that had been thrown into chaos during the Revolution. In Barrès's view, the Third Republic, as it was conceived by Opportunist politicians, similarly represented such chaos; hence his search for a hero, who, like Napoleon, could restore France to order and glory.

One of the most influential books of the time, *Les Déracinés* marked an important step in the transformation of the Napoleonic legend during the fin de siècle. It further confirmed the emergence of a personal Napoleon of the soul, divorced from history, a figure to be shaped according to each individual's needs. Yet it also presented Napoleon as a touchstone for both personal and national identity.[55] Furthermore, *Les Déracinés* marked the appropriation of the Napoleonic legend by an opponent of the Third Republic. Although Barrès, unlike some of his nationalist friends, was a republican, he opposed the parliamentary form the new republic had taken as well as the universalism it espoused. *Les Déracinés* was a critique of contemporary France, run, according to Barrès, from Paris by Freemasons, Jews, and Protestants. Barrès wanted to return to a more traditional France, rooted in the soil and the blood of his ancestors. For Barrès, the Napoleon of the soul could provide the unity and glory sorely lacking in the present day. Barrès may have been a republican, but his portrait of Napoleon contributed to the disassociation of Napoleon from the revolutionary legacy, setting the stage for the emergence, in the wake of *L'Aiglon*'s success, of an integral nationalist Napoleon, presented nevertheless as "above politics."

The representation of Napoleon in Barrès's novel also mirrored anxieties about consumer culture, itself embedded in notions of gender during the period. Barrès was especially sensitive to the "crisis of masculinity" engendered by the loss of national honor in the war as well as the perceived threats of consumerism. According to contemporaries, the feminization of society through consumerism led to widespread materialism, hedonistic excess, and individualism, qualities opposed to the male disinterestedness and selflessness of heroes.[56] Even Barrès's opponent in the

---

[55] See David Carroll on Barrès's presentation of both a personal and national Napoleon: *French Literary Fascism: Nationalism, Anti-Semitism and the Ideology of Culture* (Princeton, NJ: Princeton University Press, 1995), 39.

[56] Rita Felski, *The Gender of Modernity* (Cambridge, MA: Harvard University Press, 1995), 19.

Dreyfus Affair, Emile Zola, expressed this widespread fear. Yet as in the case of Cyrano and Joan, although Napoleon was represented as the antidote to consumer society, the Napoleonic cult was fueled by the same consumerism.

Barrès, like other intellectuals, both conservative and progressive, feared the democratization of society in which the plebian tastes of the masses would diminish the power of intellect in society; hence his search for "an intellectual Bonaparte." Such defensiveness on the part of intellectuals resulted from the increasing marginal position of literature and arts in a materialist society that associated masculinity with action, enterprise, and progress.[57] During the Third Republic, democratization was also accompanied by bureaucratization. For Barrès, middle-class men, out of touch with the land and confined to airless offices in Paris, had lost their virility. Napoleon harkened back to a time when French men were rooted in the soil and the land, leaving it only to go off to war.[58] Indeed, the rise of the neurasthenic male is one of the major themes of Max Nordau's best-selling *Degeneration*, translated into French in 1894. The professor of energy exalted by Barrès represented virility and potency at a time when some French men, troubled with neurasthenia, had lost theirs. In fact, energy was a code word for virility and potency.

At a time that witnessed the apotheosis of the military hero, Napoleon was the ultimate hero. Not only was he a symbol of France's victories, but he was also a virile man on horseback – a sexual image certainly not lost on contemporaries of the fin de siècle. Napoleon also represented the glory of the Empire, which could, depending on one's views, either be compared to or contrasted with the Third Republic's attempts to expand its own empire overseas in the colonies.[59] Finally, at a time when women threatened to blur gender lines and enter into the male, public sphere, Napoleon was a familiar and reassuring symbol of France's past glory and a society in which French men ruled both at home and abroad.

[57] Felski, 90, and Andreas Huyssen, *After the Great Divide: Modernism, Mass Culture, Postmodernism* (Bloomington: Indiana University Press, 1986), 45. For reactions of intellectuals to democratization, see Datta, *Birth of a National Icon,* "Chapter 3: Aristocrat or Proletarian? Intellectuals and Elites in Fin-de-Siècle France," 65–84.

[58] See Karen Offen on the fascination of Barrès and other intellectuals for the military: "Depopulation, Nationalism, and Feminism in Fin-de-Siècle France," *American Historical Review* 89, no. 3 (June 1984): 548–676.

[59] I owe this observation to Professor Robin Walz of the University of Alaska Southeast.

L'Aiglon

Interest in the Napoleonic legend peaked with Rostand's *L'Aiglon* in 1900. *L'Aiglon* marked the climax of the development of a more literary Napoleon, moreover, of an image that could be made to fit an individual vision. Indeed, anti-Dreyfusards like Jules Lemaître, writing about the play, although claiming to view Napoleon above politics, essentially presented a conservative vision of the emperor, one that was not necessarily intended by Rostand himself.

Writing in 1894, Francis Magnard had explained the search for heroes as a desire for "panache."[60] The use of the word "panache" is prescient because the word was subsequently associated with Edmond Rostand's *Cyrano de Bergerac*. A large part of Cyrano's universal appeal was due to his combining the qualities of an intellectual hero with those of a brave soldier. Rostand's *L'Aiglon*, which had a similar success on the Parisian stage two years after *Cyrano*, fed on the same desire for heroes, particularly in a France divided by the Affair.

In this best-known of fin-de-siècle works with a Napoleonic theme, Rostand told the story of Napoleon's son the Duke of Reichstadt (1811–1832), who died prematurely of tuberculosis at the age of twenty-one. Napoleon's nephew Louis-Napoleon was anathema to most of those inspired by the Napoleonic legend. He represented the sordidness and deception of reality, but Napoleon's son was an unknown who could embody all the hopes of those inspired by the legend. They could shamelessly indulge themselves in the fantasy of what might have been. Historians who had studied Napoleon II had been unable to reach conclusions about his personality and ambitions.[61] Thus, the French people, through Rostand, were free to speculate about the young man. Did this "French prince," transplanted to a foreign court, miss his "native land"? Did he dream of returning to France in glory? Did he suffer from the same "mal du siècle" as other young men of his generation?[62] The French public, faced with a weakened France, indulged in speculation, thus making the play a resounding popular, if not always critical, success.

---

[60] Magnard, 108.

[61] Frédéric Masson, who had earlier exchanged barbs with Sardou, wrote petulantly that "poets have all the rights" in an article in which he criticized the accuracy of Rostand's sources on the duke: "L'Aiglon," *La Revue de Paris*, no. 7 (1 April 1900): 585 and 598.

[62] These questions were asked by critic René Doumic in his review of the play. Doumic's review was originally published in *La Revue des deux mondes* 158 (1 April 1900): 698–703, and was reprinted in a volume entitled *Le Théâtre nouveau* (Paris: Perrin, 1908), 332–339.

As renowned critic Emile Faguet noted, the play was at times melodramatic and overly precious, yet it was undeniably moving.[63]

The action of the play takes place from 1830 to 1832, first in Baden in a villa occupied by the former Empress Marie-Louise (daughter of Emperor Franz II of Austria, and mother of the duke) and then in the Schoenbrunn palace, where the duke is a virtual prisoner. The play, as critics noted, does not really progress; the duke hesitates in the last act, just as he does in the first. What Rostand strives to depict is the young man's hopes and dreams. We witness his discovery of his father's feats – he must learn of them in secret, because his Austrian tutor refuses to speak of them. Throughout the course of the play, the duke insists on his French blood and rejects his Austrian heritage.[64] Such a depiction of Napoleon II must certainly have appealed to French audiences of the time.

At the beginning of the play, a member of the "Jeune France" movement offers to help the duke escape to Paris. At first, the duke refuses. Instead, he attempts, during a meeting interrupted by Metternich, to persuade his grandfather to let him assume the French throne. The following acts depict his meeting with Flambeau, a former *grognard* sent by his French admirers to watch over him in the guise of a servant. The duke finally agrees to participate in the plot to escape (from a masked ball no less!) to France and reclaim his throne. In the end, however, he hesitates, in order to protect a young woman who is in love with him. The play ends in the fantastic, on the plains of Wagram, the scene of one of his father's most glorious and costly victories (the French lost 34,000 men, the Austrians, 50,000). In it, the ghosts of Napoleonic soldiers rise up to show the duke their wounds and cry "Long live the Emperor!" The duke understands then that he must die to expiate the massacres committed by his father. The scene is melodramatic (the ghosts sing the *Marseillaise* at one point), but contemporary audiences were truly moved. As the play closes, the duke dies in agony, thereby giving the "divine Sarah" the opportunity to die onstage, a feat she also performed as Joan of Arc (Figures 3.4 and 3.5).

It is an interesting irony that *L'Aiglon* should mark the height of the Napoleonic cult, because the young Napoleon II, unlike his father, was

---

[63] Emile Faguet, *Propos de Théâtre*, 4ème série (Paris: Société française d'imprimerie et de librairie, 1907), 354–360. The review was originally published on 10 March 1900. Gustave Larroumet described the play as "not very dramatic but eminently poetic" in his review originally published in *Le Temps* of 19 March 1900 and reprinted in *Etudes de critique dramatique*, vol. 2 (Paris: Hachette, 1906), 246.

[64] Edmond Rostand, *L'Aiglon* (Paris: Charpentier et Fasquelle, 1900).

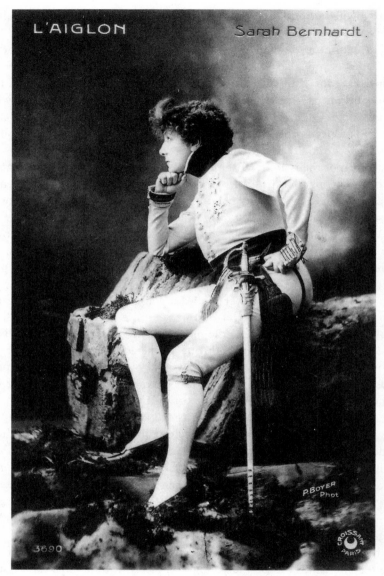

FIGURE 3.4. Sarah Bernhardt as the Duke of Reichstadt in Edmond Rostand's *L'Aiglon*, courtesy of the BNF.

a would-be man of action, unable to act because he was paralyzed by both his dreams and heritage. He rather resembled the sickly characters afflicted with neurasthenia who people the novels and plays of the period. Indeed, he has more in common with Barrès's "déracinés" than

FIGURE 3.5. A cartoon by Sem.
Caption (top): On The Battlefield of Wagram. Caption (bottom): M. Edmond Rostand to Napoleon: "Come sir, a little effort. Decorate both of them!" Courtesy of the BNF.

with the "professors of energy" who served as Barrès's heroes. One critic even described him as "devoid of energy."[65] But perhaps one can see in him a tragic hero, as did Bernhardt, who compared him to Hamlet. Contemporary audiences also viewed him as a sacrificial figure, not unlike the image of Napoleon himself following his defeat at Waterloo and exile to Saint Helena. The suffering hero was in fact a leitmotiv at the time, with such anti-Dreyfusard heroes as Colonel Henry and Dreyfusard ones as Zola, Picquart, and Dreyfus himself exalted as Christ-like figures.[66]

[65] Romain Coolus, "Notes dramatiques," *La Revue blanche* 21 (1 April 1900): 549.

[66] Dreyfus was, of course, cast by anti-Dreyfusards as a Judas. See Christopher E. Forth, "Sanctifying Dreyfus: Intellectuals, Jews, and the Body of Christ," pp. 67–102 in *The Dreyfus Affair and the Crisis of French Manhood* (Baltimore, MD: Johns Hopkins University Press, 2004). The celebrations of the St-Napoleon on 15 August, promoted by the First Empire with the help of the Vatican and continued under the Second Empire, further contributed to this image of Napoleon; see Hazareesingh, *The Saint-Napoleon*; Day-Hickman, 84–110, and Frank Bowman, "Napoleon as a Christ Figure," in *French Romanticism: Intertextual and Interdisciplinary Readings* (Baltimore, MD: Johns Hopkins University Press, 1990), 34–60.

In a similar vein, Cyrano and Christian were Christ-like heroes, as was Joan of Arc. But this view of sacrifice could also be used to impugn the manhood of both Napoleon and his son, as it was by Romain Coolus, the ardently Dreyfusard drama critic of *La Revue blanche*. Reflecting on the brutality of Napoleon – in particular, of the military hero – Coolus noted with satisfaction that Napoleon, the conquering hero, was unable to himself create one from his own loins:

Son of a father who assassinated all the joy in the world, and who desired – although without really wanting it – to become himself the Murderer, the Killer, the Hero, according to stupid human standards; who all of a sudden feels and understands himself to be destined for impotence, condemned to physical degeneration and moral misery, expiatory victim, host, because it is only just that the man whose glorious and detestable function it was to kill men was not able himself to create a real man.[67]

Another irony of *L'Aiglon* was that a woman, and a Jew at that, was playing the role of the duke. Given l'Aiglon's neurasthenia, a trait associated with the "feminine," perhaps this association seemed natural to audiences of the time. The theater was one of the few spaces in the arts that allowed women a key role, probably because acting was seen as imitative and reproductive rather than original and productive.[68] Moreover, Sarah Bernhardt used cross-dressing to express anxiety and impotence, thus making it easier for audiences who felt uneasy about transvestite parts to accept her playing male roles.[69] Interestingly enough, however, most accounts depicted Sarah Bernhardt's strength and force in the role, two characteristics at odds with the duke's weaknesses – a case that would also be made with regard to her Joan of Arc. Perhaps then, dressing as a man could not only be seen as an accommodation of gender roles, given that l'Aiglon was weak and "effeminate," but also as a subversion of them,

---

[67] Coolus, 549.

[68] Huyssen, 51. On another note, actresses were seen by critics of mass culture as symptoms of the pervasiveness of illusion and spectacle in modern life; see Felski, 20.

[69] Lenard Berlanstein, "Breeches and Breaches: Cross-Dress Theater and the Culture of Gender Ambiguity in Modern France," *Comparative Studies in Society and History* 38, no. 2 (April 1996): 362. See also Berlanstein's *Daughers of Eve: A Cultural History of French Theater Women from the Old Regime to the Fin-de-Siècle* (Cambridge, MA: Harvard University Press, 2001). The actress Virginie Déjazet had already played the duke in Pillaud de Forges and Eugène Sue's 1830–1831 production *Le Fils de l'homme*: Samuels, 135. She had earlier portrayed the young Napoleon in *Bonaparte à l'école de Brienne*. See Barbara Day-Hickman, "Cross Dress Actress Virginie Déjazet and the Napoleonic Legend during the July Monarchy," paper presented at the French Historical Studies Conference, Tempe, Arizona, April 2010.

because for the writers of the feminist *La Fronde*, Bernhardt represented the possibility of transcending, even overcoming, gender differences.[70]

Surprising too is the relative silence in the anti-Semitic press about Bernhardt's Jewish background. *La Libre Parole*, on previous occasions, had certainly taken potshots at the actress. When reviewing the play, the newspaper's critic praised Rostand's work, commenting on Bernhardt only to say that at age fifty-five, she was a bit long in the tooth to be playing the role of a young man.[71] That *L'Aiglon* was seen as a nationalist work may have made it awkward for journalists even at *La Libre Parole* to carp about the Jewish origins of the play's lead. In some sense, that a Jew should portray Napoleon's son was fitting, because the Napoleonic legacy emphasized inclusion and national unity above all.

Such tensions, although not lost on the audiences of the time, did not prevent *L'Aiglon* from becoming a huge success. It undoubtedly appealed not only to France's wounded pride at no longer being the most powerful and populous country in Europe but also to the nation's sense of glory. If Napoleon II was a would-be man of action, the real hero of the play was the aptly named Flambeau, who represented not only France's heroism on the field of battle but also her civilizing mission. Such a representation of a soldier and the army was important during a time when the army's value was being questioned. Rostand managed to praise the army and thus win the support of most nationalists without incurring the ire of Dreyfusards (with some exceptions), many of whom also claimed to venerate the army and believed themselves to be true patriots.

Whereas the two different visions of the hero, as intellectual and as soldier, had been represented by one individual in *Cyrano de Bergerac*, these two ideals were embodied by two different characters in *L'Aiglon*, although a strong case could be made for Flambeau as both an intellectual and a military hero; it is he, after all, who organizes the plot for the duke's escape to France. Yet in common with the earlier play, despite the fact that one of its major themes was politics, *L'Aiglon* was viewed as being above politics and seen as a means of national reconciliation.

---

[70] Roberts, *Disruptive Acts: The New Woman in Fin-de-Siècle France* (Chicago: University of Chicago Press, 2002), 178–179.

[71] Maurice Ordonneau, "Chronique dramatique," *La Libre Parole*, 16 March 1900. In *Disruptive Acts*, Mary Louise Roberts mentions an anti-Semitic review by Dom Blasius from *L'Intransigeant* of 17 March 1900. I myself did not come across too many anti-Semitic references in the press with regard to *L'Aiglon*. For more on Bernhardt's Jewish identity and anti-Semitism, see Roberts, *Disruptive Acts*, 210–213, as well as 107–130 on "The New Woman and the Jew."

Thus, despite the mixed reviews it received, *L'Aiglon* was a huge hit – performed 235 times in 1900 alone – earning Rostand nearly as much money as he had made from *Cyrano de Bergerac*.

Like Sardou, Rostand had a keen eye for what would appeal to fin-de-siècle audiences. The ambiguity of the duke's character allowed for widely differing interpretations of the play. Was Rostand exalting Napoleon's bloody legacy or deploring it? Or perhaps a bit of both? A moderate Dreyfusard, Rostand, like Sardou, was part of the republican establishment, *Cyrano* having earned him a Legion of Honor and other accolades (eventually, it secured his election to the French Academy). As he asserted in an interview with Ange Galdemar, published in *Le Gaulois* of March 7, 1900, he had grown up with the legend; in fact, a portrait of the young duke hung in his room when he was a child. Although Rostand was undoubtedly captivated by the legend, as a good republican, he must have been aware of the negative consequences of the Napoleonic legacy. The figure of l'Aiglon not only appealed to his poetic imagination, but the son of Napoleon could also provide Rostand with a way to represent his reservations in a sympathetic manner. In any case, the playwright was clearly attempting to use the Napoleonic legacy to celebrate French grandeur and as a means of national reconciliation, offering a little of something for everyone.

But Rostand vehemently denied writing a Bonapartist or overtly political work in a letter addressed to the French ambassador to Germany, following Prince Metternich's complaint that the play maligned his father. In the letter, written on March 3, 1899, and subsequently published in *Le Figaro* of July 21, 1902, Rostand claimed to have created a play for art's sake, without regard for party politics: "My play is a lyrical, fictional work, not a political pamphlet like a poem by Barthélemy and Méry." Indeed, the following lines, which precede the written version of the play, seem to confirm this (naïve) belief: "Good God! It is not a cause / That I attack or defend / And this is nothing but / The story of a poor child."[72]

In some ways, the reception of *L'Aiglon* corresponded to the author's expectations, but he must have been taken aback by the co-opting of the play by enemies of the parliamentary republic. In "La Légende au thé-âtre," published in *Le Gaulois* of March 6, 1900, Paul Costard noted that *L'Aiglon* united republicans and Bonapartists, who forgot their past bitter quarrels in order to place in the enigmatic figure of the roi de Rome their common hopes and dreams. Jules Delafosse, Costard's colleague at

---

[72] *L'Aiglon*, title page.

Le Gaulois and a Boulangist deputy, also marveled at the play's ability to unite, especially in the wake of the Dreyfus Affair.[73] Surprisingly, instead of dividing public opinion, the exact opposite occurred: "From the orchestra seats to the uppermost balcony, the reaction was the same, and one witnessed Jacobins, socialists, intellectuals and other anti-militarist categories rival with their enthusiasm the most fervent nationalists."[74]

These critics all explained the play's success in similar terms, taking their cue from Jules Lemaître, president of the anti-Dreyfusard Ligue de la Patrie Française and exemplar of the Ligue's conservative, academic anti-Dreyfusism. No friend of the republicans in power, Lemaître characterized the popularity of *L'Aiglon* as a sort of revenge: "There is, first of all, in the pleasure given us by these memories, an exhilaration of national pride, the joy of having once been the strongest. ... Our present-day weakness exacerbates our retrospective sense of pride. The wars of the Empire seem to us a revenge in anticipation of other wars ... because France, during the last twenty years, has been far from brilliant, we have witnessed under the Third Republic a revival of the Napoleonic cult."[75] According to Delafosse, *L'Aiglon* recalled the glories of the Empire at a time of mediocrity: "the theater-going public consoles and avenges itself, without realizing it perhaps, against the ignominies of the present day by acclaiming past glories." The taste for *L'Aiglon*, he concluded, was part of "a sentimental protest movement ... against our decline as a people."[76]

Lemaître noted that the most admired scenes of the play were those that celebrated Napoleon's military glories, but he observed that the acclamation for the emperor was based not only on his military might but also on his having inspired French men to prefer glory to life and to sacrifice themselves for noble ideals. Implicit in this statement was the belief that Third Republic politicians had little hope of inspiring such sacrifice. Lemaître felt that the character of Flambeau illustrated to the public that "the formidable egoism of the Emperor was enabled by admirable self-denial, that the work of domination and pride ... was also a work of sacrifice and love."[77] In this way, Lemaître attempted

---

[73] Jules Delafosse, "Le Culte des héros," *Le Gaulois*, 28 March 1900. Delafosse (1843–1916), who served as deputy for Calvados from 1877 to 1898 and again from 1902 to 1916, succeeded Paul de Cassagnac as the Imperialist columnist at *Le Matin* in 1886: Offen, *Cassagnac*, 290.

[74] Delafosse, "Le Culte des héros."

[75] Jules Lemaître, "Drame nationaliste," *L'Echo de Paris*, 19 March 1900.

[76] Delafosse, "Le Culte des héros."

[77] Lemaître, "Drame nationaliste."

to diminish the selfishness of the late emperor, because heroes were by definition selfless, their sacrifices made for the greater good of the nation.

Conservative Catholic commentator Joseph Cornély took a rather unorthodox view of *L'Aiglon*, observing in *Le Figaro* of March 22, 1900, that the play, which, on first glance, had seemed a Bonapartist work, did not at all exalt Napoleon's victories in war. If it were to wage war, France could not ask for a better general than Napoleon, but the play was actually a disincentive to war, because it showed that these victories had decimated the French male population. At the beginning of the nineteenth century, he noted, France had been the most populous nation on the continent but was now reduced to fourth place.[78] This argument did not sway critics of the play, nor did Lemaître's claim that the play united the actors of the Affair, such that even republican politicians "applauded like us":

At last, this drama made us experience the beneficial effect and pleasures of unanimity. During four hours, marked by the clock, revolutionaries and conservatives, Jacobins and liberals, parliamentarians and plebiscitarians, and those who during the Affair had one opinion and those who had the opposite opinion, quivered together with the same patriotic passion.[79]

Although many republican politicians applauded *L'Aiglon*, others, like Urbain Gohier, writing in the Dreyfusard newspaper *L'Aurore*, did not. The play might be a beautiful literary work, he observed, but it was certainly a bad political one. Although he admitted that Rostand was no admirer of brutal force or of war, Gohier claimed that his play was Bonapartist propaganda and prepared the way for a coup. Ardently antimilitarist and anti-clerical, Gohier felt that the Napoleonic legend, which he described as the tail end of Boulangism, had "infested" the theater of the time.[80] Charles Martel, theater critic of *L'Aurore*, was more nuanced. He praised Rostand's artistry and admired many of the scenes of the play, but he too found it strange that Rostand should present Napoleon, "the assassin of all liberties," as a friend of liberty. Without being Bonapartist, *L'Aiglon* celebrated the "sinister" Bonaparte. Yet Martel also noted that the nostalgia for the Empire was strictly a literary phenomenon. The Third

---

[78] Joseph Cornély, "L'Aiglon rend-il nationaliste?" *Le Figaro*, 22 March 1900. A monarchist, Cornély, the editor of *Le Clairon*, had earlier urged Cassagnac to rally publicly to the monarchist cause, specifically to the Comte de Paris.

[79] Lemaître, "Drame nationaliste."

[80] Urbain Gohier, "L'Aiglon," *L'Aurore*, 15 March 1900.

Republic was here to stay; the only way to witness a "retour des cendres" (revival of the Napoleonic legend) was in the theater.[81]

The reactions of Dreyfusards need to be situated within the context of the previous success of *Cyrano de Bergerac*. Although the earlier play had united Dreyfusards and anti-Dreyfusards, certain members of the avant-garde, many of them associated with *L'Aurore* and *La Fronde*, had approached the play warily, in part because among its most ardent admirers were anti-Dreyfusards.[82] Couched in this praise of Rostand and *Cyrano* was criticism of the literary avant-garde and its predilection for foreign "Northern" literatures (German and Scandinavian). Referring to this situation, Jane Misme, writing on *L'Aiglon* in *La Fronde* of March 16, 1900, observed that to applaud *L'Aiglon* as one had *Cyrano* would be to attack avant-garde writers and their clientele of cosmopolitans and Dreyfusards. Misme did not hold Rostand personally responsible, because one could not always choose one's friends.[83] Nevertheless, those who had the greatest praise for the play were conservatives, who had earlier celebrated *Cyrano* as a welcome antidote to the commercial and industrial literature of the time. Such a view presented by these conservatives must have been doubly insulting for members of the avant-garde, who themselves claimed to be the true alternative to such literature, because *Cyrano* had earned its author renown and fortune even as it decried those things. The success of *L'Aiglon* only aggravated matters.

To some extent, *L'Aiglon* foreshadowed the nationalist revival that took place in light of the increasing threat from Germany in the years immediately preceding the First World War. Furthermore, like Sardou's *Madame Sans-Gêne*, *L'Aiglon* proved, despite its author's intentions, that the Napoleonic legend best served the political aims of the opponents of the parliamentary republic. Indeed, Gyp's *Napoléonette* amply illustrated the success of integral nationalists in appropriating the Napoleonic legend. Published in 1913, on the eve of the First World War, it represents to some extent the Napoleonic legend's last hurrah. The butchery of the war would again raise the specter of Napoleon the warmonger responsible for the massacre of an earlier generation of French men.[84]

---

[81] Charles Martel, "Théâtres," *L'Aurore*, 16 March 1900.
[82] See Emile Faguet's review in *Le Journal des débats*, 3 January 1898, and that of Jules Lemaître in *La Revue des deux mondes* (1898), 695.
[83] Jane Misme, "Le Nationalisme en littérature," *La Fronde*, 16 March 1900.
[84] Gildea, 106.

Napoléonette

Like her friend Barrès, Gyp (the pseudonym of Sibylle-Gabrielle Marie-Antoinette de Riquetti de Mirabeau, comtesse de Martel de Janville), the anti-Semitic writer of popular novels, was a nationalist, but unlike Barrès, she came from a family of Legitimists. In common with her friend and other contemporaries in search of an ideal hero for a decadent age, she was fascinated by "Le brav' Général," who appeared in a number of her writings. Although Boulangism proved illusory, she could still take comfort in the figure of Napoleon, who represented the antithesis of such Third Republic politicians as Jules Grévy, the French president forced to resign in the wake of a scandal involving his son-in-law in 1887. In Gyp's eyes, not only was the Third Republic inefficient and corrupt, but it was also cowardly, in that it refused to engage in *revanche*. She also faulted the Republic for not having properly integrated the working class into its society and culture. Napoleon, of course, represented the great unifier, one who could integrate all elements of French society into a great and glorious nation.[85]

Gyp, like other writers of her time, had grown up with Napoleonic lore; for Gyp, however, such lore had personal dimensions because her beloved grandfather Colonel Aymard Olivier Le Harivel de Gonneville, a royalist, had served in the Imperial Army. During her childhood in Nancy, a garrison city, Gyp listened avidly to his war stories. So obsessed was she by Napoleon that she claimed to share his birth date (in fact, there was a difference of a day). In many ways, Gyp's *Napoléonette*, dedicated to Frédéric Masson, was her ideal biography; she herself played the lead role and that of her suitor was modeled on her grandfather.[86]

Napoléonette told the story of a young girl, the daughter of a Napoleonic soldier from a family of *ultras*, who passes herself off as a young boy, Léo de Sérignan.[87] The godchild of the emperor himself, she is forced to give up her masquerade and leave the army in order to live with her uncle, who serves as *Maître du Palais* to Louis XVIII in the Tuileries Palace. Before she leaves the field of battle, she meets a young royalist, Jean de Chalindrey, who dresses her wounds. Although he is a royalist, he

[85] Willa Z. Silverman, *The Notorious Life of Gyp: Right-Wing Anarchist in Fin-de-Siècle France* (New York: Oxford University Press, 1994), 88–91.

[86] See Willa Z. Silverman, "Mythic Representations of Napoleon in the Life and Works of Gyp," *Correspondances: Studies in Literature, History, and the Arts in Nineteenth-Century France*, ed. Keith Busby (Amsterdam: Rodopoi, 1992), 203–212.

[87] Could this be a tip of the hat to Figueur and other women who had dressed as men to join the emperor in battle?

has served in the emperor's army because, as he explains to her, "before being a royalist, I am first French: There are no longer, once they are in rank, royalists, imperialists, or republicans, but only soldiers who fulfill their duty without afterthought, because they are French and because they love their country."[88] Léo and Chalindrey are attracted to each other, although the latter is frankly puzzled by his feelings for a young boy.

The novel depicts Napoléonette's life at the court of Louis XVIII. Although the king is described as a kindly old man who befriends Napoléonette, his courtiers are castigated as sycophantic, hypocritical, and self-centered. A greater contrast could not be made with Napoleon's rule. Even the king himself admits: "Glory will never have anything in common with me or with my reign."[89] As for Napoléonette herself, she, like her godfather, is intrepid, honest, courageous, and lively. The novel ends with Napoléonette's foiling a plot against the king's life and marrying Jean de Chalindrey. In this way, Gyp "married" two of France's traditions, the monarchy and the Empire, and thereby reconciled her personal fascination for Napoleon with her Legitimist background.[90]

Although Napoleon himself only appears very briefly at the beginning of the novel, he overshadows the entire work, undoubtedly reflecting Gyp's view of Napoleon's role in French history. Moreover, her Napoleon, like that of Barrès, is both a personalized image and an essentially conservative figure, disconnected from his revolutionary legacy, despite the fact that Gyp herself was the granddaughter of the revolutionary orator the comte de Mirabeau.

Perhaps the most fascinating aspect of Gyp's novel is her equation of the novel's female heroine with Napoleon. Like her namesake, Napoléonette represented Gyp's heroic ideal, embodying such "masculine" virtues as bravery, physical force, and charisma. The case of Gyp, a female writer, a self-proclaimed feminist who felt uneasy with her own femininity and who loathed her typically "feminine" peers, is especially interesting because she endowed her female heroines with the heroic male traits she herself longed for. Her sexual uneasiness is reflected in many of her novels, not only in female characters disguised as men but also by her giving a male identity to one of her most popular characters, "le petit Bob." Willa Silverman notes in her biography of Gyp that the figure of Napoleon allowed Gyp to project personal fantasies onto the national

[88] Gyp, *Napoléonette* (Paris: Calmann-Lévy, 1913), 14 and 32.
[89] Gyp, *Napoléonette*, 331.
[90] Silverman, "Mythic Representations of Napoleon," 212.

plane. Her fascination with Napoleon was born of a need for a father figure as well as her desire to associate herself with the male traits prized by her family, who had hoped for a boy.[91] On a national level, a virile hero like Napoleon would prevent the "feminization" – read democratization – of France. Yet Gyp, like Barrès, was drawn to Boulangism, which represented the first instance of mass party politics in France. Moreover, in common with Sardou and Rostand, she profited from the very democratization she deplored, for her best-selling novels appealed to a newly formed reading public, just as Rostand and Sardou's plays did.

Conclusion

The various works that made use of the Napoleonic legend during the fin de siècle illustrate both the popularity and ambiguity of the Napoleonic legend. Not only did the Napoleonic legend appeal to writers of varying political persuasions during the fin de siècle, but more important, it struck a chord with the French public of this period, hungry for heroes and for a revival of France's past glories. The popularity of the legend, rooted in a familiar and glorious era, should not be surprising in an age that witnessed great change, most notably, the advent of a modern, mass consumer society. Ironically, the Napoleonic vogue alleviated the fear of such a society even as it fueled the commercialism it decried. Furthermore, in contrast with the legacy of the French Revolution, which was hotly contested, the legacy of the Napoleonic legend was more easily incorporated into national memory. Although Bonapartism was rejected, Napoleon himself became an integral part of the national self-image. For a nation weary of the infighting represented by the revolutionary legacy, this divorce from party politics was crucial. In this sense, the Napoleonic phenomenon was more literary than historical. Although the litterateur had clearly won against the historian in the struggle to co-opt the legend, it still remained embedded in politics in the larger sense of the term. French men and women were less interested in the facts than in an image of Napoleon they could fashion to their own needs and desires, political and cultural. Napoleon's example also served as a promise for the future at a time when heroes seemed conspicuously absent in French life.

As they did with Cyrano, contemporaries sought a virile but humanized hero for the democratic age. This hero, however, was not a typical

---

[91] Silverman, "Mythic Representations of Napoleon," 208.

manly figure but rather a husband fearing he might be cuckolded in *Mme Sans-Gêne*; a young neurasthenic who strived to live up to his father's legacy – a character played, moreover, by a woman – in *L'Aiglon*; or a young girl disguised as a boy, in *Napoléonette*. The Napoleonic legend and the manly hero were thus destabilized by authors of the fin de siècle. Similar gender ambiguity surrounded the Joan of Arc cult at this time. But whereas masculinity had been subverted in the Napoleonic legend by novelists and playwrights, it was the traditional image of femininity that would be destabilized in Sarah Bernhardt's brilliant onstage portrayals of the young maid.

4

On the Boulevards: Representations of Joan of Arc in the Popular Theater

Like Cyrano and Napoleon, Joan of Arc, the lone female hero in this trio of military heroes, became a touchstone for both gender and national identities during the fin de siècle. Indeed, the nineteenth century witnessed a revival of the Joan of Arc cult with the fin de siècle marking the apotheosis of the Joan of Arc legend.[1] Whereas the Napoleonic legacy had not always succeeded in finding a unity "beyond politics," representations of Joan of Arc in the boulevard theater, especially as she was depicted by Sarah Bernhardt, managed to unite fin-de-siècle audiences, especially during the belle époque years immediately preceding the First World War.

The memory of Joan, however, was not neutral; rather, it was divisive, reflecting long-standing divisions in French society.[2] Rosemonde Sanson and Gerd Krumeich have both argued that the struggle between right and left to co-opt Joan during the fin de siècle ultimately led to the right finally succeeding in the years preceding World War I in making Joan a symbol of political conservatism.[3] Michel Winock and Robert Gildea, on the other

An abbreviated version of this chapter, "Sur les boulevards: Les Représentations de Jeanne d'Arc dans le théâtre populaire" (translated by Céline Grasser), was published in *CLIO, Histoire, Femmes et Société* 24 (2006): 127–149.

[1] Michel Winock, "Jeanne d'Arc," in *Les Lieux de mémoire*, ed. Pierre Nora, vol. 3 (Paris: Gallimard Quarto, 1997), 4435, and Philippe Contamine, "Jeanne d'Arc dans la mémoire des droites," in *Histoire des droites en France. Vol. 2: Cultures*, ed. Jean-François Sirinelli (Paris: Gallimard, 1992), 400. In her recent work, *Jeanne d'Arc* (Paris: Perrin, 2004), Colette Beaune describes Joan as a "living myth," unlike most other heroes, whose mythification comes in the wake of their deaths, 11. In this way, Joan resembled Napoleon.

[2] Winock, "Jeanne d'Arc," 4431.

[3] Gerd Krumeich, "Joan of Arc between Right and Left," in *Nationhood and Nationalism in France: From Boulangism to the Great War, 1889–1918*, ed. Robert Tombs (New York: HarperCollins, 1991), 63–73, and Rosemonde Sanson, "La Fête de Jeanne

hand, recognize that this co-option was neither complete nor entirely successful, pointing to the emergence of Joan as a figure of national unity during the war and immediately after.[4] None of these scholars, however, address the question of Joan's gender, nor do they fully explore Joan as a cultural symbol of the time. Marina Warner, on the other hand, in her now-classic work, has presented Joan as a model of female heroism, but the focus of her study is not the late nineteenth century but rather the medieval period itself.[5] Only a study that combines cultural and political analyses, particularly one that focuses on issues related to gender, can shed new light on the Joan of Arc legend and its impact on national identity at this time.

This chapter examines representations of Joan of Arc in the boulevard theater, concentrating on two of the best-known productions of the fin de siècle: Jules Barbier's *Jeanne d'Arc*, with music by Gounod, performed in 1890 at the Théâtre de la Porte Saint-Martin, with Sarah Bernhardt in the title role, and *Le Procès de Jeanne d'Arc*, by Emile Moreau, staged at the Théâtre Sarah-Bernhardt in 1909, with Bernhardt again playing the lead.[6] These two productions, nearly twenty years apart, span the fin de siècle, and, moreover, coincide with relatively quiet moments in the struggle between right and left to co-opt the Joan of Arc legend. The Barbier play, presented in January 1890, came on the heels of Boulanger's defeat and corresponded to the beginning of the short-lived *ralliement*, which was propitious to a consensual Joan.[7] Similarly, the Moreau play, which premiered in November 1909, followed the beatification of Joan in April that year. Indeed, Joan's beatification contributed to unity around her.[8]

d'Arc en 1894: Controverse et célébration,"*Revue d'histoire moderne et contemporaine* (July–September 1973): 444–463.

[4] Winock, "Jeanne d'Arc," 4438, and Robert Gildea, *The Past in French History* (New Haven, CT: Yale University Press, 1994), 154–165. For an analysis of how fin-de-siècle authors saw Joan of Arc, the best study remains Marie-Claire Banquart, *Les Écrivains et l'histoire: Barrès, Bloy, Péguy et France* (Paris: Nizet, 1966).

[5] Marina Warner, *Joan of Arc: The Image of Female Heroism* (New York: Knopf, 1981). Other more recent works that encompass gender analyses of Joan include Bonnie Wheeler and Charles T. Wood, eds. *Fresh Verdicts on Joan of Arc* (New York: Garland, 1996), and A. J. Hoenselaars and Jelle Koopmans, eds., *Jeanne d'Arc entre les nations* (Amsterdam: Rodopoi, 1998).

[6] The corpus of materials is large. Joan has been the subject of many plays, as attested by the numerous press dossiers in the Collection Rondel at the BNF: Bibliothèque des Arts du Spectacle (Richelieu). See also the compilation of works by Jean Joseph Soons: *Jeanne d'Arc au théâtre* (Purmerend, the Netherlands: J. Muusses, 1929).

[7] Philippe Contamine, "Jeanne d'Arc dans la mémoire des droites," 411, and Gildea, 158.

[8] Gildea, 158.

An increasing external threat from Germany also forged greater national unity at this time, leading to what Eugen Weber has described as the "nationalist revival."[9]

Given Sarah Bernhardt's participation in – indeed organization of – these two productions, they were events of national importance, attended by huge audiences and covered amply by the mass press. The fact that Bernhardt, a Jew and a New Woman, was playing the virginal Joan was not without its ironies. Famous for her transvestite roles, Bernhardt, the cross-dresser, was herself playing a cross-dresser and, moreover, an androgyne. In the context of the fin-de-siècle crisis of masculinity, this gender blurring by the historical figure and the actress who portrayed her is significant. Furthermore, Bernhardt, who, by this time, had become a commodity associated with mass culture, played a role in the commodification of the Joan of Arc legend. During the fin de siècle, the figure of Joan was not only represented in the boulevard theater but was also used to hawk bonbons, soap, liqueur, and even cement.[10]

As I demonstrate in this chapter, the fact that Bernhardt played Joan of Arc contributed both to the commercialization of the Joan of Arc cult and to a certain consensus around Joan as she was played by the actress. The staging of these two plays represented an attempt by republican authors and their famous actress collaborator to create an image of Joan, the "patriotic saint," "above politics," one that could be reconciled with both the Third Republic and the Catholic Church. Bernhardt's Joan could easily be consumed by fin-de-siècle audiences, who, in an era of great social and political conflict, flocked to these two productions, as they did with *Madame Sans-Gêne*, *Cyrano de Bergerac*, and *L'Aiglon*, to find within the theater walls a unity that was often lacking outside them. But the consensual image of Joan did not come easily. Moreover, just below the surface of unity lay contentious issues, not only about politics but also about gender, mass culture, the theater, and indeed, Bernhardt herself.

Historians Mary-Louise Roberts and Lenard Berlanstein have argued that Bernhardt chose to play Joan to adopt a more respectable stance

---

[9] See Eugen Weber, *The Nationalist Revival in France, 1905–1914* (Berkeley: University of California Press, 1968).

[10] Winock, "Jeanne d'Arc," 4435. On the representation of Joan of Arc in commercial and religious art at the fin de siècle, see Marie-Claude Coudert, "Fin de Siècle," in *Jeanne d'Arc: Les Tableaux de l'histoire: 1820–1920* (Paris: RMN, 2003) and the virtual catalog by Nicole Pellegrin on the Musea website: http://musea.univ-angers.fr.

and to transform herself into a symbol of the nation.[11] This may have been the case initially in 1890, but by 1909, Sarah Bernhardt was firmly established as a national icon. A 1906 survey, published by *Le Petit Parisien*, ranked Bernhardt sixth behind Napoleon and Victor Hugo as one of the ten most illustrious French people of the nineteenth century.[12] Thus, the opposite is also true. Joan of Arc, a national figure who was often the subject of partisan quarrels, was played by an actress, who, despite the controversies surrounding her, was slavishly admired by the majority of her contemporaries.

Before proceeding to an examination of Sarah Bernhardt as Joan, it is important to examine the social, political, and cultural context in which the Joan of Arc legend developed in the nineteenth century, because the different circumstances in which the two plays were produced influenced both their staging and reception.

Joan of Arc: Between Left and Right

After a period of relative obscurity, the Joan of Arc legend was revived during the nineteenth century by liberal republican historians – above all, by Jules Michelet, who promulgated the idea of Joan not only as a heroine but also as a patriotic symbol. This vision, neither clerical nor anticlerical, but rather spiritual and patriotic,[13] led to the discovery of new documents as well as the rediscovery of previously known sources by historians, in particular, Jules Quicherat. Another republican historian, Henri Martin, popularized the findings of Quicherat, who edited volumes on the original trial as well as the rehabilitation trial. Meanwhile, liberal Catholics also promoted the cult of Joan of Arc, chief among them, Mgr. Dupanloup, the bishop of Orléans, who campaigned tirelessly to have Joan declared a saint. Because Dupanloup, who sought to adapt Catholicism to the modern world, did not necessarily associate royalism with his enthusiasm for Joan of Arc, his view could be reconciled with the populist, patriotic Joan of left-wing historians.[14] In this task, Dupanloup was seconded by Catholic historian Henri Wallon, whose name is linked

---

[11] Mary Louise Roberts, *Disruptive Acts: The New Woman in Fin-de-Siècle France* (Chicago: University of Chicago Press, 2002), 217–218, and Lenard Berlanstein, *Daughters of Eve: A Cultural History of French Theater Women from the Old Regime to the Fin de Siècle* (Cambridge, MA: Harvard University Press, 2001), 235.

[12] Cited by Lenard Berlanstein, *Daughters of Eve*, 236.

[13] Gildea, 154.

[14] Krumeich, "Joan of Arc between Right and Left," 68.

with the 1875 amendment bearing his name, which established the hybrid political system of the Third Republic, acceptable both to Orléanists and republicans.

In the wake of the Franco-Prussian War, interest in Joan as a figure of *revanche* was heightened. She was viewed, however, not as a symbol of triumphant nationalism but of its defensive variety. It was the martyred image of Joan that struck a chord with contemporaries, rather than the triumphant messianim that she also represented.[15]

The loss in the war led to a revival of an integral Catholicism, as evidenced by the rise of a new order, the Assumptionist fathers, who promulgated a mystical, emotional, and fanatical Catholicism.[16] Although the Assumptionists were retrograde in many ways – they believed that the defeat was the result of France's collective sins since the Revolution – they were modern in their appeal to the masses and their use of the press to influence public opinion.[17] Not only did they lead the way in raising funds for the building of the Sacré-Coeur, which was to serve as a symbol of national atonement, but they also organized pilgrimages, in particular, to Lourdes, and published their own newspaper *La Croix*, which played a leading role in the anti-Semitic campaigns of the fin de siècle. Meanwhile, republicans, who had recently gained control in the Chamber of Deputies (and would do so in the Senate in 1879), attempted to establish republican symbols and holidays and passed the Ferry school laws both to root the new regime in the past and to establish the primacy of a secular state.

The 1870s and 1880s thus witnessed extreme bipolarization of left and right, due to internal politics within the Catholic Church as well as a conflict between secular and religious forces. It was against this background that the collision between the 1878 commemoration of the centenary of Voltaire's death and the anniversary of Joan of Arc's execution took place. Anti-clericals used Joan of Arc to castigate Catholics as those responsible for her burning. For their part, many Catholics were outraged

---

[15] Krumeich speaks of a "defensive nationalism," *Jeanne d'Arc à travers l'histoire* (Paris: Albin Michel, 1989), 187. See Beaune on these two images, 12.

[16] As characterized by Gordon Wright, *France in Modern Times*, 5th ed. (New York: W.W. Norton, 1994), 227.

[17] See Raymond Jonas, *France and the Cult of the Sacred Heart: An Epic Tale for Modern Times* (Berkeley: University of California Press, 2001); Ruth Harris, *Lourdes: Body and Spirit in the Secular Age* (New York: Viking, 1999), 306–307; Suzanne K. Kaufman, *Consuming Visions: Mass Culture and the Lourdes Shrine* (Ithaca, NY: Cornell University Press, 2005), 140–144, all of whom highlight this phenomenon.

that the insulter of Joan – Voltaire had written mockingly of her – was being celebrated on the very day of her death. It was also within this context that republican deputy Joseph Fabre first sought in 1884 to propose a national day in honor of Joan of Arc, one that would serve as a corollary of the July 14 celebrations. Although Fabre was himself an ecumenical who saw this holiday as one of national unity, the bill was signed by 252 deputies, many of whom were left-wing republicans, who saw in it an opportunity to prevent Catholics from "co-opting" their image of a secular, populist Joan, betrayed by the king and the Catholic Church.[18] Thus, in 1885, Joan of Arc was still the sister of Marianne.[19] Fabre, however, lost his mandate, and the project was shelved until he brought it up again, this time in the Senate, in 1894. By then, circumstances had changed considerably.

The intervening years witnessed the rise and fall of General Boulanger, if not of Boulangism itself. Ex-Boulangists fanned the Panama scandal, which led to a renewal of political personnel, bringing to power a new generation of moderate republicans more willing to compromise with Catholics. The increasing threat of Socialists, who obtained forty seats in the Chamber of Deputies during the 1893 elections, also reinforced this trend, as did Jules Ferry's need for Catholic support to pursue his colonial policies. On the Catholic end, a number of events resulted in the easing of tensions. The Boulanger débâcle led some monarchists to adopt the label of conservative republicans, among them the Comte de Mun, Jacques Piou, and the Baron de Mackau. Although it was the papal encyclical, "Au Milieu des solicitudes," issued by Pope Leo XIII in 1892, that officially established the policy of the *ralliement*, signs of the new mood were already present in 1890. Although some French Catholic leaders never reconciled themselves to it, there is sufficient evidence to suggest that many Catholic voters did.[20] Indeed, in 1894, the same year that Joan was declared venerable, Fabre again proposed the bill, this time in the Senate. On this occasion, however, favorable votes came from moderates and Catholics, resulting in a slim margin of victory. However, many left-wing republicans, who had earlier voted for the bill felt wary of legislation that might give support to Catholics. This bill never made it to the Chamber of Deputies. In 1909, the same year Moreau's play was staged,

---

[18] See Sanson for a full accounting of the two attempts by Fabre to establish a national holiday in honor of Joan of Arc.

[19] Krumeich, "Joan of Arc between Right and Left," 66.

[20] Wright, 238–239.

Joan was beatified, and only in 1920, the same year as her canonization, was an official holiday established.

Although the early 1890s were relatively quiet in terms of left/right tensions, this period did witness social conflict and threats to the regime from the extreme left – witness the incidents at Fourmies and anarchist agitation. The years later in the decade proved even more contentious, due, in part, to the conflicts of the Dreyfus Affair, which led to a hardening of positions on the left and right. Boulangism, which marked the evolution of nationalism from left to right, too had long-term effects on this development.[21] Up to this time, there had been two general visions of Joan of Arc: a Catholic one, which represented Joan as the defender of the faith, and a republican one, which represented her as a child of the people. Within each group were hard-liners, who would deny the opposite group's claim to her legacy, as well as moderates, who sought to portray her as a symbol of unity. The new "integral nationalism," which had little to do with the republican messianic variety inherited from the Revolution, led to a third vision of Joan of Arc that combined elements of the radical ex-Boulangist left and the Catholic right to produce a Joan of Arc who was the standard-bearer of a defensive and exclusionary vision of France.[22] Their Joan was both republican and monarchist, as the appropriation of Joan by the "Catholic republican socialist" Edouard Drumont and the monarchist Charles Maurras illustrates.

Joan: Symbol of Unity at the Fin de Siècle?

It was during this period – from 1890 until the eve of the First World War – that the Joan of Arc cult reached its peak.[23] Many critics reviewing the revival of Jules Barbier's *Jeanne d'Arc* in 1890 noted the contemporary interest in Joan of Arc. *Le Petit Parisien* described her as "a subject

[21] On nationalism, see Raoul Girardet, *Le Nationalisme français: 1871–1914* (Paris: Seuil, 1983).

[22] Krumeich, Gildea, and Winock describe essentially these three visions of Joan, although the former two do so in slightly different terms. I myself am following Winock's definition of three different Joans, 4442.

[23] *Jeanne d'Arc à travers l'histoire*, 184–186. *Revanche*, Krumeich argues, was not the sole factor of the Joan revival, because in the immediate aftermath of the war, there was no immediate renewal of interest in Joan of Arc. Rather it was during the 1890s, at the height of the bipolarization between anti-clerical and religious factions, that the Joan of Arc cult took off. Both Winock and Contamine also point to this period as marking the apogee of the Joan of Arc legend.

of current interest," whereas *Le Gaulois* spoke of her as "in fashion."[24] The Barbier revival occurred at the same time as the representation of Joan at the popular Hippodrome theater and the dedication of a Joan of Arc statue in Nancy,[25] as well as the competing efforts of the bishops of Verdun, which contained Vaucouleurs, the site from which Joan had begun her journey, and Saint-Dié, which included her hometown of Domrémy, to dedicate statues in her honor.[26] Finally, a recent book by Ernest Lesigne, which claimed not only that Joan had done little more than inspire others to undertake their mission against the English but also that she had not been burned at the stake but had survived, married, and borne numerous children, stirred quite a controversy in the press.[27]

Francisque Sarcey, writing about the revival of the Barbier play in *Le Temps* of January 6, 1890, noted that since the play had originally been staged in 1873, the Joan of Arc cult had become even more popular, citing not only Mgr. Dupanloup's attempt to have Joan canonized, but also Joseph Fabre's efforts in 1884 to establish a Joan of Arc festival on the date of her birth.[28] Sarcey's fellow journalist Jean de Nivelle at *Le Soleil*

---

[24] "Jeanne d'Arc," *Le Petit Parisien* (unsigned), 7 January 1890, and Yveling Rambaud, "La Mise en scène de Jeanne d'Arc," *Le Gaulois*, 2 January 1890 (Dossier Sarah Bernhardt: Collection Rondel: Rt5884 1–2, BNF). All Rf and Rt dossiers cited in subsequent notes are from the Collection Rondel on the theater at the BNF Richelieu. In some instances, clippings from this collection or from the press collections at the Bibliothèque Marguerite Durand do not identify the newspaper in question or the date. Whenever possible, I have attempted to verify both the source and exact date.

[25] Although Maurice Barrès hailed the unifying qualities of the contemporary admiration of Joan as represented by the statue, this event, in fact, led to some discord when a republican historian, who called Joan a "lay saint," clashed with Mgr. Turnza, who objected to this definition of Joan. See Winock, "Jeanne d'Arc," 4451.

[26] On various Joan of Arc manifestations, see Louis Ganderax, "Chronique," *La Revue illustrée*, 19 July 1890 (Joan of Arc dossier, Bibliothèque Marguerite Durand: BMD).

[27] Ernest Lesigne, *Fin d'une légende: Vie de Jeanne d'Arc (de 1409 à 1440)* (Paris: Bayle, 1889). See the review "A Propos de Jeanne d'Arc," by R. Jallifier in *Le Journal des débats*, 29 April 1891 (Joan of Arc Dossier, BMD). The book is also mentioned in several other articles that review the Barbier play.

[28] "Chronique théâtrale," *Le Temps*, 6 January 1890. According to Sarcey, when the play was first staged in 1873 at the Gaîté theater, run by Jacques Offenbach, it was chosen as an uplifting work to revive audiences who felt "guilty" about having overly indulged in the operettas of the Second Empire. Offenbach, the name most closely associated with this frivolity, sought to stage a play with a short run. Instead, the play became a resounding success, in part, because some of the lines, like "We are fleeing the nation," had contemporary resonance. Sarcey claimed that he himself had felt little emotion watching it the first time but that when he viewed it again, this time with an audience composed largely of members of the lower middle classes, he was moved, as much by their reaction as by the play itself. He wrote a supportive review and immodestly claimed that this evaluation led to the success of the play. In the original production, the role of Joan was

noted that in 1873 the play had been a modest success. Theatergoers went to historical plays to see actors play their parts. Only now had such a play become an event of national significance.[29] Nivelle spoke especially of Joan of Arc, but his comment about the increasing interest in historical plays is worth noting. Not only did playwrights attempt to forge national unity in the theater, but there is also ample evidence that audiences, including theater critics, viewed the theater as a place for national consensus.

Whereas the Assumptionist paper *La Croix* condemned the wickedness of the theater and blamed the contemporary decline of interest in religion for recent events – from the fire at the Opéra Comique in 1887 to the current bout of influenza that raged in Paris – others in the press noted approvingly that the power of Joan had grown even stronger in light of such dechristianization. Among them were Ernest Renan and E. Le Pelletier. Indeed, Le Pelletier called Joan "a lay saint, the national saint."[30]

Whereas some Catholic observers would have rejected the description of a "lay saint," nearly all in the press spoke of Joan of Arc as an antidote to the political strife of the period. Maurice Barrès, speaking of the dedication of a statue to Joan in his home district of Nancy, described the fascination for Joan of Arc as "a new Boulangism" on the part of a public "weary of struggles, weary to the point of nausea."[31] In an editorial on

played by Lia Félix, the sister of the acclaimed actress Rachel. Félix, like Bernhardt, was Jewish, a fact that was noted without comment in a number of reviews from 1890.

[29] In his article, "La Patrie," published in *Le Soleil* of 7 January 1890, Jean de Nivelle observed that compared with the current revival, the original production of 1873 had elicited little attention. But, as he noted, during the last ten years, the French had created a cult of Joan of Arc, that is, the cult of the nation.

[30] In an editorial, "Avertissement et châtiment," from *La Croix* of 17 January 1890, Vatès, deploring such dechristianization, concluded: "Thus, isn't it quite evident that we deserve to be chastised? Theaters are burning – is this not fitting, since they damn so many souls." Others like Renan and Le Pelletier saw dechristianization in a more positive light. See Renan's interview with Jehan des Ruelles: "Jeanne d'Arc et M. Renan," *Gil Blas*, 6 January 1890 (Joan of Arc dossier, BMD), and Le Pelletier, who noted of Joan: "The crowd bows down in front of her statues. ... She is the Virgin for those who do not celebrate the month of May [a reference to celebrations of Mary]. In our scientific age, which no longer believes in legends but which knows that history repeats itself, Joan of Arc is called hope." "La Bonne Française," paper not identified, no date (probably the first week of January 1890) (Rf87543: Recueil factice d'articles de presse sur *Jeanne d'Arc* de Jules Barbier). See also Hector Pessard, reviewing the play for *Le Gaulois* of 4 January 1890 ("Jeanne d'Arc").

[31] Maurice Barrès, "Jeanne d'Arc ou la république ouverte," *Le Figaro*, 4 July 1890 (Joan of Arc dossier, BMD).

the front page of *Le Journal des débats politiques et littéraires* of January
13, 1890, André Heurteau complained bitterly of the appropriation of
Joan by various partisan groups. Heurteau was irritated that Joan was
being co-opted by the vulgar politicians of the late nineteenth century,
especially since he, like numerous contemporaries, saw her as an antidote
to the baseness of the times. He also saw her as a unifying force above
political quarrels: "It is also the soul of France, without consideration of
political parties and their petty quarrels, which moves toward her [Joan]
with a tender and invincible fervor."[32] Writing about the Barbier play in
1890, Anatole France noted not only the divisiveness of the time but also
Joan's power to overcome it: "Divided as we are by opinions and beliefs,
we are reconciled in her."[33]

Most critics saw in Joan a unifying figure, not only in 1890, but also
after the Dreyfus Affair. One commentator in 1909 noted that the Joan
of Arc cult had grown even stronger since the Barbier revival, which was
already a "distant memory."[34] Although Joan had been beatified earlier
in 1909, the same year as Moreau's play, the previous year had witnessed
considerable controversy surrounding the Joan of Arc legacy. Anatole
France's biography on the life of Joan of Arc ruffled the feathers of many
Catholics, who saw in his depiction a vilification of Joan's voices and religious convictions. Furthermore, the incidents surrounding the Thalamas
Affair took place in the winter of 1908–1909, just a few short months
before the premiere of the Moreau play. Thalamas, a professor who denigrated the Joan of Arc cult, had earlier been the target of royalist agitation
in 1904 but once again became the target of *Action française* demonstra-
tions, when he was appointed to the Sorbonne.[35]

---

[32] André Heurteau, editorial with no title on the front page of *Le Journal des débats politiques et littéraires* of 13 January 1890: "She belongs neither to one group or another.
She does not belong to journalists, politicians or to political parties. She would disdain
the crude flattery they offer her."

[33] Anatole France, "Sur Jeanne d'Arc," originally published at the time of the revival of the
Barbier play in 1890, reproduced in *La Vie littéraire*, 3ème série (Paris: Calmann-Lévy,
1898), 243.

[34] Jacques Copeau, "Le Procès de Jeanne d'Arc," *Le Théâtre*, 2 December 1909 (Fol SW
257: Caricatures et illustrations de Sarah Bernhardt dans *Le Procès de Jeanne d'Arc*,
d'Emile Moreau, BNF Richelieu).

[35] On the Thalamas Affair and the Action française, see Martha Hanna, "Iconology and
Ideology: Images of Joan of Arc in the Idiom of the Action française, 1908–1931,"
French Historical Studies (1985): 215–239. See also Nadia Margolis, "La Chevauchée
solitaire du Professeur Thalamas: Rationalistes et réactionnaires dans l'historiographie
Johannique (1904–1945)," *Bulletin de l'Association des Amis du Centre Jeanne d'Arc* 15
(1991): 7–28. But the period also announced some consensus around Joan; witness the
ecumenical vision of Joan presented by Jaurès in his 1910 work *L'Armée nouvelle*.

Writing about the Moreau play in 1909, Jean Richepin spoke in terms similar to those used by critics in 1890: "In this divided country that we are, is it not true, that despite so much dissension, we maintain an imperious need, a desire, a thirst for a common belief around which we would like to unite in brotherhood. I am simply among those who make Joan of Arc the [patron] Saint of our nation."[36] Jacques Copeau concurred. Speaking of Joan, he noted: "She glides above discords."[37] As for Charles Martel of *L'Aurore*, he spoke of Moreau with admiration in his review of the play: "For my part, I admire the author who in taking on such a heroine simultaneously claimed by republicans for having personified patriotism before their time, by royalists to serve against these republicans whom they used to malign as 'patriots,' by free thinkers as a victim of priests, and by priests as a victim of free thinkers, has been able to represent her in the theater, without excommunicating anyone. And all this, of all marvels, while maintaining historical accuracy."[38] In this observation, he was entirely correct. The reviewers of newspapers as different as *L'Action française* (monarchist), *L'Humanité* (Socialist), and *L'Action* (republican and virulently anti-clerical) all wrote favorably of the play.

Sarah, the Patriot

Before proceeding to an examination of the two plays, one must ask why Bernhardt chose to portray Joan of Arc. The choice must have been deliberate, as she played Joan not once but twice, and moreover, in productions that she initiated and over which she had great control.[39] Asked in an interview with *Le Figaro* in January 1890 why the role of Joan attracted her, Bernhardt replied:

I am a bit of a patriot [*chauvine*]; one can't be perfect, right? I adore my country and for me Joan is its purest personification – I assure you that to be on the other side of the world makes you realize how much this old corner of earth called

[36] Jean Richepin, "Le Procès de Jeanne d'Arc," *Le Gaulois*, 22 November 1909, (Rf677.22 (1): Recueil factice d'articles de presse sur *Le Procès de Jeanne d'Arc* d'Emile Moreau): "Communion in a faith, that is what the sons of this divided country are missing, without a doubt. By loving the France she symbolizes, perhaps we will come [back] to loving each other some day."

[37] Jacques Copeau, "Le Procès de Jeanne d'Arc."

[38] Charles Martel, "Le Procès de Jeanne d'Arc," *L'Aurore*, 26 November 1909.

[39] As Roberts notes, the choice "just cannot be arbitrary," 217. See also Bergman-Carton, "Negotiating the Categories: Sarah Bernhardt and the Possibility of Jewishness," *Art Journal* 55, no. 2 (Summer 1996): footnote 31, who notes that Bernhardt was well aware of the timing and the sequence of the roles she played.

France, this beloved country that cannot be removed like the sole of one's boots but which is always there, very much alive, in the depth of the heart, is loved.[40]

Bernhardt in some respects was parodying her detractors – by asserting the Frenchness they would deny her. Her description of herself as "chauvine," followed by the comment that "one couldn't be perfect" was clearly intentional and perhaps even tongue in cheek, her patriotism notwithstanding.[41] Bernhardt thus downplayed the subversiveness of Joan in order to conceal the unsavory realities of her own life. Her representation of Joan as devout and feminine was part of a personal strategy to shield herself from criticism about her Jewishness and her status as a New Woman.[42] Indeed, attacks against Bernhardt's Jewish identity were directly associated with her identity as a New Woman.[43]

In another interview in *Le Figaro*, Bernhardt played up not only her patriotism by speaking of the superiority of French actors and playwrights to foreign ones, but also her Catholic childhood. Explaining to the interviewer that she had wanted to be a nun as a child, she claimed: "It is solely to the Church that I owe my being in the theater. As a child, my imagination was struck by Church hymns, the fervor of the assistants, the mystic nature of the ceremonies."[44] Whether an accurate representation of her childhood or not, Bernhardt was clearly trying to head off criticism of those who might be shocked to see her play a role such as Joan of Arc. Although Bernhardt's mother was Jewish, she herself was a baptized Catholic. But Bernhardt always maintained her double quality as Christian and Jew, emphasizing one or the other in different circumstances. Indeed, it was this slippage between categories that made her seem so dangerous to anti-Semites.[45]

---

[40] Lahire, "A Propos de Jeanne d'Arc: Une Visite à Sarah Bernhardt," *Le Figaro*, 2 January 1890.

[41] Roberts, 210–212.

[42] Roberts, 218.

[43] Carol Ockman also notes that attacks against Bernhardt's transgressions as a woman were inseparable from anti-Semitic attacks on her such that perception of her Jewishness was conflated with other discourses, especially the fear of women in the public sphere: "When Is a Jewish Star Just a Star? Interpreting Images of Sarah Bernhardt," in *The Jew in the Text: Modernity and the Construction of Identity*, ed. Linda Nochlin and Tamar Garb (New York: Thames and Hudson, 1995), 139.

[44] Alberty, "Sarah Bernhardt: La Veille d'une première," *Le Figaro*, October 1890 (Rt5881: Sarah Bernhardt: Interviews).

[45] Bergman-Carton, "Negotiating the Categories," 58. Anti-Semites François Bournand and Raphael Viau devoted numerous pages to the actress in their *Les Femmes d'Israël* (Paris: A. Pierret, 1898).

Bernhardt, through Joan, was clearly trying to "domesticate" herself. She spoke to the *Figaro* reporter interviewing her in 1890 about repeated requests from mothers for her to play a role suitable for viewing by young girls.[46] Playing Joan allowed Bernhardt to become a national icon and was part of the strategy that led to her emergence during the fin de siècle as a respectable figure, fit for family consumption. Such co-opting of actresses by the mainstream, progressive press was part of a movement that led to their transformation from "notorious women" to "intimate strangers," as Lenard Berlanstein puts it.[47] Nevertheless, although Bernhardt certainly cloaked herself in Joan's standard, she might well have been amused to play a figure as controversial as herself. There was clearly a subversive element in her choice. Moreover, like Joan, Bernhardt meant different things to different people, and it was this very diversity that contributed to unity around both figures.

The Two Plays

Despite the consensus around them, the two plays were quite different. *Jeanne d'Arc*, with verses by Barbier set to the music of Gounod, was simplified in the revival of 1890, that is, limited to three parts: *la mission*, *le triomphe*, and *le martyre*.[48] Although the idea of tableaux set to music corresponds to the definition of a melodrama in its original sense, most reviewers likened it to a mystery play.[49] In fact, many commentators, noting its pictorial aspects – the most spectacular of the scenes staged was Charles VII's coronation at Rheims – wrote that attending the play was like seeing the pages of a missal come to life.[50] The play, however, was somewhat static and had little drama, despite the fact that Joan dies on stage.

---

[46] Lahire, "A Propos de Jeanne d'Arc."

[47] Berlanstein, *Daughters of Eve*, 209–236.

[48] In his column in *Le Temps* of 6 January 1890, Sarcey praised Bernhardt, especially in the second tableau, "where she is incomparable, is in her poetic grace. ... She is Joan, the Joan of which we have dreamed, she is ever this Joan ... yes, the legend has come to life." The grace and elegance to which he refers are not usually traits one normally associates with Joan of Arc.

[49] In an interview with Lahire, "A Propos de Jeanne d'Arc," Bernhardt spoke of the Barbier play both as a melodrama in the traditional sense and also as a mystery play.

[50] See Henry Bauër, "Les Premières Représentations," *L'Echo de Paris*, 5 January 1890 (Dossier Sarah Bernhardt, Rt5884). See also Yveling Rambaud, who used the same term in "La Mise en scène de Jeanne d'Arc." He was so struck by the visual qualities of the play that he suggested that painters and sculptors seeking to portray Joan consult the costumes and décor of the play.

Moreau's play was a more sober historical drama that focused on the trial itself, although the characterization of Bedford as a man unknowingly in love with Joan led many to carp that Moreau had fallen victim to his former collaborator Sardou's love of melodrama.[51] Moreau himself had told an interviewer from *Le Figaro* that he saw the play as Joan's revenge against her adversaries. In addition, he wanted to highlight the dramatic aspects of Joan's story. It is for these reasons that he chose to focus on the trial itself.[52] In an interview with a reporter from *Comédia*, Moreau referred to Joan's trial as "the most poignant and agonizing judicial affair in the world."[53] His readers were undoubtedly thinking of other contemporary trials, not only the Dreyfus trials but also the more recent trial of naval ensign Ullmo for treason in 1908, as well as the murder trial of Meg Steinheil, which had ended only two weeks earlier. At least two reviewers mentioned the Dreyfus and Meg Steinheil trials in their reviews of the play.[54] Here too, the visual qualities of the staging of Moreau's play were in evidence, with the splendor of the decors and costumes commented upon by critics. Indeed, Bernhardt was well known for her attention to historical detail and the splendor of the costumes and decors of her productions. In this instance too, critics described the play as the pages of history come to life.[55]

Although Bernhardt had underscored Joan's girlish qualities in the Barbier production, Joan's strengths were somewhat muted. In Moreau's play, Joan was a much stronger figure, in part due to the trial dialogue, although Bernhardt at age sixty plus still managed to portray Joan's girlishness. Moreau's Joan was more defiant, less a symbol of martyred patriotism as she had been in 1873, and even in 1890, than the harbinger of a combative nationalism that sought to expel the foreign invader.[56] In

---

[51] See the reviews of Ergaste for *L'Action française*, Léon Blum for *Comédia*, and Henri de Régnier for *Le Journal des débats*. Full references are listed in subsequent notes.

[52] Moreau interview with *Le Figaro* (no date indicated), quoted in *Le Procès de Jeanne d'Arc*, published by *L'Illustration théâtrale* (Paris: 1909), no page number indicated.

[53] In an interview with Antoine Delecraz, "Le Procès de Jeanne d'Arc au Théâtre Sarah-Bernhardt," *Comédia*, 26 November 1909 (Dossier Moreau: Rf67.722).

[54] Speaking of Joan's prison, François de Nion compared it to that of Dreyfus in a review of 26 November 1909 from *L'Echo de Paris* ("Le Procès de Jeanne d'Arc") (Dossier Moreau, Rf67.722). Steinheil, who had been the mistress of President Félix Faure, was accused of killing her mother and husband and was later acquitted. She had been tied up when the police found her, making the affair a locked room mystery.

[55] See, for example, the review by Félix Duquesnel, who had staged the Barbier production in 1890: "Première Représentation," *Le Gaulois*, 26 November 1909 (Dossier Moreau: Rf67.722).

[56] Francis Chevassau felt that Moreau had not adequately represented Joan's hesitations: "Le Procès de Jeanne d'Arc," *Le Figaro*, 26 November 1909.

addition, the figures around Joan were seen to be weak. Bishop Cauchon, who had engineered the trial, was in Moreau's rendering a quaking, cowardly "super villain," while the English regent Bedford, who had little to do with the trial, was elevated to a major player. This, however, was a Bedford subject to doubts and visions, who was, at best, transformed into a romantic hero à la Lorenzaccio (the trouser part that Bernhardt herself had played) and, at worst, a hero of melodrama.[57] So too was the portrait of young King Henry VI, who is depicted as frail and ill, almost a copy of the young Duke of Reichstadt in Rostand's *L'Aiglon* a few years earlier. Yet, significantly, in the Moreau play, it was not the French character who was neurasthenic but rather the foreign opponent. Despite this slight shift from 1890 to 1909 in the presentation of a stronger Joan, symbol of a nation more confident in itself, both the Barbier and the Moreau plays were part of the same cultural landscape in that both sought to present a consensual Joan of Arc, one who would unite rather than divide national audiences.

At the time of the Barbier revival, there had been much public discussion of hysteria and hypnosis. Bernhardt even told a reporter from *Le Gaulois* that she saw evidence of hysteria in Joan of Arc: "In the aura of her mysticism, there is a suggestion, [of] a case of hypnotism – this is my humble opinion – which can and must have a sure effect in the theater, if it is presented sincerely, especially in our time, when science deigns to step in the realm of the magical." Asked further by the interviewer if she believed in psychic experiences, Bernhardt replied in the affirmative, recounting a story of her being aware from the other side of the Atlantic that her son had suffered an injury (See Figure 4.1.).[58]

Bernhardt was trying to be different things to different people. In some interviews, she indicated that she had deep religious convictions and that she believed in the divine mission of Joan of Arc. At the same time, she was studying the latest scientific research on hysteria in order to depict Joan hearing voices. Bernhardt attended Charcot's famous Tuesday lectures and observed his patients. Furthermore, a whole series of stills by Nadar depict Bernhardt imitating the postures of hysterics in her rehearsals for *Jeanne d'Arc*. Yet in the same breath, Bernhardt

---

[57] Some critics felt that this Bedford was a politic one in light of the Franco-British alliance marked by the Entente Cordiale. See Edmond Stoullig, *Les Annales du théâtre et de la musique: 1909* (Paris: Ollendorff, 1910), 255.

[58] Yveling Rambaud, "Chez Mme Sarah Bernhardt," *Le Gaulois*, 4 December 1889 (Dossier SB: Rt5884, 1–2).

FIGURE 4.1. Sarah Bernhardt in Jules Barbier's *Jeanne d'Arc*, 1890 (Joan hears voices), courtesy of the BNF.

seemingly minimized the role of science by talking about the realm of the mysterious, by exalting the trend of spiritism, which was in vogue at the time.[59] She must have been treading a fine line here. Charcot himself was an unbeliever who sought to represent extreme religious experience

---

[59] Sardou staged a play, *Spiritisme*, in 1897. During the Bazar de la Charité fire, a medium figured prominently in predictions about the fire. A medium was also prominent during the Dreyfus Affair. In general, references to hypnotism are abundant in the reviews of the 1890 production and altogether absent from the 1909 one.

as hysteria. But Bernhardt was trying to reconcile various constituencies among her fans. It is no doubt for this reason that she appears to contradict herself. By the time of the Moreau play in 1909, Bernhardt seems to have dropped such references to hysteria, and if there are hysterics present in the latter play, they are Joan's enemies, not the maid herself.

Reviewers praised both plays for their historical accuracy, Barbier's for the authenticity of the costumes and decors and Moreau's for the use of the trial transcripts to create Joan's dialogue.[60] At the time of the Barbier revival, during an interview with Yveling Rambaud, Bernhardt spoke of how she had researched the role, reading all texts from Michelet to Martin and Quicherat: "I essentially steeped myself, so to speak, in the life of the heroine, reading all that has been written about her." She even knew what Joan looked like, replying that she was "thin and slight," a description that would bring to mind Bernhardt's own physique, although she had acquired some middle-aged girth by this time.[61] Such an image also corresponded to the contemporary ideal of Joan as a young girl. Similarly, in 1909, in an interview with *Comédia*, Moreau was careful to note the historical sources of his work, citing Quicherat and Michelet.[62] Félix Duquesnel, who had staged the Barbier production in 1890, noted that Moreau's drama was not a play but rather the trial come to life, and with Sarah Bernhardt in the title role, fiction had become reality.[63] Indeed, most of the reviews from both 1890 and 1909 commented that Bernhardt no longer seemed to

[60] Especially the Rheims cathedral where Charles VII was crowned. See Vanessa Schwartz on the fin-de-siècle craze for historical panoramas: *Spectacular Realities: Early Mass Culture in Fin-de-Siècle Paris* (Berkeley: University of California Press, 1998), 149–176. See, for example, *L'Illustration*, 27 November 1909 (Dossier Moreau, Rf677.22, 1). Henri de Régnier spoke of Moreau's "admirable concern for accuracy and truth" in "La Semaine dramatique," *Le Journal des débats*, 29 November 1909.

[61] Yveling Rambaud, "Chez Mme Sarah Bernhardt." This masculinized image of Joan as a boy-woman in the 1880s and 1890s was also evident in works by composers of the *Conservatoire*, signaling a change in the aesthetics of previous years: Jann Pasler, *Composing the Citizen: Music as Public Utility in Third Republic France* (Berkeley: University of California Press, 2009), 663.

[62] Moreau, quoted by Antoine Delacraz, "Le Procès de Jeanne d'Arc au Théâtre Sarah-Bernhardt," *Comédia*, 26 November 1909 (Dossier Moreau: Rf67.722).

[63] About Bernhardt, Duquesnel noted, "She symbolizes delightfully the figure of Joan of Arc, or even better, becomes her, since with her [SB], fiction becomes reality and her great art consists especially of 'bringing to life' the character she is portraying," Duquesnel, "Première Représentation."

be acting but rather "channeling" Joan such that the actress became the French heroine on stage.[64]

Sarah as Joan: A Stained-Glass Image

At some point, the heroine and the woman who portrayed her were united in the minds of spectators such that their image of Sarah was also swept up in this belief in Joan's purity. In her review of *Le Procès de Jeanne d'Arc*, Jane Catulle-Mendès thanked Bernhardt for taking on such an important role: "Our gratitude should be greater ... more sacred. Through her [SB], in our era of ruthless ambition, of haggling and even worse, when baseness and vulgarity are flaunted and sometimes triumph in so many theaters, alas, there is an image of beauty, purity, of an ideal, and a profoundly human image as well."[65] Given that Bernhardt was, in many ways, the personification of the commercialization of the era, such a comment seems astonishingly naïve, yet this sentiment was not atypical.[66]

This close association of the actress and the heroine was also evident in the way reviewers described Joan as divine and accessible at the same time; they were referring *both* to Joan and Sarah, who portrayed her so brilliantly. Joan of Arc was thus a saint for the democratic age, fashioned to reflect the era's democratization and belief in heroes that were accessible to the ordinary man or woman. In *La Revue illustrée* of July 19, 1890, Louis Ganderax spoke of Joan's cult in the following terms: "We devote to her ... a secret, familiar cult, as we do to a superior being, close to us,

---

[64] Francisque Sarcey, despite his reservations about the Barbier play and, at times, about Bernhardt's acting, conceded that in Bernhardt, "the legend has come to life," "Chronique théâtrale." In her article "Sarah" (paper not identified, January 1890 from Dossier Interviews SB: Rt5883, 1–4), Renée declared: "She has, through one of those psychic phenomena that escapes us, relived a life that died out a long time ago." Another skeptic, Henri de Régnier, writing about Bernhardt's performance in "La Semaine dramatique," in *Le Journal des débats* of 29 November 1909, declared that to attain such perfection in the role, "one needs a kind of intuition."

[65] This article, from the Moreau press dossier (Rf67.722), has no exact date nor is the source identified, but it appears that it was from *Femina* in late 1909 or early 1910, because Jane Catulle-Mendès wrote a theater column for that paper. I have not been able to track down the correct issue of *Femina* in which the article appeared, but Catulle-Mendès also wrote a review of the play for *L'Intransigeant* on 25 November 1909: "Le Procès de Jeanne d'Arc: Sarah Bernhardt."

[66] Lenard Berlanstein speaks about the domestication of actresses by the late nineteenth century such that they had become acceptable role models. Indeed, they were promoted by such glossy women's magazines like *Femina* for which Catulle-Mendès wrote, 219.

nevertheless, like a legendary figure we might have known, and about whom no one in the world will make us doubt."[67]

The author of a *Comédia* review of Moreau's *Le Procès de Jeanne d'Arc* in 1909 wrote the following about Bernhardt playing Joan: "Mystic and inspired, she is not the saint of a stained-glass window, who exists far removed from human concerns; on the contrary, we see her as subject to all the sensations and simple and heated emotions [typical] of adolescent hearts."[68] Finally, Jane Catulle-Mendès spoke in almost identical terms of Sarah herself: "We can only thank [SB] her for being so human and so divine, so near to us and yet so close to the greatest splendor of our dreams."[69] Writing of Bernhardt's performance in 1890, Anatole France had observed of her: "Madame Sarah Bernhardt is poetry itself. She exudes the radiance of a stained-glass window that the visions of saints had left, at least as we imagine it – on the beautiful visionary of Domrémy. She incarnates at the same time an ideal life and an exquisite archaism: she is the legend come to life."[70] In this assessment, he echoed the actress describing Joan: "My Joan is a stained-glass window saint – she is radiant, a visionary."[71]

This does not necessarily mean that Bernhardt depicted Joan in a more accessible way in 1909. She may have done so, but it is important to note that artists of the period in their images of Joan of Arc depicted her as a more human figure.[72] Thus, the idea of a stained-glass image and that of accessibility need not have been contradictory, as it was for the *Comédia* reviewer. Indeed, in 1909, the women's magazine *Femina* depicted Bernhardt as Joan of Arc on a stained-glass window on

---

[67] Ganderax, "Chronique." Similarly, Jules Lemaître, writing about the Barbier play in 1890, spoke movingly of what Joan had meant to him as a young boy growing up in Orléans. Like other commentators, Lemaître compared the story of Joan to the Gospels, which he had read at the same time. Lemaître's review, originally published in *Le Journal des débats* on 6 January 1890, is reproduced in *Impressions de theatre: 5ème série* (Paris: Lecène, Oudin et cie, 1891), 222–230. Others also compared Joan to Christ. See, for example, Henry Bauër, who wrote of Joan: "Does this woman-Christ not offer a singular analogy to Jesus of Galilee? If Jesus has invented a new cry in the world: humanity. Joan has revealed the nation," "Les Premières Représentations" (1890).

[68] The author of the review was Emery, who wrote in *Comédia* of 26 November 1909 (Dossier Moreau: Rf 67.722).

[69] Jane Catulle-Mendès, Review of Moreau's "Le Procès de Jeanne d'Arc."

[70] The idea of an image coming to life is also present in an article by Henry Bauër, "Les Premières Représentations" (1890). See also Bauër's "La Ville et le théâtre," *L'Echo de Paris*, 6 January 1890 (Dossier SB: Rt5884, 1–2).

[71] Bernhardt, quoted by Yveling Rambaud, "Chez Mme Sarah Bernhardt."

[72] Coudert, 129.

its cover.[73] So intertwined had the images of the actress and the heroine become that Sarah via Joan was now presented in a stylized version of religious art (Figure 4.2).

This idea of the interchangeability of actress and heroic figure is also in evidence in the poster Bernhardt commissioned for the Barbier play in 1890 from then-unknown artist Eugène Grasset (Figures 4.3 and 4.4). Although this would be the first and last collaboration between the actress and the Swiss artist, it did signal the beginning of such publicity posters for Bernhardt's plays by Alphonse Mucha.[74] Unhappy with the first design Grasset submitted to her for the Barbier play, Bernhardt asked Grasset for a second version. Both versions have survived, thereby providing important clues to how Bernhardt saw Joan of Arc as well as herself in the role. In the first version, the likeness to Sarah is striking. Joan/Sarah's hair, like Bernhardt's, is frizzy. She is gazing upward and has placed one hand on her chest in the declamatory gesture for which Bernhardt was well known. On the top of the poster in large gothic letters is written "Jeanne Darc" (is the fact that there was no punctuation indicative of both artists' republican sentiments?), and on the bottom, "Sarah Bernhardt", such that the two figures are equated: Sarah is Joan. In both versions, Joan/Sarah, holding the standard that unfurls behind her (bearing the legend Jésus Maria), is surrounded by arrows on the left side of the poster, and lances on the right. In the background is a stream of orange smoke – perhaps announcing her burning. The differences in the two posters are clear. The Joan of the second poster looks like Bernhardt but a more stylized version, indeed, a less "Semitic" rendering of the actress; frizzy hair was associated by anti-Semites with Jews, although it was also often used to depict women in pre-Raphaelite paintings.[75] Joan's/Sarah's hair is straight, and she gazes hypnotically at the viewer.[76] She also looks

[73] See Coudert, 129–162. In her essay on Bernhardt in the Jewish Museum catalog, Janice Bergman-Carton refers to an American observer of the time speaking of a "stained-glass Sarah." "A Vision of a Stained Glass Sarah: Bernhardt and the Decorative Arts," 99–123, in *Sarah Bernhardt: The Art of High Drama*, ed. Carol Ockman and Kenneth E. Silver (New York and New Haven, CT: The Jewish Museum and Yale University Press, 2005). In its 15 December 1909 issue, *Femina* depicted Bernhardt as Joan on a stained-glass window on its cover. Perhaps the American observer to whom Bergman-Carton refers had seen this image.

[74] As for Grasset, he was so inspired by the image of Joan of Arc that he went on to submit numerous designs and drawings of Joan of Arc, including an entry in the 1893 competition for stained-glass windows depicting Joan for the Orléans cathedral.

[75] Carol Ockman, "When Is a Jewish Star Just a Star?" 137–138 and Coudert, 142.

[76] See Coudert's description of the two posters, 140–142.

FIGURE 4.2. Sarah Bernhardt as a stained-glass saint (Joan of Arc) on the cover of *Femina*, 1909, courtesy of the BNF.

younger and is more modest in that her robes cover more of her legs in the second poster.

One similarity, however, is worth noting. In both versions, Joan/Sarah is on a pedestal, but one foot steps off it, touching the letters of Bernhardt's last name. This pose could be interpreted in a number of different ways. It could be a wink at the viewer, indicating that despite the roles she played, Sarah was always Sarah in the end. But it could also hint at Bernhardt's desire to make Joan more human and accessible and less of a heroine "on

FIGURE 4.3. Sarah Bernhardt (frizzy hair, eyes heavenward) in a Eugène Grasset poster for Jules Barbier's *Jeanne d'Arc*, 1890, V&A Images, London/Art Resource, New York.

FIGURE 4.4. Sarah Bernhardt (straight hair) in a Eugène Grasset poster for Jules Barbier's *Jeanne d'Arc*, 1890, courtesy of the BNF.

FIGURE 4.5. Sarah Bernhardt as Joan of Arc in Emile Moreau's *Le Procès de Jeanne d'Arc*, 1909, courtesy of the BNF.

a pedestal." Finally, by depicting one foot off the pedestal, ready for action, it could also suggest the active qualities of Joan, which are downplayed in the Barbier play. Bernhardt often undermined as she affirmed feminine stereotypes.[77] In this instance, Joan/Sarah is feminine and modest, and at the same time, ready for action. Similarly, in the publicity stills for the play, Bernhardt as Joan holding the standard looks anything but weak.[78] Although there was no analogous poster for the 1909 production, there are photos and drawings of Bernhardt in Moreau's *Le Procès de Jeanne d'Arc*. Whereas there were numerous costume changes in the first play, there is only one in the second. In the latter play, Bernhardt wears a cuirass covered by a tunic with the cross; here her legs are showing. The costume seems less elaborate than that of the earlier play. Bernhardt as Joan looks, perhaps because the role demanded it, both stronger and more vulnerable (See Figure 4.5.).[79]

[77] Roberts, see especially pages 173–177.
[78] My description of the posters is similar to that of Coudert, but the arguments about the significance of Sarah stepping off the pedestal are my own.
[79] As Raymond Jonas notes in his book on the latter-day Joan of Arc, Claire Ferchaud, weakness could be a strength as well: *The Tragic Tale of Claire Ferchaud and the Great War* (Berkeley: University of California Press, 2005), 8.

So interchangeable had Joan and Sarah become that anti-Semites found it hard work to attack the actress in this role. Although anti-Semites made use of Joan of Arc to juxtapose her to the "pernicious" influence of Jews in French society,[80] I have found little evidence of attempts to denigrate Bernhardt as Joan in 1890 and in 1909, barring the following assessment by Léo Taxil in *La France chrétienne* of December 18, 1889: "To represent a sublimely Christian figure, the enemies of God have chosen a Jewish actress, whose scandalous adventures currently fill the gossip-columns of the press of the Boulevards. This Jewess will deliberately play the role of Joan of Arc in the wrong way; she will present her as a hysterical woman who has hallucinations; she will make her behave in the most extravagant way; she will turn the holy girl into a mad and grotesque virago."[81]

In 1890, Dom Blasius, who reviewed the Barbier play for the anti-Semitic, populist *L'Intransigeant*, praised both Barbier and Bernhardt for their portrayal of Joan.[82] His colleague and editor of *L'Intransigeant*, Henri Rochefort, commented in passing on the Barbier play but did not dwell on Bernhardt's portrayal of Joan. Instead, he concentrated his ire on Charles VII, who seemed to him to resemble other more recent French monarchs such as Louis-Philippe, who used the people when it served their interests but soon abandoned and betrayed them. By and large, most critics found much to like in the two plays, and all of them, almost without exception, hailed Bernhardt's two performances.

In 1890, Mgr. Monsabré, when asked by a journalist what he thought of Bernhardt playing the Virgin Mary and Firmin Gémier, the role of

---

[80] Winock, "Jeanne d'Arc et les juifs," in *Nationalisme, antisémitisme et fascisme en France* (Paris: Seuil, 1990), 145–146. See, for example, Gaston Méry, "De Cauchon à Thalamas," *La Libre Parole*, 2 December 1904.

[81] Taxil, quoted in Stephen Wilson, *Ideology and Experience: Anti-Semitism in France at the Time of the Dreyfus Affair* (Rutherford, NJ: Fairleigh Dickinson University Press, 1982), 593. It is hard to know, however, how seriously to take this example, because Taxil was the ultimate prankster. A fierce anti-clerical who claimed to have converted to Catholicism, he later recanted, claiming that he had been faking all along in order to expose the dangers of clericalism. Anti-Semites at *La Libre Parole*, which had not begun publication in 1890 at the time of the Barbier performance, would later deplore it: see Roberts, 212 (and footnotes 207, 208).

[82] Dom Blasius, "Premières Représentations: Jeanne d'Arc," *L'Intransigeant*, 5 January 1890. The review of the Moreau play in the 29 November 1909 issue by André Leroy was also positive. See also Dom Blasius's review of Sarah playing the lead in *L'Aiglon* in 1900. Although he began his review with a disparaging comment on the influence of Jews in French society, he went on to praise Rostand's play and Bernhardt herself, seemingly ignoring the fact that the famous actress was often the target of anti-Semites like himself: Dom Blasius, "Premières Représentations," *L'Intransigeant*, 17 March 1900.

Christ, the priest replied that he was disturbed by famous actors, known for other roles, representing religious figures.[83] Although he was clearly no fan of Sarah Bernhardt, his objection seemed to lie in the secular nature of the play rather than in a criticism of the actors themselves. This tendency to disengage with Bernhardt as Joan of Arc rather than criticize her seems especially pronounced in 1909, when even the reviewer for *L'Action française* praised both Moreau's play, which was deemed respectful of Joan, and Bernhardt's depiction of the heroine.[84] *La Croix* did not, of course, review plays, but on November 26, 1909, the day after *Le Procès de Jeanne d'Arc*'s premiere, the Catholic newspaper published a letter from the Archbishop of Montreal denouncing the dangers of the theater. On the following day, it published an article on the building of a religious theater on the Quai de Passy. Was this perhaps a way to fight the co-opting of religious figures by the secular theater? As for *La Libre Parole*, which did have a regular theater column, it studiously avoided all mention of the play. Although this silence is perhaps coincidental, taken with *La Croix's* pointed comment about the dangers of the secular theater, one could assume that these anti-Semites were in something of a quandary about Bernhardt's playing Joan of Arc. On the one hand, they saw her as a Jew, but by this time, Bernhardt had become a national figure so beloved that it might have seemed fruitless to attack her in the pages of *La Libre Parole*.[85] The fact that *L'Action française's* reviewer praised both the play and Bernhardt's depiction of Joan is a testimony to the success that Bernhardt had in uniting around her representation of Joan of Arc all but the most recalcitrant among the extreme right.[86] But the silence of these holdouts at *La Libre Parole* and *La Croix* was also a sign of the tensions that lay beneath the surface of the consensual Joan created by Bernhardt.

[83] "Le R. P. Monsabré et les mystères," *Le Gaulois*, 7 March 1890 (Dossier SB: Rt5884 1–2). The priest couldn't help taking a potshot at the actress: "Madame Sarah Bernhardt, I am told, is a very great artist, but to know that she will portray the Virgin! Ah! Spare me from having to comment on such a painful subject."

[84] Although he criticized Moreau's "romantic anti-clericalism," the reviewer Ergaste praised Moreau for not attempting to secularize Joan: "Les Théâtres," *L'Action française*, 27 November 1909.

[85] Only the previous year, Drumont had lamented in the pages of *La Libre Parole* that his attempts to stir anti-Semitic opinion against Jewish naval ensign Charles-Benjamin Ullmo had failed.

[86] Even the anti-clerical paper *Action*, which had published articles denigrating Joan of Arc as an ignorant young peasant in 1904, now abandoned this strategy and opted for a quietly respectful review both of the Moreau play and Bernhardt's acting: Camille Le Senne, "La Semaine théâtrale," 4 December 1909.

Joan: A Heroine for the Fin de Siècle

It is no accident that the Joan of Arc legend reached the height of its popularity during the fin de siècle, a golden age of hero making.[87] Despite the different types of heroes exalted, heroism was based primarily on acts of courage, both physical and moral. Heroes, who exhibited a great strength of will, were defined by their strong sense of self, honor, and duty, along with their belief in discipline and sacrifice. They sacrificed themselves for the greater good – more often than not, that of the nation – and were held up as antidotes to the decadence of the age. Heroism also implied self-control and scorn of danger, both male qualities. Although heroism was not limited to men, as the example of Joan illustrates, heroic virtues were viewed as specifically male.[88] How then do we reconcile the celebration of Joan with an era in which males across the political spectrum were determined to maintain separate spheres for the sexes? What did Joan mean as a cultural symbol at the fin de siècle, independently of how Bernhardt portrayed her?

Joan was a unifying figure because the ambiguity of her gender gave her a transcendental power, indeed, a national power that placed her outside the gender wars of the fin de siècle. At the same time, however, this very ambiguity was also a potentially subversive force. In order to shed light on how Joan was viewed during this time, one should begin with Marina Warner's classic work on Joan of Arc as an image of female heroism. In successive chapters that treat Joan as "maid of France," "ideal androgyne," a knight, a heretic, and an amazon, among others, Warner offers explanations about Joan's contradictions and marginality in the medieval period that still resonated at the fin de siècle.

First, Joan was a young woman, complete with all the sexual characteristics of womanhood. Yet she also represented the negation of all that those characteristics symbolized.[89] A virgin who did not menstruate, she remained in a prepubescent state. In other words, she was still a child, not a grown woman, and could not pose the same threat to men that a "real" woman might have. But at the same time, this amenorrhea was seen as a source of her strength.[90] According to Joan of Arc lore,

---

[87] In an interview from 1890 ("Jeanne d'Arc et M. Renan"), Renan, asked to comment on the Joan of Arc legend, noted, "The masses are not cut out for the truth ... let them adore the idols who have replaced gods."

[88] Paul Gerbod, "L'Ethique héroïque en France (1870–1914)," *La Revue historique*, no. 268 (1982): 414–415.

[89] Warner, 19.

[90] Warner, 22.

it was not possible to desire her, because all those who did were punished. It is partly for this reason that critics of all political stripes reacted strongly against Moreau's hinting that Bedford was in "love," or at the very least, "haunted" by Joan. As one observer noted, she "wasn't even a woman."[91] Joan's indeterminate status, conversely, made her more accessible to many fin-de-siècle males who were plagued by a fear of losing their own manhood. Similarly, the fact that she was exceptional made her more acceptable to these men. The historian Ernest Renan, when asked in 1890 by a reporter whether Joan should serve as an example to young French women, replied in the negative, claiming that Joan was unique.[92] Although males and females might admire Joan's qualities, young girls could and should not emulate her.

Joan's sexlessness also allied her with the Catholic tradition of strong women, first and foremost, the Virgin Mary, and a number of female saints. Again, because these saints were not "real" women, they could be more readily accepted for their strengths, which consisted principally of martyrdom.[93] For republicans, Joan was the complement to Marianne, another figure whose sexuality was tamed in order to make her a symbol of the nation.[94] Joan's intact sexuality, even in her own time, symbolized the inviolability of a France torn apart by war.[95] It is for this reason that her image struck a chord with contemporaries of the late nineteenth century, who had witnessed the "rape" and dismemberment of France after defeat in the Franco-Prussian War. For them, Joan became a symbol of the nation before the "loss" of this "innocent" state.

Joan's virginity was one way in which she achieved androgyny. Her transvestism was another way she attained this ambiguous status; she was no longer a woman nor was she a man. By dressing like a man, Joan rejected the destiny of womanhood and usurped men's functions while rejecting the drawbacks of their sex.[96] Among the charges against Joan were dressing like a man and bearing arms, two male prerogatives. But, as the church claimed during the second trial, she needed to wear these

[91] Camille le Senne, "La Semaine théâtrale."

[92] "Jeanne d'Arc et M. Renan."

[93] Warner, 157.

[94] See Lynn Hunt, *Politics, Culture and Class in the French Revolution* (Berkeley: University of California Press, 1984), and Maurice Agulhon, *Marianne into Battle: Republican Imagery and Symbolism in France, 1789–1880*, trans. Janet Lloyd (New York: Cambridge University Press, 1981).

[95] Warner, 32.

[96] Warner, 145–146.

clothes to do a man's job and to protect her from unwanted attentions.[97] Once her mission was over, she was content to wear women's clothing. In other words, she dressed like men to do a man's job and reverted back to her "feminine" state once it was over. Such an argument was much less threatening than claims to equality of status with men.

With regard to the male art of war, Joan always claimed that she was more comfortable with her banner than she was with her sword, which has historically been associated with male potency. Moreover, she did not want to kill nor had she done so.[98] This disavowal of martial qualities made Joan easier to accept by men during the fin de siècle.[99] Instead, she inspired others, and this role of muse better fit gender categories of the era. Although some contemporaries played up her military qualities, most sought to minimize them, especially Ernest Lesigne and Anatole France, whose books caused controversy at the time of the Barbier revival and the Moreau play, respectively. Both men denied Joan's military prowess, claiming that she had been the agent of others. Objecting to this point of view, conservative critic René Doumic, in his review of France's book in *La Revue des deux mondes*, claimed that the famous author had reduced Joan to a "mannequin" and a "mascot." Similarly, critics of Lesigne's book took issue with the idea that she had merely inspired others.[100]

It is interesting to note that foremost among those who would deny Joan's agency were those of the left – some on the left dismissed her as an *hommesse* – perhaps because their opponents on the right could claim that she took her orders from God and/or the king. In this way, individuals on both sides, albeit in different ways, could deny Joan's power and

---

[97] Among the many books by Régine Pernoud, see *Joan of Arc: Her Story*, co-written with Marie-Véronique Clin, trans. Jeremy DuQuesnay Adams (New York: St. Martin's Griffin, 1998). See also the recent translation and introduction by Daniel Hobbins of the trial of Joan of Arc: *The Trial of Joan of Arc* (Cambridge, MA: Harvard University Press, 2005).

[98] Warner, 165–166.

[99] Writing about the depiction of Joan of Arc in "le Petit Lavisse," "The Nation According to Lavisse: Teaching Masculinity and Male Citizenship in Third-Republic France," *French Cultural Studies* 18, no. 1 (2007), Denis Provencher and Luke Eilderts note that Joan is depicted without the standard male signifier of the sword, 49. They also observe that agency is taken away from Joan by transferring it to men – Baudricourt, the king, as well as God, who is, after all, a male figure, 46.

[100] Doumic felt that France had underestimated Joan of Arc's psychological power by reducing her to the puppet of others, 930. Doumic also objected to France's undercutting of Joan's martial qualities and concluded that his Joan of Arc story was a story without Joan – a criticism also made of Lesigne's book: "Revue littéraire: La Jeanne d'Arc de M. Anatole France," *La Revue des deux mondes* 44 (15 April 1908): 921–933.

shape her image into one that was palatable for males of the time. The republican historian Ernest Lavisse, writing about the representation of Joan in his famous textbook for children ("le Petit Lavisse"), walked a similar tightrope in his portrayal of this figure. He depicted her heroic qualities while assuring that she was feminine enough not to excite male anxieties about powerful women in the public sphere.[101]

Because Joan was neither a man nor a real woman, she could be seen as a unifying figure. An androgyne, she united "male" and "female" qualities of heroism: on the one hand, the martial qualities of the warrior, and, on the other, the female qualities of sacrifice and self-effacement. Yet Joan, despite such "domestication," remained, as she always had been, a subversive figure who blurred the very gender categories many of the time sought to maintain.[102] Joan of Arc, like Bernhardt herself, undercut gender categories even as she affirmed them. Joan's heroic qualities were associated with a male chivalric code of honor and represented the usurping by a woman of the male prerogative of individual action in the public sphere.

Joan of Arc also transcended boundaries of class by the richness of her dress and her possession of a sword and standard, both of which were associated with nobles, specifically with knights.[103] This transcending of class must surely have caught the notice of Bernhardt, who similarly transgressed such barriers through her actress status, because the point was underscored in the Barbier revival by Bernhardt's magnificently rich cuirass (on display at the 2006 Jewish Museum exhibit on the actress). Furthermore, there was a certain provocation to Joan's dressing as a man, something that Bernhardt, famous for her *travesti* roles, had to have been aware of. Transvestism can just as easily accentuate sexuality as it can eliminate it.[104] Indeed, the aforementioned costume from the Barbier production was feminine and flowery, in part, because knights of the time dressed in this ornate fashion, but also to highlight Joan's femininity.

Above all, Joan's courage challenged the gender norms of the period. Although courage, both physical and moral, as the aristocratic women in the Bazar de la Charité fire illustrated, was not solely a male characteristic, contemporaries of the fin de siècle minimized women's

---

[101] As Provencher and Eilderts note, "while the male protagonist in Lavisse becomes the citizen-soldier and martyr for king and nation, the female protagonist is ultimately abandoned by her king and nation, and remains standing alone before God," 50.

[102] Warner, 23.

[103] See Warner's chapter "Knight," especially pp. 159–169.

[104] As Warner notes, 217.

courage by depicting it as visceral, a product of the heart rather than a conscious choice of the mind, even when actual events contradicted their words.[105]

Undoubtedly, for such individuals, direction from God or the king helped explain Joan's courage in the face of death. And they could also dwell on her "feminine" weakness, that is, her fear and recanting. But by the time of the Moreau play in 1909, in the wake of the "nationalist revival," commentators, although recognizing this "human weakness," also reveled in Joan's defiance against the enemy.

Finally, the story of Joan of Arc also fits into the classical tradition of an amazon, a virginal woman with extraordinary physical qualities. The fin de siècle feared such "amazons" and associated them with New Women.[106] But although amazons were killed in the end by male heroes, Joan was herself responsible for her death. Yet in this case too, male qualities were affirmed over female ones.[107] Joan must die so that French (male) "citizens" may live.[108] This martyrdom was a necessary quality of her heroism, and it is for this reason that Lesigne's most outrageous claim, that Joan had survived burning at the stake and had lived to give birth to numerous children, struck a nerve. Not only did he deny her martyrdom, but he also depicted her as a grown woman.

Sarah Bernhardt was undoubtedly right when she observed that the public wanted to see an idealized image of Joan; in general, this image corresponded to the ideal female of the period. In her memoirs, tellingly called *Ma double vie*, published in 1907, the actress expressed her frustration with the public for wanting to see the legend rather than the reality of such historical figures as Jesus, Napoleon, and Joan:

I have tried ... to force the audience to return to the truth and to destroy the legendary aspect of certain characters whose true nature modern historians have revealed but the audience has not followed me. I soon came to the realization that legend always triumphs over historical fact, and maybe that is a blessing for those who think with the crowd. ... We do not want Joan of Arc to be a crude

---

[105] See my *Birth of a National Icon: The Literary Avant-Garde and the Origins of the Intellectual in France* (Albany, NY: SUNY Press, 1999). In his editorial in *Le Journal des débats politiques et littéraires* (of 13 January 1890), André Heurteau noted that republicans saw Joan as a manifestation of individual conscience. This vision corresponds to the Dreyfusard view of heroes during the Dreyfus Affair.

[106] See Chapter 4, "Amazone, Femme Nouvelle, and the Threat to the Bourgeois Family," of Debora L. Silverman, *Art Nouveau in Fin-de-Siècle France: Politics, Psychology and Style* (Berkeley: University of California Press, 1989), 63–74.

[107] Warner, 216.

[108] Provencher and Eilderts, 50.

strapping peasant woman violently pushing away the rough soldier who wants to joke, mounting like a man the broad-backed draft horse, laughing freely with the soldiers' crude jests and, subject as she was to the shameless lack of privacy typical of this still barbarous era, deserving all the more credit for remaining a heroic virgin.[109]

As the reviews of Bernhardt's performances illustrate, audiences liked the accessibility and humanity of her Joan, but at the same time, this public wanted a sanitized image of the heroine, one which corresponded to the contemporary ideal of the *jeune fille*. Bernhardt, always closely attuned to the pulse of the age, noted further:

In legend she remains a frail being, led by a divine spirit. Her girl's arm, holding up the heavy standard, is supported by an invisible angel. The beyond is reflected in her child's eyes from which the warriors draw their strength and courage. It is thus that we wish her to be. And the legend remains triumphant.[110]

Note that it is not Joan who is described by Bernhardt as forceful and courageous; rather, she inspires these qualities in others. Furthermore, she is not a physically strong woman, but a frail young girl, indeed, a child, who can only hold up the heavy banner with the help of an invisible angel. Yet the publicity posters of Bernhardt as Joan show the very opposite – her Joan is all "tensile strength," in the words of art historian Kenneth Silver (See Figure 4.6.).[111]

At the time of the Barbier revival in 1890, Bernhardt was asked by a reporter how she saw Joan of Arc. After carefully asserting that she was neither a historian nor a philosopher but simply an artist, she declared, "She is a mysterious figure, above all inspired and mystical. She suffers from hallucinations, is a sort of ecstatic figure who moves toward a fatal goal guided by a will she cannot resist: a warrior, she is horrified by blood; she does not wield the sword. Once the goal is attained, the divine mission accomplished, she becomes a woman once again, and she transforms herself, and regains her human qualities. It seems to me that

---

[109] *Ma double vie* (Paris: Editions Phébus, 2000), 99–100. The translation I have used here and in the next note comes from *My Double Life: The Memoirs of Sarah Bernhardt*, trans. Victoria Tietze Larson (Albany: SUNY Press, 1999), 59.

[110] *Ma double vie*, 99–100; *My Double Life*, 59.

[111] Kenneth E. Silver, "Sarah Bernhardt and the Theatrics of French Nationalism: From Roland's Daughter to Napoleon's Son," in *Sarah Bernhardt: The Art of High Drama*, 76. See also his essay, "Celebrity, Patriotism and Sarah Bernhardt," in *Constructing Charisma: Celebrity, Fame and Power in Nineteenth-Century Europe*, ed. Edward Berenson and Eva Gilloi (New York: Berghahn Books, 2010), 145–154.

FIGURE 4.6. Sarah Bernhardt holding standard in Jules Barbier's *Jeanne d'Arc*, 1890, courtesy of the BNF.

Joan of Arc is a character shrouded in mystery much more than a tragic heroine."[112] Here, as she would later, Bernhardt affirmed Joan's human and feminine qualities rather than her martial character. Her mystic and

---

[112] Lahire, "A Propos de Jeanne d'Arc: Une Visite à Sarah Bernhardt" (1890).

religious aspects could always be reconciled with traditional notions of femininity.

Bernhardt's portrayal of Joan, a woman disguised as a man, is interesting, not only because the actress wore male clothing offstage but also in light of her fame in playing trouser parts – Lorenzaccio, Hamlet, and l'Aiglon being the most famous. François de Nion, writing about her performance as Joan in 1909, distinguished among these roles, observing that in *L'Aiglon*, where she played a young man, not for one moment did her comportment reveal *un travesti*. But with Joan, he noted, "Joan's manner under the suit of armor recalls the recent skirts of fustian, and this is the way that a young woman dressed as a boy presents herself."[113]

Bernhardt claimed she liked playing male roles because they offered more depth to the actress but asserted that the only male parts a woman could play were those of a man's mind in a weak (male) body. As Bernhardt's portrayal of l'Aiglon illustrates, Bernhardt used the trouser role to interject vulnerability into the duke's character and into the Napoleonic legend itself.[114] But at the same time, Bernhardt herself was depicted as forceful, not only in the male parts she played but also in her portrayals of Joan. Auguste Vitu, writing in *Le Figaro* of January 3, 1890, noted, "But where she surprised everyone ... was in the extraordinary, passionate and irresistible strength that she was able to give to the patriotic enthusiasm of the heroine." Jules Lemaître, writing in *Le Journal des débats politiques et littéraires* of January 6, 1890, observed of Bernhardt in the role: "She possesses an inner strength."[115] In both cases then, whether she was playing a man or a woman dressed as a man, Bernhardt was subverting, even as she seemed to maintain, traditional gender roles.[116] Bernhardt thus

---

[113] François de Nion, "Le Procès de Jeanne d'Arc."

[114] Berlanstein, "Breeches and Breaches: Cross-Dress Theater and the Culture of Gender Ambiguity in Modern France," *Comparative Studies in Society and History* 38 (April 1996): 362. Berlanstein demonstrates that trouser parts reached the height of popularity at the very moment that the idea of separate spheres between men and women became an article of faith; yet in an age of gender blurring, the notion was declining in popularity. Because men felt threatened in real life, they found the practice of stage inversion distasteful, 350–352.

[115] See also reviews from 1909 that comment on Bernhardt's/Joan's strength: Adolphe Brisson, "Théâtres: Le Procès de Jeanne d'Arc," *Le Temps*, 29 November 1909, as well as the review by Jacques Copeau.

[116] Mary Louise Roberts, who notes that Bernhardt was seen as both excessively feminine and masculine, asks if a woman could assume a man's role and still retain her femininity, what does this mean about gender roles? She concludes that Bernhardt's playing of trouser parts could be read subversively: *Disruptive Acts*, 173–174. I would extend this reading to Bernhardt's portrayal of Joan. See also Martha Vicinus, who has

embodied qualities of both sexes. Maurice Rostand wrote of her that she was both "extraordinarily virile" and "completely feminine," concluding that she was "in sum, the couple reunited."[117]

Conclusion

Joan of Arc, like other heroes of the time, was seen as the antidote to a base age of selfish consumerism. She represented disinterestedness and sacrifice at a time when French society seemed in danger of losing these qualities. It is thus ironic that Bernhardt, herself the embodiment of mass culture, a symbol of the culture of spectacle and display that promulgated new roles for women, not only in the theater but also in advertising,[118] should become so closely linked in the public's mind with Joan of Arc and represented as the antithesis of such culture. But every night, in 1890 and again in 1909, Bernhardt brought the house down with her portrayal of Joan. Commentators from both periods noted that a *frisson patriotique* (patriotic shiver) united the audience during her performances.[119] By associating herself with the image of Joan, Bernhardt accelerated but was not solely responsible for the contemporary commodification of the Joan of Arc legend. As we know, Joan of Arc was used to sell consumer products. Bernhardt too capitalized on her celebrity to hawk a variety of items from women's face powder to tonics. The actress, in some measure, also used her image to "sell" Joan to fin-de-siècle audiences. Although

---

described the subversive nature of Bernhardt's rendering of trouser roles. As she tells us, Bernhardt inspired homosexuals, both male and female: "Fin-de-Siècle Theatrics: Male Impersonation and Lesbian Desire," in *Borderlines: Genders and Identities in War and Peace, 1870–1930*, ed. Billie Melman (New York: Routledge, 1998), 172–173.

[117] Maurice Rostand, *Sarah Bernhardt* (Paris: Calmann-Lévy, 1950), 54.

[118] See Susan A. Glenn, *Female Spectacle: The Theatrical Roots of Modern Feminism* (Cambridge, MA: Harvard University Press, 2000), especially her chapter, "The Bernhardt Effect: Self-Advertising and the Age of Spectacle," 9–39, and Carol Ockman, "Was She Magnificent?" *Sarah Bernhardt: The Art of High Drama*, 55. Indeed, the entire catalog of objects from the Jewish Museum is a testimony to Bernhardt's self-promotion skills. See also Ockman's essay "Women, Icons, and Power," in *Self and History: A Tribute to Linda Nochlin*, ed. Aruna D'Souza (New York: Thames and Hudson, 2001), 103–116.

[119] See, for example, reviews by Richard O'Monroy, "La Soirée parisienne," *Gil Blas*, 5 January 1890 (Dossier SB: Rf 5884); Auguste Vitu, "Les Premières Représentations," *Le Figaro*, 4 January 1890; and "La Soirée théâtrale" in the same issue of *Le Figaro* by Un Monsieur de l'orchestre. For 1909, see Georges Boyer, "Premières Représentations," *Le Petit Journal*, 26 November 1909; René Doumic, "Revue dramatique," *La Revue des deux mondes* 55 (15 January 1909): 443–444; Un Monsieur de l'orchestre, "La Soirée," *Le Figaro*, 26 November 1909.

Bernhardt's Joan corresponded to the gender norms of the period, she also displayed great strength as well as human qualities, making her more accessible to the mass public. This was a Joan who could be "consumed" with every performance by individuals of differing political opinions.

Despite the various political battles being fought outside the theater walls, both in 1890 and in 1909, Sarah Bernhardt managed to unite the French audiences who flocked nightly to her performances. A similar situation occurred during the height of the Dreyfus Affair with Edmond Rostand's *Cyrano de Bergerac*, and a bit less successfully two years later with Rostand's *L'Aiglon*. Bernhardt herself saw the theater as both a progressive force and the stuff of dreams, as she told an interviewer in 1921.[120] The actress clearly used the figure of the virginal Joan, who was, moreover, a national symbol, to establish a certain respectability for herself and to associate herself in the public's mind with an image of "authentic Frenchness." At the same time, however, she was subverting traditional gender roles and mocking those who doubted her true qualities as a French woman. But if Bernhardt used the figure of Joan to transform her own image, the reverse is also true. The fact that Sarah Bernhardt played Joan of Arc twice in popular productions had an impact on the legend, making the heroine more human and accessible to turn-of-the century audiences who craved images of heroes to whom they could relate.

The consensual Joan of Arc, forged in part by Sarah Bernhardt, was not destined to last, because just below the surface of consensus lay irreconcilable positions on what Joan stood for. Although unity was maintained through World War I up to the declaration of Joan's sainthood in 1920, thereafter the image of Joan was increasingly co-opted by the right, although two rival visions of Joan emerged during the Second World War, pitting the Joan of Vichy against the Joan of the Resistance. In our own time, the extreme right wing in the form of the National Front has all but cornered the market on Joan of Arc imagery. But for a short time, during the fin de siècle, Joan became a saint for the democratic age. It is thus fitting that this Joan be enshrined in the boulevard theater, a symbol of the new mass culture, and moreover, played by Sarah Bernhardt, an icon of the age.

---

[120] "The theater is the great propagandist of progress, the great evoker of dreams," she told the journalist for *Le Petit Journal*, 9 October 1921: "Sarah Bernhardt, gloire de la scène française, nous raconte sa vocation et conseille des artistes de demain" (Rt5881 Interviews with Bernhardt from 1890 to 1920).

Bernhardt herself was a transcendent figure, capable of reuniting all but the most recalcitrant around her, but it is also true that during the years immediately preceding the First World War, the French people, both weary of internal conflict and anxious about an ever-present threat from Germany, increasingly sought consensus, around heroes as well as anti-heroes. Moreover, nourished on a diet of plays with larger-than-life figures and a press that blurred fact and fiction, they came to view the real-life events of the Ullmo spy affair of 1907–1908 as a national performance.

5

Opium, Gambling, and the Demimondaine: The Ullmo Spy Case of 1907–1908

> *Hegel remarks somewhere that all great, world-historical facts and per-*
> *sonages occur, as it were, twice. He has forgotten to add: the first time as*
> *tragedy, the second as farce.*
>
> – *Karl Marx*

As the fin de siècle shaded off into the belle époque, the French were more united than previously, not only around the heroic legacy of Joan of Arc, especially in 1909, but also a few months earlier, over the Ullmo spy case, which captivated national attention in late 1907 through early 1908.[1] On October 25, 1907, French newspapers were filled with reports of a naval officer accused of having stolen valuable documents concerning France's national defense. The details of his capture could not have been more burlesque than a scene from Maurice Leblanc's popular Arsène Lupin (the "gentleman burglar") detective series. Charles-Benjamin Ullmo, a naval ensign, second in command of the counter-torpedo boat *Carabine*, had been lured and then captured by officers of the Sûreté générale at the gorges of Ollioules, a secluded spot some twelve kilometers outside of Toulon on October 22. Ullmo had set up a meeting with the Sûreté agent, thinking him to be a representative of the Naval Ministry, having earlier written to the Naval Minister Gaston Thomson, offering to sell France secret documents in his possession for 150,000 francs. He would sell them to a foreign power, he threatened, if the Ministry rejected his offer.

---

[1] As I mentioned at the beginning of the book, I have generally used the term *fin de siècle* to cover the thirty-five years before the war, but I fully recognize that a shift in mood had taken place in the years immediately preceding, leading some historians to distinguish between the fin de siècle and the belle époque.

Earlier attempts to secure the money had ended in failure. For the meeting at the Ollioules gorges, Ullmo had arrived in a chauffer suit, which he had rented from a costume shop, with a mask covering his face. The officer in charge had assured him he had no weapon, but when Ullmo, in possession of a gun, let down his guard, the agent, versed in boxing maneuvers, easily overpowered and disarmed him. Thus ended the career of a rather inept spy, more the hero of a farce than a dangerous mastermind (Figures 5.1, 5.2, and 5.3).

Immediately upon his capture, Ullmo admitted his guilt. He pleaded for clemency, explaining that he needed money desperately to fund his opium habit, pay his gambling debts, and support his mistress, a well-known demimondaine named Lison (Marie-Louise) Welsch. In actuality, Ullmo's crime was more than a simple case of extortion. Headlines blared treason in mid-November, when investigators discovered that Ullmo had first tried and failed to sell the papers to a German agent. Accordingly, Ullmo was eventually accused of intelligence with the enemy. Convicted of high treason on February 22, 1908, he was sentenced to deportation for life on Devil's Island, occupying the same cell as Alfred Dreyfus had some years earlier.

Although contemporaries, especially anti-Semites, who did not fail to note Ullmo's Jewish identity, drew strong parallels between the Dreyfus and Ullmo cases, the two men could not have been more different. Unlike the innocent, discreet family man Alfred Dreyfus, Ullmo, by his own admission, was a flamboyant bachelor with drug and gambling problems as well as an expensive mistress. Although the Ullmo case, unlike the Dreyfus Affair, never became a *lieu de mémoire*, it captivated the imagination of contemporaries, who were fascinated by Ullmo's account of his betrayal of honor and country for love.[2] The French press, including such major dailies as *Le Petit Parisien*, *Le Journal*, *Le Petit Journal*, and *Le Matin*, as well as *Le Figaro*, *Le Gaulois*, *L'Echo de Paris*, *L'Intransigeant*, and *Le Temps*, along with the anti-Semitic *La Libre Parole* and *L'Action française*, the Socialist *L'Humanité*, and the leading Jewish paper *Les Archives israélites*, all covered the case in great detail, titillating readers

---

[2] A song was even composed about the two lovers, sung to the tune of a popular ditty of the time: "J'ai tant pleuré pour toi." See René Delpêche, *Amour, crime, châtiment ou la vie cachée de Benjamin Ullmo* (Paris: Les Editions du Scorpion, 1957), 34. The words were as follows: "If I betrayed [my country] for you. For love of your goddess-like body … If I ruined my life. Oh, Lison, the woman I love … I am happy all the same. Since I suffer for you."

DRAMATIQUE ARRESTATION DU TRAITRE ULLMO
DANS LES GORGES D'OLLIOULES

FIGURE 5.1. "The Dramatic Arrest of the Traitor Ullmo in the Ollioules Gorges,"
Le Petit Journal (supplément illustré), 10 November 1907 (back cover). Author's
collection.

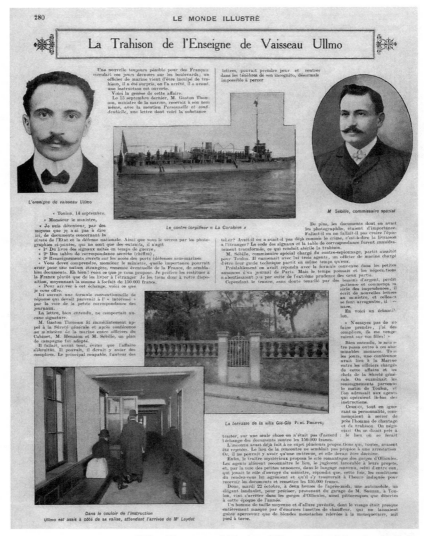

FIGURES 5.2 AND 5.3. "The Treason of Ensign Ullmo," *Le Monde illustré*, 1
November 1907 (pp. 280–281). Author's collection.

with the latest tidbits about the case. Indeed, the press even played a role
in the Ullmo affair – the would-be spy not only got his idea from reading an article about espionage in the press, but he also communicated
with both German agents and the French defense ministry by placing
ads in *Le Journal* and *La République du Var*. Despite the best efforts of

FIGURES 5.2 AND 5.3. (*Continued*).

anti-Semites to stir the tensions raised during the Dreyfus case, the Ullmo trial was a failed replay of the Dreyfus Affair.

Although the Ullmo case was not a new Dreyfus Affair, it offers an important window onto late nineteenth- and early twentieth-century attitudes about heroism, honor, and manhood, as well as their impact on national identity, by examining the opposite of heroic behavior. Unlike the celebrated heroes of the age, Ullmo had not sacrificed himself for his country but had instead attempted to sell it out for egotistical reasons. Such behavior was unpardonable, all the more so because Ullmo as a military man was entrusted both with the nation's security and with upholding national honor. Ullmo was the ultimate anti-hero whose fall served as a warning to his compatriots of the dangers of degeneration and national decline, especially because his unpatriotic behavior was linked to opium use and a "loose woman," both of which were seen as threats to national health and security. Although Ullmo was convicted of attempted treason, there was a certain amount of public sympathy, or at least pity, for the fallen solider, who was viewed as a victim of his drug habit and of a femme fatale.

Especially striking in the Ullmo case is that anti-Semitism did not play a major role. Despite the anti-Semites' best efforts, there was little public interest in pursuing an anti-Semitic agenda. Although anti-Semitism was present in the Ullmo case, it was a minor issue and was represented in a more coded way than during the height of the Dreyfus Affair. The fact that the Ullmo case did not assume the proportions of the Affair was due in great measure to the public's weariness of the internecine quarrels that had marked the earlier fin-de-siècle period. In light of an impending war with Germany, French men and women put aside such differences, thereby increasingly accepting Jews into the national consensus, as is clear from the near-universal adulation Sarah Bernhardt garnered for her portrayal of Joan of Arc in 1909. Thus, despite the continued social and political strife that marked the period, the unity the French would display during the First World War was already present during the years immediately preceding. The French could thus "consume" the Ullmo affair as a captivating *fait divers*, united in their knowledge and acceptance both of Ullmo's guilt and the extenuating circumstances surrounding his attempted treason.

The Ullmo case thus illustrates the importance of the press – in particular, the role of the *fait divers* in forging national identity during the years leading up to the war – and may be juxtaposed to the earlier Bazar de la Charité fire. Whereas the Bazar de la Charité fire, which took place on the eve of the Dreyfus Affair in 1897, ignited political tensions rather than forging a national community of mourning, the Ullmo affair was a case of treason transformed into a *fait divers*, uniting the nation as much around the consumption of the news as around the theme of national defense.

Finally, the Ullmo case offers us a fascinating glimpse into how theatrical notions of behavior gleaned both from the boulevard theater and the mass press shaped the way in which contemporaries imagined themselves and their world. The various subterfuges imagined by Ullmo – among them, exchanges of coded letters in the press, instructions to place blackmail money in the toilets of a train, and the fateful meeting where Ullmo was captured at the Ollioules gorges – seem like incidents in a boulevard production rather than events in a real-life spy case.[3] Moreover, Ullmo's lawyer depicted his client both as a victim in a national melodrama and as the author of his own vaudeville play, thereby appealing to a public enthralled by the theater.

The Politics of Social Defense

At the time of the Ullmo case, fears of threats to national security from both external and internal sources coalesced, reaching an apogee from 1906 to 1909, resulting in what Robert Nye has called the "politics of social defense."[4] On the international level, Germany posed an increasing danger in the wake of the 1904 *Entente cordiale* between the British and French. The Germans, feeling surrounded by hostile powers, attempted to split the two allies apart by challenging France's hegemony in Morocco, where the French were attempting to establish a protectorate.[5] To accomplish this goal, Kaiser Wilhelm II made a dramatic visit to Tangier in March 1905. Although the immediate consequence of the visit was to precipitate the fall from power of foreign minister Théophile Delcassé, the architect of the Franco-British alliance, the long-term effect was to reinforce British support of France and harden French national opinion against Germany.

---

[3] The Ullmo case has inspired a recent historical novel by Bernard Soulhol, *Benjamin et Lison: Toulon et l'affaire Ullmo (1805–1908)*, which recounts the details of their relationship: (Toulon: Les Presses du Midi, 2001).

[4] Robert A. Nye, *Crime, Madness, and Politics in Modern France: The Medical Concept of National Decline* (Princeton, NJ: Princeton University Press, 1984), 180–182.

[5] The British recognized French control over Morocco in exchange for French recognition of British hegemony over Egypt. After another Moroccan crisis in 1911, the French established a full protectorate in Morocco. In exchange, they ceded a large part of the French Congo to the Germans.

Beginning with the "coup de Tanger" in 1905, France experienced a "nationalist revival." No longer were nationalist concerns exclusively the preserve of an extreme right-wing party. Nationalism entered the mainstream, and even many on the left, with the notable exception of the newly unified Socialists, were at least resigned to war with Germany.[6] Thus, there was considerable unity at the time, despite evidence of political conflict in other arenas.[7] In 1914, the French, viewing themselves as the victims of German aggression, entered the war with determination, and, moreover, united around the notion of the *Union sacrée*.[8]

On the domestic front, former Dreyfusards were in power. As *La Libre Parole* noted scathingly, Georges Clemenceau was prime minister; Georges Picquart, minister of war; and Gaston Thomson, the son-in-law of Adolphe Crémieux (known for the law granting Algerian Jews citizenship), minister of the navy. Under the Emile Combes ministry from 1902 to 1905, the government attempted to republicanize the army; witness the infamous *affaires des fiches* of 1904–1905, in which a scandal ensued when the press discovered that the anti-clerical War Minister General Louis André had attempted to prevent the promotions of officers with clerical ties. Similar efforts to democratize the navy were undertaken during Camille Pelletan's tenure as naval minister during these years (from 1902 to 1905).[9] The separation of church and state in 1905 and Alfred Dreyfus's rehabilitation in 1906 marked in some ways the end of the Dreyfus era, as did a series of violent strikes from 1906 to 1909, which led to contemporary anxieties about class warfare. In contrast with the earlier Dreyfus period, which witnessed political conflict among propertied classes, these years featured class conflict between capital and labor.[10]

---

[6] See Eugen Weber, *The Nationalist Revival in France, 1905–1914* (Berkeley: University of California Press, 1968).

[7] As Edward Berenson notes, the bulk of French public opinion occupied a fluid center, which could veer to moderate nationalism or a patriotic pacifism. Thus, the French were not jingoist partisans of war at this time, nor did they seek to actively avoid it: *The Trial of Madame Caillaux* (Berkeley: University of California Press, 1992), 72.

[8] The war was thus seen as a defensive one by the French: Leonard V. Smith, Stéphane Audoin-Rouzeau, and Annette Becker, *France and the Great War, 1914–1918* (Cambridge: Cambridge University Press, 2003), 29–30.

[9] In part by using torpedo boats rather than *cuirassiers* – a disastrous policy in the long run: Philippe Masson, *Histoire de la Marine. Tome II: De la vapeur à l'atome* (Limoges: Lavauzelle, 1983; 2000).

[10] Although there were more strikes in 1906, their intensity was higher in 1907: Nye, *Crime, Madness, and Politics*, 188. In 1907 there was also a revolt against the government by

Prime Minister Georges Clemenceau, whose ruthless suppression of these strikes earned him the sobriquet of *premier flic de France* (the first cop of France), thus effectively signaled the end of the alliance of the left and center left forged during the Dreyfus years.[11]

The sense of social unrest was heightened by a fear of increasing crime and lawlessness. There was an upsurge of criminal activity, including murders and violent crime; newspapers devoted a great deal of space to them, with France's highest-circulation paper *Le Petit Parisien* leading the way. The years after 1900 witnessed an upsurge in reporting on crime, with crime stories occupying 10 percent of the surface of *Le Petit Parisien* during the period from 1902 to 1908.[12] All the major newspapers were infected by such coverage, even the sober *Le Temps*, although to a much lesser extent.[13] The exploits of gangs, dubbed *apaches* by a member of the press, along with highly public murder cases, especially those committed by women, were covered in great detail.[14]

In the weeks before the news of Ullmo's arrest, newspapers were filled with tales of murder, from the trial in July 1907 of Albert Soleilland, responsible for the brutal rape and murder of his neighbor's young daughter, to news of child killer Jeanne Weber, who had been arrested in May of the same year. These trials took place against the backdrop of national discussions about the death penalty, not only in the Parliament,

---

[11] winegrowers, suffering from overproduction and increasing foreign competition. The fact that government troops sent to quell rioting mutinied and took the side of those opposing the government only heightened fears of insecurity.

[11] Robert David Andersen, *France: 1870–1914* (New York: Routledge, 1984), 27.

[12] Dominique Kalifa, *L'Encre et le sang: Récits de crimes et société à la Belle Epoque* (Paris: Fayard, 1995), 20–21. Kalifa also notes that 1907 to 1908 was a particularly big year for crime reporting, in part because of discussions about the death penalty in Parliament, 23–24. Nye examines this debate in "1908: The Capital Punishment Debate in the Chamber of Deputies," 227–264 of *Crime, Madness, and Politics*.

[13] Historians of the press have argued that the coverage of the *fait divers*, in particular, the criminal *fait divers*, contributed to the development of a national community around the consumption of these thrilling events. See especially Kalifa, who indicates that instead of placing articles about crime in the provinces in a rubric entitled "Départements," editors henceforth put them in the category of *faits divers*. Furthermore, the Parisian newspapers sent "special envoys" around the country to report on these incidents, 21. See also the pioneering work of Michelle Perrot: "L'Affaire Troppmann," *L'Histoire* 30 (January 1981): 28–37, and "Fait Divers et histoire au XIXème Siècle," *Annales, ESC*, no. 4 (July–August 1983): 911–917. In her recent book, *Le Fait divers en république: Histoire sociale de 1870 à nos jours* (Paris: CNRS, 2000), Marine M'Sili argues that the *fait divers* contributed to the creation of a national community, especially in the local press, which far from emphasizing local cohesion over national unity, linked the two, subsuming the former in the latter, 142–146.

[14] These fears were borne out by statistics: Nye, *Crime, Madness, and Politics*, 192.

but also in the press, beginning with *Le Petit Parisien*, which launched an opinion poll on the matter – and manipulated the results to favor its own pro–capital punishment position.[15]

Stories of spies also filled the papers of the time, with Ullmo's arrest coinciding with that of former army officer Louis Berton for spying (Figure 5.4).[16] Moreover, these stories were reported in the wake of discussions about national defense, after a member of Parliament, Charles Humbert, published a book in late 1907 entitled *Sommes-nous bien défendus?* in which he accused the government of inadequately preparing the nation for war. The timing was such that on 26 October 1907, one side of the front page of *L'Humanité* was devoted to Ullmo and the other, to Humbert's book.[17] Given the convergence of these events, both domestic and international, the French public could be forgiven for thinking that crime and lawlessness were on the rise and, moreover, that the nation was potentially in peril.

The contemporary interest in murder and crime was reflected in fiction as well. The Sherlock Holmes and Arsène Lupin novels, both of which were adapted for the theater, were huge successes.[18] So too were espionage stories – in fact, one of the principal authors of the genre was General Boulanger's son-in-law, Emile Driant, who wrote under the pseudonym of Capitaine Danrit.[19] During the unfolding of the Ullmo case, *Le Petit*

---

[15] Nye, 210–211. Death sentences were resumed in 1909. On the Soleilland murder, see Jean-Marc Berlière, *Le Crime de Soleilland (1907): Les Journalistes et l'assassin* (Paris: Tallandier, 2003).

[16] *Le Petit Journal illustré* of 17 November 1907 explicitly made the link with a drawing, "A bas les traîtres," which depicted an indignant Marianne surrounded by judges, soldiers, and workers looking at portraits of the two men at their feet (as if to stomp on them?). See Figure 5.4. Unless otherwise indicated, all newspaper articles cited are unsigned.

[17] See also the front page of *L'Aurore* (Clemenceau's former paper) of 26 October 1907, with one side of the front page containing an article entitled "Sommes-nous défendus?" with a rebuttal from Minister of War Picquart, and the other showing an article on the Ullmo case, "Sommes nous trahis?" with a negative response from M. Hennion, head of the Sûreté générale. See also Antoine Sabbagh, "Trahisons à la une," in *Presse à scandale, scandale de presse*, ed. Christian Delporte, Michael Palmer, and Denis Ruellan (Paris: L'Harmattan, 2001), 184–194. As he notes, in the period immediately preceding the war, the theme of the spy and traitor was ever present in the press. Moreover, two rival publications, *Le Journal* and *Le Matin*, each one anxious to represent itself as the true patriotic paper, not only used the figure of the traitor to sell newspapers but also accused the other of false patriotism in order to stigmatize its competition (Humbert had begun at *Le Matin* and had defected to *Le Journal*).

[18] Kalifa, 29–34.

[19] I would like to thank Professor Dominique Kalifa for pointing the Danrit novels out to me. The interest in crime was also found in the nascent cinema: see Richard Abel's "The Thrills of *Grande Peur*: Crime Series and Serials in the Belle Epoque," *The Velvet Light Trap*, no. 17 (Spring 1996): 3–9.

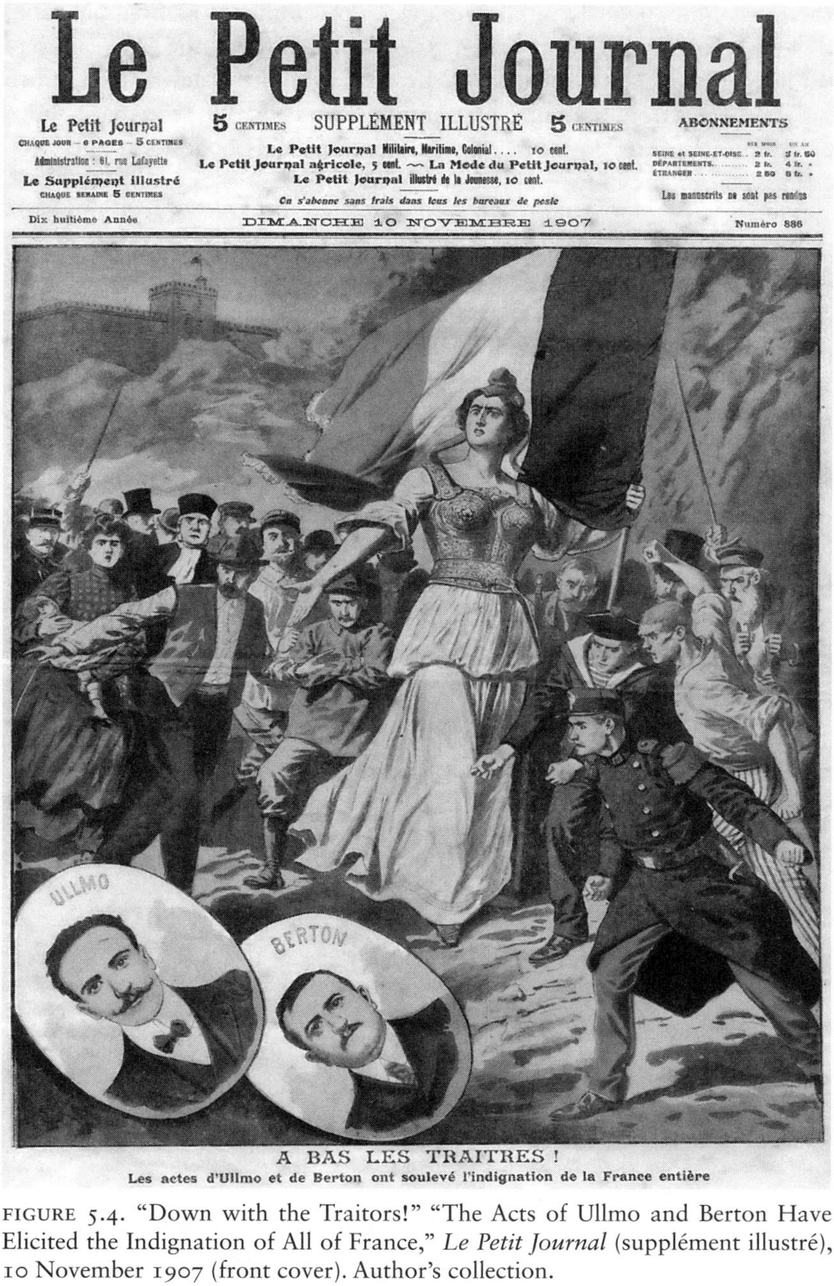

Le Petit Journal

Le Petit Journal
CHAQUE JOUR — 6 PAGES — 5 CENTIMES
Administration : 61, rue Lafayette
Le Supplément illustré
CHAQUE SEMAINE 5 CENTIMES

5 CENTIMES SUPPLÉMENT ILLUSTRÉ 5 CENTIMES

Le Petit Journal Militaire, Maritime, Colonial .... 10 cent.
Le Petit Journal agricole, 5 cent. ~ La Mode du Petit Journal, 10 cent.
Le Petit Journal illustré de la Jeunesse, 10 cent.
On s'abonne sans frais dans tous les bureaux de poste

ABONNEMENTS

	SIX MOIS	UN AN
SEINE et SEINE-ET-OISE ..	2 fr.	3 fr. 50
DÉPARTEMENTS	2 fr.	4 fr. »
ÉTRANGER	2 50	5 fr. »

Les manuscrits ne sont pas rendus

Dix huitième Année — DIMANCHE 10 NOVEMBRE 1907 — Numéro 886

A BAS LES TRAITRES !
Les actes d'Ullmo et de Berton ont soulevé l'indignation de la France entière

FIGURE 5.4. "Down with the Traitors!" "The Acts of Ullmo and Berton Have Elicited the Indignation of All of France," *Le Petit Journal* (supplément illustré), 10 November 1907 (front cover). Author's collection.

Parisien simultaneously published articles on Ullmo and a fictional serial about betrayal in the military in its *feuilleton*. Although the *feuilleton* had traditionally occupied the space below the fold of the newspaper, which separated fact from fiction, the latter increasingly invaded the space above the fold, with *faits divers* increasingly presented as fiction, and fictional accounts presented in a realistic fashion.

On the day after Ullmo's degradation in June 1908, *Le Matin* published an article about the latest Sherlock Holmes play, which it placed above the fold next to the account of the degradation ceremony. Two days later, in a complete collapse of fact and fiction, journalist Gustave Téry published an interview on the front page of *Le Matin* above the fold with Firmin Gémier, the actor playing Holmes, asking him how to solve the real-life murder mystery of the Meg Steinheil case, which had been splashed across the front pages of the papers in the preceding two weeks![20] Similarly, a few months earlier, in November 1907, *L'Instransigeant* had launched a contest, exhorting its readers to act like Sherlock Holmes by tailing one of its ace reporters throughout Paris in order to identify him and win a large cash prize.[21] This intermingling of fact and fiction also took place in the theater, with the staging of plays in theaters in Paris and the provinces based on the recent Soleilland murder trial.[22] These events,

---

[20] *Le Matin* of 13 June 1908: "Sherlock Holmes: Un Criminel!" Gustave Téry, "Un Assassinat expliqué par un détective," *Le Matin*, 15 June 1908. Gémier had garnered some notoriety in the lead role of Alfred Jarry's *Ubu Roi*. Similarly, in 1912, a few days after the killing of gang leader Jules Bonnot by an agent of the Sûreté, Léon Sazie, the author of the *Zigomar* detective stories, wrote an article also in *Le Matin* explaining how his fictional hero would have captured the real-life bandit. On this blurring of fact and fiction, see Kalifa, 34–35; Anne-Marie Thiesse, *Le Roman du quotidien: Lecteurs et lectures populaires à la Belle Epoque* (Paris: Le Chemin Vert, 1984), 20; M'Sili, 97.

[21] See, for example, "Sherlock Holmes à *L'Instransigeant*: Un Concours original" in the paper of 26 November 1907. In "La Chasse à l'homme: Une Passionnante Equipée," from 7 December, Félix Méténier, the reporter to be followed (also the author of the article), described himself as Arsène Lupin and told his readers that he would explore all the public haunts of Paris, from cafés, to stores, train stations, and theaters, thereby illustrating the visual and spectacular aspect of Parisian culture of the time. On a slightly different note, Maurice Leblanc had one of the characters (the examining magistrate) in the short story "L'Evasion d'Arsène Lupin" claim that among Lupin's many identities was that of a working-class savior in the Bazar de la Charité fire! See Vanessa Schwartz, *Spectacular Realities: Early Mass Culture in Fin-de-Siècle Paris* (Berkeley: University of California Press, 1998).

[22] *L'Instransigeant* railed against a theater in Paris that proposed to stage a play based on the Soleilland murder: see the article "Joies théâtrales," from 17 February 1908. Similarly, V. Snell in "La Mauvaise École," 17 November 1907 of *L'Humanité*, denounced a provincial theater in Blois that proposed to stage a play entitled *The Last Day of a Condemned Man*, accusing the director of capitalizing on prurient interest in the Soleilland murder

both on the domestic and international fronts, and in the political and cultural realms, shaped the public's understanding of the Ullmo case and of Ullmo himself.

Charles-Benjamin Ullmo was born on February 17, 1882. Ullmo was the son of a respected Lyon merchant, and his uncle was the founder of a famous tannery in Lyon.[23] In an interview with a reporter from *Le Matin*, shortly after Ullmo's arrest in October 1907, Ullmo's superior officer on the *Carabine*, Lieutenant Mandine, stated that his fellow officers had the impression that Ullmo was the son of the famous tanner.[24] At any rate, according to Mandine, Ullmo let it be known that he had an income of 9,000 francs per annum, not an enormous sum but more than a naval lieutenant earned in a year.[25] Both of Ullmo's parents were deceased, and he had two married sisters. The papers reported that Ullmo had squandered his inheritance.[26] Ullmo had attended the lycée Janson de Sailly before entering the Naval Academy in October 1898 with a rank of three out of seventy-four. Graduating eighth out of seventy-four in 1900, he was made ensign on October 5, 1903. Ullmo served in the squadrons of the Far East and in Indochina, and at the time of his arrest he was on provisional leave from his job as second in command of the counter-torpedo boat *Carabine*.[27]

Ullmo came from a practicing Jewish family and attended the synagogue in Lyon regularly when he was growing up.[28] The first in his family to join the navy, he entered the Naval Academy at the height of the Dreyfus Affair. Unlike army officers, officers in the navy tended to

case. Snell attacked not only the theater but also the press, accusing the press of infecting the theater: "It was inevitable! From the newspaper churning out [tales of] bloody horror for a *sou* per slice, [this sort of] debasement was bound to reach the theater."

[23] Ullmo's personal file in the archives of the Service Historique de la Marine (Vincennes, France) indicates that his father was a *négociant*: SHM: CC7 4e série moderne, Carton 480; Dossier 11. Delpêche reports his inheritance as 80,000 francs, Delpêche, 23. His lawyer Aubin quoted the slightly lower figure of 70,000 francs: "Le Procès Ullmo," *La Revue des procès contemporains*, 26 (April 1908): 213. Aubin's defense plea, along with the government prosecutor's rebuttal, and the arguments for and against closed session, was reproduced in *La Revue des procès contemporains*, 209–260.

[24] Ullmo's father, who had worked in the factory, took over as administrator after his brother's death: Aubin, 248.

[25] *Le Matin*, from 26 October 1907: "Traître: Ullmo part pour Paris: Enchaîné et tête basse."

[26] *Le Figaro*, 25 October 1907: "Arrestation d'un officier: Chantage ou folie?" by Paul Edouard, and *Le Petit Parisien* of 25 October: "Espion ou maître chanteur?"

[27] This information comes from Ullmo's personal dossier in the SHM (CC7 4e série moderne, Carton 480; Dossier 11).

[28] Delpêche, 104–105.

be either nonobservant or indifferent in matters of religion.[29] Although there may have been no blatant or systematic anti-Semitism in the navy, a fact borne out by Ullmo's marks from his superior officers, this does not mean that Ullmo did not suffer from anti-Semitic comments. Casual anti-Semitism was widespread during the time of the Affair. Ullmo's lawyer, Antony Aubin, quoting from the medical testimony at the time of his trial, declared that his client suffered from the taunts of his peers during the height of the Dreyfus Affair, until the protection of one of his colleagues put an end to such treatment.[30] As for *Le Petit Journal*, it reported that Ullmo was vocal about his Dreyfusard sympathies and that he nearly fought a duel with an anti-Dreyfusard colleague. Although it is not possible to confirm the information about a duel, Ullmo did tell a biographer years later that the period of the Affair was one of the most difficult of his life.[31]

Ullmo generally received good assessments from superior officers.[32] In the June 4, 1904, report from Saigon, his superior officer wrote: "Ullmo is a very good officer, very active, very serious, looking for every opportunity to educate himself." There was a marked change, however, in the report of February 1, 1905, in which Ullmo's behavior was described in the following manner: "mediocre conduct, he has inexplicable absences. Manner of serving: bad. M. Ullmo, the naval ensign, is an intelligent officer who could have become very good with a bit of good will and work."[33] The change in the assessments Ullmo received from superior officers appears to coincide with his making the acquaintance of Lison Welsch.

[29] William Serman and Jean-Paul Bertaud, *Nouvelle Histoire militaire de la France, 1789–1919* (Paris: Fayard, 1998), 625. Moreover, there appears to be a real difference between the composition of the army and navy at this time; fewer nobles enlisted in the navy.

[30] In his personal file housed in the SHM in Vincennes, there is no reference to his religion, which is, of course, in keeping with good French republican principles – although these principles were sometimes violated and indications of religion noted.

[31] "L'Enseigne Ullmo," *Le Petit Journal*, 26 October 1907. See Delpêche, 21, who also states that Ullmo regretted his choice of career in light of this anti-Semitism.

[32] A report from 27 July 1900 indicates that Ullmo is a "personality who is difficult to comprehend but who is intelligent and capable." SHM.

[33] The report continues in the same vein: "Since the last general inspection, he is completely disinterested in all his duties and his profession as a naval man ... this officer is increasingly inclined to indiscipline, he thinks only of his rights, [thereby] seriously neglecting his duties. For the past eight months, he has served as a bad example for the crew." The assessment is signed by Ferry on 1 February 1905. The assessment of Vice-Admiral Commander in Chief of the Far East Squadron Bayle says that the evaluation of Ullmo's immediate superior is inexact, that Ullmo is very intelligent but is nevertheless a bad officer.

In an interview with *Le Matin* from October 25, 1907, his superior officer Mandine described Ullmo as a man somewhat aloof from his colleagues, in part, because he was preoccupied by his mistress, with whom he had set up housekeeping in the sumptuous villa Gléglé (in Toulon). Ullmo spent quite a bit of money, according to Mandine, but, again, he noted that Ullmo's colleagues did not realize that Ullmo had already squandered his inheritance. Pressed by the reporter, Mandine admitted that according to other colleagues, Ullmo had on several occasions been suspected of petty theft on board ship but that the accusations could never be proven, adding that he himself had noted nothing of the sort. Several papers from the same date reported that Ullmo had left the lycée under a cloud of suspicion after having allegedly stolen a bicycle. Ullmo's father had supposedly covered up the incident.[34]

The first articles that appeared in such mainstream newspapers as *Le Matin* and *Le Figaro* depicted Ullmo with some sympathy.[35] *Le Figaro* made no mention of Ullmo's Jewish origins, and *Le Matin* only referred to them as a minor "detail." An article in *Le Figaro*, entitled "Chantage ou folie?" indicated that Ullmo was a "morphine addict" whose reason seemed to have been affected by his habit.[36] *Le Matin* also described Ullmo as yet another victim of the "Indochinese poison whose usage is becoming increasingly widespread among our naval officers."[37] All

[34] "Traître: Ullmo part pour Paris," *Le Matin*, 26 October 1907. An article from 25 October 1907 from *Le Figaro* ("Arrestation d'un officier de la marine") also mentioned the suspicions of fellow officers that Ullmo was responsible for petty thefts, but that nothing could be proved against "this young blond officer, with amiable manners and a soft, silky voice." Note the gender-encoded effeminate language here as well as in a piece in *L'Humanité* ("Un Traître"): "This is a man of small stature, with an elegant appearance and a delicate face." Other papers also reported on purported thefts by Ullmo: "Espion ou maître chanteur," *Le Petit Parisien*, 25 October, and "L'Affaire Ullmo," *Le Petit Journal*, 25 October 1907.

[35] Some right-wing newspapers were unsympathetic from the very beginning, calling Ullmo a traitor – for example, *La Libre Parole* and *L'Action française*, but also *L'Intransigeant*. Although *L'Intransigeant* was no longer an overtly anti-Semitic publication (the fact that Ullmo was Jewish was noted in passing), its staff had no love for the *bloc des gauches* and, in fact, accused Clemenceau and his ministers of a cover-up of the Ullmo case to avoid a military trial and to instead try Ullmo in a civil court. See especially an editorial by Léon Bailby, "Trahison? Peccadille!" from 26 October 1907 and "Pour sauver le traître Ullmo, on veut étouffer l'Affaire!" from 29 October (no signature but probably Bailby). Similarly, commentators in the paper had little sympathy for the opium defense: see Dr. Grasset, "Sus aux criminels, malades ou non" from 16 November 1907. Nevertheless, the staff had great respect for Ullmo's sisters and for Ullmo's lawyer, Antony Aubin. See especially "Sur le cas d'Ullmo: L'Enquête continue" from 4 November 1907.

[36] Paul Edouard, "Chantage ou folie?" *Le Figaro*, 25 October 1907.

[37] "Traître: Ullmo part pour Paris," *Le Matin*, 26 October 1907.

the papers were very hard on Ullmo's mistress, Lison Welsch, who was described discreetly by *Le Petit Parisien* of October 27 as being celebrated in "the society in which one amuses oneself."[38] The reporter for *Le Matin* held her responsible for Ullmo's opium habit: "But it is not enough for her to attract [men] through her loose morals and charming personality. In her villa in the Mourillons [a region just outside of Toulon], she has established an opium den. ... One is led to believe that it is the attraction, the passion for this woman, and the vice of opium that she peddles, that have had a negative effect on the intelligence – up to this point, solid – of this unfortunate creature."[39] Ullmo himself, admitting his guilt to blackmail in October 1907, declared: "Yes, it's true, I have committed an unpardonable error, but it is for this dear Lison! The evidence of my madness is to be found in the stupidity of my plan. I am lost, but I have no accomplices, and Lison has never doubted that I tried to make her happy."[40] The journalist for *Le Figaro* conducted an interview with the Sûreté agent in charge of Ullmo's capture, who described the young man as "a degenerate" and an "opium addict." *Le Figaro* concluded that Ullmo's act was that of a "madman rather than of a traitor."[41] Ullmo was described in the papers as having burst into tears and expressing remorse; indeed, this appears to be the leitmotiv of the press coverage of Ullmo up to this point.[42]

In mid-November, the Ullmo case took a sensational turn when investigators (there were simultaneous investigations on the part of civil and military authorities) learned of a telegram signed by Ullmo to a German agent in which he offered to sell documents containing the code to France's maritime signals. Ullmo had, in fact, contacted the German military attaché in Paris, who had duly passed the offer along to his government. Ullmo had also met with a German agent, who had refused his

---

[38] *Le Petit Parisien* of 27 October: "L'Officier escroc." The reporter further noted that Lison had disgraced her respectable family by running away with a young medical student, eventually becoming a prostitute in a brothel. *Le Temps* refused steadfastly to refer to Lison in its reporting.

[39] "Traître: Ullmo part pour Paris," *Le Matin*, 26 October 1907.

[40] Reported in *Le Figaro* of 25 October 1907 by André Nède: "La Genèse de l'Affaire."

[41] "La Genèse de l'Affaire," *Le Figaro*, 25 October 1907.

[42] Reporters described Ullmo as looking "beaten down." See, for example, *Le Temps*, "Au Jour le jour," from 27 October. On the day of his first round of questioning by the judge, Ullmo was described by *Figaro* reporter André Nède as "more depressed than ever, he seemed to walk automatically, held up rather than led by his jailers." The reporter noted sadly: "What a painful spectacle to see the evaporating of such hopes in a being that appeared destined for one of the most brilliant and noble of careers." "L'Affaire Ullmo: Départ pour Paris," *Le Figaro*, 26 October 1907.

offer, claiming that his price of 950,000 francs was too high. Thus, Ullmo had attempted, albeit unsuccessfully, to sell the plans to a foreign government. The affair then became a case of treason, and after authorities determined he had no civil accomplices, Ullmo was turned over to naval justice and transported to Toulon, where he was held in military prison to await his trial. At this point, the press's attitude toward him hardened, and the coverage of Ullmo in late November and during his trial was markedly more severe.

The Ullmo Trial

By the time the trial took place in February 1908, some of the excitement in the news about the case had died down, although crowds flocked to the courtroom the first day, especially women, as the reporter from *Le Petit Parisien* noted, commenting that women were more interested in the story of treason for love than in a case about national defense.[43] Whereas the second Dreyfus trial at Rennes had taken place over the space of six weeks, with only a few days in closed session, the Ullmo trial took place over the period of just three days, on February 20, 21, and 22, with more than half the time in closed session, after the judges voted five to two in favor of two closed sessions and one open one. Captain Schlumberger, the government prosecutor, had attempted to have the entire trial conducted in *huis clos* (closed session), arguing that one could not separate state secrets from facts that could be revealed to the public, whereas Ullmo's lawyer, Antony Aubin, argued just the opposite, hoping to bring public sympathy to bear on the military judges who would decide the case. He also warned of repeating the mistakes of the Dreyfus Affair, doing so obliquely without mentioning the Affair by name.[44] Some in the press, among them Henri Varennes, who had written about the Rennes trial for *L'Aurore* and was now writing for *Le Figaro*, issued similar warnings.[45]

---

[43] "Malgré les efforts de son avocat, le traître est jugé à huis clos," *Le Petit Parisien*, 21 February 1908. This observation was confirmed by the other newspapers. Women were often in attendance at famous trials, and the association of women with the culture of spectacle is evident in some of the comments of fin-de-siècle male contemporaries. See Katherine Fischer Taylor, *In the Theater of Criminal Justice* (Princeton, NJ: Princeton University Press, 1993), 17.

[44] Aubin implied but could not say that there might be another repetition of a trial with documents that the accused and his lawyer would never see.

[45] Henri Varennes, "Gazette des tribunaux: Ullmo," *Le Figaro*, 18 February 1908.

Such public pressure and fear of a repetition of the Dreyfus case undoubtedly played a role in the judges' decision to hold part of the proceedings in public, notably the defense plea and the reading of the *acte d'accusation*, which included the entirety of naval investigator Devarenne's report, whereas others, the indictment and the medical evidence as well as the witness testimonies, were closed to the public, although some of the papers summarized them, along with the prosecution's arguments.[46] Despite this initial bow to public opinion, the differences between a jury trial and a military one were considerable, as the reporter from *Le Matin* noted. Military judges were severe and cold; they could not be expected to view facts in the same way as juries composed of civilians, which were more apt to acquit even when the defendant had admitted guilt, especially when it came to a "crime of passion."[47]

The Dreyfus Rennes trial had taken place in a highly charged atmosphere, with many believing that the question of Dreyfus's guilt or innocence held the key to France's fate. The fact that those proceedings took place onstage in the makeshift courtroom of a schoolhouse in Rennes highlighted the trial's dramatic qualities.[48] In the case of Ullmo, who had already admitted his guilt, the dramatic impact of the trial was diminished, and, moreover, allowed for a consensus around it that the Dreyfus trial could not. Not only was more at stake in the Dreyfus Affair, but contemporaries were also curious about Dreyfus himself, who was returning from detention on Devil's Island. In contrast, Ullmo was a known quantity, his reactions and confessions having been published on a daily basis in October and November of the previous year, during the course of the investigations of his betrayal.[49]

---

[46] Although newspapers were not supposed to leak information from the closed session of the trial – it was considered treason – some did so, no doubt, because they did not fear prosecution, which would have been made more difficult by the passage of the 1881 law on the freedom of the press. Obviously, they were taking a chance, but it was a calculated one. I owe this observation to Professor Edward Berenson. As for the medical report, it was subsequently published in a criminology journal: Dr. Dupré et al., "Mémoires originaux: L'Affaire Ullmo," *Archives d'anthropologie criminelle de médecine légale et de psychologie normale et pathologique*, no. 176–177 (August–September 1908): 545–586.

[47] "Le Traître effondré," *Le Matin*, 21 February 1907. See Edward Berenson, 33–35.

[48] I have explored the issue of Dreyfus's "heroism" in an article entitled: "From Devil's Island to the Pantheon? Alfred Dreyfus, the Anti-Hero," in *Confronting Modernity in Fin-de-Siècle France: Bodies, Minds and Gender*, ed. Christopher E. Forth and Elinor Accampo (New York: Palgrave Macmillan, 2010), 217–234.

[49] Again, the press was not allowed to attend sessions with the investigating magistrate, but there were obviously leaks to the papers, with *Le Petit Parisien*, which put quotation marks around conversations a reporter had not witnessed, being the most brazen.

Although the Ullmo trial was somewhat anti-climactic, the public continued to be fascinated by Ullmo and his mistress. Indeed, many spectators in attendance during the first day of the trial stood up to get a look at the "traitor," as many called him in the press.[50] *Le Petit Journal* of February 20 described Ullmo as extremely pale when he entered the courtroom with a "jerky step." In response to questions about his name and status, he answered "in a feeble voice, his gaze vacant at times, his body quivers slightly, but his face remains impassive."[51] This composure barely remained in place as he listened to the reading of the naval investigator's report outlining the events of his case. As Henri Varennes of *Le Figaro* observed, Ullmo maintained "the immobility of a photographic pose," but he blinked, reddened, and clenched his teeth in an obvious effort to control his tears.[52] During the trial, Ullmo burst into tears on a number of occasions, exasperating some in the audience, a number of whom had been in attendance at the Dreyfus Rennes trial. In the earlier trial, Dreyfus had shown little emotion and had frustrated his supporters who had hoped for an emotional outburst or a manly tear of indignation.[53] Although tears themselves did not necessarily signal a lack of masculinity, Ullmo's excessive crying only highlighted the contemporary view of him as a child, a representation that was reinforced by his defense lawyer (See Figures 5.5, 5.6, and 5.7.).[54]

---

[50] See, for example, "L'Enseigne Ullmo devant ses juges," *L'Aurore*, 21 February 1908, and "Le Procès Ullmo," *L'Humanité* of 21 February 1908. Many of the papers, like *Le Petit Parisien*, eschewed citing the *acte d'accusation* and the Devarenne report, commenting that their contents had already been reproduced, although parts of the defense summary, described as powerful and eloquent by journalists, were widely quoted in the press.

[51] "Le Traître Ullmo comparaît devant les juges," *Le Petit Journal*, 21 February 1908.

[52] "Gazette des tribunaux," *Le Figaro*, 21 February 1908.

[53] Anne Vincent-Buffault, *Histoire des larmes* (Paris: Rivages, 1986), 185–188. Nevertheless, the line between "effeminate" histrionics and "honest indignation" was a fine one. See Christopher E. Forth, *The Dreyfus Affair and the Crisis of Manhood* (Baltimore, MD: Johns Hopkins University Press, 2004), 30, for a discussion of manhood and emotion. See also Forth, *Masculinity in the Modern West: Gender, Civilization and the Body* (New York: Palgrave Macmillan, 2008), especially pp. 141–168, and Forth and Bertrand Taithe, eds., *French Masculinities: History, Culture and Politics* (New York: Palgrave Macmillan, 2007), in particular, Forth's essay, "La *Civilisation* and Its Discontents: Modernity, Manhood and the Body in the Early Third Republic," 85–102. On honor and manhood, see Nye, *Masculinity and Male Codes of Honor in Modern France* (Berkeley: University of California Press, 1998).

[54] I do acknowledge, however, that being more childlike could be seen as a "feminine" trait, but although there may have been some implication of "feminine" behavior, it was not made explicitly nor did it dominate discussions of Ullmo.

138

Le Lieutenant de vaisseau Devarenne, auteur du rapport

La belle Lison entre au Conseil de guerre

dience en landau à deux chevaux, et dont la contenance a choqué.

La dernière audience, à la date du 22 février, a été occupée par une discussion ex-

insiste, que l'accusé n'a reconnu comme authentiques et véridiques que les pièces de l'accusation échafaudée péniblement contre lui par l'instruction civile et l'instruction maritime; les deux parquets qui ont eu à informer à son sujet ayant été d'accord pour relever contre l'accusé l'inculpation de haute trahison.

Le défenseur a répliqué, gardant l'espérance, malgré l'inflexibilité de son honorable contradicteur, que le jugement prononcé sera inspiré par l'indulgence.

— On vous a invités, Messieurs, dit alors Mᵉ Aubin, à donner un exemple, et pour cela, on fait un argument terrible de cette considération si honorable qu'il n'y a jamais eu de traître

dans notre marine. C'est pour cela, au contraire, que vous pouvez être indulgents, car il n'est besoin d'aucun exemple à cette marine restée pure, loyale et sans tache.

« Être indulgent, a dit encore Mᵉ Aubin en concluant, ce n'est pas de la faiblesse, et c'est toujours de la justice. »

Avant la clôture des débats, le président ayant demandé à l'accusé s'il avait à ajouter quelque chose pour sa défense, Ullmo s'est dressé presque automatiquement, et d'une voix que l'émotion dénaturait, il a déclaré ce qui suit :

« M. le commissaire du Gouvernement a dit que, par ma faute, en cas de guerre, nous serions en état d'infériorité. Eh bien! je puis être tombé bas, mais si bas que je sois, il y a des choses que je ne puis pas laisser dire.

« Commandant, je suis devant vous, je vous regarde, je regarde des officiers, je vous le répète en face, je suis tombé bien bas, mais je jure que je n'ai rien livré.

« Ce n'est pas vrai, commandant, je vous le jure sur cet uniforme que je porte pour la dernière fois, je n'ai rien livré. »

Ayant dit, Ullmo s'est effondré sur son siège au milieu de l'émotion des assistants.

La délibération qui a précédé la sentence n'a pas duré moins de deux heures.

Le conseil étant rentré en séance, lecture a été donnée du jugement.

« Le conseil rejette, à l'unani-

mité, les conclusions du défenseur, relatives à l'inapplication de l'article 76, déclare, à l'unanimité, Ullmo coupable d'intelligences avec un agent d'une puissance étrangère et de reproduction de documents, le condamne à la déportation à vie dans une enceinte fortifiée, à la dégradation militaire, aux frais du procès, et décide l'affichage du jugement à 150 exemplaires. »

Un frisson a circulé dans la salle après que ces paroles irrémédiables ont été entendues. L'assistance s'est lentement dispersée, puis un piquet d'infanterie s'étant rangé, l'arme au pied, le condamné a été emmené.

Paraissant inconscient, sans rien voir et sans rien entendre, il a descendu l'escalier d'un pas rapide entre deux maréchaux-de-logis de gendarmerie, son visage conservant l'impassibilité avec laquelle il avait écouté la lecture du jugement.

Il a reçu un peu plus tard la visite de son défenseur qui l'a trouvé littéralement écrasé et tout en larmes. Il a cependant pu signer son pourvoi en cassation mais en ayant peine à tracer les lettres du nom qu'il a déshonoré.

La cour, réunie en chambre criminelle, statuera sur le pourvoi et, s'il y a lieu, renverra l'affaire devant le 2ᵉ conseil de guerre permanent. Ce conseil est présidé par le capitaine de vaisseau Ribouet. Le commissaire principal de Bellegou y

clusivement juridique de la part du commissaire du Gouvernement. Le commandant Schlumberger avait compris que les défenseurs chercheraient à tirer parti de l'ambiguïté de l'article 76, en s'efforçant de transformer Ullmo de traître en espion.

En conséquence, il a combattu cette thèse, disant que la condamnation devait être non seulement une répression, mais un exemple, dans l'intérêt du pays.

Il renouvelle cette considération, sur laquelle il

La belle Lison

FIGURE 5.6. "La Belle Lison," drawing and photo of Lison entering the military court, *Le Monde Illustré*, 29 February 1908 (inside page, 138). Author's collection.

vingt minutes. Après quoi, les pauvres femmes quittèrent la prison. Malgré la peine qui les accable, elles conservent une espérance. Dans un procès comme celui du pauvre frère qu'elles continuent à chérir avec la plus touchante piété fraternelle, on peut trouver toujours un point qui laisse place à un arrêt de cassation. Il ne faudrait certes pas le chercher dans la marche même des débats, car le commandant Schlumberger, commissaire du Gouvernement, a fait remarquer que l'avocat d'Ullmo n'a présenté aucune réserve, formulé aucune conclusion. Donc, Me Aubin n'a relevé rien d'irrégulier.

Et puis, aller en cassation pour un jugement de conseil de guerre de l'armée de terre ou de l'armée de mer, équivaut à faire appel.

Reste à savoir si la cour suprême prononcera la receva-

La foule devant le Conseil de Guerre

Me Antony Aubin et Me Steinard entrant au Conseil de Guerre

Me Steinard lisant les conclusions de la défense

remplit les fonctions de commissaire du gouvernement et le lieutenant de vaisseau Guyon celles d'officier rapporteur. Le greffier est l'adjudant principal de 2e classe Roubaud.

Un cas de cassation a déjà été relevé au cours des débats. Ce pourvoi donne à Ullmo un délai d'environ deux mois.

Depuis la condamnation qui l'a frappé, Ullmo a eu la consolation d'être visité par ses sœurs qui avaient obtenu l'autorisation de pénétrer auprès de lui.

Un de nos confrères quotidiens a raconté cette émouvante entrevue tout à la louange de ces femmes admirables qui ont été les protectrices inlassables et dévouées de l'infortuné, depuis le jour où l'infamante accusation pesa sur lui.

Dès qu'il les vit, dans le parloir de la prison militaire, il se mit à sangloter, leur demandant pardon.

Cette entrevue dura près de

bilité de ce genre de recours.

Ullmo ayant signé son pourvoi en blanc, le cas de cassation n'étant pas encore spécifié. Le pourvoi aura donc dû être signifié à la justice avant quarante-huit heures, après lesquelles seront expirés les trois jours francs accordés à cet effet au condamné.

Jusqu'à ce qu'il soit statué sur son pourvoi, le condamné restera en situation de prévenu. Si la condamnation devient définitive, il ne serait astreint à aucun travail à la prison maritime. Il y attendra la terrible cérémonie de la dégradation militaire, après quoi, il sera transporté à l'endroit désigné pour qu'il y subisse la peine expiatrice, la détention perpétuelle qui le retranchera à tout jamais du monde qui l'a rejeté.

A B.

M. de Saint-Seine   M. Sulzbach   M. Sébille   M. Chardon
LA SALLE DES TÉMOINS

FIGURE 5.7. "The Crowd in Front of the Entrance to the Military Court" (top image on page), *Le Monde illustré*, 29 February 1908 (inside page, 139). Author's collection.

Lison the Femme Fatale and Ullmo the Man-Child

Given that Ullmo had already admitted his guilt, Aubin's job was difficult, because he had to argue for diminished responsibility, placing the blame both on Lison and on opium. Accordingly, after asking for the pity of the judges, he spent the first part of his plea attacking Ullmo's mistress, "the beautiful ... and for me, fatal Lison," as the woman who had ensnared Ullmo and had encouraged his opium habit to better control him. "Lison dominates this trial, in the same way she dominated Ullmo's life," he declared to the judges.[55] Although treason was not a crime of passion, Aubin sought to define Ullmo's behavior in emotional terms to garner sympathy for his client.

In murder cases tried in criminal courts, women were more likely than men to be acquitted for crimes of passion because they could be depicted as hysterical. In light of a contemporary belief in the emotional nature of women, female defendants were acquitted at a higher rate than men for crimes of passion. When men were acquitted, it was because they could illustrate that they had defended their honor and or that they had temporarily been insane.[56] Although Aubin could not prove that Ullmo's honor was at stake – national honor, which Ullmo had betrayed, trumped personal honor here – he could represent Ullmo in a way that undercut his masculinity, by portraying him as a victim of love, a depiction that was usually reserved for women defendants. This tactic had some resonance because the press had already reported on Ullmo's kleptomania – a crime viewed by most contemporaries as a feminine one.[57]

Fin-de-siècle conventions, unlike earlier Romantic ones, which depicted individuals as languishing from love, described defendants as being driven mad by love, thus giving rise to a specialized language and stylized behavior that created a melodramatic discourse of love that

---

[55] Aubin's defense plea (heretofore referred to as Aubin), 211 and 213, respectively.

[56] See Ruth Harris, *Murder and Madness: Medicine, Law, and Society in the Fin de Siècle* (Oxford: Oxford University Press, 1989), especially pp. 285–320 titled, "Men, Honour, and Crimes of Passion"; Ann Louise Shapiro, *Breaking the Codes: Female Criminality in Fin-de-Siècle Paris* (Stanford, CA: Stanford University Press, 1996), 148; and Edward Berenson, *Madame Caillaux*, 28–30. As they all note, men who committed crimes of passion had to represent themselves as having upheld their honor and also as the product of temporary madness. Harris further observes that the men involved were often portrayed as Romantic heroes, melancholic and misunderstood, 304.

[57] See Patricia O'Brien, "The Kleptomania Diagnosis: Bourgeois Women and Theft in Late Nineteenth-Century France," *Journal of Social History* 17, no. 1 (Autumn 1983): 65–77.

could be used to justify, or at least explain, certain criminal behaviors.[58] Although judicial dossiers in criminal courts were full of such accounts, it was not clear whether such a discourse would work in a military setting, but Aubin had no other line of defense. Accordingly, he represented Ullmo as a child, even quoting Lison's letters to him, in which she referred to him as "the child" and "dear child." As if to underscore his immaturity, after Aubin described him as a "poor child," Ullmo, according to the reporter for Le Matin, lowered his head and cried.[59] This "poor child" had been ensnared and enslaved by a calculating Lison, who had precipitated his downfall. Gender roles were reversed so as to get Ullmo the minimum sentence.

Thus, Lison was described as cold and calculating when she weaned Ullmo from gambling. Earlier, in the press, Lison had depicted herself as Ullmo's savior, claiming that she had tried to save him when she forced him to abandon gambling. Aubin, however, ascribed more selfish motives to Lison, whom he accused of wanting to protect her investment.

It was for this reason, he explained, that she invited Ullmo to live with her at the villa Glégié, playing on Ullmo's desire to keep her to himself. How many men who sequester the women they love are themselves enslaved, asked Aubin rhetorically. The language Aubin used to describe Lison and Ullmo's relationship only served to reinforce this image: "Lison fearing [sic] the rivalry of this passion for gambling. One gesture from her: 'don't gamble any more!' And he gives in, he obeys, he ceases to gamble ... up until the day ... when for her, he begins to gamble again – greedy for money, greedy for love." Aubin continued: "At the slightest sign from Lison, he doesn't just reject an inclination, a penchant, a habit, a passion. He gives over to her, he relinquishes all that a man has that is most precious in the world: his independence and his liberty."[60] In Aubin's account, Ullmo had sacrificed all that defined a man at this time: independence of thought and action, both of which were male qualities par excellence.[61]

---

[58] Shapiro, 143. Romantic heroes could be anti-heroes in the Byronic mode. Ullmo was more of a protagonist who elicits sympathy – unlike the typical villain. Most contemporaries focused on what Ullmo could have been and on what he was before his fall.

[59] "Le Procès Ullmo: Ses Poisons," Le Matin, 22 February 1908.

[60] Aubin, 214.

[61] Delpêche noted that although Ullmo was depicted as weak by both his lawyer and the press at the time of his trial, this characterization was false. Never since his arrival in Guyana had he shown the least sign of weakness, 65. On independence of thought and manhood, see my Birth of a National Icon: The Literary Avant-Garde and the Origins of the Intellectual in France (Albany: SUNY Press, 1999), 152–156.

In defending Ullmo, Aubin not only diminished the manhood of his client, but he also articulated a number of misogynist arguments, which may have found resonance among the judges in the Ullmo case, who too were males, and, moreover, military men who had undoubtedly had experiences with mistresses and prostitutes. Whereas Ullmo, a "gentleman" to the last, maintained that his mistress knew nothing of his selling secrets, his lawyer had free rein to describe her as "Ullmo's worst demon."[62] Aubin accused Lison of having trapped Ullmo with the semblance of married life ("the wild Lison becomes the little housewife"). In describing how Lison prepared opium pipes for her lover, Aubin referred to the chains of love with which Lison bound Ullmo, accusing her of hooking Ullmo on opium in order to control him.[63] Aubin also mentioned what he called Lison's ignominious past, chastising her for her numerous lovers, but he seemed singularly offended by her impersonation of an honorable housewife.[64] Aubin thus implied that while Ullmo treated Lison as "a young wife," she was playing a role to get his money. In a real marriage with an "honorable" woman, Ullmo would have maintained his independence, because he, as the husband, would have been in charge. The illusion of the real thing, however, only served to highlight his servitude.[65]

Aubin was especially indignant that Lison could socialize with the honorable ladies of the neighborhood. During the nineteenth century in France, prostitutes were seen as a necessary evil, to be quarantined and cordoned off from bourgeois society so as to preserve the moral and physical health of the nation.[66] At the fin de siècle, demimondaines, who occupied the shadowy space between the world of prostitutes and that of "honorable" society, set themselves up as the equivalents of "housewives" for their lovers. Especially troubling to contemporaries was the idea that a prostitute could be taken for an honorable bourgeoise and vice-versa.[67] These contemporaries viewed prostitutes who imitated "honorable women" as a poison infecting the body politic, and Aubin played on such contemporary anxieties.

[62] Aubin, 259.

[63] Aubin, 215. Aubin had already referred to Marcelle Joujou, Ullmo's first mistress, as having introduced him to opium, 213.

[64] Aubin, 214–215.

[65] Aubin, 217.

[66] Alain Corbin, *Women for Hire: Prostitution and Sexuality in France after 1850*, trans. Alan Sheridan (Cambridge, MA: Harvard University Press, 1990), 4–5.

[67] Hollis Clayson, *Painted Love: Prostitution in French Art in the Impressionist Era* (New Haven, CT: Yale University Press, 1991), 56–64.

To represent Ullmo as a victim, Aubin not only had to depict Lison as a femme fatale, but he also had to portray his client as naïve and easily manipulated. This tactic required some effort, because Ullmo was known to be a highly intelligent officer. Moreover, the image of a weak individual overcome by his passions was at odds with the ideal portrait of a military man, who was valued for his control and self-discipline.[68]

Whereas the innocent Dreyfus had been chastised by his defenders for his iron control and for being too much of a military figure, Ullmo was portrayed by his lawyer as overwhelmed by his emotions in order to mitigate his guilt. In this regard, Aubin had some help from the expert medical testimony of Doctors Dupré, Raymond, and Courtois-Suffit. Quoting selectively from their medical report, Aubin described Ullmo as "emotional, impressionable and nervous." Moreover, he embroidered on the report, emphasizing that Ullmo had lost his mother, to whom he was attached, at an early age, as well his father shortly thereafter: "Reserved and distant in appearance, he has a desperate desire for tenderness."[69] Aubin attempted to argue that Ullmo's heredity, the cruel treatment he received from his colleagues during the Dreyfus Affair, and his parents' death shortly thereafter had led to a "nervous depression" and a "mental alienation." It was in this weakened state that Ullmo had met Lison, who led to his downfall.[70] According to Aubin, such a weak man was prey to the wiles of prostitutes like Lison, whom he held responsible for his opium habit as well as of squandering his inheritance.

The medical report, however, contradicted Aubin's depiction on many points, its authors noting that although Ullmo had eight antecedents in his family with psychological problems, he did not suffer from degeneration.[71] The doctors found Ullmo to be calm and reserved, a characterization shared by his superior officers. In addition, they found no "venereal excesses" nor homosexual tendencies or "genital perversions."[72] Nevertheless, although Ullmo was not "abnormal," he did not correspond to the typical contemporary manly soldier. Unlike Aubin, who blamed Lison for the disappearance of Ullmo's fortune, the doctors castigated the naval officer for his vanity and prodigality, along with his inability to

---

[68] Datta, *Birth of a National Icon*, 156–161.
[69] Aubin, 214. The actual report says: "Ullmo describes himself as emotional, impressionable and nervous," Dupré, 555. This is also the account Ullmo gave to his biographer: see Delpêche, 20.
[70] Aubin, 244–248.
[71] Dupré, 555.
[72] Dupré, 555–556.

control his desires.[73] In their opinion, Ullmo was a lazy sensualist, possessing the soul of a gambler and fatalist.

Whereas women at the time were viewed as unable to control their appetites, men, especially military men, were supposed to be in complete control of themselves. "Ullmo appears to us to be an intelligent, educated, cultivated subject, with a clear sense of the moral value of his acts. ... But at the same time, he appears to be a man of little will, lacking in ambition and courage," they concluded in their evaluation.[74] It is worth noting that there were no signs of overt anti-Semitism in the report, although the doctors did classify Ullmo as a typical "Semitic type." Furthermore, although they did not depict Ullmo as a hysteric, they implied he was a neurasthenic and therefore weak and unmanly. Male hysteria, despite the research of Jean-Martin Charcot, who attempted to separate hysteria from the feminine, was still a "female" trait projected onto male bodies, but the bodies were in most cases those of Jewish or working-class men – in other words, not bourgeois male gentiles.[75]

Opium Dreams

Not only did Aubin have to attack Lison in his defense of Ullmo, but he also needed to make a direct connection between opium consumption and Ullmo's betrayal to rebut the prosecution's claim that Ullmo had acted with sangfroid and that he had been fully in control of his actions. Ullmo had earlier explained both to investigating magistrate Joseph Leydet and naval investigator Devarenne that he had gotten the idea for his scheme from reading about an instance of espionage in the newspaper and that he had hatched his plans under the influence of opium: "I am an opium smoker. ... It is during the course of my ecstatic dreams that the idea took root in my brain. ... Under the influence of opium, I had lost the notion of good and evil, of duty and honor. I can hardly believe now that I was prey to such an aberration and that I suffered so cruelly from such an

---

[73] Dupré, 562.

[74] Dupré, 562.

[75] It should be noted that the Jewish men were generally foreign born: Mark S. Micale, *Hysterical Men: The Hidden History of Male Nervous Illness* (Cambridge, MA: Harvard University Press, 2008). See especially chapter 3, "Charcot and *La Grande Hystérie Masculine*," and chapter 4, "Male Hysteria at the Fin de Siècle," pp. 117–161 and 162–227, respectively. See also Jan Goldstein, "The Hysteria Diagnosis and the Politics of Anticlericalism in Late Nineteenth-Century France," *Journal of Modern History* 45, no. 2 (June 1982): 209–239, and "The Use of Male Hysteria: Medical and Literary Discourse in Nineteenth-Century France," *Representations*, no. 34 (Spring 1994): 134–165.

irresistible force. Treason appeared to me to be a thing if not natural, at least not at all shocking."[76] Aubin elaborated on this statement, even citing witness testimony from one of Ullmo's colleagues stating that during this time, Ullmo was constantly smoking opium.[77]

Unfortunately, it was a difficult argument to make, because the medical testimony tended to contradict the defense's argument that opium use was responsible for Ullmo's attempt at treason. The medical experts had concluded that Ullmo did not smoke enough opium (30 to 40 pipes a day, which was the equivalent of 30 grams) to be sufficiently affected mentally and physically, citing his excellent overall health and the lack of serious withdrawal symptoms after his arrest. Moreover, they claimed that use of the drug led to indolence, a state that was at odds with the resolution required to carry out the plans that Ullmo had executed.[78] Although they did not feel that opium had led to Ullmo's attempted treason, they conceded that opium had played a secondary, indirect role, diminishing his energy and courage.[79] On the whole, this report was devastating for Ullmo, but Aubin obviously sought to make the most of the argument that opium had made an impact on Ullmo's judgment. Accordingly, the defense lawyer quoted from the report, which called for outlawing the use of opium, viewed by the experts as dangerous for the health of military men. In doing so, Aubin preyed on contemporary fears of the nefarious role of opium in the health of the nation, chastising the government for letting sales continue under state protection.[80]

Historians have viewed the Ullmo case as the trial of opium – it eventually led to the outlawing of opium use in 1916 – but Aubin's primary goal was not to argue for the criminalizing of opium but rather to divert attention from Ullmo's individual responsibility by making his case of treason part of a wider social and political debate.[81] If opium did not

---

[76] Quoted in "Il avoue: Deux Mots rayés nuls," *Le Matin*, 15 November 1907. The other papers reported the same thing, with the wording slightly different in each paper.

[77] Aubin, 219.

[78] Dupré, 577–581.

[79] Dupré, 581.

[80] Dupré, 582; see also Aubin, 219–220.

[81] Both Howard Padwa and Thomas Vincent have examined the Ullmo affair as the "trial of opium." Although I acknowledge the importance of opium in discussions of the Ullmo affair, the question of opium is secondary to my analysis of heroism and national identity. I would like to thank Howard Padwa and Thomas Vincent for sharing their work with me and refer the reader to their respective works: Howard Padwa, "Narcotics vs. the Nation: The Culture and Politics of Opiate Control in Britain and France, 1821–1926" (Ph.D. Dissertation, UCLA, 2008), especially 232–251; Thomas Vincent, "L'Affaire Ullmo (1907–1908): Le Procès de l'opium" (M.A. thesis, University of Paris I, 2003–2004). See

necessarily cause Ullmo to commit a crime, he argued, it diminished his moral energy to repulse it.[82] Such arguments, made at a time marked by a "crisis of masculinity" – during which individuals feared the diminution of national energy, as defined by the energy of its males, especially its military men – had resonance with the public and perhaps with the judges as well.

As is clear from the medical testimony of the doctors in the Ullmo case, opium was seen to lead to indolence, a diminishing of a man's "male energies" – not only because it affected his sexual appetites and therefore made him less likely to procreate, but also because it made him egotistical, and furthermore, deprived him of his judgment and agency, making him a passive victim.[83] This view was further reinforced by popular novels of the period – notably those by Claude Farrère and Jules Boissière, who depicted hapless soldiers who had lost both their manhood and humanity through opium use.[84] In fact, these authors further suggested that opium made virile white male soldiers more effeminate and thus more like "Oriental" colonized males, thereby raising the specter of the "effeminizing" influence of untamed colonies. In contrast, the mainstream qualities of an ideal male hero of the time were those of an active, virile man capable of independence of thought, who, moreover, was disinterested and served the higher good of the nation.[85]

Even though the judges rejected Aubin's opium defense, they, like members of the public, who perhaps had more sympathy for Ullmo, made explicit connections between opium use and his attempted treason. Opium was held responsible for creating both bad soldiers and bad citizens, thereby representing a double danger for the nation. Indeed, many at the time viewed the use of opium as a ploy by Germany to undermine French national defenses, weakening the bodies of individual soldiers as well as the health of the nation itself.[86]

---

also Jean-Jacques Yvorel, *Les Poisons de l'esprit: Drogues et drogués au XIXème siècle* (Paris: Quai Voltaire, 1992).

[82] Aubin, 220.

[83] Yvorel, 198–200; Padwa, 214, 219.

[84] Padwa, 209–220.

[85] As I have previously argued, Dreyfusards put greater emphasis on independence of thought as a male trait, while anti-Dreyfusards placed greater emphasis on the soldier who obeyed orders, but Dreyfusards were increasingly on the defensive with regard to discourses about manhood. By the time of the Ullmo case, both images had to some extent been united.

[86] Padwa, 209; Yvorel, 249.

Pulp Fiction?

If the first aspect of Aubin's defense plea was to represent Ullmo as a child controlled by Lison and opium, a secondary strategy was a rhetorical one designed to depict Ullmo's actions as fantastical and ridiculous, in order to counter the prosecution's charge that Ullmo had acted with sangfroid. Aubin further reinforced the idea of Ullmo as an easily misled minor by depicting him as an imaginative child so enamored of stories that he created his own spy plot, representing Ullmo as the playwright of his own vaudeville play.[87] This strategy had several advantages, because it portrayed Ullmo, albeit indirectly, as a male hysteric, unable to control himself.

Whereas the prosecution described Ullmo's calm demeanor in executing his plans, depicting a cold and calculating soldier, Aubin represented Ullmo's plan to sell documents to a foreign power as "delusional" by placing coded messages in the newspapers."[88] As Aubin recounted, Ullmo went to his meeting with the German spy in Brussels and made no attempt to disguise himself. Furthermore, in the course of sending a telegram to his German contacts, he absentmindedly signed his real name to it and even gave his own address when sending another telegram. This was no cold-blooded spy, argued Aubin, but rather a madman unable to control himself, indeed, a "veritable automaton."[89] Ullmo was so naïve and foolish that he bought a camera in his own name and a toy typewriter on which to type his correspondence to the Naval Ministry – the use of a child's typewriter was, of course, supposed to highlight the image of Ullmo as a child.[90]

Having painted Ullmo as a child, Aubin next portrayed him as ridiculous, calling his attempt to extort money from the French naval minister "burlesque" and "stupid." Accordingly, Aubin characterized Ullmo's ruses as fantastical elements right out of a plot of a vaudeville play, even using the word "vaudevillesque" when he described Ullmo's instructions for collecting money in the toilets of the train heading for Marseille. To the amusement of those present, Aubin recounted the incident of the incontinent consul who had entered the toilets and had been arrested in Ullmo's place as an episode in a tragi-comedy.[91]

---

[87] "Ullmo pointed to the next act of the play," noted Aubin, 231.
[88] Aubin, 221.
[89] Aubin, 229.
[90] Aubin, 230.
[91] Aubin, 231–232.

In his defense plea, Aubin also used the language of the theater to depict Ullmo as the victim of a melodrama, with the curtain rising when Lison came onstage and entered his life. By using the dual strategy of representing Ullmo as the playwright of a vaudeville play as well as the victim in a melodrama, Aubin emphasized the link between fiction and reality, underscoring the public's fascination with the *fait divers* and the theater, and, moreover, illustrating the near collapse of fiction and reality in both the press and the theater of the time.[92]

Another important aspect of Aubin's strategy was to claim that Ullmo's crime was the lesser charge of espionage, as defined by the law of 1886, rather than treason, as prescribed by the infamous article 76, already invoked to condemn Dreyfus, because the former implied a lesser penalty, with up to five years of jail time, as opposed to imprisonment in perpetuity. Thus, he declared that Ullmo's intention was not to betray his country and to provoke a war by trying to sell documents to the Germans but rather to obtain money.[93] In addition, Aubin argued that Ullmo should receive a lesser penalty because he had not actually succeeded in selling the documents in his possession, a view shared by some in the press, who complained about the inequities of the law such that Boulanger, who had organized a plot against the nation, could get off with the lesser charge, whereas a relatively lowly officer like Ullmo (or Dreyfus before him) could receive a greater penalty.[94] After Aubin's arguments, the prosecutor was then allowed a rebuttal in which he objected to the lesser charge and encouraged the judges to think not of Ullmo the individual, for whom they might have pity, but rather national security.

At the end of closing arguments, there was a great deal of emotion in the courtroom, especially when Ullmo, having asked permission, addressed the judges and prosecutor for the last time: "I have sunk quite low, but I cannot allow it to be said that I did this, that I supplied arms in betrayal of France. It is not true! This is the last time that I will wear the uniform, so in this climactic moment – and I understand the importance of what I say – I look you in the face, commander, and all of you officers, and I repeat: I delivered nothing!"[95] The press reaction to these

---

[92] He even recounted that Ullmo had gone to a costume shop, thinking first to disguise himself as a wolf for the meeting at the Ollioules gorges: Aubin, 233.

[93] Aubin, 213 and 233–234.

[94] Varennes, "Gazette des tribunaux," *Le Figaro*, 23 February 1908.

[95] Ullmo's speech in "L'Affaire Ullmo," *La Revue des procès contemporains*, 260. This speech was quoted by the press with varying degrees of accuracy. Some of the papers added rhetorical flourishes to the speech that are not in the original, quoted in this transcript of the public proceedings of the trial.

words was generally favorable, even among those who had earlier been impatient with Ullmo's crying – some reports indicate that Ullmo had cried, holding his head in his hands at various points in the trial, when Aubin spoke of Lison, as well as during the prosecutor's speech.[96] The reporter for *Le Figaro* declared he felt pity for the would-be traitor, noting approvingly that the formerly honorable officer seemed to resurface for the last time: "He said all this without gesturing, maintaining a pose suitable for an officer speaking to his superiors. ... He reassumed the professional attitude of a naval officer who maintains his mental focus out of a respect for discipline."[97] Even the correspondent for *La Libre Parole* expressed sympathy, in spite of himself.[98]

After a brief deliberation, the judges rendered Ullmo's verdict, finding him guilty of treason and sentencing him to lifetime imprisonment in exile. Some papers described Ullmo's initial reaction to the verdict as "impassive, glacial, gloomy," upon which he collapsed, prostrate with grief, unable to maintain his impassivity.[99] A number of journalists reported that Ullmo was on suicide watch in his cell.[100]

The Press and Ullmo

In examining press reaction to Ullmo, one would do well to begin with coverage by the two extremes, that is, the Jewish and the anti-Semitic papers. In many ways, their discourses were mirror images of each other. Already in late October 1907, Emile Cahen, the reporter for *Les Archives israélites*, like those in the mainstream press, lamented that a young man from an honorable family had sunk so low. French Jews, like French Catholics, he noted, could not be held responsible for the treason of one of their own, citing Marshal François Achille Bazaine, who

---

[96] Henri Varennes, writing for *Le Figaro*, had earlier implored Ullmo to remain silent, stating that he would have preferred cynicism to Ullmo's asking for forgiveness: "Gazette des tribunaux," 18 February 1908. For his part, the journalist for *Le Petit Journal* ("Le Traître Ullmo: L'Horreur de trahison," 19 February 1908) found Ullmo's remorse to be a cynical posture designed to help him get off lightly.

[97] Henri Varennes, "Gazette des tribunaux," 23 February 1908; *Le Matin* similarly reported that after this speech, the accused looked "less beaten down than before," "Le Traître condamné: Au Maximum," *Le Matin*, 23 February 1908.

[98] Jacques Larue, "Le Dreyfus de la Marine devant le Conseil de Guerre Maritime de Toulon," *La Libre Parole*, 23 February 1908.

[99] "Le Traître condamné," *Le Matin*, 23 February 1908; see also *Le Figaro* of 23 February 1908: "Gazette des tribunaux," by Henri Varennes.

[100] "Le Traître condamné: Ullmo en Prison," *Le Gaulois*, 26 February 1908, and "Après la sentence," *Le Petit Journal*, 24 February 1908.

had capitulated to the Germans in 1870, as an example.[101] In the same article, Cahen concluded that no bond of religious solidarity would incite French Jews to come to the aid of a guilty man, thus distinguishing the Ullmo case from the Dreyfus Affair. Cahen could also report with some satisfaction that France had progressed sufficiently such that Ullmo's religion did not make the headlines as had Dreyfus's religion thirteen years earlier.[102] Thus, the Jewish press made a real distinction between Dreyfus and Ullmo – justifying Jewish support of Dreyfus earlier and reiterating Jewish patriotism and loyalty to France.

Anti-Semites, of course, linked the two cases, with *La Libre Parole* and *L'Action française* referring to Ullmo at the outset as "the Dreyfus of the Navy." In order to underscore this link visually, *La Libre Parole* published images of Dreyfus and Ullmo at their respective degradation ceremonies in its issue of June 14, 1908, thereby arguing that all Jews were potential traitors.[103] Drumont was at first delighted at the irony that such former Dreyfusards as Clemenceau and Picquart should have to deal with their own case of treason while in power, but delight soon turned to petulance when the Ullmo case failed to turn into a new Dreyfus Affair. Anti-Semites accused the Clemenceau cabinet as well as the mainstream papers, *Le Figaro* and *Le Matin*, in particular, of covering up facts in the Ullmo case so as to minimize Ullmo's guilt. Drumont deplored the lack of anti-Semitic indignation that would lead people to take to the streets as they had during the "heroic" time of the Affair.[104]

Given that former Dreyfusards were in power, anti-Semites must have felt defeated. In an article entitled, "Le Virus juif," Drumont's colleague Gaston Méry made use of a common metaphor of medical pathology, describing France as so ill she no longer cared about her illness, instead seeking to come to terms with it. In other words, Jews had so overrun

---

[101] "Chronique," *Les Archives israélites*, 31 October 1907.

[102] See "Trop de zèle" by Cahen, *Les Archives israélites*, 12 December 1907 and "Chronique," 5 March 1908. In an article ("Variations sur un thème antisémite" from *Les Archives israélites*, 28 November 1907), his fellow correspondent H. Prague took anti-Semites to task, criticizing their lack of logic. If Jews committed treason all the time, why would one act of treason by a Jew cause such emotion, he asked.

[103] "Les Deux Cousins: Deux Parades d'exécution, hier et aujourd'hui," *La Libre Parole*, 14 June 1908, signed A.M. (Albert Monniot).

[104] See Drumont's "Ullmo et Dreyfus," in *La Libre Parole*, 29 October 1907. In another article, Drumont complained: "Today France no longer inspires envy but rather pity. Our army is in ruins. ... Religion, which had been the soul of France, has been brought down." "L'Affaire Dreyfus et l'Affaire Ullmo," *La Libre Parole*, 18 November 1907.

France that the French were hardly aware of it.[105] In an article from April 14, 1908, Drumont declared that France was no more: "Jews have triumphed, at least for the moment ... this nation – immobile, demoralized and discouraged, is incapable of interesting itself in anything." Drumont darkly predicted a second wave of anti-Semitism, which would be even more violent than the first, but despite his bravado, it is clear that for the moment, he felt defeated.[106]

Although anti-Semitism was a minor factor in the Ullmo affair, it was not entirely absent from the major newspapers, especially after Ullmo admitted to having first attempted to sell the documents in his possession to the Germans. Although the mainstream press had previously represented Ullmo as the victim of mental problems, after they learned of his attempted treason, reporters both mocked and chastised him, as did Henri Varennes of *Le Figaro*, who wrote, "Now that we know him better, the guy is more horrible; we believed him to be contemptible and ridiculous, we took him for an imbecile, but he is terrible and odious." Varennes was so disgruntled that references to Ullmo's Jewish origins, heretofore absent, were now clearly stated, with the reporter commenting: "He should have considered that his status as an Israelite imposed on him more than another the respect for his patriotic duty because he could by his crime revive recent atrocious quarrels; but what does it matter to him, he needs money."[107] *Le Matin* had earlier mentioned Ullmo's religion as a detail, but in the coverage of his trial on February 21, 1908, one can detect a note of anti-Semitism: "In these circumstances, the expression on his face is as natural as one could wish, since misery, desolation, and shame can be read on his miserable face. His hair, a bit curly, combed back, his reddish mustache, curly and tightly-wound – his hooked nose, the former lover of the 'beautiful Lison' is hardly seductive."[108] The references to Ullmo's nose and hair were coded to illustrate his Jewish origins.

The journalist for *Le Petit Journal* whose newspaper had initially depicted Ullmo with sympathy – before the discovery of his attempted treason – found Ullmo's crime "particularly odious," perhaps, in part, because he was Jewish. The writer mentioned that Ullmo's father was an Israelite, not only calling Ullmo a Judas, but also stating that opium had

---

[105] Méry, "Le Virus juif," *La Libre Parole*, 21 February 1908.
[106] "Les Zolistes et les Dreyfusards," *La Libre Parole*, 14 April 1908.
[107] Varennes, "Gazette des tribunaux," *Le Figaro*, 21 February 1908.
[108] "Le Traître effondré," *Le Matin*, 21 February 1908. The description in Henri Varennes's article in *Le Figaro* ("Gazette des tribunaux") of 21 February 1908 is nearly identical.

revealed the real Ullmo, a man for whom gold was a god and who was willing to risk everything for it, thereby forsaking a brilliant career.[109]

Despite some measure of anti-Semitism in these articles, especially in descriptions of Ullmo's physiognomy, anti-Semitism was subsumed by a sense of profound disappointment with an officer who had wasted his energies and talents and had thus brought shame upon himself, his family, and his country. In marked contrast with the Dreyfus Affair, the same articles condemning Ullmo depicted his sisters with great sympathy.[110] In this respect, the mainstream press shared an attitude similar to that of the Jewish press toward Ullmo.

Although the discourses in the Jewish and anti-Semitic press were diametrically opposed, they did find common ground, particularly with regard to the effects of opium on Ullmo. Thus, Emile Cahen wrote in *Les Archives israélites*, lamenting the state of affairs in France: "With the decline of religious sentiment, the advance of alcoholism and the increasing use of drugs, criminality is on the rise in the world"; nevertheless he concluded, "the excuse of alcohol or opium is of no value."[111] His reaction was echoed by writers for the anti-Semitic papers. In an article entitled "La Responsabilité du fumeur d'opium," the reporter Vesale deplored the current trend of viewing opium addicts not as criminals but as victims. He disapproved of those who attempted to minimize Ullmo's guilt by using opium as an excuse. He further distinguished between the "degenerative" effects of opium and those of alcohol. Unlike the alcoholic who risked passing his disease on to his descendants, the *opiomane* was unable to have children.[112]

In an article from *L'Action française*, Léon Daudet, himself a doctor, echoed Vesale, and added, "for the real opium addict, women hardly

---

[109] "Le Traître Ullmo: L'Horreur de trahison," *Le Petit Journal* of 19 February 1908. Although *Le Petit Journal* had been anti-Dreyfusard, it had not been anti-Semitic, and in the case of Ullmo, its reporting was a bit harsher than that of the other papers but was not overtly anti-Semitic. On the role of *Le Petit Journal* during the Dreyfus Affair, see Janine Ponty, "*Le Petit Journal* et l'Affaire Dreyfus," *Revue d'histoire moderne et contemporaine* 24 (October–December 1977): 641–656.

[110] See, for example, "Douloureux Calvaire" in *Le Matin* of 24 February 1908, describing the sisters' visit to their brother and "Ullmo avant et après sa condamnation," *Le Petit Journal*, 26 February 1908.

[111] Emile Cahen, "Chronique, " *Les Archives israélites*, 21 November 1907.

[112] "La Responsabilité du fumeur d'opium," by Vesale, *L'Action française*, 10 April 1908. Like Ullmo's doctors, Vesale went on to point out that opium was not the cause of violence but on the contrary lent itself to inertia. Degeneration was a subject of much discussion, not only in the medical community, but also in the popular novels of Emile Zola, who treated this issue in his Rougon-Macquart novel series.

matter. He seeks above all solitude and silence. The role of Lison in Ullmo's life diminishes that of the enchanted pipe." In his conclusion, however, Daudet, the man of science, abdicated to Daudet, the irrational anti-Semite, by stating: "Ullmo committed treason, not because he is an opium addict but rather because he is a Jew."[113] Notwithstanding such anti-Semitic comments, it is striking that the Jewish and anti-Semitic press, both of which included social conservatives who blamed the decline of religion in France for the corruption of contemporary mores, came to similar conclusions, with the two sides accepting Ullmo's guilt as well as his responsibility for his actions.

Others in the press, although they might not necessarily think that the opium defense was sufficient to acquit Ullmo of the charges against him, did have some measure of sympathy for the naval officer. Nevertheless, in common with the Jewish and anti-Semitic press, they shared a concern for the effects of opium and other drugs on the nation's youth and, in turn, on the moral and physical health of the nation. Newspapers as different as the Dreyfusard *L'Aurore*, the right-wing *L'Instransigeant*, and the middle-of-the-road *Le Matin* struck similar attitudes toward Ullmo, seeming to agree that Ullmo was more pitiful than reprehensible and that he had been the victim of opium and "nefarious" women in port cities who preyed on young naval officers by encouraging opium use.[114] The journalist for *L'Instransigeant* spoke for the majority of his colleagues when he called for the regulation of opium and morphine. For his part, the journalist for *L'Aurore* wrote an open letter to Minister of the Navy Thomson, in which he urged the minister not only to forbid the use of opium by naval men under severe penalty but also to banish such loose women from France's ports.[115] The reporter for *Le Matin*, while acknowledging that Ullmo's case was unique, also had harsh words for the women of easy virtue linked to spy rings. He, like others, feared that the flower of French youth could fall under the spell of these women, thereby simultaneously putting an end to their aspirations and careers and placing the nation in danger.[116]

[113] Léon Daudet, "L'Opium, fait-il trahir?" *L'Action française*, 8 May 1908.
[114] Even papers like *Le Temps*, which reported on the trial with little comment, quoted an unnamed officer who stated that Ullmo really could have betrayed his country because of opium, reiterating the dangers of the drug as for the military youth of the country: Pierre Mille, "Ullmo et l'opium," *Le Temps*, 27 February 1907.
[115] "L'Opium par la femme: Lettre ouverte à M. le Ministre de la Marine," *L'Aurore*, 25 February 1908. See also "L'Opium: Code et codex," *L'Instransigeant*, 26 February 1908.
[116] "Le Procès Ullmo: Ses Poisons," *Le Matin*, 22 February 1908.

Striking in these articles is the depiction of a man hooked on opium as an easily led child no longer in control of his actions, a view that had been expressed by Ullmo's lawyer to describe the naval officer. In fact, the journalist for *Le Matin* wrote that Ullmo's actions were so erratic that it was clear he was under the influence of opium. Moreover, the connection between the two sources of poison for the nation was made explicitly – through a language that linked the contamination of prostitutes to that of opium, infecting the national body by striking at its young fighting men.[117] An article from *Le Matin* of February 21 even depicted an image of a trail of smoke from an opium pipe leading to the feathers and ribbons in Lison's chapeau, literally illustrating this link in the minds of many.[118]

Lison

Whereas the press's tone hardened vis-à-vis Ullmo after he admitted to attempted treason, journalists had always depicted Lison Welsch with great disdain. When the correspondent for *Le Figaro* saw Ullmo's mistress in person in November 1907, he expressed his disillusionment: "But, oh, what a disappointment! Scrawny, dried up, no sense of style, her face armor plated with rice powder ... a suit-dress seemingly made for another, thus appears 'the beautiful Lison,' enchantress, the queen of Toulon, the one for whom Ullmo sold his honor and his conscience!"[119] The correspondent for *La Libre Parole*, no fan of Ulllmo, had a similar reaction, as did the correspondent from *Le Matin*, who lamented that Ullmo, a naval officer, had fallen so far for such a woman: "She is a svelte young woman, with shiny blond hair, brown eyes and a matte complexion. Her type of beauty is on the whole quite common and one shudders to think that it is for this dolled up fresh little face that an officer handed over to foreigners the code to our maritime signals and documents related to the national defense."[120]

Both the journalists from *Le Matin* and *Le Figaro* reported that many in Toulon felt that Lison herself should be sitting beside Ullmo on the

---

[117] "Dans les mailles de la trahison," *Le Matin*, 20 February 1908.

[118] "Le Traître effondré," *Le Matin*, 21 February 1908. Indeed, the feather boa itself, which invoked snakelike imagery, associated women with the image of the femme fatale who led men to their downfall. See Elizabeth K. Menon, *Evil by Design: The Creation and Marketing of the Femme Fatale* (Urbana: University of Illinois Press, 2006), 250–251.

[119] *Le Figaro*, 21 November 1907.

[120] "Le Traître effondré," *Le Matin*, 21 February 1908; Jacques Larue, "Le Dreyfus de la Marine devant le Conseil de Guerre," *La Libre Parole*, 21 February 1908.

defendant's bench, with Henri Varennes of *Le Figaro* calling her "the instigator of the crime."[121] Interest in Lison during the trial was thus heightened and many in the press reported that crowds followed her in a vain attempt to speak with her. The efforts of journalists themselves similarly met with little success. Lison attended the first two days of the trial covered in a heavy veil in order to hide her reactions, but journalists nevertheless attempted to gauge them, with the journalist for *Le Petit Parisien* noting that during the previous two days, Lison "snickered each time Ullmo's lawyer spoke of Ullmo's passion for her." He described this disrespect for her former lover as having provoked the violent protests of the public, concluding that it was for this reason that Lison did not attend the trial on its last day, a violation of the law that required her presence as a witness. The journalist further observed that Lison had shown the greatest of indifference to Ullmo since his imprisonment and that she had not been moved by the condemnation of her former lover, seeing the whole incident as due homage to her seductive capacities.[122] In fact, she was seen with another officer shortly after Ullmo's imprisonment, thus highlighting her fickle nature.[123]

The reporter from *Le Matin* mocked Lison for appearing before the military judges, many of whom she knew socially (and implying perhaps intimately), as timid and self-effacing.[124] Similarly, the journalist for *Le Gaulois*, in common with Ullmo's lawyer, was indignant that Lison had earlier played the role of a loyal wife.[125] Lison herself thus did not help her own case, later starring in a music-hall review in Paris, depicting a tableau of Ullmo's "opium dreams" (the show was closed down after protests).[126] Not only was she unfaithful but she also sought to profit

---

[121] "Le Procès Ullmo: Ses Poisons," *Le Matin*, 22 February 1908.

[122] "Déportation perpétuelle, dégradation militaire," *Le Petit Parisien*, 23 February 1908; Henri Varennes, "Gazette des tribunaux," *Le Figaro*, 22 February 1908.

[123] The journalist from *Le Matin*, when he learned of her new love affair with a young officer, noted wryly: "It is a calling!" "Le Traître effondré," 21 February 1908. *L'Intransigeant* reported that Lison had been asked to leave Toulon by the naval authorities and also that she had been offered a job in a café-concert: "Ullmo veut l'oubli, Lison pleure" ("Ullmo desires oblivion, Lison cries" – the headline was somewhat ironic), 24 February 1908. See also "Ullmo avant et après sa condamnation" in the 26 Feburary 1908 edition of *Le Petit Journal*.

[124] "Le Procès Ullmo: Ses Poisons," *Le Matin*, 22 February 1908.

[125] Especially because she so obviously was not loyal, given that she was going out with other men: G. De la Maisière, "L'Affaire Ullmo," *Le Gaulois*, 22 February 1908.

[126] This information was related in the newspapers of the time: see, for example, *La Libre Parole*: "Les Etudiants et la 'Belle Lison'" by A. de Boisandré, 6 March 1908; "La 'Belle Lison' supprimée," signed H. R. from 6 May 1908; and "L'Incident de la 'Belle Lison'"

from Ullmo's downfall and, more important, from a potential danger to France's security. She did not fit the ideal, whether republican or Catholic, of the faithful woman ready to sacrifice all for love of her man and country. In fact, Lison, a demimondaine, united contemporary discourses about the nefarious effects of prostitution and drugs on the bodies of individual soldiers as well as on the body politic itself.[127] In the minds of contemporaries, prostitutes themselves were symbols of addiction, and the fact that Lison was associated with Ullmo's opium use only cemented that association for those who held the "loose" women of Toulon responsible for the opium addiction of naval officers.[128]

In many ways, criticism of Ullmo's mistress was grounded in the expectation that the ideal woman occupied the private sphere – despite the fact that "respectable" women were increasingly visible in the public arena. Not only was the issue of Lison playing at the role of the loyal woman disturbing, so too was the fact that she represented, for many commentators of the period, the excesses of the society of spectacle. The author of an article for *Le Matin* described Lison as a "public woman" (the word, of course, stood for prostitute), "known" (here again, the word could have a double meaning) to the judges who questioned her "because no other woman got around Toulon more than she." He thus linked her directly to the society of spectacle, describing her as being seen "at the café, the casino, the theater, anywhere people amuse themselves and even elsewhere."[129] In a similar vein, Henri Varennes of *Le Figaro* castigated Lison for her showiness, for having arrived at the trial in a landau when everyone else was arriving on foot.[130]

For some commentators, who linked drug use to other vices, the society of spectacle was directly responsible for the corruption of mores. Former Dreyfusard Urbain Gohier wrote an article entitled, "De la pornographie à la trahison," in *Le Matin* of February 23, claiming that Ullmo was not only an opium smoker but also a pornographer: "the Chinese pipe and sadistic literature have contributed equally to degrading his soul."

by H. de Rauville, 7 May 1908. Delpêche also notes that she first performed in a café-concert in Nice before heading for Paris, where she did not last long, because she was booed off stage by an indignant public, 40.

[127] Menon, 70, 115.

[128] Even though history illustrates that it was actually the opposite – it was officers coming home from the Orient who had originally initiated the women in opium use: Yvorel, 213–214.

[129] "Le Procès Ullmo: Ses Poisons," *Le Matin*, 22 February 1908.

[130] "We had not expected tact and modesty from Mlle Lison," noted Henri Varennes, "Gazette des tribunaux," *Le Figaro*, 22 February 1908.

Ironically, Gohier, who was an anti-clerical and opposed the Catholic Church, seemed to be on a moral crusade that would not have been out of place in the pages of *La Croix*, writing: "One exhibits in Paris, in public places, as in earlier times in Rome, nudity that is neither chaste nor artistic. One gets acclimated to ferocious sports reminiscent of circus games." He specifically targeted the theater, indeed, the visual culture of the time: "Mania for the theater holds sway with the entire public, which has neither the intellectual strength necessary for reading, conversation nor meditation and which is only capable of *seeing* – seeing images in books instead of the text, pantomimes instead of dramas, films instead of [comedic] plays." Gohier concluded by recommending religion as a brake against vice. It is clear from references in Gohier's article to the *apaches* and the rise in the murder rate that he was deeply concerned by what he viewed as contemporary lawlessness. For him as well as for many contemporaries, the Ullmo case was a sign of national decadence, and only the "expiation" of a degradation ceremony would suffice to "purify" the nation, yet the ceremony, like other aspects of the Ullmo case, ironically was itself the kind of spectacle against which Gohier had railed in his article.

The Degradation

Ullmo's degradation ceremony, which involved censure by his colleagues and the removal of his military insignias, took place on June 12, four months after his trial. This event, moreover, took place just days after the pantheonization of Emile Zola on June 4 and the assassination attempt on Dreyfus during the ceremonies. The Dreyfus Affair – in particular, the earlier traumatic degradation of Alfred Dreyfus on January 5, 1895 – was clearly on the minds of contemporaries, although only the anti-Semitic press mentioned Dreyfus, drawing close parallels between the two "cousins" and "traitors."[131] Unlike Dreyfus's ceremony, which took place on a bleak January day, the atmosphere surrounding Ullmo's degradation was more like a festival, perhaps because it took place during the summer, and furthermore, in the Provencal town of Toulon, on the place Saint-Roch, with the journalist from *Le Matin* describing it as "the most joyous

---

[131] "Les Deux Cousins: Deux Parades d'exécution, hier et aujourd'hui" by A. M. (Albert Monniot), *La Libre Parole*, 14 June 1908, and "Les Deux Traîtres," *L'Action française*, 13 June 1908.

Ullmo sortant de la prison.   La dégradation.   Devant le front des troupes.
A TOULON. — LA DÉGRADATION DU TRAITRE ULLMO

FIGURE 5.8. "The Degradation of Ullmo," *Les Annales politiques et littéraires*, 21 June 1908 (p. 592). Author's collection.

of southern French festivals and the most poignant of spectacles" (See Figure 5.8.).[132]

Newspaper estimates of the crowds in attendance varied from 10,000 to 40,000.[133] Special train excursions had been arranged to bring people in from outlying areas to witness the ceremony, and the sidewalks and ramparts adjacent to the square were filled with people.[134] Surrounding trees bore the weight of curious spectators, and the density of the crowd was such that some were injured and had to be transported to the hospital.[135] Journalists noted the strong presence of women in the crowd, with *L'Aurore* castigating the demimondaines who were loudest in jeering the fallen officer. The journalist from *L'Action française* similarly noted – with some discomfort – that "women showed themselves to be the most fanatical," thereby highlighting the fear on both the right and left of angry mobs of women.[136]

---

[132] See *Le Matin*, "L'Expiation: On dégrade le traître," for example, of 13 June 1908.

[133] *Le Matin*, "L'Expiation," of 13 June: 40,000; *Le Petit Parisien*, "Expiation: La Dégradation d'Ullmo," of 13 June: 10,000; *Le Gaulois* "La Dégradation d'Ullmo" of 13 June: 20,000; and *Le Petit Journal*, "Le Traître Ullmo a été dégradé hier à Toulon," of 13 June put the figure at 30,000.

[134] According to the *New York Times*, although it is not clear who organized them – perhaps the press? See "Traitor Degraded in France," *New York Times*, 13 June 1908.

[135] See "Expiation: La Dégradation d'Ullmo," *Le Petit Parisien*, from 13 June; "Les Deux Traîtres: La Dégradation d'Ullmo," *L'Action française* of 13 June; "Le Traître Ullmo a été dégradé hier à Toulon," and *Le Petit Journal* of 13 June; and "Traitor Degraded in France," *New York Times*, 13 June 1908.

[136] "La Dégradation d'Ullmo" of 13 June in *L'Aurore* and *L'Action française* of 13 June "Les Deux Traîtres." Similarly, *Le Petit Journal* of 13 June ("Le Traître Ullmo a été dégradé

Although Dreyfus's name was not mentioned, Ullmo provided a coun-
terpoint to Dreyfus in the minds of many contemporaries, especially
reporters who had witnessed both ceremonies. During Dreyfus's degradation, tensions had been greater and the crowd, along with some in the
press, had been offended by Dreyfus's proud demeanor, firm step, and
refusal to show emotion, castigating him for what they viewed as a cynical posture. Many in the press had exhorted Dreyfus to cry in order to
show remorse.[137] In contrast with Dreyfus, Ullmo entered the courtyard
of the square assuming the posture of a guilty man. The journalist from
Le Temps described him in the following manner: "he has become thin-
ner, he walks with his eyes downcast, he is very pale [and] he advances
with an unsure step." His entry provoked jeers of "Down with the traitor," to which Ullmo reacted by reddening and crying.[138] The description from *L'Action française* was hardly different: "In the crowd, people
scream and whistle. Jeers are shouted out. Ullmo, who is pale, walks
slowly. The traitor wishes to maintain his impassivity; he makes a movement as if to straighten himself and to take up a military posture, but
all eyes in the crowd are fixed ardently on him, intimidating him; he
walks with his eyes downcast and with a livid pallor that invades his
[entire] face."[139] The journalist for *Le Petit Journal* described Ullmo after
his insignias had been ripped off: "Snug in his black frock coat, the felo-
nious officer resembles a ghost. He does an about face, takes off his cap,
and with an automatic step, he walks toward the two rows of soldiers.
Cries are heard, and Ullmo, with no strength remaining, cries silently. It
is over!"[140]

Whereas the crowds may have demonstrated their hostility to Ullmo
by hooting and jeering at him, the press accounts, compared with those
of Dreyfus's degradation ceremony, were more neutral; a number of
reporters again expressed their regret that an officer had fallen so low

hier à Toulon") noted that some officers had brought demimondaines with them to wit-
ness the ceremony and that others in the crowd had protested against the presence of
these women. On crowds, see Robert Nye, *The Origins of Crowd Psychology: Gustave
Le Bon and the Crisis of Mass Democracy* (Beverly Hills, CA: Sage, 1976), and Susanna
Barrows, *Distorting Mirrors: Visions of the Crowd in Late Nineteenth-Century France*
(New Haven, CT: Yale University Press, 1981).

137 Léon Daudet, writing for *Le Figaro*, had been outraged: "It is a terrible sign ... that there
was neither collapse nor weakness [on Dreyfus's part]. In this tragic circumstance, tears
would not have seemed cowardly." "Le Châtiment," *Le Figaro*, 6 January 1895.

138 "La Dégradation d'Ullmo," *Le Temps*, 13 June 1908.

139 "Les Deux Traîtres," *L'Action française*, 13 June 1908.

140 "Le Traître Ullmo a été dégradé hier à Toulon," *Le Petit Journal*, 13 June 1908.

and conveyed sympathy for Ullmo's family. Some of the virulence of the spectators was more ritualistic than real, as the reporter for *Le Matin* observed, commenting not only that "the insulting remarks toward the officer end in farcical jibes" but also that the crowd felt some measure of "unconscious pity for what the miserable creature had to endure."[141] Even the reporting of the anti-Semitic newspapers like *La Libre Parole* (*L'Action française* became a daily paper only in 1908) seemed much less heated than it had been thirteen years earlier.[142] Notably absent from the descriptions, with the sole exception of *La Libre Parole*, are reports of anti-Semitic taunts, although whether these epithets were absent or ignored by the mainstream press is not entirely clear. In the wake of the ceremony, Ullmo, as the newspapers reported, collapsed.[143]

After the degradation ceremony, Ullmo was imprisoned until he was deported to Devil's Island in French Guyana. Ullmo was provisionally liberated in 1923, when journalist Albert Londres, writing a series for *Le Petit Parisien* on penal colonies, met with the former naval officer on the mainland, in Cayenne, where he worked for an import-export company. Londres reported that Ullmo had converted to Christianity five years earlier and that he had subsequently been disowned by the family that had supported him in the wake of his attempted treason. Eventually pardoned by French president Albert Lebrun in 1933, Ullmo died in Cayenne on 21 September 1957.[144]

---

[141] "L'Expiation," *Le Matin*, 13 June 1908. The original French is as follows: "Les blasphèmes envers l'officier félon finissent en des lazzis." The word *lazzis* refers to comic stunts or gags in the Italian *commedia dell'arte*, which the French describe as the "Italian farce."

[142] Perhaps in part because Ullmo "acted" like the anti-Semitic caricature of the weak, unmanly Jew.

[143] See, for example, *Le Petit Journal* of 13 June and *L'Aurore*: "Le Châtiment: La Dégradation d'Ullmo," 13 June 1908.

[144] The pardon came in part because many felt that the initial sentence had been too harsh; if it had not been for the beginning of the First World War, Ullmo would have been released much earlier: René Delpêche, 211. Léon Sulpice, "La Trahison d'un marin," *Historia*, no. 245 (April 1967): 114–120. Albert Londres, *Au Bagne* (Paris: Albin Michel 1923), "L'Expiation d'Ullmo," 65–76. In his interview with Londres, Ullmo expressed the desire to expiate his crime, feeling he had done so and also showing surprise that his story was still of interest to the French public, 75. The information about Ullmo's conversion to Christianity is confirmed by Delpêche, 106–107. As for Lison, it was again Albert Londres, writing a series about the cruelty of military prisons, who found her in Morocco, married to the proprietor of a bar who did not wish to discuss the former notoriety of his spouse. Londres, noted with regret that the fat and frumpy woman before him little resembled the femme fatale of earlier years: *Dante n'avait rien vu* (Paris: Albin Michel, 1924), 18–20. My thanks to Dominique Kalifa for sharing this reference with me.

Conclusion

The Ullmo case never assumed the proportions of the Dreyfus Affair. Political circumstances in 1907 were different from those in 1894. Most obviously, the fact that Ullmo admitted his guilt allowed for national consensus, whereas Dreyfus's declaration of his innocence could only serve to divide his compatriots, if only because that innocence pointed to the fallibility of French justice. Furthermore, Dreyfusards had "won" the battle of the Affair and were now in power. Thus, anti-Semitism, although not entirely absent in the Ullmo case, no longer represented the political force it had thirteen years earlier. Moreover, the navy did not historically play the same role as the army as the touchstone for national identity, although the threat to France's security through its military men was made manifestly clear in the Ullmo case.[145] Finally, contemporaries, weary of the internecine political quarrels of the Dreyfus era, yearned for unity. In the end, Ullmo became a symbol of national decline and served to unite the French against the German enemy and what many already saw as the impending war.

The Ullmo and Dreyfus cases demonstrate the extent to which political, social, and cultural issues were intertwined and, moreover, indicate that these anxieties were linked to a discourse on the health and well-being of the nation. Thus, despite the very real differences in political circumstances between the two cases, there is a certain measure of continuity with regard to notions of heroism and manhood as well as anxieties about national decadence. Although the behavior of the two men could not have been more different, the terms used in the press to describe Ullmo and Dreyfus were remarkably similar. Dreyfus too had been described as a "specter," a "cadaver," an "automaton," and a "puppet." These were, of course, code words used to signal a loss of honor and manhood.[146] Both men were seen as unheroic but for different reasons, although there were some points of similarity. In common with each other, both were anti-heroes, in part,

---

[145] I owe this observation to M. Jean de Préneuf, one of the archivists at the SHM.

[146] Indeed, Barrès referred to Dreyfus as a "tragic Guignol," on whose strings his masters pulled every time he spoke at his trial in Rennes, and his fellow anti-Dreyfusard Léon Daudet had earlier referred to him as a "pantin." The image of a puppet to describe a man during this time was a reference to powerlessness and thus effeminacy; it was a way of denying him manhood: Barrès, *Scènes et doctrines du nationalisme* (Paris: Editions du Trident, 1987), 119; Léon Daudet, "Le Châtiment," *Le Figaro*, 6 January 1895. Witness the use of the word to disparage Oscar Wilde years earlier (*Birth of a National Icon*, 128) and to denigrate representations of a devirilized Napoleon, dressed in his dressing gown as played by actor Félix Duquesne in Victorien Sardou's *Mme Sans-Gêne*.

because they were represented as victims – by supporters, in the case of Dreyfus, and by his lawyer, in the case of Ullmo (anti-Semites saw Ullmo and Dreyfus as villains). They both lacked agency.

Nevertheless, there were also some important differences. For anti-Semites, Dreyfus's guilt and his lack of manhood were both seen as a function of his Jewish identity. This was not necessarily the case for Ullmo. The threat to Ullmo's manhood came less from his own body than from the outside – in the form of drugs and women who were seen as agents of Germany. To be sure, certain doctors (and anti-Semites, who argued that all Jewish bodies were diseased) of the time argued that a weakened diseased body was fertile terrain for drug use, but others argued the exact opposite.[147] It is worth noting that it was Ullmo's own lawyer who made the case for degeneration and that this view was rejected not only by the doctors who examined him but also by the judges and the public, although they drew different conclusions.[148] The Ullmo case suggests that even if the anti-Semitic prejudices of the earlier era had not disappeared, they were by then less important than external threats from Germany. Furthermore, Ullmo's emotional displays as opposed to Dreyfus's icy control elicited greater sympathy from contemporaries, although the ensign's excessive crying did begin to wear thin at times. Perhaps this change reflects an evolution in attitudes toward male hysteria and, especially, toward drug users, who, as many in the press noted, were increasingly depicted as victims rather than criminals. Although Ullmo's crying made him less manly, it did not necessarily make him more womanly but rather more childlike. Moreover, it was not the crying itself that was at issue but rather its excessive nature. The Ullmo trial also points to an evolution of gender stereotypes in the years since the Dreyfus Affair. Already during the Affair, certain of Dreyfus's supporters had deplored the fact that he had not depicted more emotion, wishing him to shed a manly tear. By the time of the Ullmo case, a male was actually expected to show emotion – just not excessively, thereby indicating a greater fluidity in gender codes.

Although the French public condemned Ullmo's attempt to betray his country, they did have some sympathy for him, not only as the victim of a pernicious opium habit, which was viewed as a corrupting

---

[147] Yvorel, 200–201.

[148] The judges therefore that Ullmo was fully responsible and therefore guilty, whereas many members of the public believed that Ullmo had fallen prey to outside influences – drugs and women – which were largely responsible for his downfall.

influence on the French military, and thus a threat to national defense, but also as the pawn of his mistress, Lison Welsch, whom they viewed as a femme fatale. Lison was the antithesis of ideal French womanhood at the time and represented the threat to national security of "dangerous" women, an image that would emerge fully during the First World War in the person of Mata Hari. A great deal of public indignation was thus directed toward Lison, illustrating the era's concern for the role of women as well as men in upholding national honor and serving the nation. Although contemporaries clearly viewed Lison as a villain, they viewed Ullmo, at best, as a tragic fallen hero who had sacrificed his good name and a promising career, and at worst, as a pitiful man-child, meriting pity as much as censure. Gender roles were to some extent reversed in the national melodrama of the Ullmo case. Such a view of a man as a victim may be seen as a remasculinizing strategy, designed to absolve men of unmanly and unpatriotic behavior in the context of an impending war.

Theatrical notions of behavior found in both the boulevard theater and the mass press informed the public's view of appropriate behavior, thus contributing to the greater sympathy that Ullmo elicited, as opposed to Dreyfus.[149] Ironically, because the innocent Dreyfus did not act like a theatrical hero, he therefore was not viewed as sufficiently heroic, even by some of his supporters. The more emotional Ullmo better fit contemporary notions of expected behavior. Moreover, his clever lawyer, realizing that he could garner sympathy with the public, represented Ullmo as a victim in a melodramatic plot as well as the author of his own vaudeville play. Whereas Dreyfus's worldview resembled that of a stoic classical hero straight out of the pages of Corneille, Ullmo's imagination was clearly shaped by the hyperbolic conventions of the boulevard theater and the mass press, as his fantastical plot against the Naval Ministry illustrates. In some sense, the play enacted on the national stage during the Ullmo trial mirrored the performances in the theater of the time, marking the era as a great age of the theater in every sense of the term. Not only did theatrical conventions influence the perceptions of contemporaries with regard to expected codes of behavior, especially that of men, but the theater itself had become such a key element of the culture that a potential national crisis was viewed as a performance, even a divertissement.

---

[149] As the journalist from *L'Humanité*, writing at the time of the Ullmo trial, observed: "Le Triomphe de Sherlock Holmes," *L'Humanité*, 8 June 1908, p. 2.

The Ullmo case illustrates the important place of the theater in French culture as it also highlights the ever more important role of the mass press in French society. The press, which had come of age even before the Dreyfus Affair, served up a court-martial trial as a commodity to be consumed by a public anxious for examples of "spectacular realities."[150] The drama and excitement of the Ullmo case as a *fait divers* was more compelling than any arguments the anti-Semites could offer. Although French men and women did rally around the idea of the nation in danger in the Ullmo case, they were equally united as consumers in the new age of mass culture.

[150] This expression comes from Vanessa Schwartz's *Spectacular Realities*.

Conclusion

From One War to the Next: The End of Heroes?

My father spoke in 1897, to a generation weaned on faith; he felt in some mysterious way that this was a generation destined to die. ... These young men who listened to him, these hearts who would submit to the soul of Cyrano, console themselves with his panache, these are already the condemned men of 1914.

Thus wrote Maurice Rostand in his memoirs published in 1948. Fifty years earlier, Edmond Rostand had exhorted young schoolboys at his alma mater to imitate the panache of Cyrano. There is certainly evidence to indicate that many young French men entering into battle during the First World War had taken this lesson to heart. Notwithstanding the hyperbolic nature of Rostand *fils's* comment and the hindsight involved, it is true that French soldiers took copies of *Cyrano de Bergerac* to the front with them and that they also performed the play in the trenches.[1] Rostand himself regularly received letters from *poilus* (soldiers), who saw the great author as a national icon, indeed, an honorary uncle.

If Rostand was France's cherished elder statesman, his friend and fellow icon Sarah Bernhardt was her grande dame, a personification of France itself. Bernhardt, who by this time was in her seventies, lost a leg to amputation in 1915. Once again, however, the great actress mixed fact and fiction. She performed for *poilus* at the front in 1916, telling the reporter for the *New York Times* – she was on a propaganda tour designed to encourage the Americans to join the war effort – that these

---

[1] Maurice Rostand, *Confession d'un demi-siècle* (Paris: La Jeune Parque, 1948), 35. Rostand had a voluminous correspondence with soldiers during the First World War, as the various Rostand dossiers at the BNF Richelieu attest.

French soldiers, "fresh from the greatest melodrama of the world ... were quick to sense any insincerity of art."[2] She also played the role of wife and mother of soldiers in the epic war film *Mères françaises* (1917). Filmed on location in the theater of war, it included several scenes in the trenches. One scene depicted her character, appropriately named Jeanne, before the statue of Joan of Arc at the actual site of the war-torn Rheims cathedral praying for her family to be spared.[3] Where did reality stop and fiction begin? Many of those who saw the film were moved by her performance, but most of them must also have had in mind her brilliant portrayal of Joan of Arc.[4]

Nearly fifty years earlier, during the Franco-Prussian War, Bernhardt, ever the patriot, had organized a military hospital at the Théâtre de l'Odéon. After that catastrophic war, which led to a resounding French defeat, the cult of the hero gained great popularity and manifested itself in every aspect of national life. Only heroes could recall the bygone glories of France's past and assure French men and women that the traditions of heroism and courage still reigned in France. The loss in the war, however, was not the only reason for the rise of the heroic cult. Although the Third Republic, born of the defeat and the civil war of the Commune, lasted seventy years, its history was marked by intense political, social, and religious strife. The Dreyfus Affair, which culminated in the separation of church and state in 1905, represented the apogee of these conflicts. But other events – the Boulanger episode in the 1880s, the anarchist bombings in the 1890s, and the wave of strikes between 1906 and 1909 – were all moments of high tension.

The fin de siècle also witnessed the rise of the feminist movement and the figure of the New Woman, both of which threatened to blur traditional gender lines and assume a greater role in the heretofore (mostly) male public sphere. Changing gender roles, along with a decline in the national birthrate, gave rise to a "crisis of masculinity." This crisis was exacerbated by the emergence of modern consumer culture, which was

---

[2] "Sarah Bernhardt Writes of Trip to the Front," *New York Times*, 15 October 1916.

[3] See *Le Courrier cinématographique* of 20 January 1917. I am grateful to Florence Rochefort and Annie Metz for pointing this image out to me. It is part of an exhibition catalog for the month of photography in Paris in November 2010, *Photos, femmes, féminisme: La Collection de la Bibliothèque Marguerite Durand*.

[4] Others might have been thinking of her dramatic reading of the wartime poem by Eugène Morand entitled "Les Cathédrales," in which a soldier dreams of the great cathedrals of France, which appear to him in allegorical form: Leonard V. Smith, Stéphane Audoin-Rouzeau, and Annette Becker, *France and the Great War, 1914–1918* (New York: Cambridge University Press, 2003; 2008), 1–2.

associated with the feminization and concomitant emasculation of French society. The cult of heroes, even female ones, was a way of offsetting such changes. Ironically, however, heroes revealed cracks in the ideal of strictly delineated gender categories, as many heroic traits – selflessness, sacrifice, and devotion – were generally seen as female characteristics.

Equally ironic, although heroes were depicted as selfless and perceived as antidotes to the selfishness of rampant consumerism, they themselves – Joan of Arc, Napoleon, and Cyrano de Bergerac, chief among them – became objects of commodification. Manifesting itself in the recently Haussmannized Paris, the emerging consumer society was defined by the *grands boulevards*, cafés, and department stores. The twin pillars of this society were the mass press and the boulevard theater, which reached unprecedented numbers of citizens, male and female, especially during the years immediately preceding World War I. It was here that the cult of the hero flourished.

Journalists, playwrights, actors, and, at times, political leaders used both the theater and the press to forge national identity around consumption, in the first case, of the news and, in the second, of plays, many of which were melodramas with historical content. History was transformed into a spectacle to be consumed in the boulevard theater and magnified by the mass press. In the same manner, incidents like the Bazar de la Charité fire and the Ullmo trial were transformed into national melodramas by a mass press that often fictionalized real-life events, transforming them into *faits divers*, thus blurring the line between representation and reality.

As illustrated by the five debates or causes célèbres about heroism examined in this book – not only in the real-life cases of the Bazar de la Charité fire and the Ullmo trial but also in the fictionalized representations in the boulevard theater of Cyrano, Napoleon, and Joan of Arc – the search for heroes was not a neutral enterprise but was fraught with controversies. Historical figures like Napoleon and Joan of Arc were the objects of dispute, along with contemporary heroes. In each case, opposing political groups, claiming to represent the "true" vision of the hero, articulated different visions of the nation. The Third Republic leaders used heroes to transcend political, social, regional, and religious differences in order to forge national unity. Similarly, political foes of the republic posited an opposing vision of the nation, rallying around other heroes, although both groups grappled for control of the legacies of Napoleon and Joan. These political groups, however, were not successful in creating a unified vision of the nation. Little wonder then that the French people, weary of political quarrels and uneasy about consumer culture, which increasingly wrought changes in gender relations, sought heroes who could forge national unity "beyond" politics, finding refuge in the fictions of the theater and the press.

The process of finding heroes or anti-heroes who could bring the French together "beyond" politics was not a linear one, although a growing threat from Germany and an increasing impatience with internecine political quarrels gave rise to a desire on the part of the French public for greater unity during the years immediately preceding World War I. The *faits divers* aspects of the Ullmo spy case in 1907–1908 united the public, along with Sarah Bernhardt's portrayal of Joan of Arc, which rallied audiences in 1909. As they did with Bernhardt's representation of Joan, contemporaries rejected the partisan politics of anti-Semites, which would have focused exclusively on Ullmo's Jewish identity. Instead, they were fascinated by his opium habit, his demimondaine mistress, and his gambling problems, viewing him as a fallen hero whose example served as a lesson against the dangers of national decline.

Such national cohesion was notoriously absent in the 1897 Bazar de la Charité fire, which took place on the eve of the Dreyfus Affair. Although the French public consumed various titillating aspects of the incident as a *fait divers*, this event of national mourning, which should have united the nation, only served to reveal political, class, and religious differences. Although some in the press spoke of national solidarity forged by the union in the fire and in death of the heroic aristocratic women and their working-class rescuers, the controversy over the perceived behavior of the male aristocrats present precluded a national consensus. So too did different understandings of the significance of the tragedy. Catholics tended to see the fire as retribution for France's failure to follow the true (Catholic) path, while populist papers were envious that the passing of aristocratic women should elicit so much sympathy when the near-daily incidents that killed workers attracted little attention. The left-wing papers also castigated the Catholic Church, along with the moderate republicans who had formed an alliance with Catholics during the *ralliement*. They mocked the cowardice of aristocrats, holding up the working-class heroes as exemplars of French heroism. Aristocrats and elite males, on the other hand, were on the defensive, feeling the need to uphold their own personal honor, which they associated with that of France itself.

These tensions of class, religion, and politics would take center stage during the Dreyfus Affair, at a time when Rostand's *Cyrano de Bergerac*, which premiered in December 1897, was playing to sellout audiences. The story of Cyrano, unlike the incidents of the fire, managed to unite the public, in part because Cyrano rehabilitated the aristocratic males whose honor had been found wanting in the fire. French honor – long associated with aristocrats – was refurbished in the play. The opposing views of heroism, which were the subject of intense debate outside the theater walls, were also joined in the figure of Cyrano. Not only could Dreyfusards admire Cyrano's wit and intellect, and anti-Dreyfusards, the military hero, but the two groups could also revel in his courage, both moral and physical. Finally, Cyrano belonged to the distant heroic past of the seventeenth century. Moreover, because the real Cyrano was relatively obscure, Rostand had more latitude to create an ideal fictionalized character than would be possible for those representing Joan of Arc and Napoleon, although they certainly took liberties with these two well-known historical figures.

At around the same time – Sardou's play dated from 1893 and Rostand's from 1900 – republican playwrights like Sardou and Rostand attempted a similar feat with the figure of Napoleon, humanizing the legend and "depoliticizing" it by emphasizing its unifying aspects. The Third Republic leaders, attempting to root the new regime in the heroic past, tried to co-opt the Napoleonic legacy once it was safe to do so – in the wake of the defeat of Bonapartism and Boulangism. Although Sardou and Rostand, especially the latter with *L'Aiglon*, whose lead was played by Bernhardt, had much success in bringing their compatriots together around these theatrical representations, they were not entirely successful. Although the Napoleonic legacy was no longer linked to a political party, it remained embedded in politics. For many on the left – both Sardou and Rostand were moderate republicans – Napoleon would forever remain the dictator responsible for the deaths of so many men and not the heroic revolutionary figure of moderate republicans. He was also a part of a recent past, its wounds too fresh for many whose grandparents had participated in the events of the revolutionary and Napoleonic eras. The suspicions of the left-wing republicans were largely confirmed by the appropriation of the Napoleonic legend in the end by the nationalist right, including such writers as Barrès and Gyp, despite the efforts of Sardou and Rostand. Both Barrès and Gyp divorced Napoleon from his revolutionary legacy and presented him as an opposition figure to the parliamentary republic. Thus, the image of Napoleon as a symbol of unity "beyond" politics was only partially successful.

Like Cyrano and Napoleon, Joan of Arc was one of the most popular heroes of the fin de siècle, a touchstone for personal and national identities. Unlike Napoleon but in common with Cyrano, Joan of Arc, as

Sarah Bernhardt portrayed her, managed to successfully unite fin-de-siècle audiences, both in 1890 and in 1909 – despite the fact that Joan was the object of political disputes outside the theater walls. In common with Cyrano, Joan was a figure from the distant heroic past; the English, who were then the enemy to be booted from France, were easily replaced during the late nineteenth and early twentieth centuries by Germany. Although the two plays took place during relatively quiet moments in the struggle to appropriate Joan of Arc, much credit must go to Bernhardt, who succeeded in harnessing her own popularity to that of Joan, transforming the legend into a commodity to be consumed by fin-de-siècle theatergoers. The reactions of spectators and reviewers to her representation of Joan, especially in 1909, also attest to the power of her acting, as she created a *frisson patriotique* (patriotic shiver) among members of the audience.

By the time of the Ullmo spy case in 1907–1908, the conventions of the theater and of the *fait divers*, which played an ever more important role in the society of the time, had done their work. They nearly collapsed fact and fiction in the eyes of French contemporaries, accounting as much for the consensus around a view of Ullmo as a fallen hero as did changes in political circumstances, both foreign and domestic. Weary of political quarrels and machinations, the French preferred to consume a spy case, which constituted a potential security threat, as a national melodrama akin to the performances in the theater and the *faits divers* in the newspapers. The same *frisson patriotique* that moved theatergoers to tears watching Sarah Bernhardt as Joan of Arc in 1890 and 1909 here thrilled the armchair detectives following the Ullmo affair in the national press.[5] Thus, a spy case that could easily have been a cause for national disunity – as had been the Dreyfus Affair – instead was the source of cohesion among the French, who saw it as a warning of the dangers of national decline. A chronological shift had taken place by the time of the Ullmo case so that the external enemy was more important than internal quarrels.

The desire for heroes at the time was inclusive, bridging differences of politics, class, religion, and gender. Heroes thus came from all classes. The popular classes were represented by the working-class rescuers

---

[5] A similar preoccupation would engross the French public in the summer of 1914, during the weeks leading up to the declaration of the First World War, when the French seemed more interested in the details of the assassination of *Le Figaro*'s editor Gaston Calmette by Henriette Caillaux, wife of Radical politician Joseph Caillaux, than in the guns of war. Moreover, in this case, the journalist had himself become part of the story. See Edward Berenson, *Madame Caillaux* (Berkeley: University of California Press, 1992).

in the Bazar de la Charité fire and the peasant Joan of Arc, and even by the provincial parvenu Napoleon, whereas the aristocratic women in the Bazar de la Charité fire and Cyrano celebrated aristocratic honor. Jews too were incorporated into the national consensus – not only Bernhardt, who played both Joan and l'Aiglon, but also Ullmo, whose identity exclusively as a Jew was rejected in favor of a view of him as a fallen *French* hero.

These heroes all represented national unity, albeit in different ways. The working-class rescuers sacrificed themselves to save the aristocratic women, whereas Joan, a peasant, served both her king and country. The aristocratic women had died trying to help the poor (it is true that the working-class papers rejected the Catholic noblesse oblige view of charity), whereas the aristocratic Cyrano rejected aristocratic privilege and sympathized with the humble and destitute. As for Napoleon, he was an upstart who established his own aristocracy based on merit, thus uniting the revolutionary and monarchical traditions, although not always successfully. Ullmo, on the other hand, united by serving as a counterexample.

Not only were heroes from different social classes, they were also ecumenical. Thus, although republicans and Catholics may have each had their own pantheon of heroes, they shared a common need for heroes as well as similar ideas about what constituted heroism.[6] Heroes sacrificed for the greater good and exhibited courage, both moral and physical. France is a Catholic nation, and it is not unreasonable to think that republicans, who opposed Catholics, nevertheless shared with their opponents a similar view of heroes as martyred figures, an attitude that corresponded to the defensive national mood after the loss in the Franco-Prussian War. The most successful heroes were those who succeeded in becoming secular Christ-like figures. The aristocratic women in the fire – who were compared to Joan herself – were perhaps too closely allied with the Catholic Church to be able to unite completely. But Joan of Arc, especially as she was played by Sarah Bernhardt, who represented herself both as a Catholic and as a Jew, became a lay saint. So too did Cyrano and his other half, the aptly named Christian. Both sacrificed themselves for the woman they loved and for each other, as well as for their country. Napoleon himself had been represented as a Christ-like figure following his defeat at Waterloo and exile to Saint-Helena, but the fin-de-siècle twist to this theme depicted him through his son l'Aiglon, who died to

---

[6] There were some important differences, as I've argued in my earlier work, *Birth of a National Icon: The Literary Avant-Garde and the Origins of the Intellectual in France* (Albany: SUNY Press, 1999).

expiate the sins of the father. As for Ullmo, he too was in some sense a sacrificial figure, a foolish young man who was made to "pay" for the dangers of drugs, gambling, and loose women for military men, with whom rested the honor of the nation and its future in an impending war against Germany.

Heroes also married the two genders, although most of the era's heroes were men, with the aristocratic women in the fire and Joan of Arc remaining the exception. Furthermore, these heroes all reflected the gender ambiguity of the time, combining male and female traits. Nevertheless, although the possibility of female heroism was accepted, it could not supersede or supplant that of males. It is for this reason that the discussions of heroism in the Bazar de la Charité fire were so problematic. The events seemed to pit working-class male heroes against aristocratic male villains. Moreover, they threatened gender stereotypes, by contrasting female heroism with male cowardice. Not only could women be heroes, but certain "female" qualities like self-sacrifice were actually heroic. The discussions of heroism during the fire also illustrate the cracks in strictly delineated gender traits. The women had demonstrated the so-called male qualities of sangfroid, whereas the aristocratic men had displayed panic, a supposedly female quality. Furthermore, for those who would dismiss women for their emotional and visceral reactions, it was this very same *cran* or guts that the women and working-class heroes had exhibited in saving others. Although the entire incident ended in a whitewash of the aristocratic men's alleged cowardly behavior, the events of the Bazar de la Charité fire served to illustrate the increasingly fluid nature of gender categories at the fin de siècle.

Cyrano de Bergerac more successfully rallied the public in its presentation of heroism than did the events of the fire. First, Roxane, although heroic, did not overshadow Cyrano. Furthermore, in Cyrano, Rostand united the Dreyfusard ideal of an intellectual hero with the anti-Dreyfusard ideal of a military one. Nevertheless, Rostand's portrayal of Cyrano was more subversive than most members of his audiences realized. In the character of Cyrano, Rostand succeeded in complicating traditional notions of heroism. On the one hand, Cyrano displayed great courage, both moral and physical. He was also a master of words and wit, male qualities par excellence in the French context. Yet these very "manly" traits were destabilized, because in the end, Cyrano was a failure. He was also an incomplete hero, needing the handsome but inarticulate Christian to "complete" him. Christian, for his part, was a "puppet" controlled by another man and therefore not sufficiently manly. Together, these two men formed one half of a couple with each other as much as with Roxane. Neither, moreover, managed to consummate his relationship with her. Finally, both Cyrano and Christian displayed the typically "feminine" quality of self-sacrifice, displaying Christ-like qualities. In the context of the fin de siècle, during which many contemporaries associated Christianity with women, this trait only highlighted their unmanliness.

The masculinity of the ultimate macho hero Napoleon was also destabilized by litterateurs and historians of the fin de siècle. On the eve of the First World War, Gyp's *Napoléonette* represented the Napoleonic legacy through a fictional goddaughter. Playwrights like Sardou and Rostand played a key role in this process. The former undressed the legend and depicted him as a potential cuckold, who, moreover, is bested by the brash wife of one of his marshals. But once again, it was Rostand, who challenged and further complicated gender norms of the time, through the figure of Napoleon's son, played, moreover, by the cross-dressing Sarah Bernhardt. Napoleon's son, unlike his father, was a dreamer. In common with Cyrano (and also with the aristocratic men of the Bazar de la Charité fire), he was all talk and no action. Physically, l'Aiglon was weak, dying in the play – as he had in real life – of tuberculosis at age twenty-one. He was also an expiatory, Christ-like figure, a trait viewed as feminine. The use of a female actor *en travesti* to portray such a character in order to interject a note of anxiety and impotence could be seen as conventional. Yet Rostand's choice of Bernhardt for the part was inspired, because the great actress was also known for the power she bestowed on all the characters she played. What did it mean for definitions of male and female if a woman in drag played the main role but portrayed this weak character with force? Traditional notions of gender were nonsensical in such a context. Bernhardt's own transcendent quality allowed her to overcome gender differences, a feat she also accomplished in her tour de force performance as Joan of Arc, especially in Emile Moreau's 1909 *Le Procès de Jeanne d'Arc*.[7]

Joan of Arc was herself a transcendent figure, because the ambiguity of her gender gave her a unifying power that placed her outside the gender wars of the fin de siècle. At the same time, however, this very ambiguity, which stemmed from her virginity – indeed her sexlessness – coupled with her transvestism, was potentially subversive, a fact not lost on Bernhardt.

---

7 I am following the line of thought outlined by Mary Louise Roberts in *Disruptive Acts: The New Woman in Fin-de-Siècle France* (Chicago: University of Chicago Press, 2002), 173–174.

The great actress, who was by this time a national heroine, linked her own popularity with that of Joan, to the point that contemporaries could hardly distinguish between the two.

Joan of Arc combined in her person the martial qualities of the warrior with the feminine qualities of self-sacrifice. Again, the fact that she was a potential Catholic saint – although the left laid claim to her as well – reinforced her "feminine" qualities. Many at the fin de siècle sought to "feminize" Joan of Arc by denying her agency and representing her as the passive agent of her God and king, as a muse rather than a leader. Although Bernhardt gave lip service to Joan's "feminine" qualities, describing her as a frail young girl, she played her, as she did l'Aiglon – perhaps even more so – with fierce strength and determination. Critics of the time were not mistaken in seeing in Bernhardt's Joan of Arc male and female traits. Both Joan and Bernhardt were, in Maurice Rostand's words, the "couple reunited," at once masculine and feminine.[8]

The would-be traitor Ullmo also combined the masculine and the feminine, albeit in a different way. Whereas the women in the fire, Cyrano, Napoleon, and Joan of Arc were heroic figures, Ullmo was an anti-hero. Unlike the male aristocrats of the Bazar de la Charité fire, who were seen as villains, however, Ullmo was viewed as a potential hero who had fallen from grace. The relatively sympathetic attitude toward Ullmo was in part the result of an evolution in gender norms that led contemporaries to accept both male and female qualities in a man – more important, in a military man – without necessarily dismissing him as effeminate. Moreover, the exaggerated, at times, melodramatic, conventions of the theater and press had their effect. Ullmo elicited sympathy because his emotionalism better corresponded to the behavior contemporaries expected of their compatriots.

Such conventions were already at work during the Dreyfus Affair, when Dreyfus's sympathizers had hoped for tears from the tightly controlled army captain. Both Dreyfus and Ullmo were represented as victims, a trait generally viewed in opposition to heroism. Moreover, similar words like "puppet," "automaton," and "cadaver" were used at the time of their degradation ceremonies. Yet, whereas Dreyfus, as a result, was immediately dismissed as unmanly, this was not always the case of Ullmo, who was viewed with greater sympathy and sometimes represented as a fallen hero, the victim of an evil woman. In part, this difference was due to the lesser role that anti-Semitism played in the Ullmo trial. During the

---

[8] Maurice Rostand, *Sarah Bernhardt* (Paris: Calmann-Lévy, 1950), 54.

Dreyfus Affair, anti-Semites had dismissed Dreyfus – indeed all Jewish males – as unmanly, both unworthy and incapable of incarnating French military virtues.

Although anti-Semitism, at times expressed in coded references to Ullmo's "effeminacy," was not entirely absent from the latter case, in most instances contemporaries focused on Ullmo as a French soldier rather than as a Jew – hence an attitude that would uphold French honor and manhood through its military men. The public preferred to treat Ullmo as a fallen hero rather than a coldblooded, dangerous spy or an effeminate male. If they did the latter, what would that say about French soldiers and through them about French honor in general? The doctors who examined Ullmo presented him as a lazy sensualist, unable to control his appetites – a trait usually associated with women. Furthermore, opium, which deprived a man of his sexual and moral energy, had the power to diminish his manhood. Nevertheless, the French public exculpated Ullmo, putting the blame squarely on his mistress, Lison, whom they viewed as having hooked her lover on a substance that constituted a danger for all French military men. Due in large part to his lawyer's defense, Ullmo – although he was convicted – was seen as a pitiful man-child (like l'Aiglon) ensnared by a cunning femme fatale, in a reversal of traditional gender roles. This view of Ullmo was the one that could best unite the French public in the years immediately preceding the war. Just as the quest for heroes brought together French men and women around representations of heroes, both male and female, the Ullmo case presented a man and a woman as counterexamples of the French heroic ideal, albeit it the former with much more sympathy.

Ullmo the anti-hero was a human figure, as were the heroes of the era – lay saints for a democratic age, played by the most charismatic stars of the era. Although their heroism made them figures of admiration, it was their flaws that made them seem accessible. The ordinary men and women who consumed images of heroes inserted themselves into myths around these national icons. The mass press and the boulevard theater – in which the exaggerated conventions of fiction, especially of melodrama, flourished – created a place for an imagined heroism in the mundane social relations of those caught up in this mass culture. A shared vision "beyond" politics and gender firmly incorporated women as well as men into the national community (although women in France did not receive the vote until after the Second World War), helping to explain why and how the French entered the First World War with such unity.

Uncertain times call for heroes.[9] The years following defeat in the Franco-Prussian War were just such a period in French history. The French were obsessed with heroes and sought them in every aspect of daily life. The First World War would put an abrupt end to the fin-de-siècle cult of heroes, and in the aftermath of that conflict, a new heroic cult would emerge. But on the eve of the war, French soldiers carried into battle images of Cyrano, Joan, and Napoleon, heroic symbols of a France that would soon become part of a long-ago belle époque, a time before the ruins of the trenches and the carnage of war.

[9] The hunger for heroes seems to be acute in our own twenty-first century, especially in the post–9/11 world. The firefighters and police personnel who died saving lives in the Twin Towers, along with the ordinary citizens who struggled with their captors to divert their plane from a major target in Washington, D.C., were widely celebrated in the wake of the events. The last few years have seen a growth industry of heroes in the media – witness the popularity of the television show *Heroes* on NBC, which had more than 14 million viewers in its first season, and the phenomenal success of the Fox series *24*, with Kiefer Sutherland in the lead role of the morally ambiguous hero Jack Bauer, who seems to better correspond to the increasing cynicism of the aftermath of the Iraq debacle. Both series, incidentally, have reached an end. *Heroes* was canceled in May 2010 due to flagging ratings, whereas *24*'s last episode the same month drew in huge audiences.

Selected Bibliography

Primary Sources

I. Archives

Archives de la Préfecture de Paris, BA/1313–1314 series: Bazar de la Charité
Bibliothèque Historique de la Ville de Paris (BHVP):
  A.R.T. (Association des Régisseurs de Théâtres) Collection, *Cyrano de Bergerac*
  Collection des Actualités: Bazar de la Charité and *Cyrano de Bergerac*
Bibliothèque Marguerite Durand (BMD): Joan of Arc Dossier
Bibliothèque Nationale de France, Richelieu (BNF): Collection Rondel (on the theater):
  Fol SW 257: Caricatures and illustrations of Sarah Bernhardt in Emile Moreau's *Le Procès de Jeanne d'Arc* (1909)
  Rf677.22 (1): Press articles on Moreau's *Le Procès de Jeanne d'Arc*
  Rf 71.5333: Interviews with Rostand
  Rf71.534: Cambo Dossier
  Rf87543: Press articles on Jules Barbier's *Jeanne d'Arc* (1890)
  Rt5881: Sarah Bernhardt: Interviews
  Rt5883, 1–4: Sarah Bernhardt: Interviews
  Rt5884, 1–2: Sarah Bernhardt Dossier
  Rt6620: Coquelin Dossier
  SR 951530 and RJ 4192: *Cyrano de Bergerac* dossier, 1897–1898
Service Historique de la Marine (SHM), Vincennes, France: Ullmo Dossier: C7 4e série moderne, Carton 480, Dossier 11

II. Journals and Newspapers

Action
L'Action française
Les Archives israélites

L'Aurore
L'Autorité
Comédia
La Croix
L'Echo de Paris
L'Eclair
L'Ermitage
Femina
Le Figaro
France
La Fronde
Le Gaulois
Gil Blas
Les Hommes d'aujourd'hui
L'Humanité
L'Illustration
L'Intransigeant
Le Jour
Le Journal
Le Journal des débats politiques et littéraires
La Justice
La Lanterne
La Libre Parole
Le Matin
Le Mercure de France
Le Monde illustré
Le National
New York Times
La Paix
La Patrie
Le Petit Journal
Le Petit Journal illustré
Le Petit Parisien
La Petite République
Le Rappel
La Revue blanche
La Revue bleue
La Revue de Paris
La Revue des deux mondes
La Revue illustrée
La Revue indépendante
Le Soir
Le Soleil
Le Temps
Le Théâtre
Le Voltaire

III. Books

Barrès, Maurice. *L'Appel au soldat*. Paris: Plon, 1926.

    Les Déracinés. Paris: Union générale d'éditions, 10/18, 1986.

    Scènes et doctrines du nationalisme. Paris: Editions du Trident, 1987.

    Mes Cahiers: 1896–1923. Paris: Plon, 1994.

Bernhardt, Sarah. *My Double Life: The Memoirs of Sarah Bernhardt*. Translated by Victoria Tietze Larson. Albany: SUNY Press, 1999.

    Ma double vie. Paris: Phébus, 2000.

Bourgeois, Léon. *Solidarité*. Paris: Armand Colin, 1896. 7th ed., 1912.

Bournand, François, and Raphaël Viau. *Les Femmes d'Israël*. Paris: A. Pierret, 1898.

Doumic, René. *Le Théâtre nouveau*. Paris: Perrin, 1908.

Dreyfus, Alfred. *Carnets (1899–1907)*. Paris: Calmann-Lévy, 1998.

Dubois, Louis-Marie. *L'Incendie du Bazar de la Charité: Mystère en deux tableaux*. Paris: Librairie salésienne, 1899.

Faguet, Emile. *Propos de théâtre*. Paris: Société française d'imprimerie et de librairie, 1907.

Fesch, Père Paul. *Mortes au champ d'honneur: Bazar de la Charité*. Paris: Flammarion, 1897.

France, Anatole. *La Vie littéraire, 3ème série*. Paris: Calmann-Lévy, 1898.

Grand-Carteret, John. *L'Aiglon en images dans la fiction poétique et dramatique*. Paris: Charpentier et Fasquelle, 1901.

Gyp. *Napoléonette*. Paris: Calmann-Lévy, 1913.

Huret, Jules. *La Catastrophe du Bazar de la Charité (4 mai 1897)*. Paris: Juven, 1897.

    Tout yeux, tout oreilles. Paris: Charpentier, 1901.

Jeudon, L. *La Morale de l'honneur*. Paris: Félix Alcan, 1911.

Larroumet, Gustave. *Nouvelles Études de littérature et d'art*. Paris: Librairie Hachette et cie, 1894.

    Etudes de critique dramatique. Vol. 2. Paris: Hachette, 1906.

Lemaître, Jules. *Impressions de théâtre: 5ème série*. Paris: Lecène, Oudin, 1891.

    Impressions de théâtre, 8ème série. Paris: Société française d'imprimerie et de librairie, 1897.

    Impressions de théâtre, 10ème Série. Paris: Société française d'imprimerie et de librairie, 1898.

Lesigne, Ernest. *Fin d'une légende: Vie de Jeanne d'Arc (de 1409 à 1440)*. Paris: Bayle, 1889.

Londres, Albert. *Au Bagne*. Paris: Albin Michel, 1923.

Moreau, Emile. *Le Procès de Jeanne d'Arc*. Paris: L'Illustration théâtrale, 1909.

Moreau, Félix. *Le Code civil et le théâtre contemporain: M. Alexandre Dumas fils*. Paris: L. Larose et Forcel, 1897.

Reinach, Joseph. *Histoire de l'Affaire Dreyfus*. Vol. 2. Paris: Editions Robert Laffont, 2006.

Renard, Jules. *Journal*. Vol. 2. Paris: Union générale d'éditions, 1984.

Rolland, Romain. *Mémoires*. Paris: Albin Michel, 1956.

Rosemonde, Gérard. *Edmond Rostand*. Paris: Charpentier, 1935.

Rostand, Edmond. *L'Aiglon*. Paris: Charpentier et Fasquelle, 1900.

   Discours de Réception à l'Académie française, le 4 juin 1903. Paris: Charpentier et Fasquelle, 1904.

   Cyrano de Bergerac. Paris: Gallimard, 1983; 1999 (Folio edition with preface and notes by Patrick Besnier).

Rostand, Maurice. *Confession d'un demi-siècle*. Paris: La Jeune Parque, 1948.

   Sarah Bernhardt. Paris: Calmann-Lévy, 1950.

Sarcey, Francisque. *Quarante ans de théâtre*. Paris: Bibliothèque des annales politiques et littéraires, 1901.

Sardou, Victorien, and Emile Moreau. *Madame Sans-Gêne*. Paris: Librairie Ollendorff, 1912.

Stoullig, Edmond. *Les Annales du théâtre et de la musique: 1909*. Paris: Ollendorff, 1910.

Tarde, Gabriel. *L'Opinion et la foule*. Paris: PUF, 1989.

IV. Other Contemporary Printed Sources

Aubin, Antony. "Le Procès Ullmo." *La Revue des procès contemporains* 26 (April 1908): 209–260.

Dupré, Dr. et al. "Mémoires originaux: L'Affaire Ullmo." *Archives d'anthropologie criminelle de médecine légale et de psychologie normale et pathologique*, no. 176–177 (August–September 1908): 545–586.

Secondary Sources

I. Books

Accampo, Elinor, Rachel G. Fuchs, and Mary Lynn Stewart, eds. *Gender and the Politics of Social Reform in France, 1871–1914*. Baltimore, MD: Johns Hopkins University Press, 1995.

Agulhon, Maurice. *Marianne into Battle: Republican Imagery and Symbolism in France, 1789–1880*. Translated by Janet Lloyd. New York: Cambridge University Press, 1981.

Albanese, Ralph. *Corneille à l'ecole républicaine: Du Mythe héroïque à l'imaginaire politique en France: 1800–1950*. Paris: L'Harmattan, 2008.

Amalvi, Christian. *Les Héros de l'histoire de France*. Paris: Phot'œil, 1979.

   De l'art et la manière d'accommoder les héros de l'histoire de France: essais de mythologie nationale. Paris: Albin Michel, 1988.

Anderson, Benedict. *Imagined Communities: Reflections on the Origin and Spread of Nationalism*. London: Verso, 1983; 1986; 1991.

Andersen, Robert David. *France, 1870–1914: Politics and Society*. London: Routledge and Kegan Paul, 1984.

Andry, Marc. *Edmond Rostand: Le Panache et la gloire*. Paris: Plon, 1986.

Apostolidès, Jean-Marie. *Cyrano: Qui fut tout et qui ne fut rien*. Paris: Les Impressions nouvelles, 2006.

Aron, Jean-Paul, ed. *Misérable et glorieuse: La Femme du XIXème siècle.* Brussels: Editions Complexe, 1984.

Bancquart, Marie-Claire. *Les Écrivains et l'histoire: Barrès, Bloy, Péguy et France.* Paris: Nizet, 1966.

Barish, Jonas. *The Antitheatrical Prejudice.* Berkeley: University of California Press, 1981.

Barrows, Susanna. *Distorting Mirrors: Visions of the Crowd in Late Nineteenth-Century France.* New Haven, CT: Yale University Press, 1981.

Beaudoin, Steven M. "'Et les beaux rêves d'avenir?' Victorien Sardou and Fin-de-Siècle Attitudes on the French Revolution." M.A. thesis, University of Maine, 1990.

Beaune, Colette. *Jeanne d'Arc.* Paris: Perrin, 2004.

Becker, Jean-Jacques. *1914: Comment les Français sont entrés dans la guerre.* Paris: Presses de la Fondation nationale des sciences politiques, 1977.

Begley, Louis. *Why the Dreyfus Affair Matters.* New Haven, CT: Yale University Press, 2009.

Bell, David A. *The Cult of the Nation in France: Inventing Nationalism, 1680–1800.* Cambridge, MA: Harvard University Press, 2001.

Ben-Amos, Avner. *Funerals, Politics and Memory in Modern France, 1789–1996.* New York: Oxford University Press, 2000.

Bénichou, Paul. *Morales du grand siècle.* Paris: Gallimard, 1948.

Berenson, Edward. *The Trial of Madame Caillaux.* Berkeley: University of California Press, 1992.

  Heroes of Empire: Five Charismatic Men and the Conquest of Africa. Berkeley: University of California Press, 2010.

Berenson, Edward, and Eva Giloi, eds. *Constructing Charisma: Celebrity, Fame and Power in Nineteenth-Century Europe.* New York: Berghahn Books, 2010.

Berlanstein, Lenard. *Daughters of Eve: A Cultural History of French Theater Women from the Old Regime to the Fin-de-Siècle.* Cambridge, MA: Harvard University Press, 2001.

Berlière, Jean-Marc. *Le Crime de Soleilland (1907): Les Journalistes et l'assassin.* Paris: Tallandier, 2003.

Bonnet, Jean-Claude. *Naissance du Panthéon: Essai sur le culte des grands hommes.* Paris: Fayard, 1998.

Bowman, Frank. *French Romanticism: Intertextual and Interdisciplinary Readings.* Baltimore, MD: Johns Hopkins University Press, 1990.

Brooks, Peter. *The Melodramatic Imagination: Balzac, Henry James, Melodrama, and the Mode of Excess.* New Haven, CT: Yale University Press, 1976; 1995.

Brown, Frederick. *For the Soul of France: Culture Wars in the Age of Dreyfus.* New York: Alfred Knopf, 2010.

Burton, Richard D. *Holy Tears, Holy Blood: Women, Catholicism, and the Culture of Suffering in France, 1840–1970.* Ithaca, NY: Cornell University Press, 2004.

Carroll, David. *French Literary Fascism: Nationalism, Anti-Semitism and the Ideology of Culture.* Princeton, NJ: Princeton University Press, 1995.

Charle, Christophe. *La Crise littéraire à l'époque du naturalisme: Roman, théâtre, politique*. Paris: PENS, 1979.

Le Siècle de la presse (1830–1939). Paris: Seuil, 2004.

Théâtres en capitales: Naissance de la société du spectacle à Paris, Berlin, Londres et Vienne: 1860–1914. Paris: Albin Michel, 2008.

Charle, Christophe, and Daniel Roche, eds. *Capitales culturelles, Capitales symboliques: Paris et les expériences européennes*. Paris: Publications de la Sorbonne, 2002.

Charnow, Sally. *Theatre, Politics, and Markets in Fin-de-Siècle Paris: Staging Modernity*. New York: Palgrave Macmillan, 2005.

Clayson, Hollis. *Painted Love: Prostitution in French Art in the Impressionist Era*. New Haven, CT: Yale University Press, 1991.

Clébert, Jean-Paul. *L'Incendie du Bazar de la Charité: Roman vrai*. Paris: Denoël, 1978.

Corbin, Alain. *Women for Hire: Prostitution and Sexuality in France after 1850*. Translated by Alan Sheridan. Cambridge, MA: Harvard University Press, 1990.

Datta, Venita. *Birth of a National Icon: The Literary Avant-Garde and the Origins of the Intellectual in France*. Albany: SUNY Press, 1999.

Day-Hickman, Barbara Ann. *Napoleonic Art: Nationalism and the Spirit of Rebellion in France (1815–1848)*. Newark: University of Delaware Press, 1999.

De la Motte, Dean, and Jeannene M. Przyblyski, eds. *Modernity and the Mass Press in Nineteenth-Century France*. Amherst: University of Massachusetts Press, 1999.

Delpêche, René. *Amour, crime, châtiment ou la vie cachée de Benjamin Ullmo*. Paris: Les Editions du scorpion, 1957.

Delporte, Christian, Michael Palmer, and Denis Ruellan, eds. *Presse à scandale, scandale de presse*. Paris: L'Harmattan, 2001.

Duclert, Vincent. *Alfred Dreyfus: L'Honneur d'un patriote*. Paris: Fayard, 2006.

Dwyer, Philip. *Napoleon: The Path to Power*. New Haven, CT: Yale University Press, 2008.

Englund, Steven. *Napoleon: A Political Life*. Cambridge, MA: Harvard University Press, 2004.

Felski, Rita. *The Gender of Modernity*. Cambridge, MA: Harvard University Press, 1995.

Forth, Christopher E. *Zarathustra in Paris: The Nietzsche Vogue in France, 1891–1918*. De Kalb: Northern Illinois University Press, 2001.

The Dreyfus Affair and the Crisis of French Manhood. Baltimore, MD: Johns Hopkins University Press, 2004.

Masculinity in the Modern West: Gender, Civilization and the Body. New York: Palgrave Macmillan, 2008.

Forth, Christopher E., and Elinor Accampo, eds. *Confronting Modernity in Fin-de-Siècle France: Bodies, Minds and Gender*. New York: Palgrave Macmillan, 2010.

Forth, Christopher E., and Bertrand Taithe, eds. *French Masculinities: History, Culture and Politics*. New York: Palgrave Macmillan, 2007.

Friedman, Lawrence M. *The Horizontal Society*. New Haven, CT: Yale University Press, 1999.

Fuchs, Rachel G. *Contested Paternity: Constructing Families in Modern France*. Baltimore, MD: Johns Hopkins University Press, 2008.

Geyl, Pieter. *Napoleon: For or Against*. Translated by Olive Renier. New Haven, CT: Yale University Press, 1967.

Gildea, Robert. *The Past in French History*. New Haven, CT: Yale University Press, 1994.

Girardet, Raoul. *Le Nationalisme français: 1871–1914*. Paris: Seuil, 1983.

Nationalismes et Nation. Brussels: Editions Complexe, 1996.

Glenn, Susan A. *Female Spectacle: The Theatrical Roots of Modern Feminism*. Cambridge, MA: Harvard University Press, 2000.

Grazia, Victoria de, and Ellen Furlough, eds. *The Sex of Things: Gender and Consumption in Historical Perspective*. Berkeley: University of California Press, 1996.

Guilleminault, Gilbert, ed. *Prélude à la Belle Epoque*. Paris: Denoël, 1956.

Harris, Ruth. *Murder and Madness: Medicine, Law, and Society in the Fin-de-Siècle*. New York: Oxford University Press, 1989.

Lourdes: Body and Spirit in the Secular Age. New York: Viking, 1999.

Dreyfus: Politics, Emotion and the Scandal of the Century. New York: Metropolitan Books, 2010.

Hazareesingh, Sudhir. *The Legend of Napoleon*. London: Granta Books, 2004.

The Saint-Napoleon: Celebrations of Sovereignty in Nineteenth-Century France. Cambridge, MA: Harvard University Press, 2004.

Hemmings, Frederic William John. *The Theatre Industry in Nineteenth-Century France*. New York: Cambridge University Press, 1993.

Theatre and State in France, 1760–1905. New York: Cambridge University Press, 1994.

Hobbins, Daniel. *The Trial of Joan of Arc*. Cambridge, MA: Harvard University Press, 2005.

Hobsbawm, Eric, and Terence Ranger, eds. *The Invention of Tradition*. Cambridge: Cambridge University Press; Canto, 1983; 1992.

Hoenselaars, A. J., and Jelle Koopmans, eds. *Jeanne d'Arc entre les nations*. Amsterdam: Rodopoi, 1998.

Holmes, Diana, and Carrie Tarr, eds. *A "Belle Epoque"? Women in French Society and Culture, 1890–1914*. New York: Berghahn Books, 2006.

Hunt, Lynn. *Politics, Culture and Class in the French Revolution*. Berkeley: University of California Press, 1984.

Huyssen, Andreas. *After the Great Divide: Modernism, Mass Culture, Postmodernism*. Bloomington: Indiana University Press, 1986.

Irving, William D. *The Boulanger Affair Reconsidered: Royalism, Boulangism and the Origins of the Radical Right in France*. New York: Oxford University Press, 1989.

Jeanneney, Jean-Noël. *Le Duel: Une Passion française, 1789–1914*. Paris: Seuil, 2004.

Joll, James. *The Origins of the First World War*. New York: Longman, 1984.

Jonas, Raymond. *France and the Cult of the Sacred Heart: An Epic Tale for Modern Times*. Berkeley: University of California Press, 2001.

The Tragic Tale of Claire Ferchaud and the Great War. Berkeley: University of California Press, 2005.

Jourdan, Annie. *Napoléon: Héros, imperator et mécène*. Paris: Aubier, 1998.

Kalifa, Dominique. *L'Encre et le sang: Récits de crimes et société à la Belle Epoque*. Paris: Fayard, 1995.

La Culture de masse en France, 1860–1930. Paris: Editions de la Découverte and Syros, 2001.

Kaufman, Suzanne K. *Consuming Visions: Mass Culture and the Lourdes Shrine*. Ithaca, NY: Cornell University Press, 2005.

Kelly, Barbara, ed. *Music, Culture and National Identity in France, 1870–1939*. Rochester, NY: University of Rochester Press, 2008.

Krumeich, Gerd. *Jeanne d'Arc à travers l'histoire*. Translated into French by Josie Mély, Marie-Hélène Pateau, and Lisette Rosenfeld. Paris: Albin Michel, 1989.

Landry, Marc. *Edmond Rostand: Le Panache et la gloire*. Paris: Plon, 1986.

Larkin, Maurice. *Religion, Politics and Preferment in France since 1890*. New York: Cambridge University Press, 1995.

Lehning, James R. *Peasant and French: Cultural Contact in Rural France during the Nineteenth Century*. New York: Cambridge University Press, 1995.

The Melodramatic Thread: Spectacle and Political Culture in Modern France. Bloomington: Indiana University Press, 2007.

Levillain, Philippe. *Boulanger, fossoyeur de la monarchie*. Paris: Flammarion, 1982.

Lloyd, Sue. *The Man Who Was Cyrano*. Bloomington, IN: Unlimited Publishing, 2002.

Lorcey, Jacques. *Edmond Rostand*. 3 vols. Paris: Atlantica, 2004.

Lucas-Dubreton, J. *Le Culte de Napoléon, 1815–1848*. Paris: Albin Michel, 1960.

Manuel, Jean-Baptiste. *Edmond Rostand, écrivain imaginaire*. Paris: Atlantica, 2003.

Margadant, Jo Burr, ed. *The New Biography: Performing Femininity in Nineteenth-Century France*. Berkeley: University of California Press, 2000.

Margerie, Caroline de. *Edmond Rostand ou le baiser de la gloire*. Paris: Grasset, 1997.

Martin, Henri-Jean, and Roger Chartier, eds. *Histoire de l'édition française. Vol. 4: Le Livre concurrencé: 1900–1950*. Paris: Fayard, 1991.

Martin, Marc. *Médias et journalistes de la république*. Paris: Odile Jacob, 1997.

Masson, Philippe. *Histoire de la Marine, tome II: De la vapeur à l'atome*. Limoges: Lavauzelle, 1983; 2000.

Maugue, Annelise. *L'Identité masculine en crise au tournant du siècle, 1871–1914*. Paris: Editions Rivages, 1987; Payot, 2001.

Maza, Sarah. *Private Lives and Public Affairs: The Causes Célèbres of Prerevolutionary France*. Berkeley: University of California Press, 1993.

Melman, Billie, ed. *Borderlines: Genders and Identities in War and Peace, 1870–1930*. New York: Routledge, 1998.

Menon, Elizabeth K. *Evil by Design: The Creation and Marketing of the Femme Fatale.* Urbana: University of Illinois Press, 2006.

Micale, Mark S. *Hysterical Men: The Hidden History of Male Nervous Illness.* Cambridge, MA: Harvard University Press, 2008.

Miller, Michael. *The Bon Marché: Bourgeois Culture and the Department Store.* Princeton, NJ: Princeton University Press, 1981.

Mistacco, Vicki. *Les Femmes et la tradition littéraire: Anthologie du Moyen Age à nos jours.* 2 vols. New Haven, CT: Yale University Press, 2006.

Mollier, Jean-Yves. *La Lecture et ses publics à l'époque contemporaine: Essais d'histoire culturelle.* Paris: PUF, 2001.

Mosse, George L. *Nationalism and Sexuality: Middle-Class Morality and Sexual Norms in Modern Europe.* Madison: University of Wisconsin Press, 1985.

M'Sili, Marine. *Le Fait divers en république: Histoire sociale de 1870 à nos jours.* Paris: CNRS Editions, 2000.

Nicolas, Pierre. *Martyrologe du Bazar de la Charité.* Paris: Ed. Pierre Nicolas, 2000.

Nochlin, Linda, and Tamar Garb, eds. *The Jew in the Text: Modernity and the Construction of Identity.* New York: Thames and Hudson, 1995.

Nora, Pierre, ed. *Les Lieux de mémoire.* 7 vols. Paris: Gallimard, 1984–1992; Quarto Edition, 1997.

Nye, Robert A. *The Origins of Crowd Psychology: Gustave Le Bon and the Crisis of Mass Democracy.* Beverly Hills, CA: Sage, 1976.

Crime, Madness, and Politics in Modern France: The Medical Concept of National Decline. Princeton, NJ: Princeton University Press, 1984.

Masculinity and Male Codes of Honor in Modern France. New York: Oxford University Press, 1993; Berkeley: University of California Press, 1998.

Ockman, Carol, and Kenneth E. Silver, eds. *Sarah Bernhardt: The Art of High Drama.* New York/New Haven, CT: Jewish Museum and Yale University Press, 2005.

Offen, Karen. *Paul de Cassagnac and the Authoritarian Tradition in Nineteenth-Century France.* New York: Garland, 1991.

Orr, Linda. *Headless History: Nineteenth-Century French Historiography of the Revolution.* Ithaca, NY: Cornell University Press, 1990.

Padwa, Howard. "Narcotics vs. The Nation: The Culture and Politics of Opiate Control in Britain and France, 1821–1926." Ph.D. diss., UCLA, 2008.

Paoli, Dominique. *Il y a cent ans: L'Incendie du Bazar de la Charité.* Paris: Mémorial du Bazar de la Charité, 1997.

Pasler, Jann. *Composing the Citizen: Music as Public Utility in Third Republic France.* Berkeley: University of California Press, 2009.

Pedersen, Jean. *Legislating the Family: Feminism, Theater, and Republican Politics, 1870–1920.* New Brunswick, NJ: Rutgers University Press, 2003.

Pernoud, Régine, and Marie-Véronique Clin. *Joan of Arc: Her Story.* Translated by Jeremy DuQuesnay Adams. New York: St. Martin's Griffin, 1998.

Perrot, Philippe. *Fashioning the Bourgeoisie: A History of Clothing in the Nineteenth Century.* Translated by Richard Bienvenu. Princeton, NJ: Princeton University Press, 1994.

Petiteau, Natalie. *Napoléon, de la mythologie à l'histoire*. Paris: Seuil, 1999.
Phélippeau, Eric. *L'Invention de l'homme politique moderne: Mackau, l'Orne et la République*. Paris: Belin, 2002.
Ravel, Jeffrey. *The Contested Parterre: Public Theater and Political Culture, 1680–1791*. Ithaca, NY: Cornell University Press, 1999.
Rein, Irving, Philip Kotler, and Martin Stoller. *High Visibility*. New York: Dodd Mead, 1987.
Rioux, Jean-Pierre, and Jean-François Sirinelli, eds. *La Culture de masse en France: De la Belle Epoque à aujourd'hui*. Paris: Fayard, 2002.
Roberts, Mary Louise. *Disruptive Acts: The New Woman in Fin-de-Siècle France*. Chicago: University of Chicago Press, 2002.
Rothney, John. *Bonapartism after Sedan*. Ithaca, NY: Cornell University Press, 1969.
Samuels, Maurice. *The Spectacular Past: Popular History and the Novel in Nineteenth-Century France*. Ithaca, NY: Cornell University Press, 2004.
Schickel, Richard. *Intimate Strangers: The Culture of Celebrity*. New York: Doubleday, 1985.
Schivelbusch, Wolfgang. *The Culture of Defeat: On National Trauma, Mourning, and Recovery*. Translated by Jefferson Chase. New York: Picador, 2004.
Schwartz, Vanessa R. *Spectacular Realities: Early Mass Culture in Fin-de-Siècle Paris*. Berkeley: University of California Press, 1998.
Serman, William. *Les Officiers français dans la nation (1848–1914)*. Paris: Aubier Montaigne, 1982.
Serman, William, and Jean-Paul Bertaud. *Nouvelle Histoire militaire de la France, 1789–1919*. Paris: Fayard, 1998.
Shapiro, Ann-Louise. *Breaking the Codes: Female Criminality in Fin-de-Siècle Paris*. Stanford, CA: Stanford University Press, 1996
Shattuck, Roger. *The Banquet Years: The Origins of the Avant-Garde in France, 1885 to World War I*. New York: Vintage Books, 1968.
Showalter, Elaine. *Sexual Anarchy: Gender and Culture at the Fin de Siècle*. New York: Viking, 1990.
Silverman, Debora. *Art Nouveau in Fin-de-Siècle France: Politics, Psychology and Style*. Berkeley: University of California Press, 1989.
Silverman, Willa Z. *The Notorious Life of Gyp: Right-Wing Anarchist in Fin-de-Siècle France*. New York: Oxford University Press, 1994.
    The New Bibliopolis: French Book Collectors and the Culture of Print, 1880–1914. Toronto: University of Toronto Press, 2008.
Sirinelli, Jean-François, ed. *Histoire des droites en France. Vol. 2: Cultures*. Paris: Gallimard, 1992.
Smith, Leonard V., Stéphane Audoin-Rouzeau, and Annette Becker. *France and the Great War, 1914–1918*. French sections translated by Helen McPhail. Cambridge: Cambridge University Press, 2003; 2008.
Soons, Jan Joseph. *Jeanne d'Arc au théâtre*. Purmerend: J. Muusses, 1929.
Soulhol, Bernard. *Benjamin et Lison: Toulon et l'affaire Ullmo (1805–1908)*. Toulon: Les Presses du midi, 2001.
Sternhell, Zeev. *La Droite révolutionnaire: Les Origines françaises du fascisme, 1885–1914*. Paris: Seuil, 1978.

Surkis, Judith. *Sexing the Citizen: Morality and Masculinity in France, 1870–1920*. Ithaca, NY: Cornell University Press, 2006.

Taylor, Katherine Fischer. *In the Theater of Criminal Justice*. Princeton, NJ: Princeton University Press, 1993.

Thérenty, Marie-Ève. *La Littérature au quotidien: Poétiques journalistiques au XIXème siècle*. Paris: Seuil, 2007.

Thiesse, Anne-Marie. *Le Roman du quotidien: Lecteurs et lectures populaires à la Belle Epoque*. Paris: Le Chemin vert, 1984.

Thomson, Richard. *The Troubled Republic: Visual Culture and Social Debate in France, 1889–1900*. New Haven, CT: Yale University Press, 2004.

Tiersten, Lisa. *Marianne in the Market: Envisioning Consumer Society in Fin-de-Siècle France*. Berkeley: University of California Press, 2001.

Tombs, Robert, ed. *Nationhood and Nationalism in France: From Boulangism to the Great War, 1889–1918*. New York: HarperCollins, 1991.

Tulard, Jean. *L'Anti-Napoléon: La Légende noire de l'empereur*. Paris: Julliard, 1965.

Le Mythe de Napoléon. Paris: Armand Colin, 1971.

Vincent, Thomas. "L'Affaire Ullmo (1907–1908): Le Procès de l'opium." M.A. Thesis, University of Paris I, 2003–2004.

Vincent-Buffault, Anne. *Histoire des larmes*. Paris: Rivages, 1986.

Walker, David H. *Outrage and Insight: Modern French Writers and the 'Fait Divers.'* Oxford: Berg, 1995.

Walkowitz, Judith. *City of Dreadful Delight: Narratives of Sexual Danger in Late-Victorian London*. Chicago: University of Chicago Press, 1992.

Warner, Marina. *Joan of Arc: The Image of Female Heroism*. New York: Knopf, 1981.

Weber, Eugen. *The Nationalist Revival in France, 1905–1914*. Berkeley: University of California Press, 1968.

Peasants into Frenchmen: The Modernization of Rural France, 1870–1914. Stanford, CA: Stanford University Press, 1976.

France Fin de Siècle. Cambridge, MA: Belknap Press of Harvard University Press, 1986.

Wheeler, Bonnie, and Charles T. Wood, eds. *Fresh Verdicts on Joan of Arc*. New York: Garland, 1996.

Williams, Rosalind H. *Dream Worlds: Mass Consumption in Late Nineteenth-Century France*. Berkeley: University of California Press, 1982.

Wilson, Stephen. *Ideology and Experience: Anti-Semitism in France at the Time of the Dreyfus Affair*. Rutherford, NJ: Fairleigh Dickinson University Press, 1982.

Winock, Michel. *Nationalisme, antisémitisme et fascisme en France*. Paris: Seuil, 1990.

Wright, Gordon. *France in Modern Times*. 5th ed. New York: W. W. Norton, 1994.

Yvorel, Jean-Jacques. *Les Poisons de l'esprit: Drogues et drogués au XIXème siècle*. Paris: Quai Voltaire, 1992.

II. Articles/Book Chapters

Abel, Richard. "The Thrills of *Grande Peur*: Crime Series and Serials in the Belle Epoque." *Velvet Light Trap*, no. 17 (Spring 1996): 3–9.

Accampo, Elinor. "Private Life, Public Image: Motherhood and Militancy in the Self-Construction of Nelly Roussel, 1900–1922." In *The New Biography: Performing Femininity in Nineteenth-Century France*, edited by Jo Burr Margadant, 208–262. Berkeley: University of California Press, 2000.

Alexander, R. S. "The Hero as Houdini: Napoleon and Nineteenth-Century Bonapartism." *Modern and Contemporary France* 8, no. 4 (November 2000): 457–467.

Auslander, Leora. "The Gendering of Consumer Practices in Nineteenth-Century France." In *The Sex of Things: Gender and Consumption in Historical Perspective*, edited by Victoria de Grazia and Ellen Furlough, 79–112. Berkeley: University of California Press, 1996.

Berenson, Edward. "Fashoda, Dreyfus and the Myth of Jean-Baptiste Marchand." *Yale French Studies* 111 (2007): 129–142.

"Unifying the French Nation: Savornan de Brazza and the Third Republic." In *Music, Culture and National Identity in France 1870–1939*, edited by Barbara Kelly, 79–112. Rochester, NY: University of Rochester Press, 2008.

Bergman-Carton, Janice. "Negotiating the Categories: Sarah Bernhardt and the Possibility of Jewishness." *Art Journal* 55, no. 2 (Summer 1996): 55–64.

"A Vision of a Stained Glass Sarah: Bernhardt and the Decorative Arts." In *Sarah Bernhardt: The Art of High Drama*, edited by Carol Ockman and Kenneth E. Silver, 99–123. New York and New Haven, CT: Jewish Museum and Yale University Press, 2005.

Berlanstein, Lenard. "Breeches and Breaches: Cross-Dress Theater and the Culture of Gender Ambiguity in Modern France." *Comparative Studies in Society and History* 38, no. 2 (April 1996): 338–369.

"Historicizing and Gendering Celebrity Culture: Famous Women in Nineteenth-Century France." *Journal of Women's Studies* 16, no. 4 (2004): 65–91.

"Selling Modern Femininity: *Femina*, a Forgotten Feminist Publishing Success in Belle Epoque France." *French Historical Studies* 30, no. 4 (Fall 2007): 623–649.

Blum, Antoinette. "*Les Loups* au Théâtre de l'Oeuvre: Le 18 mai 1898." *Revue d'histoire littéraire de la France* 6 (November–December 1976): 883–895.

"*Les Loups* de Romain Rolland: Un Jeu théâtral sur l'histoire." *French Review* 66, no. 1 (October 1992): 59–68.

Bold, Stephen C. "Rostand's *Cyrano de Bergerac* and Seventeenth-Century France." Paper presented at the Western Society for French History, Boston, November 1998.

Chanet, Jean-François. "La Fabrique des héros: Pédagogie républicaine et culte des grands hommes de Sedan à Vichy." *Vingtième siècle* 65 (January–March 2000): 13–34.

Charbonnier, Jean. "Le Code Civil." In *Les Lieux de mémoire*, vol. 1, edited by Pierre Nora, 1331–1352. Paris: Gallimard Quarto, 1997.

Charle, Christophe. "Les Théâtres et leurs publics: Paris, Berlin, Vienne, 1860–1914." In *Capitales culturelles, Capitales symboliques: Paris et les expériences européennes*, edited by Christophe Charle and Daniel Roche, 403–420. Paris: Publications de la Sorbonne, 2002.

Contamine, Philippe. "Jeanne d'Arc dans la mémoire des droites." In *Histoire des droites en France. Vol. 2: Cultures*, edited by Jean-François Sirinelli, 397–435. Paris: Gallimard, 1992.

Coudert, Marie-Claude. "Fin de Siècle." In *Jeanne d'Arc: Les Tableaux de l'histoire: 1820–1920*, 129–161. Paris: RMN, 2003.

Crook, Malcolm, and John Dunne. "Napoleon's France: History and Heritage." *Modern and Contemporary France* 8, no. 4 (November 2000): 429–431.

Cubitt, Geoffrey. "Martyrs of Charity, Heroes of Solidarity: Catholic and Republican Responses to the Fire at the Bazar de la Charité, Paris, 1897." *French History* 21 (2007): 331–352.

Datta, Venita. "Passing Fancy? The Generation of 1890 and Anarchism." *Modern and Contemporary France*, no. 44 (January 1991): 3–11.

"Romain Rolland and the Theater of the Revolution: A Historical Perspective." *CLIO* 20, no. 23 (Spring 1991): 213–222.

"'L'Appel au soldat': Visions of the Napoleonic Legend in Popular Culture of the Belle Epoque." *French Historical Studies* 28, no. 1 (Winter 2005): 1–30.

"Sur les boulevards: Les Représentations de Jeanne d'Arc dans le théâtre populaire." *CLIO, Histoire, Femmes et Société* 24 (2006): 127–149.

"Superwomen or Slaves? Women Writers, Male Critics, and the Reception of Nietzsche in Belle-Epoque France." *Historical Reflections/Réflexions historiques* 33, no. 3 (Fall 2007): 421–427.

"From Devil's Island to the Pantheon? Alfred Dreyfus, the Anti-Hero." In *Confronting Modernity in Fin-de-Siècle France: Bodies, Minds and Gender*, edited by Christopher Forth and Elinor Accampo, 217–234. New York: Palgrave Macmillan, 2010.

"Heroes, Celebrity and the Theater in Fin-de-Siècle France: *Cyrano de Bergerac*." In *Constructing Charisma: Celebrity, Fame and Power in Nineteenth-Century Europe*, edited by Edward Berenson and Eva Giloi, 155–164. New York: Berghahn Books, 2010.

Day-Hickman, Barbara. "Cross Dress Actress Virginie Déjazet and the Napoleonic Legend during the July Monarchy." Paper presented at the French Historical Studies Conference, Tempe, Arizona, April 2010.

Delporte, Christian. "Presse et culture de masse en France (1880–1914)." *Revue historique* 605 (January–March 1998): 93–121.

Duclert, Vincent. "Dreyfus, de l'oubli à l'histoire." *Cahiers de l'Affaire Dreyfus*, no. 1 (2004): 63–91.

Dwyer, Philip. "Public Remembering, Private Reminiscing: French Military Memoirs and the Revolutionary and Napoleonic Wars." *French Historical Studies* 33, no. 2 (Spring 2010): 231–258.

Forth, Christopher E. "'La *Civilisation*' and Its Discontents." In *French Masculinities: History, Culture and Politics*, edited by Christopher Forth and Bertrand Taithe, 85–102. New York: Palgrave Macmillan, 2007.

Fuchs, Rachel G. "Paternity, Progeny, and Property: Family Honor in the Late Nineteenth Century." In *Confronting Modernity in Fin-de-Siècle France: Bodies, Minds and Gender*, edited by Christopher E. Forth and Elinor Accampo, 150–168. New York: Palgrave Macmillan, 2010.

Gerbod, Paul. "L'Ethique héroïque en France (1870–1914)." *La Revue historique*, no. 268 (1982): 409–429.

Goldstein, Jan. "The Hysteria Diagnosis and the Politics of Anticlericalism in Late Nineteenth-Century France." *Journal of Modern History* 45, no. 2 (June 1982): 209–239.

"The Use of Male Hysteria: Medical and Literary Discourse in Nineteenth-Century France." *Representations*, no. 34 (Spring 1994): 134–165.

Hanna, Martha. "Iconology and Ideology: Images of Joan of Arc in the Idiom of the Action Française, 1908–1931." *French Historical Studies* 14, no. 2 (Fall 1985): 215–239.

"France and the Great War, 1914–1918," *H-France Review* 3, no. 119 (October 2003): 525–529.

Hughes, Michael J. "Making Frenchmen into Warriors: Martial Masculinity in Napoleonic France." In *French Masculinities: History, Culture and Politics*, edited by Christopher E. Forth and Bertrand Taithe, 51–66. New York: Palgrave Macmillan, 2007.

Joly, Bertrand. "La France et la revanche (1871–1914)." *La Revue d'histoire moderne et contemporaine* 46, no. 2 (April–June 1999): 325–347.

Krumeich, Gerd. "Joan of Arc between Right and Left." In *Nationhood and Nationalism in France: From Boulangism to the Great War, 1889–1918*, edited by Robert Tombs, 63–73. New York: HarperCollins, 1991.

Kuchta, David. "The Making of the Self-Made Man: Class, Clothing, and English Masculinity, 1688–1832." In *The Sex of Things: Gender and Consumption in Historical Perspective*, edited by Victoria de Grazia and Ellen Furlough, 54–78. Berkeley: University of California Press, 1996.

Lambron, Marc. "Le Mythe Cyrano." *Le Point*, no. 916 (9 April 1990): 8–12.

Mansker, Andrea. "Shaming Men: Feminist Honor and the Sexual Double Standard in Belle Époque France." In *Confronting Modernity in Fin-de-Siècle France: Bodies, Minds and Gender*, edited by Christopher E. Forth and Elinor Accampo, 169–191. New York: Palgrave Macmillan, 2010.

Margolis, Nadia. "La Chevauchée solitaire du Professeur Thalamas: Rationalistes et réactionnaires dans l'historiographie johannique (1904–1945)." *Bulletin de l'association des amis du centre Jeanne d'Arc* 15 (1991): 7–28.

Mazgaj, Paul. "The Origins of the French Radical Right." *French Historical Studies* 15, no. 2 (Fall 1987): 287–315.

Morand, Paul. "Le Bazar de la Charité." In *A la fleur d'oranger*. Vevey: Les Clés d'or, 1946.

Nora, Pierre. "Lavisse, instituteur national." In *Les Lieux de mémoire*, 7 vols., edited by Nora Pierre. Paris: Gallimard, 1984–1992; Quarto Edition, 1997, vol. 1, 239–276.

Nye, Robert. "Western Masculinities in War and Peace." *American Historical Review* 112 (April 2007): 417–438.

O'Brien, Patricia. "The Kleptomania Diagnosis: Bourgeois Women and Theft in Late Nineteenth-Century France." *Journal of Social History* 17, no. 1 (Autumn 1983): 65–77.

Ockman, Carol. "When Is a Jewish Star Just a Star? Interpreting Images of Sarah Bernhardt." In *The Jew in the Text: Modernity and the Construction of Identity*, edited by Linda Nochlin and Tamar Garb, 121–139. New York: Thames and Hudson, 1995.

"Women, Icons, and Power." In *Self and History: A Tribute to Linda Nochlin*, edited by Aruna D'Souza, 103–116. New York: Thames and Hudson, 2001.

"Was She Magnificent?" In *Sarah Bernhardt: The Art of High Drama*, edited by Carol Ockman and Kenneth E. Silver, 23–73. New York/New Haven, CT: Jewish Museum and Yale University Press, 2005.

Offen, Karen. "Depopulation, Nationalism, and Feminism in Fin-de-Siècle France." *American Historical Review* 89, no. 3 (June 1984): 648–676.

Ozouf, Mona. "Le Panthéon." In *Les Lieux de mémoire*, 7 vols., edited by Nora Pierre. Paris: Gallimard, 1984–1992; Quarto Edition, 1997, vol. 1, 155–178.

Perrot, Michelle. "L'Affaire Troppmann." *L'Histoire* 30 (January 1981): 28–37.

"Fait divers et histoire au XIXème siècle." *Annales, ESC*, no. 4 (July–August 1983): 911–919.

Pomfret, David. "A Muse for the Masses: Gender, Age, and Nation in France, Fin de Siècle." *American Historical Review* 109, no. 5 (December 2004): 1439–1474.

Ponty, Janine. "*Le Petit Journal* et l'affaire Dreyfus." *Revue d'histoire moderne et contemporaine* 24 (October–December 1977): 641–656.

Provencher, Denis, and Luke Eilderts. "The Nation According to Lavisse: Teaching Masculinity and Male Citizenship in Third-Republic France." *French Cultural Studies* 18, no. 1 (2007): 31–57.

Puymège, Gérard de. "Le Soldat Chauvin." In *Les Lieux de mémoire*, 7 vols., edited by Nora Pierre. Paris: Gallimard, 1984–1992; Quarto Edition, 1997, vol. 2, 1699–1728.

Rioux, Jean-Pierre. "L'Aigle de légende." *L'Histoire*, no. 124 (July–August 1989): 94–100.

Roberts, Mary-Louise. "Gender, Consumption and Commodity Culture." *American Historical Review* 103, no. 3 (June 1998): 817–844.

Rogers, Juliette M. "Feminist Discourse in Women's Novels of Professional Development." In *A 'Belle Epoque'? Women in French Society and Culture, 1890–1914*, edited by Diana Holmes and Carrie Tarr, 183–195. New York: Berghahn Books, 2006.

Sabbagh, Antoine. "Trahisons à la une." In *Presse à Scandale, scandale de presse*, edited by Christian Delporte, Michael Palmer, and Denis Ruellan, 184–194. Paris: L'Harmattan, 2001.

Sanson, Rosemonde. "La Fête de Jeanne d'Arc en 1894: Controverse et célébration." *Revue d'histoire moderne et contemporaine* 20 (July–September 1973): 444–463.

Sapin, Louis. "L'Incendie du Bazar de la Charité." In *Prélude à la Belle Epoque*, edited by Gilbert Guilleminault, 271–332. Paris: Denoël, 1956.

Sauvy, Anne. "La littérature et les femmes." In *Histoire de l'édition française. Vol. 4: Le Livre concurrencé: 1900–1950*, edited by H. J. Martin and R. Chartier, 269–281. Paris: Fayard, 1991.

Schudson, Michael. "News, Public, Nation." *American Historical Review* 107, no. 2 (April 2002): 481–495.

Shaya, Gregory. "The *Flâneur*, the *Badaud*, and the Making of a Mass Public in France, circa 1860–1910." *American Historical Review* 109, no. 1 (February 2004): 41–77.

Silver, Kenneth E. "Sarah Bernhardt and the Theatrics of French Nationalism: From Roland's Daughter to Napoleon's Son." In *Sarah Bernhardt: The Art of High Drama*, edited by Carol Ockman and Kenneth E. Silver, 75–97. New York/New Haven, CT: Jewish Museum and Yale University Press, 2005.

    "Celebrity, Patriotism and Sarah Bernhardt." In *Constructing Charisma: Celebrity, Fame and Power in Nineteenth-Century Europe*, edited by Edward Berenson and Eva Giloi, 145–154. New York: Berghahn Books, 2010.

Silverman, Willa Z. "Mythic Representations of Napoleon in the Life and Works of Gyp." In *Correspondences: Studies in Literature, History, and the Arts in Nineteenth-Century France*, edited by Keith Busby, 203–212. Amsterdam: Rodopoi, 1992.

Sulpice, Léon. "La Trahison d'un marin." *Historia*, no. 245 (April 1967): 114–120.

Taithe, Bertrand. "Neighborhood Boys and Men: Changing Spaces of Masculine Identity in France, 1848–1871." In *French Masculinities: History, Culture and Politics*, edited by Christopher Forth and Bertrand Taithe, 67–84. New York: Palgrave Macmillan, 2007.

Tulard Jean. "Le Retour des cendres." In *Les Lieux de mémoire*, 7 vols., edited by Nora Pierre. Paris: Gallimard, 1984–1992; Quarto Edition, 1997, vol. 2, 1729–1754.

Vicinus, Martha. "Fin-de-Siècle Theatrics: Male Impersonation and Lesbian Desire." In *Borderlines: Genders and Identities in War and Peace, 1870–1930*, edited by Billie Melman, 163–192. New York: Routledge, 1998.

Weber, Eugen. "About *Thermidor*: The Oblique Uses of Scandal." *French Historical Studies* 17, no. 2 (Fall 1991): 330–342.

Wilson, Michael L. "'Capped with Hope, Clad in Youth, Shod in Courage': Masculinity and Marginality in Fin-de-Siècle Paris." In *Confronting Modernity in Fin-de-Siècle France: Bodies, Minds and Gender*, edited by Christopher Forth and Elinor Accampo, 192–212. New York: Palgrave Macmillan, 2010.

Winock, Michel. "Un Avant-goût d'apocalypse: L'Incendie du Bazar de la Charité." In *Nationalisme, antisémitisme et fascisme en France*, 83–102. Paris: Seuil, 1990.

    "Jeanne d'Arc." In *Les Lieux de mémoire*, 7 vols., edited by Nora Pierre. Paris: Gallimard, 1984–1992; Quarto Edition, 1997, vol. 3, 4427–4473.

Index